They Danced All Night

GETHRO JONES

Copyright © 2016 Gethro Jones

All rights reserved.

ISBN: 1523393181
ISBN-13: 978-1523393183

A NOTE FROM THE AUTHOR:

I wrote this book for my conscience to ease the pain I had to endure through life. The loss of Kim to cancer at the tender age of 23, to acknowledge my friends who are with me no more, to honor what they brought to the scene, to tell a different story, one through my eyes of life in the seventies and my journey onto the Northern Soul scene. I pull no punches but one thing drove me to keep going, to drag the memories to these pages, to release the pain in my heart. I would only write the truth, I had to tell it exactly like it was. We can't bring back the past but for a brief moment we can relive a memory in a photograph and a thought in our heart. This in its own way releases a smile. This book is for you, it's my side of the story, it tells of the love and respect we had for each other from the dance floor. This book is the dancer's side of the story. Without Linda, my second wife, pushing me, giving me strength in my darkest hours to complete my journey there would be no book. My friend, Glenn Walker Foster, who spent hours, even days dating every record I mentioned to keep the book authentic. Brent and Irish, Scatty and Mona, invaluable friends who helped jog my memory of the times we had. To Kristen who helped put it all together. To all of the above, I owe a tremendous gratitude.

This book came from my diary and memorabilia from 1974. Through its pages I have tried to transfer my feelings and emotions of that time. Forty years have passed since I looked at those pages. I don't possess a degree in English literature nor a mastery of the English language. This book reflects in the simplicity of my writing that comes straight from the heart. I have tried to protect people's identity, my descriptions of them are brief, even at times changing their names due to the nature and content of this book. In some cases, I have gone a step further and built events around them but always staying true to the circumstances as they unfolded. Friendships that spanned forty years, I would not want to jeopardize them in a book. I write as if you were by my side, I want you there with me on this journey. If I make you laugh or wipe a tear then I have touched your heart and in truth, reached my goal. As you too will know when you look me in the eyes a connection to my soul. X

GETHRO JONES

CONTENTS

	Foreword by Glenn Walker-Foster	iv
1	A Childhood With No Dreams	11
2	A Vision of Freedom and Hope	28
3	Happy Birthday to You	35
4	A Canal Bridge and The Girl Across The Street	38
5	Nowhere to Run, Nowhere to Hide	44
6	Get It On – August 1971	49
7	The White Boy Didn't Run	53
8	Cavendish First Time – Street Life	57
9	Late 1971	61
10	Gladys MK 1	63
11	Move On Up	65
12	The Octopus Spring 1972	71
13	The Ship and Rainbow	76
14	Two Div's and a Dance Floor	86
15	Cavendish Christmas Party – 1972	94

16	The Octopus – Start of 1973	98
17	March 1973 – Cats First Time	100
18	Turf Wars	109
19	Cats on a Wednesday Night	115
20	Rumpy's Saturday	127
21	Wolvo Boxing – Early August 1973	135
22	The Ship – Pay Back	140
23	VA-VA Bolton	142
24	Too Late	161
25	Anything You Want, Anyway You Want It	171
26	Our First Contact With Wigan Casino	175
27	We Were Made For Each Other	179
28	What Goes Up, Comes Down	202
29	Out On The Floor	212
30	There's No Stopping Us Now	237
31	The Diary of a Soul Boy (One That Doesn't Lie)	241
32	February 1974	246

33	March 1974	251
34	Leeds Soul Festival April 6th 1974	256
35	There's Nothing Else to Say	266
36	Beachcomber, Wolvo, and Wigan	272
37	The Mecca and Northern Divide	278
38	Black and White Divide	293
39	Who Are You	299
40	Center of Our Universe	301
41	Just a Little Misunderstanding	308
42	In More Ways Than One	319
43	The Shoebox	325
44	The Night of the Anniversary	331
45	Looking For You	337
46	Keep On Keeping On	358
47	Top of the Pops	363
	Poem by Shirley Donkersley	368

FOREWORD BY GLENN WALKER-FOSTER

Music means so many different things to so many different people, and of course each individual interprets music they love in different ways. Some choose to listen at home , some choose to listen to music live , some choose to play music to an audience and some choose to dance , I myself in 1973 made the choice to be a DJ and play music , the reward being the smiles on people's faces as they dance often singing away as they move across the dancefloor . The book you are about to read comes from the perspective of a dancer and after watching people dance for over 40 years to almost every genre of music I can say that the author of this book happens to be one of the finest dancers to grace a dancefloor to his chosen genre Northern Soul music and many people on the "Northern" scene would confirm that. From a turmoiled childhood Northern Soul music was my good friend Gethro's escape and he engrossed himself dancing to the music he loved and still does to this day. The book is very candid with no pulled punches, it is without question that Gethro writes from the heart with sometimes shocking honesty. "THEY DANCED ALL NIGHT" is a rollercoaster ride of ups and downs that maybe only those that were there will understand , Northern Soul music is quite unique in that it is a scene of music that by the main were American R n B failures and just not hits and often B sides of records that were not hits , The natural 4 x 4 beat was tailor made for dance floors and the music was adopted by the UK at clubs like The Catacombs in Wolverhampton , The Twisted Wheel and The Pendulum in Manchester, The Howard Mallet in Cambridge , The Golden Torch in Stoke and so many more . In 1973 when several clubs had closed down a club opened in Wigan which exposed Northern Soul to a wider audience and this book focuses on those that experienced the manic all night scene of Northern Soul dancing and written by a man that was there and stamped his authority and a place in Northern Soul history. It is my honour to write the foreword to this truthful interpretation of life on the dancefloor in the glory days of Northern Soul and my pleasure to remain a close friend of the Author for over 40 years. Glenn Walker-Foster

Chapter 1

A CHILDHOOD WITH NO DREAMS

"No love of a mother or father, no birthdays for you!"

The old black Riley trundled along the seats creaking in rhythm with the engine. Buddy Holly filtered across the airwaves of the crackling radio filling the car with the warm glow of music. Wood and chrome caught the odd street light, complementing the smell of worn leather gave the car an atmosphere all its own. It felt safe and indestructible, like the bow of a ship moving through the sea of darkness. Pushing all aside as if never to let you down, to go on moving forward forever. The dials on the dash burning bright and comforting you, telling you everything was ok. Sitting in the back seat, lost in the melody I gazed out of the window watching trees flicker by. Odd streetlights capturing moths in a fluttering dance, a spiraling tornado of insects closing out another day.

The engine slowed as we turned, a large open iron gate appeared in the headlights stretching long, fingered shadows fading to darkness, sucking us into a black hole. We hesitated and moved forward, the ivied wall and ironwork closing to shut out the outside world, the normal world where I had been for a day. A tear trickled down my cheek then another. I felt the rush of despair resting upon my shoulders, I couldn't straighten up thinking only of my helplessness. I wanted so much and had so little, my dreams shattered, left in reality where they never come true.

"You have to be brave. You have to be brave." The voice of my invisible friend whispering softly but I wasn't brave, I had seen happiness and love.

"Hey what's up? You're not crying, are you?"

"No sir." My tearful reply hidden as best I could.

"Come on, it's not that bad." The driver's gentle voice trying to ease his pain as well as mine.

The car came to a halt at a stone gatehouse, a pale yellow light filtered to a gravel pathway. Lights on either side displaying an oval wooden door, a remnant belonging in some medieval castle, the door knocker a lion's head defying all to enter.

"Hey Philip, I won't be long. I've just got to check something, stay here and don't touch anything, all right?"

"I won't." My murmured reply.

"Ok, I'll be back in a minute." Taking the keys the driver left me alone.

"Wonder why we stopped? What's going on?" Wiping a circle of mist from the window I watched as he entered the open door, my eyes straining in darkness something caught my eye.

There in the bottom window surrounded in soft light, a silver Easter egg as big as me. Across the centre, a large red bow, scattered around the bottom smaller eggs of different colors. A sign I couldn't read must be a present or something. Transfixed, my eyes would not move. Look at all that chocolate. I imagined dividing it up into endless neat lines, being careful to save some to share with my friends. It would last me forever. I could have chocolate every day and never run out, my mind racing with thoughts of what I would do. The driver returned, firing the engine as the radio crackled to life. His darting eyes in the mirror avoiding eye contact as if something were on his mind. The car lurched forward, frustrated hands crunching gears to find their slots. I gazed out of the back window as the lights of the gatehouse faded out of sight.

Four large Victorian cottages appeared in the shadows. Their tall, slated roofs overhanging ornate, leaded scrolled windows. Each one alight in a sea of children's faces, their cupped hands peering into the night. Slowly we passed them by, scurrying figures darted from window to window. Feeling uneasy, I turned away. At the last cottage, in the light of a half open door, an arched figure shielded their eyes. An elderly woman, tubby and rounded, neatly dressed in a white apron. Her graying hair pushed tightly into a bun. I continued to study her as she approached the car, her waving hand beckoning me to come out. "Why are we stopping here? I don't live here," I thought. Jumping down from the seat and leaving the warmth of the car, her voice was sharp and clear.

"Hello Philip, you must be the new boy I've heard all about. My name is Mrs. Mathews, I'm your new house mistress and this is your new home now. You have been moved to cottage number four." My heart sank, so my feelings had been right. I had been happy in the other cottage, all of my friends were there and now I was being put with the older boys. My stomach felt empty, gripping me in fear. Staring at the ground I wanted to become invisible. This wasn't happening to me, surely they had made a mistake! I couldn't move, I had seen how they bullied the younger boys. I had always been safe as I looked on from a distance but that was no more.

"But Miss, I don't want to," my voice trembling as hot tears filled my glasses and trickled down my face. I tried to fight them back but I couldn't control them anymore.

"What are you crying for? Grow up, you are a big boy now. Stop sniveling!" Her voice was laced with severity, impatient from being around so many children. I was one of many and many were too much.

I can't remember how long I had been at the orphanage. I knew of no other life and I felt totally alone. I had been abandoned at birth, never having a mother or father. What had I done that had been so wrong? Why can't I have happiness and a home like everyone else? A million thoughts ran through my mind all racing in different directions, returning with no answers. I couldn't run away, I had nowhere to go. I looked up from the ground, my eyes blurred with tears, I watched as the car turned and drove away into the darkness. I wanted so much to be in that car, to leave this place and to have a home. Mrs. Mathews placed her hand upon my shoulder and eased me to the steps. My head bowed, staring at the ground, an unknown force pushed me forward, holding me in a vice of fear.

"We have to get you washed up and into bed. Now stop crying or I'll give you something to cry about! We don't cry in this cottage, this is for the big boys!" Her voice echoing in my head.

As we ascended the steps the children's voices growing louder and louder. Rubbing my eyes, wiping my tears with firmness the damp handkerchief quickly returned to my pocket. I didn't want them to see me crying, taking a deep breath once more trying to control my nerves, my head level with the door handles. Mrs. Mathews pushing the door open, the warmth and smell of the room wrapping itself around us. Reaching down she grasped my hand, hers a wrinkled and hard road map of veins gnarled by time.

The noise instantly subsided as all attention now turned to us paused on the top step. Gripping Matron's hand tighter I looked around the room. Younger children in pajamas, endless faces returned my gaze. Benches stacked at the far end against the back wall along the left-hand side, closed shuttered windows, and a counter for serving food. Trays piled high, knives, spoons, forks, cutlery all neatly marked in corresponding boxes. A huge pine table worn and battered with age stood in the center of a polished red tiled floor. Long thin cords hung from the ceiling, chrome shades of dust illuminating dancing shadows upon pale yellow walls.

Around the table older children knelt on benches playing board games as others raced to retrieve overthrown dice, glancing inquisitively as they returned to their games. Younger boys stood motionless studying blank faces holding my gaze. Their searching eyes making me feel uneasy. Nudging and whispering, pointed fingers in my direction as silence descended upon the room.

"This is Philip, he is going to be living with us so make him feel welcome." All eyes now focused on us as a glow of embarrassment came over me. Hiding in the folds of Matron's freshly starched apron I tried to avoid eye contact. Her sideways glance at the clock on the wall was followed by clapping hands, informing them "30 minutes to bed time!" Her voice was lost in the reemerging chatter as games were instantly abandoned. Boards flipped and folded to be put away by the older children as younger ones in pajamas ran to the stairs on the right. Like a herd of rampaging buffalo, the thick, scrolled, wooden banister creaking with the nightly onslaught. Shouting, giggling children raced to be first to the top. "I want no mess left here and keep the noise down!" Mrs. Mathew's voice of authority rose above the unseen commotion.

One of the older girls gingerly approached, a girl's body of adolescence, not yet a woman. Tall and slim with long blonde hair, a softness to pale features with deep brown searching eyes.

"Betty, take Philip to the kitchen and tell Cook to find him something to eat. And hurry, it's late!"

Taking my hand we descended into the room, Betty leading me along a narrow hallway with doors on either side. The warmth and smell of baking making me hungry, drawing me in through the cracked doorway to a large, open kitchen. Pots and pans blackened from use hung from the thick, beamed ceiling. Either side of a window stood old stone sinks, their ornate iron legs standing on a spotless floor. Polished brass taps clung to the walls separated by wooden work surfaces. In the far corner large cream colored stoves bellowed heat from their cast iron plates topped with pots and kettles in a constant musical rattle, one against the other. Nervously, we approached the table, Betty taking the lead.

"Matron sent us, Cook. He needs something to eat before bed." An old lady hurriedly turned from a sink, crossing the room in a fluster, wiping her hands on her apron. Throwing them into the air explaining how late it was and how not to eat this late before bedtime! Reaching into a tall cupboard, retrieving a large plate of iced cakes, pausing before placing them on the table "Go on, I won't tell but be quick." She smiled as Betty took two, biting one then putting the other in her pocket. I picked mine from the plate. "Sit for a minute we aren't going to eat you," my startled expression drawing her remark. We both sat down counting the iced cakes as cook returned placing two cups of milk upon the table.

"What's your name?" she asked in a soft voice. Her pale blue eyes dulled by the passing of years, a gentle face lined with sincerity. "Philip," I whispered.

"Philip what?"

"I don't have a second name Miss, just Philip," my whispered reply.

A voice bellowed from the big room "I want everyone down for inspection in 10 minutes. It's bedtime!" Betty's face suddenly becoming alert with fear.

"We have to go now, thanks Cook. Come on Philip, we have to get you to the dorm." I hastily drank the milk and cursed for not putting the other cake in my pocket. As we left I turned and waved to see Cook, her back to us, head bent as if wiping her eyes. I am sure she was crying.

"Come on Philip, we have to hurry!" Betty pulled as we raced along the corridor, the noise growing louder as we approached the main room and upon reentering I couldn't believe my eyes!

Around the edge of the large table was a single file line of smaller boys my age in pajamas, chattering excitedly, pushing and shoving, poking fun with those around them. Others shuffled along in silence in two hands their underwear spread apart being kept in line by some of the older boys.

"Betty, what's was going on?" I whispered as we passed the line, making our way to the front. The children were now quieter and more organized but I squeezed Betty's hand holding it tighter than ever before.

"Inspection, everybody gets inspection!" There was no embarrassment, after all it was normal to parade with your underwear in front of Matron. How else would we have clean bottoms for little boys?

"Oh, there you are." Mrs. Mathews sat at the corner of the table, a tall chair giving her an elevated position. "Quiet on down. You boys there, quiet I said!" a pointed finger searching the line as a hush fell upon the room. "Where's Robert?"

One of the older boys approached "Here Miss."

"Take," there was a pause for a brief moment, "what's your name?"

"Philip, Miss."

"Take him to the dorm. Oh, before you go come here Philip." I stepped forward, by her side on the table sat a giant jar of golden colored liquid. She reached for the silver spoon standing inside and told me, "Open your mouth!"

The treacle like substance defied gravity. Upon extraction the spoon spinning in fingers, plunged into my open mouth. Her hand tucked under my chin in one sweeping, effortless movement closing it to deny me any second thoughts as the bittersweet taste of the liquid "that is good for growing little boys" slid gently down my throat.

"Robert, bring him to me in the morning. Now wash up and off to bed." Mrs. Mathews returned the spoon to the jar, turning to inspect the next boy's underwear held open for all to see.

"Come on slowcoach!" Robert leading me to the stairs, racing to the top two at a time. My fascination held, surveying the flickering scene through the rails of the banister, children assembled in lines as I ascended to the top of the creaking stairs.

"You, come here!" Robert stood by an open cupboard. On the top shelf were neatly folded pajamas marked in various sizes. Reaching inside he pulled a pair down, holding them against me. "No, too long. Aha! These look like they will fit," leaning down he held them by my side. "Perfect, here you'll need this!" Handing me a yellow toothbrush. "It's yours so don't lose it."

"Thank you," my hand squeezed it tightly, hoping it all would dissolve and I would wake up in my old bed and all this would be a dream, but it was still there.

"Come on, this way to the bathroom." We walked a little further along a corridor, the peeling walls dimly lit by the glow of shadeless bulbs. Numerous framed pictures of black clothed, adult figures surrounded by seated children all dressed the same. Crossed hands of motionless, sitting blank faces, their staring, peering eyes reflecting from the walls. Stopping at a large bathroom, Robert pointed inside.

"Go on, brush your teeth and use the toilet and get ready for bed. I have to see to the other boys, I'll be by the dorm. Come see me when you're done and I'll show you to your bed." His face broke into a smile. "If anyone starts on you, come get me. They might, being as you're new."

Old white sinks in the shapes of troughs lined the walls with mirrors of equal length. Tubes of paste and soap, one of each were set out for each sink with colorless worn towels hooked on racks at either end. I could hear the noise of the other boys my nerves gripping me as they started to enter. Some looking in angry stares before racing to find empty sinks. I looked away, not holding their attention. The bathroom becoming crowded with bodies, the noise of splashing water hastily washing faces. Brushed teeth checked in the mirror, all done in a flurry of movement as spotless children raced through the doorway, screaming towards the dorm.

I placed my belongings on a wooden bench as I stripped and quickly changed into my pajamas. The warmth of the cupboard was trapped in their softness giving me comfort. I made my way to the lower sink I had seen the smaller boy's use, the tiled floor felt cold upon my feet. Leaning forward, I began brushing my teeth. A tightness suddenly gripped my neck, holding me under the running tap. "Come on, it's that new kid. Duck him!" Cold water poured over my head, running down my neck and back. I struggled to breathe and break free yelling at them to, "Leave me alone!" Older boys entered the bathroom, laughing as they imitated my squeals. "You'll learn to be quicker next time little boy! Let's dump his head in the shitter!" I didn't know what this meant but with the distraction I broke free. My heart pounding running through the open door, I ran down the hallway, my clothes in hand to the light of the dormitory. Already I had lost my toothbrush and I wasn't going back for it! "Come on, you're going to have to be a lot quicker than this," Robert studying me as breathless I began to cry.

"What's up?!"

"The older boys!" He started to laugh. "I told you not to hang about, it's your own fault and hey! We don't tell tales here so shut it!" A poking finger added to my pain.

Inside the dormitory, beds were scattered everywhere. Some in neat lines others tucked in corners, many occupied by the smaller children, clothes folded neatly by their sides. A bucket in the center caught my eye.

"What's that for?"

"Stop you lot pissing the bed, Matron hates boys who piss the bed. Here's yours, fold your clothes and put them here."

"But there's someone in it?" Another boy occupied one end, he looked older than me his face of anger slid under the covers.

"I know, you have to share with him. You sleep this end and he gets the other. Now, get in." I looked around as I climbed into bed and noticed other boys were two in a bed also. "Here's your pillow."

"Thanks," Robert placing it under my head, there was no headboard and I pushed my feet deeper into the sheets. My soaking wet pajamas sticking to my skin I shivered, drawing my feet towards me to fight the cold. I felt a hard kick then another. I kicked back, Robert had gone away. Another kick hitting my ankle, anger began to well up inside. "Pack it in!"

"Why? What are you going to do? This is my bed!" My occupant's defiant reply.

"We have to share!" I pleaded.

"Well, I don't want to so get lost, find another bed!" I moved my feet to the side as another kick landed where I had been.

"I'll get you tomorrow. You won't want to sleep in this bed, you'll see." Shaking with cold and fear, I tried to sleep as screams whispered all around me softly at first, then louder.

"He's going to get you, he's coming to get yooou" echoing, haunting voices with eerie screams. I buried my head deeper in the sheets, pulled the edges tighter to lock my safe cocoon. I could hear laughter around the room. Inquisitive, I ventured my head above the sheets to peer into the darkness. The glow of the moon pushing its way to silhouette shapes in the dormitory. Straining my eyes I could see a small boy had tried to use the bucket, he ran away back to his bed crying and afraid to the delight of his tormentors. The older boys adding more screams and echoes to the room. I hated them, I would show them! I tried to settle down, eventually the warmth of the bed and the tiredness of the day let me escape. Reciting the words of a lullaby to hide their screams, the only one I knew. Over and over I recited "Bah, bah black sheep, have you any wool?" my voice in a quiver, tears gently rolling down my cheeks. Finding strength in the line "the little boy who lives down the lane," I drifted to sleep.

I had dreams, the sort of dreams that make you wake up covered in sweat. Those of a long, dark tunnel but there is something at the end. I am running fast, as fast as I can to the door at the end, only the closer you get the further away it becomes. Finally you burst into a room, you turn to get out the door has gone! Now there are four walls and you spin around looking for the door but the more you spin the more the walls close in. Everything is getting closer and closer! So you stay in the middle, they get closer and closer so you push and push, sitting down with your arms and legs pushing then you wake up covered in sweat.

The sort of dream with no mother or father to hold you tight and tell you it's ok, wiping the tears and sweat away, rocking you in their arms and talk to you softly, "It's ok. It's ok. It's only a dream." Only you wake up to a room full of beds and a bucket and you want to go but you can't move as the voices grow louder and louder so you just piss the bed! That sort of dream, only it wasn't a dream! As I woke up punches pounded my head "You little bastard! He pissed the bed! He pissed the bed! Get him!" The boy at the top shouting as loud as he could. "Fight! Fight!" Rang out as everyone came running, there was a flash as my neck creaked backwards to an explosion of pain my nose streamed with blood. I tried to fight back like a windmill, wailing my arms screaming in pain as other boys joined in. One punch, just one punch! I had to hit someone. I tried again protecting my face with my arm, more punches hit me, more and more "Leave him, he has had enough!" Everything stopped.

"Go on, move. Move it I said! You, come here!" Someone yanked me from the bed dropping me on the floor. "Come on, you clean up! "My legs weak, careless hands pushing me forwards I couldn't stand, tears filled my eyes. My whole body ached with pain running like an express train slamming to a halt at my head. I was pushed into the bathroom, blood splashing into the sink, trickling through my cupped hands. Crimson red droplets, drip after drip stretching to weird shapes, a twisting, swirling, red river vanishing out of sight. My head yanked backwards, I couldn't breathe as a cold towel smothered my face, fingers pinching my nose, a voice whispered in my ear.

"Little boy ran into the door, you have to be more careful around here!" My nose aching and throbbing, hair matted with blood and once more I was plunged under a cold tap.

"We don't tell tales now, what did you do?"

"I ran into the door sir."

"That's it, you remembered. Wash up, they won't hurt you for now. They had their fun, let's see," he wiped my face pushing toilet paper into my nose. "We should call you rubber nose, it's not broken," the smirk of a predator in his voice.

Other boys came in imitating my windmill punches looking at me laughing, covering their heads, "Perfect punch Billy. Got him good, said he would. Got him perfect." I looked at them, all older and bigger than me. As if to glean some victory, something to hold on to, my pain eased for a second as if to tell me I had tried. I didn't just take their bullying they were bigger, stronger but one day my day would come. For now though pain was to be my friend and he had no mercy.

The orphanage became a game of survival as simple as black and white, there were rules you followed, not written but the sort you learn and fast. By watching, looking and being quiet, your senses sharpen, they say you can sense danger well it's like you felt danger. You could touch it, instantly knowing when it was there. You learnt fast never to be alone when older boys were around, keeping well out of their way. I learned to fight as they goaded me to a split lip or bloody nose with cheers from a surrounding crowd. I fought with other boys my age, their twisted lies manufactured fights for their brutality had no boundaries.

Only the winner was admired so you made sure you didn't lose and I made sure it wasn't me! I was skinny, not tall, but had fast hands. You hit first, you had to. Don't bother to push and shove or argue, biting your tongue to kill pain that came your way. Anger surging you forward with everything you have got. Sometimes crashing through the circle as you drove opponents to the ground. I learned to be quick and not get hurt just speed and surprise, either that or they would hit you. What choice did I have? There was no room for pity in this merciless world, what's that? You felt no remorse, this was someone else who you would blame in your conscience for they carried the shame of what you had become. You never cried, not in front of the others, if you did you were a cry baby, a wimp. You were weak and would attract attention like a magnet, then more bullying would come your way and no one ever saw a thing. Who could you turn to, who?! No one! There was only you. "You're a big boy now! We don't tell tales here!" the voices echoed in my mind sharp and clear.

I had started to settle and stand up for myself getting a reputation amongst boys of my age. I had been moved out of the bed I shared. Feeling the full fury of Mrs. Mathews shouting and screaming at the "dirty little boy who wets the bed." Telling all who wanted to hear, her voice travelled across the room "this is what wet beds get!" Smacking my legs with one hand, holding my arms up high like a trained wrestler knowing my every twist and move. Soon I became immune to the daily routine. I now had my own bed, it was small but my own, the peeling metal frame was low to the floor so I could climb on and off with ease. A hard plastic sheet was placed on the bottom. The crunching noise keeping me awake as I tossed and turned between the sheets. I had been moved nearer the bucket to the corner of the room with other boys my age, all I needed now was courage to fight their screams.

I cried at night in the blanket of darkness, finding safety in the silence of the room. They didn't know where the sound came from. Your head burying in the pillow not making a sound, just quiet tears at first then fighting them till your stomach aches as tension grips to hold them back. "Stop or they will hear you." Your chest hurts, heart pounds, your muscles tense, every part of you joins the fight. Squeezing your eyes dry to yet more silent tears, the ones that come from your soul, from deep within. You can't hold back so you try to push them away but it makes them worse, they won't stop. Voices constantly reminding you, telling you how hopeless it all was "You are on your own, no one love's you. You are worthless, you don't deserve a family. It's your own fault no one wants you, why should they?" In the silence a thousand taunting voices whisper to tell you it's the way it is. Tears that drain a well of your broken heart and leave me tossing and turning. Sweat rolls down your cheeks till sweat and tears become one.

At last the aching in my head subsides and tiredness takes me away to peace. A place where no one could hurt you as your dreams take over, surrounding you in a shell of safety and love. To a family with dogs and a house with brothers and sisters, you make them laugh, they love you. I have a bike, playing in the street riding around and around. It's yours, gleaming new wheels shining in the sun as you peddle through puddles. Laughter and voices loud and clear, you're hugging a dog. Feeling his love, he likes you, pushing you to the ground hot breath and kisses washing your face. Toys, my toys and being told how clever I am because I could draw and write. Your guard was down, you were normal again, there was no pain here, no fighting. You were a good boy, the one you knew you were. You felt happiness as your mother held you in her arms, sheltering you, holding you tight. It felt secure and safe, everything was there, you could feel the warmth of sunshine, reach and touch things, smell life itself. Only to be woken by a bell, louder and louder every morning, that same noise opening my eyes to the reality of another day. Sheets ripped from the bed, surrounded by staring faces."

"Told you! He's still pissing the bed!" A raised fist about to come my way.

"No I haven't!" I blurted as fast as I could to halt my tormentor.

"What?"

"I haven't pissed the bed, look!" my voice stuttering with fear.

I jumped out of bed and by now a few of the older boys had gathered around and stared at the dry sheets, tearing them back to expose the worn rubber sheet below. It was dry, their faces in disbelief. It had seemed like an eternity, so long with the pain and bullying.

"He's right! Look!" I had overcome my fear, I had won I had beaten them at last. What had been so hard was now so stupid and so easy. Why? Why hadn't I been brave before? Why had I tortured myself?

"See, I haven't," my voice enthusiastic, as others came to witness this great event. No punches this time just pats and pushes as more boys gathered around.

Slowly, I recalled last night, I had eased the blankets back, the creaking rubber sheet defining my every move. Moving gently, trying not to make a sound as I crept forward into the blackness then ran. Screams were all around me but I kept running, straining my eyes looking for the bucket. "I must be near. Where is it! Where is it?!" There in the half light at last, fumbling in darkness, tingling with fear as the voices of the dead echoing around the room. "He's going to get you. Behind you, look behind you!" Voices exploding in my ears but to turn back was too far, I was here now and I wasn't going back. Their taunts drowned out by the splashing as I relived myself. The smell of stale urine reaching out from the darkness and wrapped itself around me, clinging to me, covering my mouth I held my breath. Returning fast as I could to the safety of my bed, it beaconed me, willed me, as my heart pounded and I gasped for breath. Then I pulled the warm sheets tightly over my head. Shivering, I found sanctuary, my cocoon blocking out their taunts. Their voices could harm me no more and now I had won, I had won, so surely they wouldn't bully me anymore.

"Come on, let's tell Mrs. Mathews." Trevor, the lead boy, led me out of the dorm with his hand on my shoulder. "If you keep this up you will go to Pathelle. We all go." His face breaking into a smile with excitement.

"What's that?"

"Let's see what Mrs. Mathews says first, it's up to her to decide."

Double stepping the stairs my hand skimming the banister, smooth as glass, polished by a thousand hands before me. Jumping the bottom two steps landing at the side of Trevor. Today I would not be punished, exuberance bursting in my heart. We descended into the main room, an ant's nest of activity as we approached the serving hatches along the far wall.

"Where's Mrs. Mathews?" Trevor asked a boy his age holding an empty tray.

"Why, what's he done now?"

"Nothing, we have a surprise for her."

"Main kitchen last time I saw her," the boy shouting over his shoulder turning away.

We moved along the open serving hatches, my neck straining to view above the counter. Older boys and girls were busy chattering, some buttering toast, others wiping knives and spoons oblivious to us. The warm smell of food followed as we passed them by. Big steel pots with ladles hooked on their side. Chipped blue and white bowls spread in neat rows steaming and shining with the heat of cleanliness. Military lined for porridge to be added one hungry mouth at a time. The next hatch stacked with mountains of toast, giant jars of golden marmalade stood by their side. Long spoons submerged in thick peel, a measured amount given to each child. In the center of the room the big pine table benches surrounding the sides ready to receive the hoard of children at the sound of a breakfast bell. An aroma to the commotion, the warmth of food, the smell of fresh bread, the hustle of noise everyone working with precision. Homeless synchronized puppets all with a job to do. I saw Betty, her face inquisitive as we passed by.

"Come on Philip, stop dawdling, haven't you seen food before?!" I hadn't, I had never been down before bell. Feeling hungrier by the minute we moved around the table to the hallway. The main kitchen lights drawing us past the faceless pictures, their eyes glaring at us but even they seemed happier now.

"Mrs. Mathews!" Trevor shouted in a loud voice pushing the door gently open, the heat rushing by as we entered the kitchen to the constant rattle of pots and smells.

"Who's shouting my name?" Mrs. Mathews asked turning around, her face instantly changing to anger. Hastily she approached her steel grey eyes fixed straight at me. I tried to hide behind Trevor and looked away as I knew that face and what was to come. Behind her Cook looked down with sadness as if she wanted to rescue me.

"Not Philip again?! I don't know what I am going to do with you boy!"

"But Miss!" Trevor shouted, his voice nervous at his challenge to her authority "He didn't wet the bed, its dry Miss." I sheepishly looked up at her.

"What? After all this time?" There was a silence of disbelief. "Are you sure? Did you check the bottom sheet, the plastic one?!"

"Yes Miss, it was bone dry."

"Are you sure??"

"Yes Miss." Trevor's voice emphasized his point.

Her face changed to gentleness, a smile crossed her lips. "At last! At last! He can do it once, he can do it twice!" Mrs. Mathews throwing her hands in the air, kneeling down to my level. "Philip, come here," her voice softer now.

Slowly I moved forward, my face beaming with smiles as she rubbed my head. A glow of pride rushed through my body as I rocked from side to side, happy at last I had done something good! Even Cook joined in, clapping her hands together with excitement.

"We'll make you special toast today!"

"Philip look at me!" Mrs. Mathew's firm, cold eyes holding my attention, hands pressing on my shoulders keeping me still. "If you keep this up I will let you go to Pathelle."

"What's that Miss?" My voice curious, I had no idea what she was on about.

"Well, we all go to the seaside for a whole week but only good boys can go. Do you promise to be good and not to wet the bed? We can't take wet beds, do you understand?"

"Yes Miss. I promise Miss. Please Miss, please let me go." I pled, happier now than I had ever been. What was the sea like? And sand, did it have sand? And birds? Can we swim? So many questions. "Miss, can we swim?" I blurt out from nowhere.

"First, you have to be good. Then we will see."

I couldn't even swim but I would try. She straightened up and looked at

Trevor. "Take him to the main room and Trevor, find him something to do after breakfast. Give him a little job."

"Yes Miss." His voice impatient at all the fuss for this little boy.

"Philip." Cook smiled and held a plate of fresh toast from the oven covered in butter and marmalade. "Here, take this, it's for being a good boy."

"Thank you Miss." We turned and left the kitchen "I told you he could do it," their voices fading away as we moved along the corridor stopping at the bottom of the stairs.

"Go and change and hurry! Here, give me your toast, no one will steal it." Trevor held out his hand as I reluctantly passed it to him. "Hurry, the bell will be going in a minute!"

His voice lost in my head as I flew up the stairs two at a time. My bathroom routine done at speed, ignoring comments around me. Hastily, I rejoined other children queuing at the top of the stairs hoping to retrieve my toast before Trevor ate it.

"Christopher, what's it like at Pathelle?"

"What do you want to know?" The older boy was intrigued frowning curiously. "It's the seaside. A bus comes and collects us, we go for a week."

The sound of a breakfast bell igniting the tidal wave of children, all of them surging forward, pushing and shoving. Squeals and laughter descending into turmoil in the room below.

"Calm down you lot! Stop pushing!" a monitor shouted grabbing one of the younger boys, pulling him to the side to calm him down. The room buzzing with excitement, everyone had one question, "Are you going to Pathelle?" I pushed toward my place at the table questions from every direction went unanswered. As I drew near, Trevor stood smiling looking at me with an empty plate tipping it upside down as if to emphasize his point.

"You never leave things around here." His face covered in marmalade shaking his head with laughter. "You should know better little boy!" Bending down a fist gripping me tightly as he dusted his mouth on my shoulder drawing me closer. "Remember little boy, we don't tell tales," his face hidden in the crowd. I instantly kept quiet "now go get breakfast and see me later." Everyone was talking but I never heard a word eating my toast as fast as I could. Hands grabbing in every direction till the stack had gone.

You learned to eat fast, either that or you had none it's just the way it was. At the end of breakfast my chore was to help clear tables, soiled cutlery placed in trays at the ends of the counters.

"Philip!" A girl's voice called my name, Betty appearing behind me, it seemed like an eternity since I had last seen her. She knelt to one knee as I ran to her open arms. Her face bursting in smiles the warmth of a hug giving me security of love, of hope. She was someone I could trust, I remembered her from my first day.

"Betty, where have you been, I missed you?!"

"In cottage number one helping with the little ones." My old cottage, how I wished I was back there with all my friends.

"How's Ryan and Thomas?" She ignored my question releasing me from her arms, "Philip you going to Pathelle?"

"I don't know, depends how good I am. I have to stop wetting the bed," my voice softer tears welling inside of me. I could feel my face reddening with shame as I looked at the floor. She paused for a brief moment, "It's not your fault. It's not you, look at me." Her finger lifting my chin her voice sterner now, slowly I raised my head to look into her deep brown eyes. I could see the pain in her expression as she parted her hair with one hand, the other reaching forward touching my face. Her flat palm against my cheek, a mother's touch, feelings I could not understand and had been denied, that can only come from someone given with love.

The flowers on her dress adding to the smell of fresh soap, of pureness, the gentleness of a girl trying to be a mother. "You will do it. When they try to frighten you think of me by your side. I will protect you, you have to come I will miss you so much if you don't." Her voice giving me courage, igniting an inner strength a gift I never knew. "Then I will try harder Betty, I promise. I won't let you down, I want to be with you." She was my best friend, the only one I had. No one else in this cottage bothered with me, I was just a face in a sea of many faces. It was up to me to survive in this home of broken hearts. Betty was much taller and older than me putting her arm to my shoulder she gently kissed my forehead. Feeling uneasy at the affection I mumbled, "Have you been?"

"Oh yes, we have campfires and sing songs and picnics, but you have to be good or they won't let you go."

"I will try my best but they keep picking on me. Why won't they leave me alone?!" Her voice dropped to a whisper, cupping her hands to draw me closer. "Stay away from the older boys, they will only get you in trouble. They do that to everyone, they are so spiteful and I hate them all, I want you to come."

"Betty, I have never seen the sea or been on a holiday," a note of resentment in my voice. She knew the only life we had was the orphanage, it's all I knew, it's all I could remember. "When do they leave?"

"In two weeks, I am so excited." She took my hand, I could feel her trembling.

"Philip! Clear the table!" A voice broke our silence. Trevor shouted from across the room waking me from my daydreams of Betty and the sea. I squeezed her hand to look once more into her deep and gentle eyes searching for answers to questions I could not ask. "Was this love the love of a sister? What was love?" She smiled as I turned away, back to the tables to collect more cutlery, faceless names all with a job to do.

I would be good, I had to go. My mind was set, I would do whatever it took, I was going to Pathelle. Time passed so slowly for a little boy every second dragged, two weeks taking forever. I stayed out of trouble holding my temper when taunted to fight. Never wetting the bed, ignored their voices and screams, they couldn't hurt me anymore. Betty was by my side, hidden in my dreams and each day she would smile or wave to give me the strength and courage to beat them all.

Chapter 2

A VISION OF FREEDOM AND HOPE

"Come on, we're going on holiday!!!!" Groups of children from every direction raced to assemble leaving everything behind tugging and pulling, squealing in delight. Cheers interrupting monitors, their voices drowned by a hundred thundering feet all charging to the main room. Even they were caught up in the excitement as the place burst into life clapping their hands, hurrying children to go, "move now or be left behind!"

I scrambled downstairs grabbing the banister for support taking two or three stairs at a time, it didn't matter all of us landing in a heap at the bottom. Bodies untangling, laughing, running to line up by the big table. Children gathering around jumping up and down uncontrollably, chatting about the time to come and what we all would do. Everyone talking at once in a crescendo of noise and happiness, at last we were on our way! My first adventure, I was leaving this place that had imprisoned my childhood to be a normal child or as normal as I could be. Now I would be free, so long I had waited I came alive injected by strange feelings giving me energy that I could not control. A surge of joy, I could feel it, taste it all around me, wave my hand in the warmth of it. The sensation engulfed me as pure elation and happiness now entered my dismal world.

"Calm down! Or you won't be going anywhere!" The monitors fighting to control the commotion, pushing boys back in line. "Quiet! Stand still! I said stand still! We have to count you or you won't be going anywhere!" I immediately froze as they moved along the line, tapping heads and counting out loud. Misbehavior as always switched to a punch ending in squeals or tears. All around us older children packing laundry baskets with everything that makes a holiday. Mountains of clothes, shoes and swimwear, sheets and blankets piled high. The main doors were wide open Mrs. Mathews pausing to give encouragement and rules, recounting children as we passed by.

At the top step an orderly queue descended into brilliant sunlight and the clear blue sky of a summer's day. We moved along not daring to attract attention as we waited patiently to board one of the sharabangs. At the front set in the grill, the face of a Red Indian Chief. His feathered headdress beautifully polished staring straight ahead as if to call unseen spirits to guide us safely along the way. The engine ticking in an endless mechanical rhythm as if the beating of his heart. Grabbing a chrome rail I scrambled up the steps, the smell of leather greeting me as I ran to find an empty window. Throwing myself in the seat I immediately began pulling faces at those in line.

"Is everyone ready for Pathelle?!" One of the monitors asked. A mighty cheer went out to the roar of the engine and finally the door was closed. We moved forward slowly passing the cottages that were our home. In the last one a small, kneeling child waved from a top window. I wondered, "Why she had been left behind?" As we turned the corner Mrs. Mathews stood alone, her distant figure fading out of sight. To a young boy the journey seemed to take forever as we left the town to the open countryside and sounds of "One Man Went to Mow and Old McDonald." We sang for what seemed like hours, finally I succumbed to the hypnotic creaking of the coach as I fell to a deep sleep.

"PHILIP! Wake up! Wake up, we're here!" Betty leaning over me shaking me like a rag doll, her smiling face enlightened with excitement. Throwing the bed covers aside I stumbled forwards, wiping the sleep from my eyes. The sound of a morning bell still echoing in my ears as my dreams vanished and reality woke me to this new day.

"Betty, where am I? What? What's that strange smell!?!" Pinching my nose in disgust at the aroma surrounding me.

"Philip, you're in the girl's dormitory, all the young boys have been placed in here," Betty bursting to laughter at my twisted face.

I was in a freshly painted wooden hut with iron bunk beds lining the walls.

Neatly laid out numbered grey lockers sat at the foot of beds creating a centre aisle. The mist of excited morning chatter escaped from a bathroom at the far end of the room as girls in nightdresses carrying bundles of clothes disappeared through a swinging door.

"Don't worry, we'll look after you." Betty recapturing my attention, sensing my relief that older boys couldn't bully me here.

"Now wake up, we have to go to breakfast!" Hurriedly thrusting my clothes towards me as she turned to attend to other children nearby. I made my bed, it was the first thing you ever learned, double checking the mattress to make sure I hadn't pissed it. A bounce now in my stride at my accomplishment, I entered the crowded bathroom full of laughter and squeals.

"Philip! Over here, have my sink!" Ryan, my friend from cottage one stood back admiring his reflection. His mass of curly hair protruding in a horizontal explosion held in place by ears that God had decided should come out of his head sideward. Not quite my height, of a plump build, I felt sorry for him after all he would be joining my cottage next year.

"Philip, have you seen Thomas? What's happening? When can we go out to play?" Our conversation abruptly halted as Betty entered the room.

"Philip, you know better, sinks are for brushing teeth! Go shower and hurry up. Come on, I'll be waiting." Her voice now showing impatience. Joining other children I hurried to an empty stall showering as fast as I could to be dried off in minutes. Betty's unforgiving hands spinning me around, the rough towel digging into my ears, blocking her voice as she idly chatted away.

"Now put these on and line up by the door, make sure you're not last." Her scolding tone was that of an elder sister. The warm water igniting my senses, I was now so close to my dreams. "What colour was the sea? What did sand look like?" I wanted all my questions answered. Leaving the bathroom to join Ryan by the doorway, my timing was impeccable as our breakfast bell just rang.

Our orderly queue of small children soon finding the hut that was to be our canteen. Following the smells drifting towards us of a fried breakfast and the clatter of plates as we entered through the open door.

"For His kindness we ensure ever faithful ever sure." The morning hymn echoing around the old wooden hut and we sang faster than I can ever recall. Voices hurriedly answering to God and His grace at the end to be drowned by questions of when can we play? Where is the sea? Excitement filled the air mixed with the smell of breakfast and fresh creosote which gave the room a smell all its own. "More bacon! More eggs!" Voices behind the counter repeatedly shouted, hardly heard above the din as the noise grew louder. I turned in my seat to watch as other children formed a line with trays and plates to emerge with breakfast piled high. Each table taking turns as I tried to find other friends I had missed, to wave and shout, "I'm here! Come sit here!"

"Philip, be quiet now!" Betty shouted tapping my head as she walked by to cajole another table in an relentless battle to quiet the noise. Ryan fell into the seat by my side much to my excitement and amusement then Thomas his blond hair ruffled, untouched by a morning comb. His drawn, featureless face was deep and searching as if he needed to eat ten breakfasts, not one to add weight to his skinny frame. "Table Eight!" A voice shouted as we hastily grabbed breakfast returning to eat as fast as our forks could carry the food to growing, hungry mouths.

Betty stood at the end of the table looking down at us, placing her hands to the side. "The monitors have spoken to Mr. Davies, who is in charge, he said you can go to the beach after breakfast. Your swimwear and towels are in your lockers if you need them." We hardly looked up as we gorged our food to see who would finish first. Asking to be excused from the table, laughing and squealing as we sprinted to our hut changing in minutes to be ready for our new adventure. My heart bursting inside, I waited for no one, "At last all my questions would be answered."

I raced out the door into the brightness of a cloudless sky, the morning sun added warmth to my face. Passing dunes, their tall grasses bent and swayed in an unending dance with the breeze. Gulls glided effortlessly above my head tilted wings following me crying for attention I could not give. Half buried, twisted, grey fences led my way to a steep pathway hidden in sand from the night before. The roar of the ocean waves calling me I pushed forward, mounds of sand dragging me backwards in an avalanche. Finally I reached the top, my heart pounding, bursting to the explosion of beauty that lay before me. Shielding my eyes to look upon the ocean itself. Sunlight reflecting in radiant diamonds, glistening upon cresting white waves, constantly rolling, turning to a never ending roar before crashing upon a golden shore.

The deep blue ocean stretching as far as I could see. I was lost in my new world, my shadow my only friend as I raced down to the water along the shimmering sand. Gulls dived effortlessly pulling fish from the sea as sand pipers scattered before me dancing in and out of the waves, as if chasing their reflection in an eternal game of hide and seek. Then silence to be broken by shells rolling in the surf to crash again all around me filling the air with salt to be carried in the wind. Standing alone a little boy with a dream, I had found my escape. What lay on the other side beyond the horizon? I stood transfixed in amazement at the wonder of it all. I knew in my heart one day I would travel. I vowed to myself this was the beginning of my life and I wanted more.

"Philip! Philip! Over here!" A voice I instantly recognized snapped me out of my dream. Thomas calling me from a rocky point in the distance. Ryan stood at his side franticly waving a small net above his head. I raced towards them, scampering over rock covered seaweed their voices clearer as I drew near.

"Betty gave us these, look what we've caught!" Thomas thrusting a small bucket with both hands towards me, his face wild with excitement. There swirling around in the murky water amongst the pebbles were small crabs and shrimp.

"Here, let's try this pool." Thomas bent over lifting small rocks as I joined in by plunging my hands into the ice cold water. Crabs scurried away chased by Ryan's net as the dust of a sandstorm hiding their escape. All three of us inspecting our catch. We spent hours lost in our quest for bigger game moving from pool to pool our shirtless backs burnt from the cloudless sky.

"Here you all are." Betty approached, her loose dress flowing in the wind, clinging to the slender frame of a young woman. Preoccupied hands fighting the gentle breeze to parted hair revealing her pale complexion now caught by the blazing hot sun. I smiled as all three of us stared at her, she really was a creature of habit.

"You have to give the net and bucket to the other children now."

"Oh Miss!!" All three of us shouted at once. The disappointment clear in our voices.

"You can borrow it again tomorrow." I knew it was useless to complain, her voice was in a firm no nonsense tone.

"We share, remember, now don't argue other children have to play as well. Come on, its dinner time so go join the others over there." We looked in the direction she was pointing, other children were sitting on blankets having a picnic. We ran to the water's edge tipping our bucket, releasing our catch to the freedom of the ocean. Our day dissolved in the happiness of long shadows and playing in the sea.

Pathelle was everything I wanted it to be, better than my wildest dreams. All those nights of waiting faded away to reality. I was here at last, my spirit set free to run wild, to meet nature one to one. The shadows of my past left behind as I opened a door to the innocence of childhood. Beauty rushing in surrounding me with a love of life I had always dreamed of as I wandered aimlessly in my new world. The week had gone by so quickly, I so wanted time to stand still, to leave me here forever.

"We will be back Philip. Be brave." Betty could see the sadness in my face tenderly wiping my tears, placing her hand upon my shoulder. I turned to look once more, to say goodbye to this place that had been my home.

Old wooden RAF huts silhouetted against a blazing sky as the sun dipped into the ocean, leaving a cascade of colors to illuminate all around me. The gentle wind caressing tall grasses that lined the rocky shore line to the high pitched chorus of gulls dipping and floating on the evening breeze. Memories of the ocean, of buckets and nets, sandcastles and shrimp. Evening campfires and sing songs as embers danced in the stars of a moonlit night. The tides of tomorrow washing away the memories of today, all of this had come to an end and now I returned to the orphanage and the life I had left behind.

I became totally depressed, not having the strength to fight the bullies as they made my life hell. Often I could be found sitting alone banging the side of my head against a wall. Starting with a gentle thud then harder and harder till the pain became numb, only to change sides. Slowly increasing the tempo sometimes till a trickle of blood would run down my face. Totally in despair, my world had fallen apart. I had felt love and happiness and it had slipped through my fingers, now this living nightmare was all I had left. I became a loner, isolated, withdrawn, closing out the outside world.

One day I was trying to tie my shoelaces, I remember it clearly. Sitting on a wooden bench I could not master the art and was being scolded. I rebelled finally being yanked from the bench to receive slaps around my legs, my short trousers adding little protection the woman shouted my name. A girl much older than me appeared from nowhere immediately springing to action. Tall and of a skinny build she jumped on the woman's back pulling her hair causing my scolding to stop, screaming "Leave my brother alone! Leave him!" Her arms locked around the woman's neck pulling her backwards, forcing her to release the grip that she had held so tight. She had the same red hair as me, my eyes locking into hers, that same deep blue. As I looked at her in shock she yelled again, "Leave my brother alone!" Punching and kicking, lashing out at anyone who came near me. Finally she was dragged away, later I was told, "That was your sister, she's new here." I found out her name was Margaret, from that day I never saw her again.

Those are the scars that I talk about, the ones on the inside that bleed the most, that don't go away. I want you to look into my heart, to see who I am, what I became and what I endured as a small boy in that sea of darkness that was my childhood. To not be capable of accepting real love, to deny it for the rest of your life, to treat love with distrust and never to understand it since I never felt it as a small child yet I always to search for it. We go through life and build character making us strong for the times ahead so we can bend in the wind and ride the storm of life that will come our way. I was raised in an orphanage, a simple sentence with a thousand hidden scars, this was my childhood. Shortly after the incident with my sister I was moved to a home with five other children, more bullying would come my way only this time I had an answer. It was here that I would suffer a different type of abuse, one that would damage me for the rest of my life.

Chapter 3

HAPPY BIRTHDAY TO YOU

"Happy birthday to you. Happy birthday dear Geoffrey happy birthday to you."

I was eight years old my first birthday party and now I had been given my real name. I didn't like it, after all I was Philip, but not anymore. I was in a foster home with two girls, Ann and Christine, aged fourteen and three boys, two of them brothers. I settled into my new home, attending a different school even being allowed at certain times to play in a street. In the normality of my surroundings I soon made new friends.

For the first time in my life I wasn't encased in a wall, but once again the bullying started from one of the older boys. I was no match for the pounding fists of a fourteen year old as he threw me around like a rag doll. I tried so hard to give as good as I got but in the end I gave in. Now I had a solution when I got beaten my answer was simple, I would dish the same out to the younger brother Howard, who was my age. I became a bully making his life a misery at school. In the end the two older boys had a fight and at last my bullying stopped. I was glad as I hated what I had to do to him, but what choice did I have?

The foster home consisted of two houses joined into one. A young couple, Mr. and Mrs. Morris were the house wardens who kept us all in line with strict house rules. We had a cook and our food was delivered once a month. Television viewing had to be earned, pocket money was only given after completed tasks. I had to clean everyone's shoes each night before bedtime. For this I was given a shilling at the end of the week, half of which had to be saved. I learned the value of work and to respect money even at this early age.

My problem started after about six months. We had erected a tent in the back garden and one of the girls who had been pushed away by the older boys came to investigate. What started as a gentle hug from Ann, who I looked upon as my big sister soon turned to something else. I missed Betty and turned to her for affection, only she led me down a pathway to depravity as she stripped my innocence of childhood away. Replacing it with all the inquisitiveness of a fourteen year old girl, probing hands searched my body in the seclusion of blankets and canvas.

Stolen games of doctors and nurses and hide and seek as she led me into the darkness of empty, quiet rooms. Her searching hands inspecting what she found, stroking my tiny penis as she pulled her clothing aside. My small fingers held deep between her legs. There was a strange, sweet smell to her hot breath as her knickers became moist to the touch. I wondered what had happened to her as she wasn't the same as me. At first I felt uncomfortable, as if we were doing something wrong, but slowly I became immune. I looked forward to our encounters as she showed me affection and love. After two months we finally got caught by the house mistress who dragged me downstairs screaming, "You dirty little boy! You should be ashamed of yourself!" I was only eight and a half years old, the girl was fourteen but with a low mental age, she went to a special school for backwards children. Who was the abuser? Was it her? Was it me? Who was to blame? Was she taking revenge for what had been done to her? Was this love? The love of a sister, how they treated a brother? Betty had never treated me like this and now I was the filthy little boy who should be ashamed of himself?

Shortly after the incident I was moved from the foster home to foster parents. The pain I suffered at those wandering hands destroyed my innocence never allowing me to flower and grow, to discover the wonders of youth. Flashbacks of darkened rooms haunted my dreams. I felt dirty, perverted whenever I wanted to show affection, even at the slightest touch. I just could not open my heart to anyone anymore as all I had received was rejection and pain.

I would be asked many times, do you ever want to meet your parents? My answer was always the same, no. Why not? If you have a child, that child deserves to know who their parents are. I would travel the ends of the earth to find my child. I may not always be there for them but they at least would know who their father was. No man abandons his blood, his child! To suffer the hardships and abuse I had to endure. For both my parents to leave me to face life alone, there are no excuses and never will be forgiveness as they denied me a childhood and broke my heart.

Chapter 4

THE CANAL BRIDGE AND THE GIRL ACROSS THE STREET

It's strange how a day locks in your mind that even after all these years you remember it even clearer than yesterday, a day that changed your life forever, that one moment when you know in your heart, "my life changed on that day." My life would embark on a new course in a new direction leaving the memories of the past behind, that would lead me to heights I never dreamed of or could have imagined. To touch on many lives, to say, "I knew you."

The sun felt good as I paused on the canal bridge feeling the slight breeze of that summer's day. Taking a deep breath I had time to look around at my new surroundings, I hadn't a care in the world. Old factories staring at the canal overgrown with weeds, their cracked painted walls, faded advertisements telling us of goods we didn't want any more. Dirty, broken windows guided shafts of sunlight to empty rooms where machines and men once stood. Factories lost forever neglected left to fend for themselves even industry had turned its back on you now. You didn't belong this was the seventies, times were moving forward technology was on the way.

Yet not a ripple on the canal as tall reeds stood motionless in the heat of the day casting shadows on the mirror of still water below me. There in my reflection the face of a sixteen year old boy. What lay ahead of me? What would I be like in 10 years? I wonder what old skin feels like. My face soft and smooth to the touch. A smile looking back in the reflection, mindless thoughts passed slowly through my head. I turned and walked away leaving them all behind.

Now free of all the shackles that had been my childhood, I was an apprentice with a local company finding independence, a freedom I had been denied all of my life. I had started to save and buy clothes, paying rent to my foster parents the rest to spend as I wanted. My hair cropped, now spiky to the touch I felt smart in my button down shirt. My jeans turned up to reveal red socks with 16 hole cherry reds, Dr. Martens boots polished to perfection from the night before. I had swapped a denim jacket for them they were now my pride and joy.

I looked like a skinhead but I didn't feel like one, I was just following the fashion at the time. I was on my way to my Uncle's I loved him as a father and he treated me as his son. He was blind but you would never know, and my Auntie a fiery little woman with the temper of a volcano. They were part of my new foster family they had two children and accepted me as their own, opening their hearts showing me a love I never felt at home.

As I turned the corner to cross the street three girls stood chatting by Newsagents, one of them caught my eye. Not being shy I walked toward them never taking my eyes off the girl in the red skirt. Short in stature, her slim figure and beautiful legs attracting my attention, she had the body of a goddess. I hesitated in my step, I had never been out with a girl or had a girlfriend, what was I doing? Her eyes avoiding mine as I approached lifting to reveal the face of a beautiful young girl. Long, brown, wavy hair her features so pure and simple, I was looking at the face of an angel. Her hazel blue eyes holding my gaze lighting a hidden smile of pure innocence.

"My name's Gethro. What's yours?" A squeaky nervous tone in my voice, immediately all three girls started to laugh. I could feel my face redden in embarrassment, I felt stupid their laughter irritating me as I asked again not backing away, "what's your name?"

"I don't speak to strangers. Didn't your mom tell you that?!" a sharpness in her voice showing irritation at my persistence as she turned to walk away.

"I was just asking," once more I persevered. "I think you're beautiful," blurted from my lips. Immediately she turned around. Where did that come from? I had lost control of my voice, I felt uncomfortable with no way out of the silence between us. Once more I gathered my thoughts refusing to give in, "at least give me your name." Ignoring their immediate surrounding laughter.

"Find out Gethro." She teased, a softness to her voice in a strange way questioning me.

"Do you go to the East Park?"

"Never heard of it." I felt really stupid my chat up lines were useless, totally unrehearsed. "Why had I said that?" My mind racing to think of something new to say "Will I see you there tomorrow?"

"Maybe if we can find it," she turned and walked away, her friends leaning on her shoulders, cupped hands to silent whispers laughing at her side. I stood alone my heart racing, frozen in time unable to move as she gave me a second look before I carried on my way immediately running to my Aunt's.

"Where's Robert?" I yelled as I charged through the half open door.

"It's Geoff mall!" Uncle Ron standing at the sink washing crockery, stacking them neatly to his side. "Robert, Geoffrey's here!" Auntie Marry explained always using my full name as Robert entered the kitchen.

"Rob, who's that girl at the Newsagents?"

"What girl? What's she like?" His voice inquisitive.

"Really pretty, about this high with long brown wavy hair," my hand extended, trying to guess her height.

"Oh yea!! I have seen her, dead pretty. Kim I think, yea! Her name's Kim." His face breaking to a smile of mischief.

"What do you know about her?" I wanted more, I wanted to know.

"She hasn't been here long. She's from London, they just moved in down the street to number thirty-eight I think." I felt a little happier now, I knew she lived near my Auntie.

"I just arranged a date with her over at the park." I replied trying to impress him and boost my shattered confidence.

"Nice girl Geoff, bit young for you though." A confused smirk emphasizing his point.

"What? What do you mean Rob?"

"I think she's thirteen."

What! My heart sank, no way could I date a girl thirteen and me sixteen. She's still at school, me a cradle snatcher, the lads would kill me. I had to find out how old she was. I had to know?! But at least now I had her name.

A few days passed and I still couldn't get her out of my head. There was just something drawing me to her. So her name was Kim, that's all I had to go on. I passed the small row of shops on the way to Rusty's many times hoping I would see her but she wasn't there.

Rusty and I had grown up together, he had become one of my closest friends. We had formed a small crew, just a load of mates that knocked around together, calling ourselves Twenty Nine Crew. All of us were skinheads, taking our name from the local bus route that ran into town. We would all meet at Brooklyn's Parade, a row of shops local to where we lived. Our evenings spent walking the streets posing in our new clothes or going to the park to walk in endless circles to cause trouble if we could find it. I was at Rusty's in no time to be greeted by his mom at the open door.

"Hello Mrs. Smallman. Is Rusty here?"

"Peter, your friend's here!" Her voice travelling the hallway. You could see right away why they called him Rusty, with copper coloured hair and a freckled face, the nickname suited him well. Even his last name a cruel twist of fate. He was only five foot four, mind you, he could cause chaos at times. It's always the little guys that do.

He was our leader in a way as he dressed the smartest and had all the latest clothes. I immediately felt uncomfortable as he approached. Impressed by the smartness of his presence my blue nylon ski jacket, faded jeans, "Tesco Tearaways," with RAF shoes. A cheap imitation of what he was. No match for the black Harrington button down shirt and polished royals of my immaculate friend. It was all about labels in the world of the Skin, of which I had none.

"You ready mate? Where we going?"

"The park. Let's doss down there for a while." Rusty bidding his parents goodbye, chatting along the way as we went to meet the rest of the lads. Fozza, Dave G, Goggsy, Mick in playful fights one trying a surprise attack on another, to be broken up by a third. "Where we going Rusty?" Mick shouted, dodging a kick as we approached.

"Park. Gethro's got a date."

"What you tell them that for? Cheers Rusty!" Shit, that's the last thing I wanted them to know. Now they would take the piss out of me all the way.

"Bet she's fat and ugly!" chipped in Dave G.

"What, like your sister?"

"Bet she's still at school!" I tried to hide my feelings, already they had touched a nerve.

"I haven't got a date. Just got to see someone, that's all!" Their endless, probing questions irritating me along the way.

We soon arrived at the park making for the bandstand in the center where we always hung out. Turning the corner I noticed a young girl struggling with someone, screaming as he pulled her to him. "What the fuck!" I yelled running at full speed to the commotion in the distance, pulling to a halt recognizing him right away. "Leave her alone Davies!" He was a powerfully built kid and had a reputation as a fighter but my fear had gone out of the window.

"Why, what you going to do?" His fist clenched in rage, the fire of anger in his eyes, his friend now standing at his side.

"I said, fuckin leave her!" Smashing my hand down, breaking her free of his grip as I stood between them with clenched fists. I recognized her as she turned away, a face full of shame and resentment. Those same steel blue eyes reddened, full of tears her lips now trembling with fear. "I don't want to go out with him." Her quivering voice in a whisper, he could not hear.

"You heard me. Leave her alone, she's with me. That's my bird!" Not taking my eyes off him, fixing him with that same icy stare. One that said I wasn't backing down.

"Since when?!"

"Since now!"

"You ok mate? What's up?" Rusty now standing by my side ready to fight.

"I'm ok, it's this wanker!" Both of us holding his stare, the crew gathered in a circle waiting for him to make the first move. He was dead meat and he knew it.

"Fuck you, I'll see you around." Throwing his hands in the air, turning away in frustration.

"I told you, she's with me Davies. Fuck off!" The crew now turning their attention to him as he backed away to exchange insults of next time, pointing his finger at me.

"Remember me Gethro. You'll be alone sometime, then you're mine!" I didn't care, turning around looking into the face of a beautiful young girl. I wiped the tears from her eyes, lost for a moment in the pureness of her natural beauty to ask tenderly this time, "what's your name?"

"Kim."

"Kim what? What's your last name?"

"Tell me you won't laugh." Her face searching mine for an answer.

"I won't, I promise." My voice reassuring, one of trust.

"Kim Habbits." I started to laugh, changing to a stupid grin to burst out laughing again. I couldn't help it. A flash of raging anger crossed her face to annoyance in her voice.

"What's so funny? That's how important you are, I forgot your name?!" Standing in defiance, placing hands on hips I knew I had overstepped my mark.

"Gethro," Sorry, it's just that, that's a really unusual name."

"Gethro! What sort of names that! Gethro what?!"

"I don't have a last name. It's a long story I will tell you one day. Kim, how old are you?" My hands reached for her shoulders trying to calm her down, feeling the softness of her hair on my face as she came towards me. I leaned forward to kiss her for the first time to be left in midair as she turned away, avoiding my lips. The warmth of her breath gentle on my neck as she whispered softly in my ear, "You shouldn't have laughed Gethro. I'm not telling you."

Chapter 5

NOWHERE TO RUN, NOWHERE TO HIDE

My home at this time was Heath Town, a sprawling complex of tall, high-rise flats with elevated walkways connecting to balconies of lower structures at street level. A gray city of concrete, a faceless repetitive design, shapeless windows and same coloured doors, drawing you along narrow glass lined walkways overlooking concrete lawns. Manicured trees to mirror a city of the future with little thought for the people who lived in the dingy boxes they had created. A mass of rabbit's warrens to interconnecting alleys, spiral staircases to overpasses, a jungle I would get to know like the back of my hand.

Families fought drunken battles on balconies into the night to the amusement of those around. The roots of society tearing itself apart, trapped in this new city of the future. Music and shouts echoing along dim passageways ending in urine stinking lifts. Walls full of graffiti, proclamations of hate to us all. Neighbors hurrying by, a silence between us, frightened faces avoiding eye contact never speaking a word. I was a newcomer to this slum in progress and it would only get worse. You can't house people like this, it was always going to blow and it did. I hated being in that concrete shoebox they called a home, being given no choice. My foster parents had decided we didn't need a house with a garden like normal people, this now was to be my new home.

As I wandered around my new surroundings a name that was well known in the area was Kibble and the way I met him was typical of the times I lived in. It was inevitable that I ended up at the local youth club, more out of curiosity than anything else. Each time I had visited, the place was empty, a few small kids outnumbered by social workers and Christian do-gooders. They held no interest to me at all but one thing it did have was a football machine and these were all the rage.

The next time I met Twenty Nine Crew I told them of my new find, answering their countless questions, telling them how empty and safe the youth club was. Excited that at last we had a new place to hang out we all agreed to go. I was getting sick of walking around the park in circles posing in our skinhead gear and wanted them to share in my new found world.

It was a nice summer's evening, we looked smart all dressed in similar style boots and football scarves which were the fashion. Cropped hair and button-downs, rolled up Levis and cherry reds, all of us feeling the togetherness of a crew as we laughed and joked along the way. As we approached my city of the future I could tell by their faces they weren't impressed, sensing their uneasiness as we stood waiting for the lift to arrive.

"This place is a shithole." Dave G looking more worried than the others, surveying my concrete jungle with infinite passageways, a nervous tone to his voice as we entered through the open door.

"Come on give it a chance, you haven't even seen it yet." His comments irritating me as I leaned forward pushing the button to the second floor. The smell of disinfectant and piss mixing with Brut stinging our nostrils as we ascended. All of us clinging to the center trying to avoid the dried phlegm of the spit covered walls.

"Are you sure about this place Gethro?" Rusty reading the graffiti that surrounded us, he too now with a worried face.

"No one uses the place. I haven't seen anyone, trust me it's deserted."

"Who's this Burton St. Mafia?" The door of the lift opened, a hand reached in grabbing Dave G by his scarf, smack! A perfect punch as his nose exploded in blood then more kicks rained upon him slamming him backwards into the lift, all of us standing in shock.

"Get the bastards, come on!" A gang of skins. I glanced at a face as I dived forward lunging for the button. I knew I had to hold it or we were going to get a real kicking, the door closing to pounding kicks. We stood for what seemed forever before descending to the floor below. Dave G holding his jaw, shaking his head his scarf now covered in blood!

"Who the fuck was that!" All of us exiting the lift in a panic to shouts above our heads, figures now running along balconies to cut us off.

"Come on lets have 'em!"

"Come on you wankers!" For me I wasn't hanging around and neither were the lads. I knew how to count and it wasn't looking good. We ran as fast as we could back to where we came from finding safety from this madness at last to take a rest, all of us panting for breath. "You set us up you bastard!"

"You said it was empty!" All their anger now directed at me I stood my ground.

"Fuck you, I don't know who they are! I've never seen any of them before!" I pleaded my case but they were having none of it. In the end I knew it was pointless to argue. I turned and walked away, our friendship over, their taunts still ringing in my ears. Saying a silent goodbye to what little security I had, finding safety in the darkness as I wandered back to my new home. The faceless windows towering above me illuminated in the still of the night. Now I was trapped and alone, what friends I had now lost with enemies on either side.

I became withdrawn keeping a low profile, staying in my room. The square walls of a cell closing in on me fueled by imagination, trapped in a nightmare of fear. A shadow that I had to overcome, I couldn't stop in forever. I had to get away from my foster parents, their moaning about my attitude and the relationship I had with Kim. A constant bombardment, taunts of venom from my foster mother, "She's a stuck up little snob, too young for you! Go find a girl your own age!" Adding to my turmoil playing heavy on my conscience. I had to overcome my fear! I had to break out of this room!

In the end, curiosity got to me and I headed straight back to the youth club. This time with Kim on a date, hoping they wouldn't beat me up in front of her. I had made up my mind to go down fighting, it would be over quickly and take whatever comes. It was the only place we could go feeling embarrassed by her youth. She was so young and as no one there knew me, I didn't feel like the cradle snatcher that I was. Someone had put some Motown on an old record player that stood in the corner, the sounds of the Four Tops drawing me to it. I liked Motown, The Supremes, The Four Tops, that Detroit sound.

"Watch this Kim," making her smile as I stepped in a diamond formation that I had seen them do on TV. Trying to impress her with my new found move look it's easy. "One, two, three." Suddenly the mood in the room changed, descending to silence. A figure stood watching by the open door surrounded by a gang of skins. A face I instantly recognized as he came up to me, my stomach hitting my neck.

"You were in that lift, weren't you? Where's your shit out mates?!" A coldness in his voice, his lips tightened adding vengeance to an ice cold venomous stare.

"I don't have any mates, they think I set them up!" I tried to be calm, I had to be strong Kim looking in sadness as I braced myself for what was to come. His face cracked into a smile, changing in a flash to one I found hard to read. His emotionless eyes going straight through me, a face that knew no fear. Deep inside I wished I was like him but I wasn't.

"What's your name, Mr. I haven't got any friends?!"

"Gethro."

"Well Gethro, show me that move you just did." He burst out laughing at my look of terror as I too now saw the joke.

"You're not going to have him John?" Another skin asked.

"No, leave him he's all right. He hasn't got any friends remember!" His voice in a mimicking tone to their laughter, looking for a reaction but by now I didn't care. I could see in Kim's eyes she felt my shame.

Slightly shorter than me stocky with muscular powerful arms, cropped hair and the looks of a real skinhead, he had a reputation. Kibble was like a bowling ball, anyone got in his way they went down. He backed away from no one and would knock you out for the slightest excuse. His moods could change in a flash, he just loved to fight. You made friends with Kibble if you had any sense. I got to know him well and although he had the reputation for fighting which he lived up to every chance he could get, he also loved music and especially Motown.

I started to practice dancing at the youth club, often he would join at my side. Slowly, I became accepted by him and his mates keeping my distance and always giving him respect. I soon realized Kibble was a useful friend to have as I wandered around my city of concrete, finding safety in his name. They seemed to love fighting, looking for it at every opportunity that came their way. Finding strength in that crew mentality. Look at me, I'm a skinhead, I'm hard, reveling in the fight. Telling tales of bravery of kicks they had landed close encounters they had won.

I had been brought up within the brutality of the orphanage and lived with violence every day as I struggling to survive. It wasn't new to me you had to be tough, you were a skinhead. My problem was I wasn't tough and I hated the way I was feeling. Trying to keep my sanity as my surroundings fought battles with painful memories in the playground of my mind. I couldn't breathe in this environment, everywhere around me reminders of my childhood of bullying from the past. Sure I could stand up for myself if I had to, but I hadn't got a clue who I was supposed to be. In the end, I too drifted into their insanity as I became a skinhead no better than any of them.

My feelings reflected this as life at home was no different from any other adolescent. I ate and slept there, but with us as a family all communication had broken down. We all lived our separate lives without any acknowledgment of the other. I was rebellious and hard to control, giving them a life of hell. Often to be threatened with, "you can go back to where you came from!"

In the relationship with my foster parents my adolescence hit them like an express train, mood swings I could not control. Everything they said I couldn't have or do, I did! As I vented my anger punishing them for the childhood I had been denied. I heard things but nothing stayed in my head, it was with this background that I began to develop. I thought I knew it all yet I knew so little, I had my own destiny in front of me. I didn't care what they said there were no rules in my world. I would self-destruct in my own way. I hated being around them and headed straight out the door every chance I could get. Seeking new adventure to the heart of Wolverhampton, "The Town Centre" alone and never once looking back.

Chapter 6

GET IT ON - AUGUST 1971

Wolverhampton in the early seventies was a mixture of sub-cultures. The streets of the town center echoing to the sounds of motor scooters, "scrotts" as we called them. Mirrored Lambretta's and Vespa's, hairdryers you wouldn't be seen dead on, appearing from nowhere to cruise around the town. With their Florida's and backrests of chrome, silhouetted side panels and flags waving in the breeze showing allegiance to their crews. Mirrored crash bars, fly screens and tank aerial, Lambretta GP200s, TV175s cruising machines lined the streets, parking for all to see.

I envied them as I stood looking at their sleek machines glistening in the summer's sun. T. Rex were making a name with "Get It On," The Who with, "Won't Get Fooled Again." Dave and Ansell Collins "Monkey Spanner," Tami Lynn, "I'm Gonna Run Away From You," music of the day. Slade, a Wolvo band, were riding high in the August charts "Get Down And Get With It," blasted from jukeboxes of crowded bars. The George's Tavern in the town, The Greyhound, The Valhalla, The Exchange. Pubs and bars I got to know well as I wandered around the town.

I had made new friends now, one of my best mates was Chimp. He was tall with long arms, his nickname suited him well. With our cropped hair, button-downs, cherry reds and bracers we looked every inch a couple of skins. We visited many places together in the crowded bars he opened doors for me to new faces, "Everyone knew his name." This is how I got to know some of the main players that circulated in the town. One of my favorite places to visit being The George's Lounge on Saturday afternoon. All the lads from The North Bank would be there as we took the roof off singing and chanting Wolves' songs often led by Eka, a face well-known around the town. A brilliant mate I had got to know well, hard, fair and straight and I hit it off with him right away. Eka was Eka, a natural born leader often to be found standing on a table leading us all in a drunken chorus of "Alouette" or "I Do Like To Be Beside The Seaside." Lost in the sea of drink, egged on by the surrounding crowd.

All of us competing with Glen's Pomeranian Dogs standing two legged on a table nearby. Their howling increasing in tempo, fighting to find the perfect notes as our singing intermingled with theirs. Snapping at anybody stupid enough to come near to kisses and hugs of love from their master. Tabletops of drinks fueling the atmosphere, figures swaying in the smoke filled room. The place was always jumping, full of characters from around the town. There was never any trouble here unless it came through the door, even then it never lasted long. This was a Wolvo pub, the heart of The North Bank used it so the cops left the bar alone, feeling happier we were all in one place.

Local discos at the Conaught Cavendish, The Civic were playing sounds from The Four Tops, The Supremes, Isley Brothers, Chairmen Of The Board. "Your Love Keeps Lifting Me Higher," by Jackie Wilson, a record grabbing my attention, putting feet on the dance floors and Motown on the map. Wolvo shook off the cobwebs of the 60s and moved forward with music and fashion dictating a new beginning, as the town now came alive. Mods and skins intermingled to dominate by their sheer numbers as, "the mood of youth moved in a new direction," "making violence the fashion." With the army of skins taking over with a renewed vengeance where the mods had left off.

In the town you had many gangs, crews, mafias, call them what you want. Wolvo was no different from any other town at this time. Here you had the Temple St Mafia, one of the biggest gangs in the town also The West Park, mostly black guys some of who I became close friends with and got to know well. Red hankie, red socks, Levis or Wranglers, short sleeved button-down shirts. Fred Perry's, colored bracers, Dr. Martens boots, our beloved, "cherry reds." This was your uniform of Wolvo Town Centre but other crews were fighting for that same spot.

One was the Queen St Mafia, they were older white guys dressing in the latest fashion, always with the best gear. Nice Ben Sherman's, blue full length crombies, Everpress trousers, plain brogues or royals. A statement in their fashion, none of us could afford but there were more. Stow Lawn from Bilston a really big crew, Low Hill from Bushbury with the Crutchlies, Kibbles crew led by their leader who knew no fear. Ashmoor Park and The Poets from Willenhall and many more all fighting for recognition. If you went on their territory you had better be crewed up, a big crew not only gave you numbers but protection.

I found this out the hard way as Twenty Nine Crew, all six of us, clashed with The Poets at Willenhall Market. Being totally outnumbered I actually cleared a market stall, jumping straight over it to escape my attackers, "no hero here mate!" They came from everywhere. I didn't meet The Poets but I felt them and their hatred of Temple St. The red socks were all they needed as one booted me up the arse to help me on my way. What made me mad was I wasn't even in the Temple St. at that time. Fashion could get you in a lot of trouble and I was learning fast and the hardest way.

Skinheads dominated the town, sweeping all out of their way as Wolvo, like others, became a town with attitude swept along by the violence of football on a Saturday. I, too now attended the games. Wolves were riding high in the first division. The team of Dougan, Richards, Hibbitt, McCalliog, and their fans were a match for any one at home. In 4th place we were attracting opposing fans of the time Tottenham, Chelsea, or Manchester United. We backed away from no one as The North Bank terraces rang to the chants of, "Knees Up Mother Brown" and "Alouette" with all of us as one an army of skins. Standing, swaying in the crowds a sea of scarves held high as different crews chanted their names and allegiance to our team. The gold and black of Wolverhampton, wanderers with fights breaking out on the open terraces, "as randomly as our songs."

The Mander Centre would be packed with Saturday shoppers trying to avoid the disgusting hooligans as we leaned on the side railings to gather before the matches. A mass of skinheads with cropped hair, boots polished to perfection ready to fight over the slightest excuse. If you stood in someone else's spot or they wanted your scarf, this was usually good enough. It was all about being hard, being tough, and not backing down in the eyes of your mates. Rolling strangers was common sort of "begging with attitude," we all did it often breaking into open fights. Crashing into doorways, scattering shoppers out of the way as boots and punches rained in on opponents. Our answer to those who fought back and wouldn't pay. Getting the first punch in as you knew what was to follow. Steaming became a way of life to us, we never attacked one to one. A blue uniform was all we needed as cops would come to move us along or arrest someone to be met with head on battles. All of us joining in as they and their reinforcements struggling with this new wave of violence that exploded all around them, as we openly protested our hatred of them, society and the blue uniform of authority that they wore.

Chapter 7

THE WHITE BOY DIDN'T RUN

On this particular Saturday we were to play Manchester United at home, they always brought fans, lots of them, and Wolves knew they had a battle on their hands. That day I was just wandering around town and came upon The Mander Centre. Conroy was there and Danny, two faces I knew well from the West Park Crew. Conroy was a big guy easily recognizable standing out in the crowd. The broad shoulders of his powerful muscular frame filling his denim bib and brace overalls. Thick arms and neck a body chiseled by youth he looked exactly like he was someone you didn't mess around with. We were good friends he knew I was different we used to talk a lot about dancing and music and I had told him about my new girl Kim.

Danny was of similar build, tall but the opposite. He didn't like me, neither did a few of his mates, questioning why the white boy should stand anywhere near their spot. Coming over to where I stood his face in anger waving his arms his voice getting louder and louder now only feet away. I didn't understand his patuwa blood clat white boy attitude, my look of confusion making him worse. His ranting and raving drawing attention "pussy clot bummba clot!" More insults in anger. I was about to get into a fight I knew I wouldn't win. To my relief Conroy came over to talk to me. "I don't like you!" Danny pointing his finger, glaring at me as he moved away turning his attention to someone else.

"What's up?" Conroy asks.

"Oh nothing, just Danny. You know him." Conroy smiled.

"You're cool man, don't worry about him. He won't touch you while I'm around." A breathless figure comes running toward us. "Quick! Let's go down to the ground, a special's just come in with loads of United fans queuing at The South Bank."

Suddenly a buzz erupts all around me. I feel a slap on my shoulder as Conroy starts to laugh, attracted by my look of terror. "Stick by me, you'll be ok."

There were about fifty of us, my stomach turned over, my mind racing with here we go. I knew this wasn't going to be good. Straight away the word was passed, nobody run or you would get a kicking. Either way I was going to be in a fight. The chant of, "Temple St." rang out. Looking around me it felt safe to be with the crowd. We moved forward to do battle, leaving The Mander Centre and picking more fans up as we moved on through the town.

The ground was only a short walk as we marched down to the South bank entrance. The chanting of "UNITED! UNITED!" faint at first, growing louder as we drew nearer to our prey. All of us hiding our scarves, keeping our silence, turning the corner to face a mass of Manchester United fans, a sea of red and white. All that separated us was a fence which Conroy leapt over to square up to a big white guy rushing forward "Come on! Come on!" One punch that's all it was, feeling the full power of Conroy as he hit the deck. Conroy turning to face a circle of fans as they rushed forward into the attack. We had to help him as more of us climbed over the fence to back him up. Sticking together, not questioning my emotions, no time to think just rushing forward I too had cleared the fence. All around me bodies falling, screaming in pain to be kicked and punched as they fell. All of us lashing out at anyone in red and white not even aiming punches, just grabbing, kicking opponents, a fight for survival now. I didn't care as we all surged forward into the fight.

I had to stay I was with Conroy and Danny, the white boy had to stay on his feet. We were outnumbered with nowhere to go and more United fans were fighting back, but the pure ferocity of our push into them split them up. Fights raged to the left and right, if you went down it was over you would be kicked senseless. There was no way we would let you get up. We rained kicks and punches from every direction this was the world of a skin, a battleground that they loved. Ours was a fair fight, boots and fists your only weapons dominated by aggression and held together with a brutal pride. The togetherness of a crew, the gold and black of our team.

Eventually we got the better hand, a gap appearing between us, punching stragglers as they crouched and fell. Others chased to a bloody ending, leaving them battered on the ground. Finally, left in the middle of the car park my body aching, fighting for my breath. Bent over in pain, sweat streaming down my face, a lump on my lip and side of my cheek. My head spinning, feeling the adrenaline of what we had done, a smile of self-satisfaction.

Why? What satisfaction? I didn't get any joy from this, I hated what I had become, sucked into this pit of stupid senseless violence, why? So I was a big man, tough, hard, not really. I had proved to myself I could be brave but that was all gaining some respect, even a nod from Danny, "The white boy hadn't run."

Things got worse at the end of the match as the United fans now regrouped. This fight was far from over. The police with German shepherds barking, snapping at fans, horses locked into the madness trying to keep us apart. Violent clashes erupting all around them, the town center falling apart. Fighting in shop doorways, running, battling at blocked intersections, crews looking for combat, scarves held high, and chants ringing around the town. Skirmishes scattering shoppers in a trail of broken windows leading to running battles on many streets, different crews from The North Bank joining together standing their ground.

The town center feeling the full force of United as bars erupted in an explosion of violence. They brought a lot of fans. With their sheer numbers they left a mark finally subsiding hours later, a calmness returning to the streets. I waited in a shop doorway, there on the opposite side of the street a lone figure staggering back to the train station, his shirt and face covered in blood. A United fan I recognized, alone and battered but having my respect, giving him a nod, that same kid who Conroy had hit. Catching my reflection in the window my scarf threaded through the loops of my jeans. Boots dull, tarnished with violence, a bruised cheek, thick lip where someone had hit me. Medals of the battle, my uniform of a skin, "a mirrored reflection of the times."

The night matches were just as bad, if Wolves hadn't got anybody to fight they fought amongst themselves. The different crews settling turf wars and old scores on the open terraces of The North Bank. Crystal Palace were playing on a night match, everyone knew they wouldn't bring any fans and the police had dropped their usual numbers, expecting no trouble. How wrong they were! With The North Bank packed to capacity you knew it was only a matter of time as we fought for room to stand on the open terraces. I dodged a knife, "You mad bastard! Ralphy!" His face smiling, prodding strangers making them move as we fought for room. All of us laughing at his antics crashing into one another, falling forward into the sea of gold and black.

Bodies with arms held high, clapping hands in unison, jumping up and down on the terraces in a swaying chanting mass. "Temple Street! Temple Street! Ha! Ha! Ha!" Stow Lawn as they mimicked our chant pushing to the back of The North Bank as we surged forward to meet them head on. Fighting breaking out all around us, the terraces now alight large gaps appeared in the crowd. Crews battling each other as skins rained in with windmills of punches. Boots flying from all directions into figures locked in desperate fights, cops trying to come into the crowd.

A thin line of blue uniforms, even they had lost control to be turned on by the fans they were trying to protect. Insanity took over, they backed off and let us fight it out. This continued all through the game and after as Stow Lawn went on the rampage chanting through the town. To be met at the top of Broad St. as they tried to take The George. Toe to toe, running battles as Queen St. and Temple St. joined together to protect our bars around the town. Black Mariars flew by, blue lights flashing, reflecting in shop windows tearing into the night. Heading off in all directions to arrest any stragglers and loners they could find. I was now a cog in the lunacy of this clockwork violence, "that just never seemed to stop."

Chapter 8

CAVENDISH FIRST TIME - STREET- LIFE

You had three main discos in Wolvo that I knew of at this time. The Lafayette, a club playing mostly charts music, The Conaught Hotel, a function room on a Friday, and on the opposite week The Cavendish on a Saturday. My favorite was The Cavendish, built on to the side of the old Vic Hotel and being more or less in the center of the town. With a line of scrotts outside whenever it was on, some now their side panels showing allegiance to Temple Street Mafia. Now more than ever I wanted to be part of that crew and ride around the town.

On my travels I had bumped into Twenty Nine Crew and although I was now more of a loner sticking with the town boys. I still knocked around with them "being forgiven for the disaster at Heath Town." We held on to that crew mentality, finding protection in each other's company as we visited local discos. It was as simple as that. The town had a bad feel to it, especially late at night as we wandered to our bus stops finding strength in our numbers dealing with fights that came our way.

Discos had attitude, you looked at someone the wrong way or bumped into someone or spoke to a girl there would be trouble. Skins were the fashion and like a shadow, trouble and violence just followed them around. Crews didn't mix then only occasionally at the matches but in the discos it was more territorial and easily plain to see. Black guys hung with the black guys, whites with whites. Everyone stayed in their crews with no trust from one to the other, often fighting at the end of the night, especially over girls.

I had crossed that dance floor making friends with Conroy being told, "If anyone gives you trouble to come see me" and letting those around him know I wasn't to be touched. I wasn't much of a dancer then as girls danced around, they're bags in the meat markets of the discos, and to dance alone was a little unusual. The reggae of Dave and Ansell Collins "Double Barrel", The Harry J All Stars "The Liquidator" this was our music of the skins. Although I danced to them it had more to do with trying to attract a girl's attention than anything else. As skins, we danced in a group often in semicircles swaying in a mass as we filled the floor. Our footwork was very minimal, all body movement with no style for the individuals to express yourself to the music, at times all of us doing the same moves.

Other records were now making an impression on me pulling me onto the floor Johnny Johnson and the Bandwagon "Breaking Down The Walls Of Heartache", The Foundations "Build Me Up Buttercup", Tammy Terrell and Marvin Gaye "Two Can Have A Party", The Fascinations "Girls Are Out To Get You", The Supremes "Love Is Like An Itching In My Heart" and of course Earl Van Dyke "Six By Six", a record that changed my style of dancing. This record would always put Conroy and me side by side as we tried to shuffle along the back of the dance floor. Twisting our feet, moving in a straight line trying out new steps together. Our bond was music, falling in love with that infectious Motown beat. We laughed at each other's antics and the way we were trying to dance even getting the same coloured shoes red, white, and blue. After our first time on the floor with these we soon realized they were a big mistake but why not, we wanted the same thing to be different to stand out on the floor.

Under Conroy's protection I was tolerated in The West Park corner but often I felt uneasy. I was not liked by many of his friends with the looks of anger and comments from the side whenever he could not hear but it wasn't all one way. Often I would be questioned by the whites for hanging around with the blacks with just as much venom, but to me I didn't care. I had no time for their bullshit and ignored the comments from either side, but even I had to face reality as this became evident one Saturday night.

Brillo, a black guy I had only just met a real nice kid had started to hang around with Twenty Nine Crew. With the looks of a church goer and an infectious smile he was as innocent as you could get. What happened that night in the Cavendish wasn't a gang thing, there was only six of us. Really we were a joke as a crew! He was black, we accepted him for who he was and didn't see colour, I only saw a friend. He got beat up in the toilets for hanging around with "the white boys."

This was the first time I had ever seen racism. Sure I had felt it against me as I danced in Conroy's corner. I was white, I accepted that but I had never seen it against a black guy, black on black. When I looked into his battered face and saw the pain in his eyes, the cry for help I felt nothing but shame. I had been raised in an orphanage where you had nothing no matter what colour you were, you got treated all the same. It affected me deeply there was no colour in my world, we hadn't got the numbers and there was nothing we could do. I felt anger, ashamed of myself for being a coward, for not helping him and wished I had the courage, "the bottle" and done more. It would not be the last I would see of this. With skins' crews being white and black gangs black we were in dangerous times.

The Cavendish to me was a disco with a disco mentality then and it showed. As I stood on the steps by the bar to look across that divided dance floor blacks and whites stayed apart. Invisible lines drawn across the dance floor with tension and violence one step away. Again I asked myself, why? To a question I lacked courage to answer and one I could not understand. That night left a bitter taste in my mouth, one I would never forget.

Another disco I attended was The Conaught on Tettenhall Rd. Here you also had attitude. You had to be careful if you went there, as Twenty Nine Crew found out the hard way one Friday night. I had become more of a town boy now, mingling with the bigger crew of Temple Street that ran around the town. I would often see them and at some time in the night Rusty and I would always hit the dance floor together. Especially to any Motown that was being played. They had some new members now, they were still my mates so at the end of the disco I waited for them outside to catch up with old times and walk back through the town. Mick, one of their new members came staggering towards me holding his jaw screaming in pain. He was only a skinny kid with no meat on him at all.

"Mick, what's up?!"

"They croak my gore." he mumbled. His face twisted, all pushed to the one side and completely out of shape.

"What? Who?" I was totally confused.

"Gore mates!" Pointing his finger at me in panic with a look of terror on his face.

As I turned and ran back inside I met Conroy coming down the steps with his mates. Conroy had a temper that could snap like a twig at the wrong word. I had seen people on the receiving end, I was out of my league and knew it but I had to ask him for help.

"Conroy! My mate just got slapped about!"

"Who? Which one?" I pointed to Mick.

"Shit! Were they your mates? Sorry man." He ran back inside to stop the lads getting battered. Twenty Nine Crew were totally outnumbered and didn't stand a chance. Emerging untouched outside to looks of confusion as I told them to, "Go just go!"

Conroy returned dropping twenty pence into my hand. We burst out laughing we both knew what had happened, he got rolled I mean what could I do really!" I was nobody and although I felt sorry for Mick it could have been worse. Conroy crossed lines that night and I never forgot what he did for me and my friends. They hadn't got a clue how lucky they were.

The Conaught also had that disco mentality and now it was getting on my nerves. I couldn't breathe in this environment of total unrest. Slowly I was changing, my love was music. I was finding happiness out on the dance floor, all I wanted to do now was dance. The crews, the constant fighting battles at the end of the nights over what?! Their territorial bullshit held no meaning to me. I had been going around the town now for a while and made many new friends and soon realized to survive it was who you knew. I had moved with the times, but it was obvious and plain to see, not all of us had.

Chapter 9

LATE 1971

"Turn that bloody racket down!" The annoyed voice of my foster mother slamming my bedroom door as, "Heaven Must Have Sent You" slid from records in the stack. The mellow notes of The Elgin's filling my bedroom once more. Moan! Moan! That's all I ever heard. If it wasn't about Kim, it was my music; everything I did irritated them. I turned the volume down, making me smile knowing I had pissed them off once more. Pushing my notes to the side letting my attention wander as I tried to revise for my first year's exams.

I stayed away from The Cavendish and The Conaught for a long time, my life now was odd trips to the roller dome. Sometimes with Rusty and the lads or to meet Kim on a secret date. Her mother banning us from seeing each other, smuggled love letters and secret notes keeping our love alive. I missed her when she wasn't around, there was just something that stopped me letting go. I shared my love with other girls, searching for what she could not give. Always to be left with emptiness, a feeling I could not explain. At times I felt alone and sadly missed her, remembering the night we parted so many months ago. Words spoken between us, the vision still clear in my mind.

Her gentle face etched in sadness, swollen hazel blue eyes filled with tears.

"Kim, when shall I see you?" My heart pleading for an answer, one she could not give.

"I don't know." Her tearful whispered reply.

"I never thought I would ever hear you say that, it's horrible. I wished I had seen you more often now." Our warm tears mingled as one, a softness in our lips lost in a final kiss to slip gently through my arms. Fading figures lost in a fog of darkness, a blown kiss on fingers of silent whispers to say "I love you," the distance between us tearing our love apart.

Did I really love her? Would I ever see her again? Was that goodbye? Was she really the one for me? I don't know! I don't know! Endless questions I could not answer swirling in the cauldron of my mind. "Little Darling" the soulful words of Marvin Gaye making me miss her even more. "Come on concentrate! Get back to work!" The voices of my conscience dragging my mind back to reality and the importance of my task. Returning me with a vengeance to my books, scattered notes upon the bed.

I had to pass these exams and move forward with my life. Focus on my apprenticeship, one goal at a time. If I passed I would buy a scrott, a reward I would give myself. "Screw them!" Their words echoed along empty walls. "You can't have a motor scooter!" Can't I? We will see! Why should I take any notice of them! No love of a mother or father here, no guidance when I needed it most. I had a sixth sense. I didn't trust my foster parents, why should I? To them I was just a paycheck, a boarder, a faceless lodger who paid his rent. Too many words had been spoken between us, I had felt their anger as they had mine. With the mouth of a loaded machine gun I had a bullet for every fight. Now this bomb was ticking, it was only a matter of time before I would be shown the door.

I knew if I fell into the gutter no one would pick me up. This was all the motivation I needed as I passed my first year exams, becoming student of the year. Even Kim's mother had now relented, letting us see one another with a time table of early nights and days off between us but at least we were together again. Kim would be fifteen in April, our ages growing nearer by the day. As I looked out into the crowded room at college, turning to collect my prize there was only one face looking back at me, Kim's. No one else turned up or cared. She was all I had in my life really and I loved her with all of my heart.

Chapter 10

GLADYS MK 1

The wind felt strange on my face, my eyes straining in the darkness streaming full of tears, the cold biting into my fingers as I struggled with the controls. "Please, please change." The traffic lights obliging as I sped through, unable to stop.

"Pull the clutch in Gethro! Hit the brakes!" My mate Paul Walker hardly heard above the roar of the engines of our scrotts as we raced along side by side. Laughing at my antics I had never been on a scrott, let alone ride one and now here I was. The splutter of the engine slowed to a gentle purr as I eased forward, a slight wobble keeping the bike as straight as I could. Turning the throttle even more, a rush of adrenaline raced through me lunging forward I glanced at the speedo feeling the power of my reward.

The brightness of the headlight reaching into darkness I smiled in satisfaction at the freedom it would bring. I was now a scooter boy. Well at least I had got one and felt totally different from the foot soldier of a skin. We had been to Dudley to collect it. Twenty quid, he had wanted more but I had got my prize. A nineteen sixty four Lambretta LI 150 all it needed was some tender loving care. I would take care of that and couldn't wait to show Kim my new toy. Once again I stalled at the lights as Paul came to my side. "Clutch, brake Gethro. It will come, you're doing ok mate. Clutch, brake." Paul laughing at my face of frustration, at least this time I had stopped. I jumped off to kick start the engine. Once again rings of smoke surrounded me, the lights glowing in the darkness as we sped off into the night.

Keeping to the side roads, staying out of the town, not seeing a cop with no paperwork or license, luck was on my side. We finally made it home as I pushed my pride and joy into the shed. One problem, my foster parents. I didn't care, they would find out soon enough. I felt different, independent and now one of the lads. I now would ride around town smiling at the happiness that would bring and the girls. They all loved a scooter boy. Even though I knew I was in the shit, man life was good! For me but not my foster parents. They were furious at the battle they had lost as I came tearing down the pavement on my reward. Their faces in shock and anger. I continued on my path of self-destruction, one that had no rules.

For now all my time and money went on my scrott, even giving it a name. This was Gladys. She was old but had grace. With the help of an adjustable spanner I had a good collection of car mirrors, four now on either side. Front and back crash bars. The backrest, a final touch it was now starting to look like a real scrott. I had resprayed the side panels, our nights spent together Kim watching tirelessly as I worked on my new project. Often to be rewarded with rides on the back till I got busted by the cops. Much to the amusement of my foster parents, "I told you so!" Maybe they did! But I never heard them the distance between us growing wider every day.

I was on my second year at college and now with transport I could work Saturdays. Saving the extra money this gave me keeping a low profile. I wanted my trade more than anything else, the foster home had taught me well. Once I had my certificates in my pocket I would break free from their oppressive negativity and start a new life of my own. No matter how hard that was going to be I had reached that decision quietly in my mind.

Chapter 11

MOVE ON UP

"Christmas had been and gone and now it was time to come back to life again Nineteen Seventy-Two would be a good year, a new beginning I just felt it. I just knew."

Willenhall Baths, a short bus ride out of town was a local disco held on Monday nights that everyone used to go to. Playing mostly charts music T. Rex "Telegram Sam", Slade "Look What You Done", Chicory Tip "Son Of My Father". Although high in the charts this music of the day held no interest to me at all. Into the mix you had, Al Green "Let's Stay Together", Chi-lites "Have You Seen Her", Chairmen of the Board "Give Me Just A Little More Time", San Remo Strings "Festival Time" with a few bits of Reggae and Motown thrown in. Soul, if you want to call it, was slowly creeping into discos but attitudes were still the same. The nights there typically ended in fights. It was here that I took Kim on our first real date, she had never been to a disco and next month she would be fifteen.

At last I had got the Everpress suit jacket that I wanted, bottle green, they were all the rage. With my faded jeans, a check Jaytex shirt, red silk hanky in the top pocket I felt immaculate in my new clothes. I had tried to impress Kim, she too had dressed in a similar style, button-down shirt, Staypress trousers, a crombie and monkey boots. We looked the perfect couple, a statement to our fashion embodied in our youth.

Kim's face bursting to a smile of delight as we entered the disco, a lover's look between us sharing our happiness. My heart bursting with pride at her natural beauty, shining for all to see. The Formations "At The Top Of The Stairs" filtered onto the dance floor, soulful beats filling the crowded room. The place was packed, it had a small bar and a temporary dance floor.

Although big, stretching the full length of the room it was awkward to dance on. The uneven surface reminding me of the last time I had been. I was always weary of coming here after my previous encounter with the Poets. Immediately feeling at ease as I recognized Conroy, Danny, and Venton on the far side of the dance floor with some of The West Park Crew. They were not alone, more faces appearing as we made our way past the crowded bar. Eka, Pete Scory, Mac Roberts, Paul Walker, Aggy, Toddy, Eggy, and Gordon Stokes who always dressed immaculate. Scooter boys from The George, faces from around the town. I smiled at least if it came on top we had the numbers this time.

We made our way around the edge of the dance floor towards the DJ feeling the tightness of Kim's hand daring not to let mine go. Her face in a look of bewilderment, passing groups of motionless girls, their handbags glued to the floor. A nod of recognition to the girl watchers, more faces that I knew. There in the middle of the crowd at the front of the stage I noticed a guy, he captured my attention right away. He had long hair, well longer than mine, he wasn't a skin, wearing a blue vest with white edging. A couple of his mates stood around him, a short blond haired girl standing by his side. The driving beats of Curtis Mayfield "Move On Up" filling the sides of the floor.

His dancing making me stop dead in my tracks. "Kim, watch him look!" All you could see was a blur, his hands in a strange position held tightly at his side as he spun effortlessly on the spot. Breaking into circular footwork of stepping feet turning to repeat the move once more, to spin faster a second time. I was mesmerized, I couldn't believe my eyes.

"Did you see that, look at him dance! Fuckin brilliant." A gentle whisper passed from my lips, I was totally blown away.

"Who is he?" Kim asked.

"I don't know, I've never seen him before, but he's a brilliant dancer." We watched till the record finished, my eyes transfixed on what I had seen.

"Where's Conroy?"

"Oh you want to meet my mate do you? Ok, so long as you behave." My voice in a playful teasing tone.

"Come on lover, he's over here." Taking her hand easing our way through dancers across the crowded floor.

I soon found him, you couldn't miss him dancing with Venton and Danny along the side of the floor. Conroy was a big guy for his age. He had an air about him that commanded respect from the sheer size of his muscular build yet light and fast on his feet.

"Conroy!"

"Gethro!" A beaming smile as I approached, his outstretched arms greetings given in hugs as old friends do.

"Hey what's up man? Where you been?"

"Oh, college. You know, my exams. I've brought my girlfriend, the one I told you about. This is," turning around Kim hiding behind me, stepping forward a nervous look upon her face. Her beauty hidden in shyness as she stepped forward.

"She's beautiful, man." Her outstretched hand totally ignored. Conroy placed his hands on her shoulders gently kissed her cheek, turning to me, a big grin on his face.

"You know I'm gonna steal her man!"

"No way, she's mine!" Both of us throwing our arms around each other in a playful fight, bursting out laughing at Kim's face full of fright. Conroy and I were tight, he was a good friend of mine. I liked being around him, there was just a bond between us one I could never explain.

We hit the floor together as we always did but I didn't feel comfortable anymore in the way I danced. Kim standing at the edge of the floor watching people around her, lost in her new found world. I couldn't take my eyes off that guy in the blue and white vest and his mates at the front of the stage. We danced to Donnie Elbert "I Can't Help Myself" a record filling the floor. I loved the happy beats of this Motown classic but to dance to it was hard to do. The uneven floor gave me nothing as I tried to slide my feet, shuffling in a line to match the bouncy tune.

Frustrated at my dancing, in the end leaving Conroy with the same deal. Curiosity got to me, I walked over to the front of the stage Kim now by my side. The group I had seen earlier had stopped dancing, turning to greet us as we approached.

"Nice spinning mate. What's your name?"

"I'm Chris, and this is Gonk." The spinner pointing to his friend at his side. As we exchanged names I scrutinized their appearance, both of them were not tall, they had long hair and dressed, so different from everyone else. They didn't wear jeans but cords. In the center of their vests a black badge with a golden fist holding a flaming red torch surrounded in a two circles of gold "The Torch Stoke on Trent" in bold white letters. To me it was a beautiful badge, like nothing I had ever seen.

"How do you do that turning on the spot?" I asked.

"Spin? It's easy Gethro." Chris replied.

We stood to the side as he danced once more his feet drifting in a circular motion then one flick and bang a perfect spin. This time ending with more footwork then dropping to the floor with bent knees his hands now at the side. I just wanted to dance like him. Watching his every move I had never seen anyone dance like this. Finally, the record I didn't recognize finished. Chris came over to speak once more.

"What's that move you just did?" Again my inquisitiveness unforgiving.

"A drop-back. It's easy, you need to come to The Torch on a Saturday night if you like this music."

"What's that?"

"A club in Stoke. It just started all-nighters, it's on from 8 till 8."

"What's one of them?" I had never heard of an all-nighter.

"They play Northern Soul music all night." Chris breaking to a smile.

"What? You travel all the way to Stoke for music?!" Emphasizing my question. I hadn't a clue what he was on about, feeling embarrassed at our conversation telling me of records and artists I didn't know and to "keep the faith," as we shook hands in a crossing motion. I turned away, my mind now totally confused trying to find a piece of dance floor as Kim Weston "Helpless" came on.

One of my favorite records and that's exactly how I felt. I loved her soulful voice, the addictive Motown beats I tried to copy his style of dancing with feet I could not control. Kim standing to the side smiling at my efforts taking everything in, too frightened and shy to dance. We spent time with Conroy and wandered around for faces I knew, eventually finding the lads at the back of the floor. Rusty was a good dancer but I smiled at the rest of the crew standing, watching at his side. I didn't see much of them now but they were still my mates.

"Nice jacket man." Rusty noticing straight away.

"Everpress," my face full of pride, unbuttoning the jacket showing the black label inside. Even I realized it was all about labels, the right clothes, imitations just didn't cut it, only originals would do. I was doing well, telling them of my scrott and my exams as we laughed about the market stall and our clash with the Poets that Saturday afternoon. It was getting towards the end of the night now as we made our way to the door, Kim's mom's words ringing so clear in my ears, "Look after her." Kim was like a porcelain doll, an only child with no father. Her mother was protective and would "cut my balls off," if she came to any harm.

When the fights started outside it was over nothing. As we stood watching I became irritated at the stupidity of it all. Why? Just because someone wore a leather jacket and had long hair? That was it really! I felt sorry for the Greboes, they didn't stand a chance and what the skins did proved that they were tough. Not to me. It was a one sided fight, the numbers were with them. It was soon over, ending in the chip shop with a chair over someone's head but as I stood watching I had to laugh. I just turned away with Kim on my arm, "unless someone hits me Kim I don't want any part of that."

My attitude towards violence was changing. Sure I was a little bit wild at times, I turned and looked at Kim. She made me smile at my thoughts, maybe she would calm me down. I wouldn't go looking for trouble, I wasn't a big guy. Slim and with no weight at all. I wasn't an Eka, Kibble or Conroy, I wasn't hard it just wasn't in me I didn't enjoy fighting. Once again fashion was getting people into a lot of trouble. I was beginning to question who I was, a skinhead maybe but only on the outside? I couldn't get over what I had seen on the dance floor that night. It was my first contact with Northern Soul, they were different from another world. One thing stuck in my mind, I was determined to dance like Chris and that drifting style I had seen. There would be others but he was the first. I was hooked and wanted to know more, what did he mean? "Keep the Faith?" Little did I know the journey we had just begun, one that would last twelve years and the tiny footsteps we had just made. As we walked away into the night I felt different, more now than ever a misfit. Sure I had my scrott, I was a skin just one of the sheep, but deep inside an emptiness. I knew this wasn't for me. I wanted to dance, to stand out on a floor and be like him, be different. I had to find out more about this music he called Northern Soul. That club in Stoke, "The Golden Torch?" I had the feeling I belonged there, now it was up to destiny to show me the way.

Chapter 12

THE OCTOPUS SPRING 1972

If I wasn't working on Saturday I would ride around town on my scrott, especially if Wolves were playing away. The town center would be that much quieter and I wouldn't have to dodge the opposing fans. This Saturday was no different as I parked by The Exchange Pub joining the line of other scrotts, some I recognized from their side panels. I felt a glow of pride, Gladys didn't look so bad now. With my front crash bars mirrored to perfection a new fly screen and tank areal, she looked as good as any of the others and blended right in line.

A new bar had opened a short distance away called The Octopus, during the week DJs Blue Flame and Barmy Barry played mostly chart music. Swoz, a friend of mine who used to hang around in The George had been given a chance to DJ there. He was the driving force behind a new venue that opened on a Saturday dinner time billing it as the "Saturday Soul Show." On just before the matches, it hadn't been open long and had captured my interest as I now knew Swoz was into Northern Soul.

The Octopus wasn't hard to find, set right in the center of town. You entered through two ornate doors on the side of The Queens Pub, descending a few steps into a large room that opened up before you. A small bar area to the right illuminated the darkness of the room. Shelves had been added along the walls to rest drinks upon, complementing a few tables and chairs scattered around the dance floor with two black columns set along the left hand side. The floor wasn't big by any means, being wide but having no length, taking up most of the room and not made of wood. Faint speckles imprinted into the dance floor gave the place a disco feeling. Adding to this at the back of the room above the DJs decks hung a large smiling octopus surrounded with fishing nets and starfish. His tentacles reaching out above the dance floor. A welcome sign to all who came through the door.

It was always empty at first, playing records like The Tams "Hey Girl Don't Bother Me", Eddie Holman "Hey There Lonely Girl", The Supremes "Nathan Jones". The place didn't impress me and neither did the music but I begin to use it to get away from the match day madness of The George.

A few faces were beginning to filter in on Saturdays and Kim and I would often meet up with Twenty Nine Crew to spend our afternoons in there. It became our regular meeting place, our bar in a way but other people were appearing, faces I didn't know. They weren't skins but older guys and dressed differently from us. Some in long leathers or bomber jackets, others wearing bowling shirts with soul badges like the one I had seen at Willenhall Baths. They all seemed to know each other and it was this group that I wanted to get to know, but they were a tight circle and I was on the outside looking in.

From the very first time we used the bar it was evident it was different and although we were accepted we had to tread carefully. Keeping a low profile as you knew even as skins if it came on top you would be on the losing side. The older crowd that were in there looked like they could handle themselves and were totally uninterested in our little skinhead crew. They had their scene, we had ours, and having cropped hair, boots and bracers instantly put a label on my head. In the world of Northern Soul I was a "Div" and knew nothing about the music or the scene. The label fit well as that's exactly what I was. Only by going each week and slowly getting to know people would I become accepted. By hanging around in The Octopus I was starting to learn about the Northern Soul scene. Over time Swoz became a good friend of mine but he would bore me to death with endless information on labels and records I hadn't heard of. What little knowledge I had of records was of Motown and Soul from the charts.

To me he was a record maniac with fingers twitching at lightning speeds, he could index a record box in no time at all. His face of intense concentration looking for that one illusive find, reminding me of a mole as he dug through countless titles. Removing the odd record to a bursting smile, holding it to the light for a closer examination of his latest find. They were like a drug to him going to any lengths, no matter what the price to get a record on a specific label. Swoz attributed his knowledge of records to his close friend Blue Max. A DJ from The Catacombs, a club in Temple St, Wolvo with its roots embedded in the Northern Soul scene.

It was clear from the start, you had two sorts of people on the Northern scene, record collectors and dancers. Swoz was a record collector but he wasn't the only one amongst the crowd in The Octopus. In my heart I was a dancer, there was a big difference and to me we were miles apart. He seemed to know everyone that came through the door and slowly introduced me to people he knew from the scene. They were so distinct from everyone else, totally ignoring the Skinhead Reggae revolution that was going on outside the door. Fashions of the high street, mainstream street life held no interest to them. The film Shaft had been out for a while now and the small crowd in The Octopus seemed more related to that.

It was through Swoz that I made my second real contact with the Northern scene as one day he introduced me to Smokey. You heard of Smokey before you met him, he was just that type of a guy. I had seen him in the bar but we had never spoken. I was aware of his reputation as a fighter and always kept my distance, but he was someone I wanted to meet. Smokey used to go to The Torch and The Catacombs and was a well-known face around Wolvo. Smoke was a little taller than me, of stockier build, the sharp features of his face parted by long, straggly hair. A hooked nose with dark, penetrating eyes, the looks of a hawk that searched your soul as if looking for fear.

Smoke looked like he could handle himself, he had that demeanor. An air about him with a personality that could change in a flash. With his long, flowing, leather V-neck jumper and cords, he was different. I suppose he looked like a Soul boy but I didn't know what a Soul boy was. He told me about sounds to watch out for from the dancer's side of the label. Swoz told me records to collect because of the rarity of the label. I hadn't the money then and had little interest in collecting records but I listened to both. Smoke was the one who over time influenced me the most. He also had a reputation for his dancing, earned on the floors of both The Catacombs and The Torch. He was regarded by many as Wolvo's best dancer, but up to now I had never seen him dance. He kept telling me about the all-nighters that had just started at The Torch and the live acts he had seen there. The Drifters, Oscar Toney Jr., Edwin Starr, the sounds they played and he always had time for me and Kim.

I was young and still learning about the scene but I loved the music and he could see as I tried to dance, it was in my heart. Some weeks even bringing records with him for Swoz and the other DJs to play. Philip Mitchell "Free For All", Jimmy James "A Man Like Me", the slow drifting beats of the

Cooperettes "Shingling" and the soulful voice of Smokey Robinson "Whole Lot Of Shaking In My Heart". These are the records that inspired me as a dancer and made me get out on the floor.

Although I couldn't dance that well these were the ones I loved. I didn't care about the rarity of the record or the label, it was the actual record itself, that's what mattered to me! How it made me feel. The music passing through me, affecting me deeply inside, touching my very soul. I really wanted to go to The Torch but I had no choice. The older crowd had security in their age. I was seventeen, I wasn't going to sacrifice mine. My trade was my future, I knew in my heart night clubs and all-nighters was not the way to go. I held back, I would watch and learn from a distance. A decision I would regret later but only for a little while. The dancing fascinated me, I was on the sideline looking in but time and youth were on my side.

By being in The Octopus I got to know more people. Ric-Tic, a quiet sort of a guy, a smart dresser, a nameless face amongst the crowd with a tremendous knowledge of records and the Northern scene. Telling us of local clubs he had attended Up the Junction Crew, The Chateau Impney Drotwitch, and others The Blue Orchid Derby, The Pink Flamingo in Liverpool. The Twisted Wheel in Manchester, a legend of a club they used to go to until it closed last year. By making connections Kim and I were learning about the Northern scene from the people who were actually in it. Bob Lacey, Bagger, Dave Priest, Paul Roberts, Johnny Cromwell, Jimmy Cleary, Frankie Baggott, and Ray Webster, Ric-Tic to name just a few. Soulies from Wolvo who travelled to other Northern clubs, not just The Catacombs. By being around them I found out about this new world of underground music, the Northern Soul scene.

With the help of Blues and Soul magazine we were learning more about the artist's music, DJs, and clubs. Long articles written about certain nights spent at clubs, the odd name of Soulies highlighted giving them instant fame. I wanted to be like them, to break into this underground scene and get my name in that magazine.

Although still with Twenty Nine Crew I was very slowly breaking away. They were still locked into the fashion of being skins and the mentality that followed it. I was now, more than ever, a loner and to me I belonged to no crew and spent my time with Kim. Only occasionally popping into The George to catch up with my mates from around the town. I knew a lot of people, but I now lived in two different worlds. Although I still went to the matches, "Wolves were in my blood" it wasn't to fight. My new love was music, slowly it was taking over my life.

I would dance in The Octopus trying different footwork, even then I didn't like just dancing one style. Many times Rusty would join me, his moves so different from what I was trying to do. He too was into this new music, as always his crew just stood to the side. I would often receive a few snickers from on-lookers at my efforts as I tried something new. A hopping, circular footwork that I just couldn't seem to master or let go of but I didn't care, all I wanted to do was dance.

One thing I had was confidence, a determination, a belief that I could through dancing express myself to this music I loved. Then I too would stand out on a crowded floor. I watched all the older guys from Wolvo, how they danced, Smokey especially, but of the two Chris with his spinning was the one who impressed me the most. As I copied the moves of both dancers I was slowly improving and developing my own individual style. Weeks turned to months but I never left the dance floor, I knew I had a long way to go, nothing would come overnight. My footwork in an arc always coming back to the same spot, often in a hopping motion would lead me along a different avenue, over time it would develop and change.

It would be a year before I would finally gain recognition and I would do it my own way through my feet on the dance floor. Kim too started to dance as we fed off each other, our bond was plain to see. The dance floor became our new home, both of us one to one immersed in the music of Northern Soul. One Saturday in The Octopus, Rusty told me about a new place they had found, a pub called The Ship and Rainbow that played Soul music. I hadn't been out with them in a while so decided to join them for a night out agreeing to meet up there. After all, the least I could do was check it out.

The Octopus still wasn't crowded, it had been going for six months now and still hadn't taken off but these were early times. Northern Soul was still very much underground, it just wasn't being picked up by Main Street. It was clear to see just by walking around Wolvo not everyone was into Northern Soul, but like a seed it had started to grow. It would take a year before The Octopus would really start to come alive. Swoz never relented and was instrumental in turning his "Saturday Soul Show" into the first bar in Wolvo to play just Northern Soul. He became a real close friend of ours, but I learned in time to never talk to him about records!!

Chapter 13

THE SHIP AND RAINBOW

The Ship and Rainbow was an old pub on Dudley Road leading out of town. They held discos on a Sunday nights. Travelling DJs provided the lineup, changing every week so you never knew what you were going to get. It was advertised as a Soul Night so the music must be good. I had this on my mind as we entered through the black double doors to be greeted by a bouncer standing in a tiled foyer at the bottom of a wide staircase to his left. The cream painted walls and faded paintwork of the foyer blending with aged mahogany. A worn, ornate, Victorian banister swept to the main room upstairs. The smell of stale smoke and beer hung heavy in the air adding to the surroundings, creating a unique smell of their own. The place had history, a battered feel to it and I wasn't expecting much.

The bouncer was a big guy with a Teddy boy haircut combed back, shining, full of grease. His purple velvet coloured suit jacket stretching in all directions, which must have fit in his younger days. A lace tie and purple shirt adding to a look straight from the fifties. "I wonder what the breaking strain is on that jacket." The thought making me smile as I searched my pockets for money for us to get in.

"Thirty pence please." His voice in a polite full tone, collecting our money and depositing it into a tin on a table at his side. To his right, a misted glass door with the scrolled letters of saloon all that separated him from a crowded bar of revelers, shouts and laughter of a Sunday night. The soulful voices of The Supremes "Where Did Our Love Go" drifted down the wide staircase calling us to the room above.

"Maybe this won't be so bad Kim." My voice upbeat at what we may find.

"I just want to be with you, there are no bad times." Her soft voice ever thoughtful and reassuring, a face full of optimism and happiness. Just being together was all we ever wanted, our love so young and free. My spirits lifted by the music that floated towards us. "Come on lover." Kim reaching for my outstretched hand, holding it tightly as together we assented the worn carpeted stairs. The sound of a lazy sax snapping Motown beats getting louder as we neared the top.

Two more bouncers dressed in similar style and bigger in stature stood by the open doors that led to the main room in front of us. There was a bar area to the right and I headed in that direction looking for the lads. I wanted a pint of Shandy, it was my favorite drink and made my way past a bunch of skins to the crowded bar. I didn't know anyone in there and felt uneasy. I ordered our drinks, looking around for faces I might know only to be met with blank icy stares. Lots of skins that you don't recognize was not a good combination in those days. These weren't town boys and already I was getting the eye and we had only just come in! It was evident this was their disco and they didn't want us here, but I just blanked it and grabbed our drinks.

We had come to dance and nothing was going to stop us. Stepping around more skins to whispered insults and stares we made our way towards the main room. I felt pissed off and frustrated. When was I going to get away from this territorial bullshit?! Lost in my anger, we walked past the bouncers through the open double doors into the main room. Both of us were surprised at the size of the room that opened up before us. I immediately turned to Kim, "look at this dance floor!"

The wooden floor was big with length and breadth, a good size. A large disco ball hung from the ceiling, casting a revolving soft speckled light onto the empty dance floor. The room had a feel to it as if it had been used. With four black columns set around the edge of the dance floor on two sides, giving it the feeling of a miniature ballroom. The Chiffons "Sweet Talking Guy" drifted from speakers set on a large illuminated stage at the far end of the room. In the center a DJ caught in the lights, his silhouette the only dancer across the empty polished floor.

We made our way towards the lads on the far side of the room, giving them a wave of recognition. Getting a feel for the floor, twisting my feet with ease as I walked across it for the first time. The dim lights along the back walls gave the place a mellow feeling all of its own. It wasn't modern and didn't feel like a disco, it had heart and I could feel it as soon as I walked in. The black columns along the sides of the floor and seating set back to the walls wasn't what I had expected. I looked at Kim to a face of pure delight. She couldn't wait to dance, her shyness now gone. We both knew at last "we had found our floor." We had been practicing at her home dancing in a line with footwork, adding steps to twisting feet. That was to be our style but she could sense my uneasiness.

I had a sixth sense, born of the orphanage I could smell trouble a mile away and it had kicked into overdrive. A group of skins from the bar followed us in and stood by the open doors, others along the side looking in one direction. Some pushing each other, pointing at us with long blank stares following us, watching our every move. This was their territory and I knew a fight was only a matter of time. If it came on top we would have to battle our way out of this one. Being totally outnumbered we were dead meat and I knew it. Asking myself, "Where's Conroy and Eka when you need them?" But for me it was too late now. We found an empty table and deposited our drinks, placing my suit jacket on the back of an empty chair. "If I'm going to get into a fight there's no way I'm ripping this Everpress suit jacket!" The thought crossing my mind as slowly I moved to the edge of the floor.

"Dance or fight?" I came to dance and on this floor no one was going to stop me. I wanted to ram their stupidity down their throats and show them up with my feet. The Ship was full but the dance floor was empty. "Nothing But Heartaches" the powerful intro of The Supremes, a record we both knew and loved. Turning to Kim, my face in a beaming smile the pounding Motown beats ignited my very soul. I had to dance, there was just something about Motown that gave me an inner feeling and electrified my feet. We had to dance, let them see who we were, what we could do. This was our time. Nothing was going to stop us. The powerful voices of The Supremes so pure, echoing around the room. Neither one of us was shy or nervous as we moved out onto the empty floor.

My arms moving in time to the beats as my feet slid across the polished floor that instantly gave back to you. Ignoring my surroundings, lost in the music as my feet responded twisting in a line. Kim now at my side, together, but totally apart. I turned to repeat the move in a different direction of stepping footwork, my feet feeling the emotion of her voice. "…nothing but heartaches…" words so true to the feelings I had in my heart.

Kim feeling every note her arms and feet as mine, expressing her sheer joy as we danced together one to one. Skipping steps, so light on her feet, floating along reaching out with soft hands lost in the melodic beats. Two dancers, our shadows our only companions out on the empty floor. It was the first time we really danced together where we had space on an open floor. I couldn't take my eyes off her as I shuffled my feet, drifting in a line along the edge of floor. My footwork responding in movement to that pounding Motown beat. All eyes were on us. Faces full of anger, others just stood in amazement at our expression of pure love for each other wrapped in the music we loved. The bouncers now standing in the room looking across at us as we stopped dancing at the end to just gently clap at what they had just seen. Punching the air in defiance I ignored the crowd by the doors. I had been like you, now we had made our statement.

We came to dance, that's all, just dance. I despised there stupid looks and insults, I was affiliated with no crews! I belonged to no one and never would again. A loner, that's all I wanted to be! Turning to give Kim a hug, lifting her in the air swinging her around and around our smiling faces said it all. At last we had found a floor! A gentle kiss upon the cheek, the love I felt tearing me apart, bursting inside. Our happiness so simple and pure wrapped in our own world. Smiles of "just you and me."

We looked around the room once more and I noticed a guy leaning against a column. Tall with glasses and a skinny frame in a way with one of my mates Winston a face from around the town. We returned to the table to get our drinks, there was a look of surprise on the faces of Rusty and my old mates from Twenty Nine Crew. A smile of respect, they had never seen Kim or me dance like that together on an empty floor. Music was the most important thing in our lives, they more than anyone else could see how we had changed.

"Gethro! Kim! This is my mate Darb." We turned around to face Winston, a stranger now stood at his side. The guy in glasses who had been watching us dance from the far side of the room. Darb looked bigger close-up. Tall, a slim build with a soft face, his gentle features complemented a broad smile. His glasses giving him an air of intelligence, a face of trust.

Darb dressed bang on to the fashion at that time. A smart suit jacket, button-down and Staypress trousers. In polished brogues he dressed in style and I could tell straight away he was different. A smile as we introduced ourselves, the outstretched hands of friendship the firmness of our grip "a reflection of our hearts." I introduced Kim, I could see he was blown away by her looks of pure innocence. Her doll like features and pale blue eyes holding his gaze, the gentleness of her natural beauty reflected in her youth. Winston stood smiling at his side. Once more I looked across the room, more skins now gathering along the sides of the dance floor. It wasn't looking good but what could I do? Again I felt anger, "Why can't they leave us alone? What had we done? We had come to dance, that's all."

The fast intro of the Isley Brothers instantly made me move back to the dance floor, "Why When Love Is Gone" their melodic voices in perfect harmony to the music blasting from the speakers, as the room exploded to the sound of Soul. Kim, Darb, and Winston joining me as we returned to the empty floor once more with all the room we could ever want. The smoothness of the floor allowing me to move faster to beats that demanded fast feet.

I altered my footwork to the hopping style that I had practiced in The Octopus. A smile of recognition from Darb, impressing him with the footwork so different from before. Straight away I knew I had just met someone special. Darb moved well with his feet. Dancing with that same boldness, a confidence to get out on the floor. That same expression, a love for music. Trying to match beats that came from every direction with passion, a rawness that only comes from the heart. Smiles of pleasure between us as we danced side by side for the first time, to the music we obviously loved. The DJ playing more records with soulful beats happy, at last, to have someone out on the floor. First Choice "This Is The House Where Love Died" and Barbara Miles "Queen Of Fools" a few more dancers joining us, handbags littered the floor. The Tams "Be Young Be Foolish But Be Happy", Sue Thompson "Paper Tiger", The Newbeats "Run Baby Run", Spencer Davies Group "Gimmie Some Lovin", Johnny Johnson and the bandwagon "Honey Bee" and The Showstoppers "Ain't Nothing But A House Party", we danced to them all. "Stop Her On Sight" the soulful driving voice of Edwin Starr so pure.

The hypnotic beats driving me wild, the solo piano, powerful vocals pushing me harder in my dancing. Darb and I testing each other for the first time to see what we had, what we could bring to the floor. Driven by the music I bumped into him, embarrassed apologies from either side. Agreeing we would have to watch that as we laughed at our antics both of us lost for words. Kim laughing at our collision as we all poured our hearts out to Motown that ignited the floor.

More skins catching my eye, gathering by one of the columns spilling beer as they crossed the dance floor. Moving ever closer to our table their eyes in one direction, the circle of fools watching our every move. Darb stopped dancing, breaking away to talk to a crowd of skins at the side of the floor. He seemed to know them all and was obviously part of their crew. Throwing his arms in the air, pushing some of them backwards, arguing with them. His face in frustration and anger at pointed fingers in my direction. My hands tightened to a fist, "load of fucking wankers!" whispering insults under my breath. To me it was a simple equation, you're going to turn me over then you had better stay out of The George. I had a lot of friends around Wolvo and there would be a payback. It was as simple as that!

Darb returned to my side, a worried look upon his face. "What's going on mate?" My eyes following another skin as he crossed the room.

"Watch him Gethro. That's Froggy, he's the one that's going to kick it off. They will be over you like wasps, be careful mate they are going to steam you." His voice now full of concern. "They were going to have Twenty Nine Crew last week. That's why they brought the numbers this time." He paused then smiled. "Rumor is you're the leader."

"What! Fuck me Darb, anymore good news?" My stomach turned over, I was about to get a kicking and it would come hard and fast. I had been in their shoes, I knew how to steam a routine. I knew only too well and for what! Winston, joining our conversation, standing at my side.

"Doesn't look good Gethro." A gentle frown crossing his forehead as he nodded to skins gathering nearby.

"I know if it kicks off Winst, take care of Kim. Move her towards the stage mate, it's me they want."

"You sure? I'll help you out man." His voice defiant.

"No Winst, take care of Kim." Looking at Darb I could see embarrassment in his face, then a smile of encouragement. At least he had tried to help me, I knew I wasn't alone. Glancing at Rusty I could see a few of the lads placing bottles and glasses under the tables. Our eyes met, an anxious look between us, as if to tell me, "they were ready to fight."

I surveyed the room, we were totally outnumbered and trouble was just one step away.

A bouncer now stood on the stage talking to the DJ as the music suddenly changed, Slade now filled the room. "Momma We're All Crazy Now" a record riding high in the charts. Cherry reds packed the dance floor, faded Levi jackets, skinners boots and bracers, feathered haircuts of the girls, the uniform of the skins. Dancing in semi-circles scattered groups around the room. Their feet glued to the dance floor, bent knees swaying, twisting bodies moving in time to the music their dancing so different from us.

Turning away from the dance floor we finally sat down to talk.

"Darb, you into Soul?" I asked, trying to ease my thoughts away from the fight that was coming my way.

"I like Motown. That's Soul, why you ask?" His voice inquisitive. "Ever heard of Blues and Soul or Northern Soul?"

"No, what's that?" Shaking his head in a look of confusion.

"It's a magazine. It advertises Soul music, venues, and all-nighters that play Northern."

"What's that? I've never heard of it?"

"You got to come to The Octopus Darb. They play it on Saturday, dinner time. You'll hear the difference." My face bursting to a smile.

"Hey, they won't like you talking to a Soul boy." I gestured to his mates, now out on the floor.

"What do you mean, Gethro?"

I shook my head, "I don't belong to any crew mate. I just came to dance."

"Which crew you with Darb? Them?"

"I'm not now!" We burst into laughter, crossing our hands to the amusement of Kim and Winston sitting at our side.

"Gethro, keep your head down when Jeff Beck comes on."

"Why's that, Darb?" Shaking my head with a puzzled expression, seeking more.

"You'll see." His face now breaking to a smile.

"Who are they?" I asked, gesturing to the floor wanting more.

"Parkfield and Blackenhall skins, they are a big crew from around here."

"I've never heard of them. Who's the leader?"

"Gary Watson."

"Where is he? I want to meet him." As I stood up Darb looked surprised, Rusty joining us he too with a startled look upon his face, showing concern.

"Watch him Gethro. I've heard about him, he's a hard bastard."

"Cheers Rusty, that's nice to know."

"Trying to help you man! Just be ready for him to kick it off."

I was sick of being stared at and for what reason, because I didn't belong there? Because I hadn't asked their permission to dance. Fuck them! When would we be able to go out without this disco skinhead shit? It really was getting to me, it gnawed at me deep inside. Darb could see it in my eyes, we weren't giving up this floor. I wasn't going away.

"Winston, watch Kim for me mate."

"I got her Gethro. I'll look after her." A look of trust between us, Kim's face now pale with anxiety standing at his side.

"It's ok lover. I'll be ok." A gentle kiss between us, a worried look upon her face. Darb jumped up, "It's up to you Gethro. I got your back, that's all I can do." There was a slight pause between us as I emptied my glass, taking a deep swallow of courage. Darb leading the way to his mates on the far side of the room. We crossed the floor to the sound of Judge Dread "Big Six" another record riding high in the charts. Reggae of the skins ever popular, more boots packing the floor.

Gary was a big for a white guy, broad shouldered, a powerful build and well over six feet tall. Dressed in a steel grey tonic suit jacket, a collarless shirt, boots and jeans, the fashion of that time. A group of his mates broke their laughter, an uneasy tension as we approached. Placing his beer on the bar, slowly he turned around to face me for the first time staring straight at me. Our eyes clashed in silence, my nerves tearing me apart. I was either going to get decked or my plan would work and I was sure I had heard his name in The George. As Darb introduced me, his tight circle of friends closing in surrounding us, ready to pounce.

"Do you know Eka from The George, Gary?" Controlling my fear as best I could.

"Eka. That mad bastard, you don't know him do ya?!"

"Yea, he's a good mate of mine and Tina, do you know her?" A weary smile crossed his face.

"Eka's a good kid, hard bastard though. Leads The North Bank, goes in The George. If you know Eka then you're a mate of mine!" Throwing his arms around me, lifting me off the floor with ease. "What's your name again?"

"Gethro."

"Well come on, Gefrooo. Let's have a pint, it's your round." All three of us laughing as he slapped me on the back, nearly sending me through the bar. A cheap price to pay for the escape I had just made. Our friendship sealed in a handshake as we talked about The George, dropping names of faces we knew. Darb relaxed a smile, no words spoken between us. We both knew how close it had been. Recognition of our handshake, I just felt he would have helped me if it had gone the other way. Once again it was who you knew, a face as simple as that. Just one name, Eka. We crossed the dance floor, returning to Kim, relief now on her face smiling in an expression of love.

"That was close Darb!" Shaking my head in anxiety.

"I know. Too close mate! You're lucky, I've seen him deck someone for a bad joke!"

"Well, anyway I'm too good looking to have my face rearranged."

"I know Gethro. You're nearly as good looking as me!" All of us burst into laughter, turning to Winston stroking his chin at our side. His beaming smile and charming good looks, the image of a young Sam Cook. Winston was good looking, there was never any doubt about that! The word spread to leave us alone as tension slowly left the room and charts music once again filling the air.

Later in the night all hell broke loose, Jeff Beck's "High Ho Silver Lining" igniting the room. All the skins rushed to the middle of the floor chanting their crew's names, singing in unison to the chorus "High ho silver lining everywhere we go theirs agro!" Pushing and shoving till scuffles and fights broke out, to be broken up by the bouncers on the riot of the beer stained dance floor we had left not so long ago.

I got to know Gary really well, he wasn't a troublemaker just his mates got him into trouble and he finished it off. He never picked on any of us and his crew over time became good friends.

Northern Soul was still very much unheard of, it just wasn't being picked up in the discos. Skins were still the dominant fashion, their music was Slade and Reggae that's what filled the discos at this time. Soul like us was fighting for a place on the dance floor. Little did they know that running at the side of the skinhead revolution was Northern Soul, a totally underground scene. One of no violence frequented by people with a different passion, their love was music and dancing. We were just starting to dance then. It was all about footwork and feeling the music, that beat passing through you as your feet expressed the feelings you had, the emotions so deep in your heart. We all danced in our own individual way, you could see we were on to something but we were raw.

Sometimes our dancing just didn't fit the music, out of step and mistimed but we had something, a style of our own that was unusual from main street skins. Nothing happens overnight, our dancing would go in its own direction, our music and our feet would lead the way. All we were at the moment was different, even then we stood out with the energy we brought to the floor. I knew in my heart as we turned and came off the dance floor that night we had just made two special friends without even saying a word.

Darb never left my side for seven years after meeting that night, he became one of five of us that would leave our mark on the Northern dance scene. All we had to go on was we loved to dance and that pounding beat drove us on. Little did I know we would spend four years on this floor, as it gave us the room to practice and dance and it was to become to me, "the best floor in Wolvo." At the start full of crews and that mentality, not everyone had changed.

It took nearly a year to claim that dance floor, when we got it we never gave it back. For now we would patently wait and time was on our side. We were still chasing the Northern scene and because of The Octopus we were now closer than ever to it. At last we had found our floor, it meant so much to me and Kim to be able to dance to the Motown and Soul we loved. There were four of us now, a little crew in a way but we belonged to no one. We became inseparable. Winston and Darb became two of our closest friends, shadows who never left my side. Darb was like me, we were lost. Both of us knew where we wanted to go we just didn't know how to get there. Once again destiny had played her hand. Our life would move as fast as the music, a Northern dance floor had our names on it and Jackie Wilson was calling my name.

Chapter 14

TWO DIV'S AND A DANCE FLOOR

It was now late September, the summer had passed us by and a new football season had kicked off. The town was coming alive again to the clashes of opposing fans. Saturday was now a day I would have to myself and call for Kim at night. She never had that possessive nature that was common with girls her age and gave me space to breath. That was good in a way. My childhood had affected me deeply.

Slowly I came out of the shell I had put around me for protection in the orphanage, in the fragrance of adolescence like a flower I was starting to bloom. I was like any other seventeen year old, selfish in love. I wanted the best of both worlds and would play around with girls that came from every direction. A smile here, a wave there, I had that cheeky personality. I wasn't shy around girls.

Chasing any skirt I could, arranging to see them on nights I didn't see Kim. To be with my mates in the day and see a girl on the night was my answer to love, but really what I was chasing wasn't love at all. I only felt in love at certain times, the emotion switching on and off. Staying with one girl was virtually impossible for me at this time. Love and lust are two very different words, never the two shall meet as love will always outlast lust. A lesson I would learn the hard way as Kim really loved me, but at this time I couldn't control my emotions as the two fought battles with a conscience I didn't have.

The Ship was now our base for dancing and slowly I was being accepted on the dance floor for the dancer I was to become. Meeting with Twenty Nine Crew, the nights we went there sometimes all of us hitting the floor. Even mingling with Parkfield, who we would meet as individuals on our travels but as a crew never appeared around the town. It was simple really, Skins were very territorial just two crews ran Wolvo. Temple St and Queen St with West Park floating in the background, no other large crews were tolerated. Wolvo town center became mine and Darb's playground as we would meet up in Rumpy's cafe or The Wimpy and wander around the town. Darb and I would visit all the old haunts: The George, The Greyhound, The Tavern in the Town, The Gondolier but The Octopus was our favorite with an atmosphere all of its own.

Fashion became the most important thing to us, our age dictated that but more than this, following the Northern style of being individual, being different, putting your own spin on what you found. We didn't want to be dressed like everyone else. To us we weren't Skins, Suede Heads or Brolley Boys, call them what you want. I classed myself as neither, a misfit looking for an identity and the Northern scene was giving us that.

We were obsessed with clothes and always on the lookout for unusual items right from the start. What we couldn't find we had made. If you had a plain V-neck, I wanted a V-neck with my initial on it! I couldn't find one so Kim knitted me one. A red V-neck jumper with my initial G on the front of it. A simple change but it gave me identity, I was different and Darb was exactly the same. We wanted to create our own style, to us it wasn't just about dancing you had to stand out in the crowd. We would get deeply involved with this as we progressed onto the scene creating our own styles, reflecting the individuals that we were and Kim would be very influential in this.

On our travels on a Saturday some of the local shops would catch our eye: Rosenshines, Woodall's, or Village on Victoria St, but we both knew if you wanted clothes in Wolvo there really was only one shop. Eddies Forty Six sat just down from The Mander Centre entrance on the same side as Beatties. The brightly painted double fronted shop stood out a mile you couldn't miss it. Stocked with the latest clothes from London it was a place we would always go.

This Saturday was like any other as we stared into the window, one of our mates John Venn, the assistant, waved us in. John was also on the Northern scene and had been for a few years telling us of someone called Farmer Carl Dene and Toney Jebb from the Blackpool Mecca Highland Room. Names of two DJs we had never heard of, a place we had never been and filling us with information on clubs and history of the scene.

He was always dressed immaculate and today was no different. His clean cut features complementing a long sleeved V-neck mohair jumper, a striped tie with button-down shirt. His tapered single pleated trousers matching black royals polished to perfection. He dressed typical of the shop, a statement of fashion at that time. The clothes there weren't cheap. You brought quality and style and he couldn't wait to show us the latest arrivals from London.

"Wait till you see these lads!" Hastily, he scurried away to the back of the shop leaving us surrounded with the latest clothes. Button-down shirts, red and blue check Jaytex, roll collared Ben Sherman's with a neck loop plain or chalk striped. Real quality long and short sleeved yellow being a favorite colour of mine. Full length royal blue crombies and champagne tonic suits, four button sleeves inside ticket pockets with 2 center vents. Everpress bottle green suits, V-neck patterned jumpers long and short sleeved. Pharile's were also coming in but this was typical of the main street fashion. This time moving in the direction of suede heads, a spin off from the skins. "Gethro, I thought John had gone out the back." Darb pointing to the dummy in the front window to laughter between us, even he was dressed smarter than us.

"Check these out lads!" John remerging with three boxes hurriedly placing them on to a chair. "I've only got nines left, look at these we sold out as soon as they came in Solatio's from London!" His face in exuberant excitement a shoe held flatly in his hand.

"Shit, they're smart man!"

"The dog's bollocks Gethro." Darb captivated in the moment mesmerized as me. A double pleated leather shoe crisscross with patterns, blue and black, maroon and black even spats white on black they looked brilliant. All leather lace-ups with a more rounded front than royals. They were all the rage and I needed some dancing shoes but already he had sold out of our size. Although we loved the clothes in Eddies and we did in truth, they were at prices our youth could not afford. Bidding our farewell as we opened the door to the ringing of a bell another customer entering the shop.

"Those are smart shoes Gethro."

"You're not kidding mate, perfect for dancing but eleven pound fifty is a lot of money, Darb."

"I know that's a week's wages. You could buy four pair of RAFs for the price of them, be all right if you were an octopus."

"Now that would be a sight on the dance floor mate!" My smile driving the thought further.

"Eight RAFs with metal steggs on you would hear him coming a mile off Gethro." Our laughter lost in the moment as we messed around with our minds.

"Fuck it Darb. We don't need fashion just some shoes for dancing, funny you mentioned it though."

"What?" His face in a look of confusion.

"The Octopus. Come on, I want to find out about that guy John keeps on about."

"Who? Farmer Carl Dene?

"Yea that's him, Ric Tic will know. Anyway I could murder a pint."

"Your round Gethro!" Darb seizing the moment.

"No it's not?!"

"It is remember The Ship last week?"

"Do you remember everything?"

"Yea I do since I teamed up with you."

"You're as bad as Kim, she remembers everything."

"Who do you think I got it off?" Our steps quickening to more laughter between us. The midday sun lifting our spirits along the way.

I opened the door for Darb as we walked into The Octopus descending the few steps that led onto the dance floor clutching our copies of Blues and Soul. At the far end of the room Swoz playing records his small frame barely visible as he looked up from behind the decks.

"Gethro! Darb! Wait till you hear this!" Turning to a record box at his side. A flurry of fingers stepping through records pausing to pull out his latest find.

"Look! "Our Love Is In The Pocket" by Darrel Banks!" his face in an expression of pure love as if holding some precious artifact, a gentle wipe before sweeping it onto the decks. We stood bemused, my head spinning trying to view the title of another record we had never heard of.

Darb and I always came here, now spending afternoons in The Octopus. The atmosphere so different from The Ship. There was no skinhead mentality here, no bad vibes, the older guys from The Torch ran this bar. Although we were accepted around them my sixth sense never switched off. Here there was no set fashion and The Torch and Cats boys stood out a mile. A few Soul badges illuminated in the room, it had been going for a while now but it wasn't full by any means, just a typical Saturday afternoon.

Ric Tic came over as we stood by the decks his black blazer displaying the embroiled badge of The Catacombs which he had specially made. We both wanted that badge so bad I could see it in Darb's face as he could mine. Badges were everything to us, they gave you history of which we had none. If you had a Cats badge you went to The Cats, same with The Torch you wore the badge of that club. You had danced on that floor, you could instantly date someone and their time on the scene. The Northern scene had one rule, if you didn't go to that club you never wore their badge. He never did tell us where he got it made. Here it was all about being individual and Ric Tic was, that's another way you stood out on the Northern scene. The clothes of the Soulies were so very different with really no set fashion at all. Why?

Northern was a scene driven by music and dancing, nothing else mattered really other than you being out on that dance floor. Ben Sherman's and tapered trousers of The High St made you look good, but for us as dancers over time they just weren't going to cut it. Fred Perry's, Slazenger's bowling shirts, vests, and cords created a different style dictated to you by the dancing. You had to be able to move so baggie clothes were a must, more casual with a looser fit. You definitely had two cultures raging at the same time, one progressing underground making its own styles by being individual and if anything it was the opposite of The Main Street shops. The other moving in the direction dictated to by fashion with styles of the high street changing all the time.

Not many people here had cropped hair, even I had started to let mine grow.

Now very slowly I to was changing, the music and dancing pulling me in. Punna, a dancer we knew, who used to go to The Cats was practicing some moves out in the middle of the floor. Sprinkling talcum powder to improve his spins, losing control on the now icy floor. The mellow voice of Jackie Wilson "I Get The Sweetest Feeling" filling the half empty room.

"Swoz is on a roll now Darb" emphasizing my point in recognition to the music.

"I know he's picking up on the sounds every week.

"Did you see his face though, Darb? Looked like he had just come over the last one."

"No wonder he wiped it Gethro!" The laughter between us drowned by another record now filling the room. Catching a smile from Swoz passing on our way to the bar as he looked out with pride from behind the decks. More dancers now venturing onto the floor, acknowledging the sounds he was playing. Punna was a good dancer and a few times he hit a spin Mulley, one of his mates, came over pushing him off balance laughing as he joined in. "Quit the chart crap put some Northern on!" Teasing Swoz to exchanged V's from the center of the floor.

They were about the same age as us regulars, we had come to know who used to just mess around. The Octopus was that kind of place. We had seen them in here a few times, both of them wore Cats badges upon their vests. Another guy was with them standing to the side, tall and skinny with shoulder length black hair. I knew him as Squeak with a reputation as a spinner from The Cats. A nod of recognition between us as we made our way across the dance floor placing our drinks on one of the columns. Ric Tic rejoining us as we watched other dancers out on the floor.

"Look, check his feet out Gethro." Darb pointed to Punna as we tried to see how he kept his balance in a spin. His arms and feet entirely different from the style I had seen Chris do.

"Hey Ric Tic what do you know about Farmer Carl Dene? Only John mentioned him." I felt embarrassed by asking but I had to.

"He's been around for years Gethro. DJ'd at The Cats and The Chateau Impney in Droitwich." Darb and I looking on giving him the attention he deserved.

"He discovered loads of records on the Northern scene, Richard Temple "That Beat And Rhythm", Doris Troy "I'll Do Anything", and Leon Haywood "Baby Reconsider". There's a story about that, though he leaned forwards to emphasize his point.

Farmer Carl lent that record to Graham "Docker" White who took it to The Wheel for Rob Bellars the DJ to play. After that it became massive.

"Hold on Ric Tic, you're losing me. I've never heard of him or that record."

"You would if you went to The Torch Gethro," his face breaking to a knowledgeable smile.

"Can't mate, I've got my exams."

"What do you know about Roger Eagle?"

"I've never heard of him either." Darb nodding, a confused look between us. Both of us listening intently wanting more.

"He's the guy who started it all off but he never got the recognition he deserved. The first DJ at The Wheel Manchester he was playing rare Soul from the States before anybody had even heard of it."

"What happened to him? Where's he now Ric Tic?"

"Gethro I don't know, he just drifted away from the scene. No one was doing it before him. He started it all with records like Sam and Dave "You Don't Know Like I Know". He was the first person in UK to ever play that."

"How do you know all this crap Ric Tic? I mean, you know a lot of info!" Darb at my side, he too nodding his head.

"I collect records Gethro. It just comes with collecting records mate." His face breaking to a broadening smile.

The records were starting to flow now, the atmosphere picking up, hand claps coming from the floor drawing our attention the dancing more intense. The Vibrating Vibrations "Surprise Party For Baby".

"Gethro we got to dance to this!" A gentle nudge from Darb placing his beer on one of the columns.

"Brilliant tune man! Catch it!" Our enthusiasm infectious, hitting the floor together to a record we both loved. We didn't care what we looked like, all we wanted to do was dance.

"Come on Ric Tic!" My hand gesturing him to join us.

"I'm ok, I want my energy for The Torch tonight Gethro. Anyway, I'm a collector man." We smiled at his shyness, leaving him chatting at the side of the floor.

To me footwork was everything, the key, the foundation that we would build upon. The start of the expression of love for the music as we connected with the floor. Darb and I locked into our similar style of hopping footwork, neither one of us could quite master to match the Northern beats. A nod of respect to Punna and Mulley out dancing us with every step.

We looked good at The Ship but this was a Northern floor and here we were just two Divs. Neither one of us wearing a Soul badge, staying in the background, just two faces a dance floor and daring not to spin. "Temptation Walk" by Jackie lee keeping us locked to the beats as we moved around the floor. The Drifters "Saturday Night At The Movies" a sound that had recently left the charts, Rose Batist "Hit And Run", The Flamingos "Boogaloo Party", Mitch Ryder and The Detroit Wheels "Breakout", Edwin Starr "Back Street". The Octopus coming alive now Swoz bringing energy to the room reveling behind the decks. Northern Soul taking the dance floor on a typical afternoon The Octopus slowly establishing itself, new faces appearing all the time.

With the sounds being played at The Octopus and the pull of The Catacombs getting stronger we were about to hit the Northern scene together. Little did we know two people were about to arrive with ideas of their own and they would change it all. Kim and I still hadn't been to a Northern Soul club, just as we got our memberships for The Cats it had closed for refurbishment. Everyone was talking about The Cats and a local club The Torch and I knew we had to go, it was just a matter of time. The clock of life was ticking but time, like our youth was not always on our side.

Chapter 15

CAVENDISH CHRISTMAS PARTY - 1972

Flurries of snow twisted in a downward spiral caught in the streetlights. It seemed to be coming faster now in a never ending swirl. Fighting the chill, adjusting the collar of my crombie my hands frozen by a sharp north wind. I stood watching other couples race to be greeted by a bouncer standing at a half open door. Where is she? Tapping snow from my shoes I checked again to make sure I had the tickets, pulling them out of my pocket. There in bold letters Cavendish Xmas Party Nineteen Seventy-Two as Kim came around the corner and ran into my open arms. I smiled at my prize, her beauty holding her tightly as I lifted her off the ground.

The warmth of her face against my skin, gentle to my touch. The sweet smell of perfume engulfed me, finding softness in lips as we folded in passion to kiss as only young lovers do. We had been seeing each other for a while now, fourteen months and I missed her when she wasn't around. Sure I don't deny I was a cheat and a liar, I didn't deserve the love of the girl I held in my arms but the power of her love was shining through.

Blowing away the cobwebs of a childhood that had only ever known loneliness and pain. My heart crying on the inside at the love I could not reach and the guilt of my lifestyle, an emotion I would not face. Was I falling in love? As I held her in my arms right here, right now I had my answer but I would back away from it time and time again! I protected my heart that had never felt love. Slowly, Kim was turning the key to unlock the memories of the past. Fighting to release the love she knew I held so deep inside.

The Cavendish had reopened on once a fortnight, it was now one of my favorite places to go. The music had improved, playing more Motown and Soul with one of Wolvo's bigger dance floors I knew we would have room to dance. With Temple St and Queen St getting along there was no attitude here unless you brought it with you. The bouncers here were big guys standing out a mile and wouldn't put up with any crap, as some people found out the hard way. You just had to behave that's all and I dreaded being turned away as we climbed the stairs to go in. Kim still looked so young and refused to wear any make-up. Getting us a second look from the bouncer, collecting our tickets his face breaking to a smile as he waved us in.

A well-known DJ was on tonight Barmy Barry his voice lost in the noise of the crowd as we entered the smoke filled room. Saturday night in Wolvo, the place was packed. Suit jackets and tonic trousers, button-downs and Solatios that were the fashion. This was a place to show off, you dressed smart drifting clouds of Brut after-shave hanging heavy in the air. I felt good, especially now I too had a pair of tonics, riding the wave of fashion tonight I had dressed the same. The Cavendish was stylish, set in a large room longer than it was wide. The dance floor surrounded in tall, draped windows with seating and tables set along the sides. I squeezed Kim's hand so as not to lose her, turning to our right we made our way through the crowd climbing the few steps leading up to the bar. Pausing halfway, leaning on the handrail I stopped dead to look around, the crowded room and that divided dance floor of not so long ago.

Old attitudes had changed, there was no black or white anymore. No more invisible lines across the dance floor. You still had crews but everyone mingled together. There was a new feeling, a different atmosphere, it didn't feel like a disco. "My Man Is A Sweet Man" by Millie Jackson had just ended "Here I Go Again" from Archie Bell and The Drells, Northern beats filling the dance floor. Soul blasting from the speakers igniting the dancers in movement. A few Soulies from The Octopus, the odd spin to a certain move, faces easily recognized; Soul boys taking the floor.

Northern Soul had crept onto the dance floor, here at last. It was part of the night. I was looking for Smokey, a long leather, that's what he always wore, you couldn't miss him. A leather that's all I needed. Where's Smokey?

My gaze wandering around the room, "No, that's Selwyn," another of my mates, a small guy, a hustler with charm and I smiled as I passed his attention. Robbo, more faces in the crowd, his thick black beard a Prince of Wales check suet ending in black and white Solatios, reminiscent of a gangster stepping from the scene of shaft. Brentford and Venton chatting to girls standing at his side. All people I had got to know by being a town boy and accepted me for who I was. West Park, some of their crew now danced hitting the floor together "Get Up In The Morning" from Desmond Dekker and the Israelites, reggae beats bouncing around the room dancers swaying on the crowded floor.

There was always a crowd around Conroy, I waved as I caught his attention he easily stood out in the room. James Brown "There Was A Time", more sounds of Soul now hitting the floor. The Cavendish had changed with the rest of us and become a good venue. Soul had made a footprint on the dance floor and music had led the way. "There's Smokey, Kim. See the guy in the long leather."

I liked to watch him dance. I had practiced his footwork. To me I had been a good pupil, that's how you learned to dance but it was a style of dancing that I as an individual would not pursue for long. Standing at his side Eggy, Pete Scory, Aggy, Ray Webster, Paul Roberts, faces I knew only too well. I used to work with Paul, he gave me a perfect black eye one day for running my mouth. All he did was hurt my pride and kept me quiet for a while, well at least till it had gone away. I was always weary of him after that, he was one of the older guys from The Torch. I learned very early on some you can trust, others you can't, a lesson I would use later to my advantage. One I would never forget.

I smiled, it's Christmas "so he must be in a good mood."

"Come on, no standing on the stairs!" the bouncers moving us along as I knew they finally would. Acknowledging faces along the way we edged forward into the crowded bar. Twenty Nine Crew sitting in the corner, a tabletop full of glasses everyone buying drinks "Gethro!" "Rusty! Look at this!" Bending my knees, twisting my feet on the carpet to shouts and laughter between us. Dave, Fozza, Emma, and Mick we went way back. Kim and I joined our circle of friends. Spending time together, soaking up the party atmosphere that only Christmas brings. Friendships bonded with memories lasting into the night.

Listen Kim, "…people were standing all around…", the voice of Roy C's "Shotgun Wedding" a record that had just come into the charts.

"Come on lover!" Kim's shyness gone, her face lit up with excitement pulling me forward, gathering our drinks. The dance floor going wild, Conroy calling our names as we descended into the crowded room. I don't know what it was about this record, I just loved it. It made me happy. Joining Conroy and his girl everyone now hitting the floor, a small space at the back of the room. The floor sent into a frenzy of swaying bodies' bullets echoing around us the heavy base pounding the dance floor.

Shooting each other to laughter between us, smiling faces wherever you looked. Conroy, Venton, and Ralphy feeling the warmth of their friendship, a smile from Danny, a shared joke between us. Even the white boy hadn't run. Sharing time with Conroy, the bond of our friendship stronger than ever, more records hitting the floor. Later in the night Al Green his beautiful voice screaming so full of pain and sorrow pleading with your emotions. The heavy sax drifting from the speakers engulfed us in a room of Soul. "I'm So Tired Of Being Alone" the dim lights of the room adding feelings to the music, so true to my heart.

The party nearly over Christmas Nineteen Seventy-Two drawing to a close. I turned to Kim taking her hand to join the floor with other couples wrapping ourselves around each other. Shyness in our dancing, wandering hands held back by the tenderness of our youth. Losing our bodies to each other, two lovers gently swaying in the rhythm of love. The rest of our life in front of us, a gentle kiss upon the cheek. A dance etched in our memories, forever folded in the pages of time.

Chapter 16

THE OCTOPUS - START OF 1973

Conroy had now left Wolvo and I missed my old mate, we had spent many happy times on the dance floor together and I would never see him again. The New Year's Eve party had slipped through my fingers. I hated that as The New Year was always a special time to me. A new start, a new beginning but I had been left no choice, I had been revising. My trade was still the most important thing in my life. This year one set of my final exams out of the way and I was finally to let loose, nothing was now holding me back.

Feelings of a new beginning, the winds of change, a freshness that only a New Year brings although a little late at last I could now relax. Unbeknownst to me this year was going to be a very special one. I didn't know the significance of what was going to impact my life forever, destiny had taken over and now she would deal her hand.

Lots of clubs and discos were springing up around the town. The French Duck, a bar we would visit with a small dance floor downstairs run by our mate John Venn. The Cats had re-opened, The Pink Elephant, The Civic on a Friday night to name just a few. Kim and I would dive into all of them with Winston and Darb at our side. Little did I know she had been practicing her dancing but I would soon find out. Wolvo was alive, the town felt different it had a new energy to match the new music.

Northern Soul as I knew it was mixing with popular music, changing the face of dance floors scattered around the town. Even The Octopus was picking up, it had been going for a year now. A younger crowd had made its way through the doors and with it came a very special guy.

Jimmy Little appeared in The Octopus one day by the side of Winston and I fell in love with his infectious personality right away. I just loved being around him. With his passion for music and dancing we formed an instant friendship and he immediately joined our little band. Standing well over six foot three with his hair in the Afro style of that time, a frame of natural youth and strength he was a big guy. Younger than me his chubby features and gentle face hiding those wicked eyes, that could flash anger often directed at Winston but only ever in a playful way.

Kim took all of them in her stride as Jimmy took the piss out of anyone of us, to the amusement of the others nearby. Often cowering away from Kim's wagging finger to be given as good as he got, as laughter just followed us around. We never argued or fell out, that was the strength of the friendship we had. A respect for each other born only of individuals that bonded together as brothers along the way. Jimmy too would become an accomplished dancer for the big guy he was. Leaving a footprint on many Northern dance floors with a completely different style of dancing to anything we would do. One of the two dancers that would join us as we embarked on our journey on to the Northern Scene.

No one messed with Jimmy, you just knew that would not be a good idea, he had that air about him and gave us a sense of security. People thought twice about us now with Darb, Jimmy, and Winston by my side we were a formidable little group. I had back-up, the days of the black eyes were over, as now if it kicked off I knew we could give as good as we got. Darb and Jimmy both over six feet tall, Winston stocky with a powerful build, all of us fit well together. Right from the start we had each other's backs, we gave each other protection. This would come in handy for the future, that's how uncertain I felt around some of The Torch boys and I had every reason to feel that way as I would soon find out.

Chapter 17

MARCH 1973 CATS FIRST TIME

"Dancing in the rain"

Kim and I stood under the dimly lit sign that hung above a doorway of what seemed like a semi-derelict building in Temple Street Wolvo. We watched other couples on the opposite side of the street, some carrying skates as they made their way to the roller dome on the corner. We used to go there with Twenty Nine Crew, remembering old times as we waited for our friends reminiscing about smuggled love letters and secret dates that now seemed so long ago.

A yellow and black Dolomite Sprint startled us, appearing from nowhere screeching to a halt under a streetlight. I watched with interest, there standing on the pavement the lone figure of a girl waving goodbye the car speeding off into the night. She approached, a slight hesitation before coming towards us looking straight ahead quickening her step as she crossed the road. Tall with long blonde hair, a short fur coat, white trousers clinging to her figure the looks of a model. I smiled as we always do at the sight of a pretty girl moving to the side as she entered through the doorway and vanished out of sight. The fragrance of her lingering perfume captured in the coolness of March night air.

My thoughts immediately broken with the sound of laughter as Winston,

Darb, and Jimmy came towards us with their girlfriends. Greeting each other with hugs and handshakes as we always did.

"Is this it?" Jimmy started laughing, "Where you brought us man?!" Even I had to smile at his enthusiasm as I pointed to the sign above the door.

The once red letters now pink and faded proclaiming in a circle Catacombs Club Temple St in the center w-ton 28682. We entered through the open doorway following the trail of perfume. Graffiti covered walls, lasting memories of The Torch and Wheel leading to the top of the stairs. Little did we know as we passed through that door and up those stairs that our lives would change forever and would never be the same again. We could hear the muffled sound of music as we stood at the top of the stairs but where's the door? And how do you get in? All of us joking, laughing at our predicament. In the end, I tapped on the kiosk window which immediately slid open. A young girl with short hair and slim features, a sharpness to her voice asked, "Memberships please!"

Our cards were returned, numbered, and dated our first memberships, holding mine with pride as we all paid in. Kim showing me hers, pink on one side white on the other with number 2241 dated 72-73 telling me in a soft voice. "Told you I looked eighteen" a sense of relief came over me, she would be sixteen next month, but we were in!

> NAME ......Kim....HPERTS....
> ADDRESS ...28...HEWINGS..DRIVE....HERTH TOWN
>
> Membership No. ..2241.
>
> RULES:
> 1. Members must be over the age of 18.
> 2. The management reserves the right to refuse admission.
> 3. The management accept no responsibility for members' belongings lost or damaged on the premises.
> 4. This card is non-transferable.
> 5. The management reserve the right to refuse admission to anyone improperly dressed.
> 6. This card must be produced on request.
>
> **THIS CARD IS VALID FROM** 72 **TO** 73

The door to our left opened, the wall of sound blocked by a gorilla in a gray suit standing at the doorway. We had met The Bank's, a family of bouncers in Wolvo who ran the door at The Cats. I whispered to Kim, "He makes Jimmy look little," making her laugh as we ventured through the open door into a wall of heat and sound. The Cats sucking us in The Funky Sisters "Do It To It" the slow haunting beats adding to the atmosphere, calling us forward into the darkness of the club. The blacked out windows and painted walls dripping with condensation fueled by the heat of the night. We paused in the dim lights of the bar our smiling faces said it all, I turned to Kim feelings of total happiness engulfed me.

"At last! At last!" We had arrived on the Northern Soul scene. "We're here man, look at this place!" Wrapping my arms around Kim, squeezing her with enthusiasm my feet itching to get to the floor.

"Hear it man?! Hear it?!" Jimmy's beaming face in pure delight, pushing and nudging each other with sheer excitement as we gave our coats to the same girl who worked the kiosk. With our blue and white vests we felt like Soul Boys and instantly began to feel the energy of the club, "it had a feeling all its own."

"You Hit Me" by Alice Clark, her voice so powerful echoing all around us so much emotion in the words tearing into my heart. It was that kind of club, the records just picked you up touching your very soul! The Torch had closed and would never reopen and this was the number one club on the scene, the center of Northern Soul. Working behind the decks: Blue

Max, Alan Smith, and the new DJ Pep, carrying the flag for pure Northern.

Set right in the heart of Wolvo with the crowd from The Torch and other clubs from around the country, this club wasn't packed, it was heaving. We tried to make our way through the darkness passing the crowded bar supplying endless drinks to steaming bodies that had just left the floor. Moving in step with Soulies around us, shuffling our way deeper into the heart of the club. Music pounding in my ears, calling us forward, clapping in front of us as we edged nearer to the noise of the dance floor. At the end of the bar on our right two arched, bricked, alcoves created separate rooms in the shape of long tunnels ending at a blank wall. The cream painted brickwork conflicting with black tables in the center with matching benches on either side. Smooth painted walls shining with condensation, reflecting the soft glow of a single bulb from the domed ceiling. Caught in motionless air a spiral of smoke gently rising from a smoldering ash tray. Abandoned Coke bottles littered tabletops, empty deserted tunnels, Soulies who had returned to the floor.

"Man this place is packed!"

"I know Darb, it's killing me. I can't breathe! I can't move! Kim this way!"

We edged nearer into darkness, shapeless figures and bodies, the crowd stacked deeper as we neared the floor. This club was old, giving you the feeling of being sucked into a "pitch black mine". Out of the darkness a tall figure came towards us, his head nearly touching the low ceiling. The slim frame of his body matching the drawn features of a face covered in sweat. On his darkened vest two badges, The Twisted Wheel and the badge of The Torch. With his hand outstretched and a beaming smile he leaned forward.

"My name's Big Willie. Welcome to The Cats!"

We stood in shock, shaking his hand engulfed by his friendly nature earning our instant respect. A face we would remember and one we would get to know well. We had never felt atmosphere, this was our first real club. My body soaking wet just with the heat of the club and bodies around us. Our heads were spinning, still trying to take it all in, every one of us lost for words.

"Now just to take it up a notch!" The DJs muffled voice barely heard above the noise around us "The Laws Of Love" The Volcanoes! Instantly clapping surrounded us as we swept forward with a surge of people racing towards the floor. Kim in front of me leaning forward into the darkness, constant clapping to the beats, shouts from the dance floor the wall of sound increasing with every step. Finally, we stood looking at the sea of people in front of us. We could hardly move held in a spell at what lay before our eyes.

You didn't just walk onto this floor, you earned it! Caught in the light of the dance floor the girl we had seen earlier dancing by the stage. Her body of youth soaked in sweat, a clinging figure of beauty "etched with curves of desire." By her side a guy in white skinners, his yellow top a patchwork of dripping emotion, he too wearing a Torch badge. His face intense, locked in a glazed wide-eyed expression.

"Darb, look at that guy!" He did a drop-back and spin, to drop again he had it all. I watched him dance and envied his every move.

"That guy can dance Gethro! Look at his badge he must be a Torch dancer."

With everyone dancing on the spot you had to have perfect timing or you were just swallowed up in the sea of people. This was The Cats floor and drop-backs to us were impossible. If you wanted some room you had to be special, standout be a good dancer. My gaze glued to the floor watching every move. Squeak, Punna, and Mulley catching my attention, holding the middle of the floor. Suddenly they parted. Squeak did a spin, his long hair electrified, standing on end like a chimney brush. Sweat spraying in all directions arms at his side, tightness to his body spinning like a top. All you could see was a blur as he drilled holes in the dance floor. The florescent lights reflecting the white edging of his blue vest making him stand out even more.

I had never seen anyone spin as fast as that staying in one spot to repeat the move again only faster this time. In this crowd that was impossible to me, what I was seeing was totally unreal. I nudged Darb who was completely spellbound, speechless by what we had just seen neither of us daring to move. To my right in the dim light of the DJ booth a single table full of cassette decks with mics taping every sound. Kim was dancing in front of us, somehow she had found a small piece of floor. I felt so proud of her, she was the first one of us to actually dance in The Cats. Her new dress ruined, matted soaking wet hair a face drenched in happiness lost to the music, the atmosphere swallowing her alive.

"As requested. One of my favorites!" The DJs voice fading to a strange sound of a train growing nearer the slow introduction louder all the time. Suddenly, the mood of the club changed, to move only as The Cats could. Pep's voice screaming down the mic "Mr. Saxie Russellllll! Psychedelic

Soulllll! The anthem of The Cats!" Moving to the side of Darb I grabbed an inch of dance floor joining the mass of dancers in front of us. We had to dance to this, finding a small space by the speakers, we moved to the edge of the floor. This was a full house. You couldn't stand still in The Catacombs, the infectious atmosphere sucking you in, sweeping us onto the floor. We were blown away with the energy of the place as the dance floor erupted in all directions.

We had never seen anything like this, the best dancers the scene had to offer right before our very eyes. The atmosphere in the club intensified. That lazy sax the deep rhythmic beats was exactly what fit the crowded club. Surrounding us with Soul rebounding off the walls, pounding feet from the dance floor echoed to beats around the room. The black fist of The Catacombs badges of the dancer's soul pouring onto the floor. Bodies locked into the music moving in time all around us. The intensity of the dancers, a mass of bodies turning, spinners in unison hands held high at the end of a move igniting the crowded floor. Along the sides of the dance floor, on the stage, everywhere you looked bodies swayed the floor bouncing in rhythm with dancers.

The club packed to capacity, one mass of energy and spontaneous movement with endless faces in the crowd. The heat of the dance floor unbearable, more Soulies joining the floor. Condensation from the low ceiling trapped heat on the dance floor, soaking bodies of dancers below. I tried to get Robbo's attention on the far side of the room but when Saxie Russell was on not even Venton could get his attention. Both of them dancing in a line of fast shuffling feet, faces from The Octopus swallowed in the crowded room. The heart and soul of the Northern Scene beating as one on the dance floor. A sea of arms and clapping hands before me holding us in total ecstasy. Lost in the voice of Saxie Russell "Psychedelic Soul". Only to be followed by more, there was no rest for anyone.

On this floor you had to dance! The driving intro of "Too Late" from Williams and Watson hit me, picking up my very soul and just blew me out the door. We had never heard any of these records before! Debbie Dean "Why Am I Loving You", The Vel-Vets "I Got To Find Me Somebody", Lenis Guess "Just Ask Me", and Connie Clark "My Sugar Baby". Infectious records we didn't know driving us forward with energy to dance like never before. Grabbing what breaks we could, chatting to Soulies at the side of us, shared drinks upon the floor. Hoagy Lands "The Next In Line", Nolan Chance "Just Like The Weather", and The Velours "I'm Gonna Change" sounds from The Torch driving the floor wild.

As the night grew longer Pep's voice grew louder until in the end his voice was hoarse with screaming down the mic. Driving the atmosphere to the limits and showing no mercy to the dancers. Every record played ended in a mass of outstretched arms, clapping hands from the dancers shining faces reaching into the light. The intensity of the dancing sucking you in making you want more and more! The atmosphere unique to The Catacombs, the dancers going wild with the long intro of David and the Giants "Ten Miles High". Squeak, in a blur, tearing onto the floor, more dancers spinning like tops the heat of the club at boiling point.

Fighting to catch my breath, my body aching, burning inside with heat gasping at a slight breeze from an open emergency exit. "You ok Gethro?!" The smiling face of Darb, my mind lost in the music screaming at me to come off the floor. The flood of records kept coming that never seemed to stop! The Gems "I'll Be There" driving me on, the beats pushing me to limits of energy I never knew I had. Richard Temple "That Beatin' rhythm" and Cindy Scott's "I Love you baby", her soulful voice filling me with emotion, tearing me to shreds.

Pep and Max now taking the roof off, cheering, thundering clapping from the floor! Mamie Galore "It Ain't Necessary", Johnny Moore "Walk Like A Man", Lou Pride "I'm Com'un Home In The Morn'un", The Invitations "Skiing In The Snow", Sam Ward "Sister Lee", Jackie lee "Darkest Days", The Soul Twins "Quick Change Artist", N. F. Porter "Keep On Keeping On", Jackie Wilson "Nothing But Blue Skies", Bobby Hebb "Love Love Love", The Shakers "One Wonderful Moment", Earl Wright And His Orchestra "Thumb A Ride", Shirley Ellis "Soul Time", Mel Wynn & The Rhythm Aces "Stop Sign", Christine Cooper "Heartaches Away My Boy", The Vogues "That's The Tune", and Moses Smith "The Girl Across The Street". My emotions welling up inside, a record so close to my heart the words so true to how I met Kim.

In the end, exhausted I had to leave the floor turning into the crowd, taking Kim's hand working our way back through the darkness. Grabbing a Coke from the bar, my heart pounding, diving into an alcove saturated and breathless we sat on the edge of a table at last to finally rest. Steam rising from our soaking, aching, bodies the arched walls of painted brickwork glistening in yellow light. Shining jewels of condensation, rivers of soul trickling down the walls. The whole building shaking, feeling the heat and energy of The Cats vibrations from the dance floor "the building itself had come alive." Kim, as me, shattered from our dancing, speechless lovers watching Soulies passing us by.

The music like a magnet drawing us right back onto the floor. Smokey, Robbo, Venton, Selwyn, Paul, Pete, Scory, Brentford, Ray, Ritchie, Eggy,

THEY DANCED ALL NIGHT

Bagger, Aggy, Ric Tic, Big Willie, Forbesy, Esher, Dave, Gonk, Chris, Punna, Squeak, Mully, Knave and Swoz stopping at all of them and more. To be showered with the friendship that was Wolvo, the brotherhood of The Northern Scene, The Catacombs. Only for it to end so soon. The night over as the club emptied, spilling out onto the street below.

The light rain felt good as we stood on the pavement outside, steam rising from our bodies. All of us not caring, cool water washing sweat from our faces. Still trying to take in what we had just been through what we had seen and heard.

Alice Clark, Lenis Guess, and "Psychedelic Soul" ringing in our ears, records we had never heard of. Our first Northern Soul club, the people, the clapping, the atmosphere.

"Did you see that guy spin?"

"Which one Darb?"

"Punna and his mate Squeak, see how fast he was?"

"I know and he never moved off the spot! And that guy doing drop-backs with The Torch badge and the other guy in the red and white vest."

"He was a brilliant dancer Gethro."

"We got to practice man. We need practice bad." Both of us knew we now had a long way to go after seeing the floor that night. This was a turning point for us. The Cats was on twice a week and we would be back on Wednesday to dance once more.

A new world had opened up right on our doorstep and now we would go every week. We just grabbed hold of the music with open arms no matter what colour it was. Black artists and white artists sounded the same, they all sang their hearts out with soul. It never really was accepted for what it was. A totally underground scene with an atmosphere all its own, we had never felt it before, never seen it yet in The Cats it wrapped itself around you. You could taste it, reach out and touch it with your bare hands! It was clear from the start The Cats had something The Ship did not.

We thought we could dance but not anymore. Moves we had seen still fresh in my mind. It seemed strange to me, we had just come out of a club and we were on about dancing in the next one.

"Come on Kim, let's walk home." Holding Kim in my arms our happiness for all to see. Lovers whisper's between us catching Jimmy's wicked smile.

"Gethro, you're bad man!"

"I know Jimmy. I know." His smiling face said it all. We parted to hugs and handshakes, our friendship built on love.

It was Sunday morning, not even the rain could cool us down. The streets were empty now the odd taxi drifted through endless puddles, headlights breaking the stillness of the night. Two kids walking home in the dampness of morning air. I swung around a lamp post to dance to "Singing In The Rain" splashing about in puddles, remembering what I could.

My reflection lost in the pure happiness of the love I had found to the delight and laughter of Kim. Pausing to hold each other in the midst of a streetlight, two bodies entwined. The gentleness in her face, those pale steel blue eyes pulling me forward to fall into passionate, gentle lips. To kiss as one lost in our youth holding each other closer tighter than ever before, a kiss forever in our memories locked away in the vault of time. The love of the music bringing us closer together. We moved forward once more into the silence of morning air all around us echoing, swimming in our heads the music we had discovered. Cindy Scott "Love You Baby" a record still ringing in my ears. Singing what we knew and remembered wrapped in our new world, a love for each other and the music of Northern Soul. Skipping in darkness together dancing hand in hand, laughter to our music two lovers "Singing In The Rain." X

Chapter 18

TURF WARS

The Ship and Rainbow on Dudley road was my stepping stone to the Northern Scene. An unlikely place and never getting the recognition or respect for what it did for the Northern Scene in Wolvo. I found it by sheer chance after talking to Rusty and the lads that afternoon in The Octopus. They told me to go and I immediately fell in love with the dance floor there.

The Cats had the sounds, you can't dispute that, becoming one of the top clubs in the country when The Torch closed. The music was totally underground, rare Soul from the United States collected by the DJs and played at certain clubs. Blue Max, Pep, Alan Smith, Farmer Carl dene some of the best DJs on the Northern Scene at that time played at The Cats but The Ship had the dance floor and for me as a dancer The Cats could never match it. It became our second home.

We went to The Cats for the music but early on struggled to dance on the crowded floor. Whereas The Ship gave us room to explode to the pressings that would later come out of records from The Cats. It was here that we learned to express ourselves, to practice and practice the moves that we saw at The Cats and over time would make us stand out on the dance floors to come. Our week was now broken up and set in stone, a routine we never deviated from. Saturday and Wednesday at The Cats, Sunday and Tuesday The Ship and Saturday dinner time, The Octopus.

One advantage we had because of the reputation of the Parkfield skins not many people travelled out of the comfort of the town center. So Soulies from The Cats never came to The Ship at this time. This was good news for us as we could practice all we wanted and develop new moves we had seen to match our own style without Soulies copying from us. Dancing had taken over our lives, it really was that competitive in Wolvo. Dance floors were a battleground, everyone wanting to be the best. I would never go anywhere without hitting the dance floors, no matter what music was being played. This was the strength of our dancing.

At this time I alone was working on three different styles of footwork. Later on I would turn this to my advantage as I came up against many Northern dancers, who because of their own reasons wanted to blow me off a floor. The mistake they made was they could only dance in one style.

Even the bouncer collecting our money at The Ship was surprised at the excitement of me and Kim as we ran up the stairs and straight into the main room. Darb was across the far side of the room, noticing us straight away, he came over meeting us in the middle of the floor. We looked smart in our matching black blazers, button-down shirts and tapered trousers there was neatness about us and it showed. On mine I had red braiding around the edge with the badge of a red rose on the top pocket. I had got the idea off Rusty and just made it one of my own. Kim once again had shown me another of her talents, she could sew. Darb and I dressed alike on purpose we wanted to look like brothers but also to be different which to us we were.

Tonight I couldn't wait to dance, we had heard this guy was a Northern DJ. We left our girls to talk by the side of the floor and approached him on the stage. Philip Mitchell "Free For All (Winner Takes All)"? Lenis Guess "Just Ask Me"? Cindy Scott "I Love You Baby"? His blank face said it all as we bombarded him with some of our favorite records from The Cats. It was obvious it was going to be a long night. I looked across the empty floor, my heart sadden by the simple fact we had no real music. Once again we chased Northern sounds, a beautiful dance floor and none of the music we loved. This was reality for us, at The Ship Northern was nowhere to be found. Tonight we got lucky, the DJ Ian St John promised to play some sounds we had mentioned and others he thought we might know.

We were starting to hold our own, our time spent in The Cats was paying dividends on the floor. We had finally progressed from the hopping footwork of a circle and changes we made had smoothed it out. Now we added steps, sometimes keeping to a half moon but with twisting footwork. Folding our legs into the music and moving at speed. Dancing on your toes, sliding your feet in response to the beats put another edge to some of the moves. Dancing on the ball of your foot freed up the movement of your feet. Now twists and turns could be added, extra crossing steps made you float along the floor. Here we had room to do this, in The Cats we had to condense everything and it affected the way we danced.

The footwork we were starting to master, other moves were not so good. Not everyone at The Cats was into our style of dancing often being told we wanted too much room as many dancers there were just obsessed with doing spins. I couldn't spin that good at this time, neither could Darb we just couldn't get it to fit with what we were trying to do. Our strength was our footwork and even at this early stage on an open floor not many dancers around Wolvo could match us step for step. With all the dancing we were doing we never realized but we were getting fit. Our dancing required long periods out on the floor, record after record improved our stamina and suppleness with the moves we were trying to do.

We just carried on at The Ship staying in the background improving every week. Even here we began to get noticed as we danced to certain records and as the DJ had promised sounds we loved now filled the room. "Just A Little Misunderstanding" by The Contours, when he played it we all hit the floor just as Jimmy and Winston burst into the main room.

"Hear it man! Hear it!" Jimmy skipping towards us, a beaming smile wagging his finger at us in excitement immediately joining us on the edge of the floor. I loved this record by The Contours, a Motown classic that just made me tear into my dancing, breaking out on the floor in a wide circle of footwork. Kim and Darb at my side beats jumping at you from the decks, their voices so crystal clear. The backing singers so strong, the chorus always there in the background, it's a tune that just made you dance. The fast beats fit our footwork to perfection, Kim never missing a beat. She too was becoming a very accomplished dancer. Once again it was her footwork, a fast skipping style.

A smile of affection between us our arms held wide, singing, pleading with each other in laughter as we passed on the open floor. The DJ could see we were different as our little band now took over the floor and began to play a few of the other sounds we had asked for. Ike and Tina Turner "Dust My Broom", another record Darb and I loved. The intro alone let you wind into the beat, let you drop into different footwork as it sped up and slowed down. Her strutting voice pleading her case just folded me in half, the room bouncing full of Soul. To this record I would change my footwork and dance in a line of stepping feet, one crossing over the other moving in a straight line along the edge of the floor. Whatever the right foot did the left would do on the way back speeding up or slowing down. At times stepping in a diamond formation with one foot, the other sliding naturally to the side. Moving along the edge of the floor bouncing on your toes, again bending your knees dropping into the beats. Even bringing my feet together to stop dead and sway at a certain time.

The floor at The Ship was brilliant and let you slide with no effort as all. These were two basic styles Darb and I were working with as we helped each other along the way. At The Ship we looked good but there was no structure to our dancing, it was too sporadic. Slowly, spins and splits were being integrated into our style with moves we had seen at The Cats but they were a disaster. If I did a drop-back or Darb we virtually stopped on the spot, did the move then carried on with footwork. The same with spinning, it looked too stiff as you tried to get your balance and your feet right before launching into a spin.

Easily losing control there was no flow to any of our moves, no cohesion. The most we could do was two or three and nothing like at the speed we had seen Squeak do. Spins, off balance splits with bent knees, we were shit at these moves and we knew it. We couldn't get it to match our footwork yet the answer would come in a simple way. Just by adding two simple moves we would link it all together but for now we hadn't found the key.

I wanted to be the best I could feel it in my heart. I connected with the music deep inside a feeling, an emotion. The music became one to one to me but my body was still learning how to respond and my feet to connect to my heart. No matter how long it was going to take I wanted perfection so started to push myself in that direction. Doing the same moves over and over again Kim and Darb as addicted as me. Jimmy too was starting to work on his own style. He knew he was too big to throw himself around so did a sliding footwork with Winston always by his side. A style of dancing he would improve on as he danced to it over time. Rubin Parker "You've Been Away", Gene Latter "Sign On The Dotted Line", The Velvelettes "Needle In A Haystack", and The O'Jays "Looky Looky (Look At Me Girl)" a record that would get me recognition later and one that just blew me away, "what a record!"

A challenge to any dancer matching our footwork to the fast tempo. It wasn't easy but we mastered it over time. These were the early records we danced to as many of the travelling "Soul" DJs brought them to The Ship. The empty floor didn't bother us but tonight it was really empty, yet the bar was packed. Something didn't feel right, still it just meant we had even more room. Jimmy and Winston had stopped dancing, hardly able to stand through laughter holding each other up at the side of the floor. Annoyed, Inquisitive I stopped dancing.

"Hey what's up?!"

"It's Darb, Gethro! Look!" Winston crying with laughter as I approached, pointing to Darb oblivious in the middle of the floor. I started laughing, noticing straight away. Holding my emotions I couldn't resist it as a mate, I knew he would have done the same to me.

"Darb! How long you been into women's knickers?!" I just burst into laughter. The back of his trousers wide open from going too low in the splits. Waving to get his attention he immediately came over, a confused look between us.

"Your trousers mate, look!!" Darb, in a half turn grabbing the back of his trousers, chasing his tear in circles.

"Shit! How bad is it Gethro?!"

"Oh, it's bad man. It's all the way up!" We doubled up in laughter around him, a torrent of abuse from Jimmy, no mercy from any of us. I felt for my mate but I couldn't help it, it's just the way we were.

"We got to get some looser trousers man. Tapered ain't going to cut it Gethro!"

"I know we got to go to Jacksons." Suddenly shouts at the far end of the room caught my attention, a jostling crowd spilling into the room.

"Darb, what the fucks going on here?!" Girls screaming, pushing, and pulling. Wild kicks and punches exchanged, fierce fighting erupted, skins piling into the room. Bottles and glasses flying in every direction, shattering on the dance floor. Bodies crashing into tables, running battles in the middle of the floor. Separate fights breaking out amongst them, a flow of bodies falling towards the stage. The music instantly stopped, pushing our girls behind us we stood to the side and looked across the room. Everywhere pools of beer, the dance floor now covered in broken glass.

"Look at this shit Jimmy! Man they piss me off!" I pointed across to the far side of the room. We just watched as the fight unfolded in front of us. I looked at Darb, I could see he wanted to join into help some of his mates.

"Darb, it's nothing to do with us! Forget it man, you don't belong there anymore!" A look between us of anger, frustration written all over his face. I knew he would have joined the fight, now I was really glad he had split his trousers or all of us would have been out on the floor. The bouncers at The Ship were good guys, they never bothered you and were always polite.

There was no "I am a bouncer here, get out of my way" attitude with them. They were all ex teds though and could handle themselves as a few people would soon find out.

We stood and watched the fight now breaking into separate battles mostly at the front of the stage. Four bouncers now rushing into the room diving into the middle of the fight. Trying as best they could to bring calm to the riot around them Parkfield fighting another crew. One guy tried to bottle a bouncer and was caught red handed as he spun around and got a right cross square on the chin. His body buckled as he flew backwards sliding in his crombie along the full length of the floor. Crashing into the tables still clutching his bottle, totally out cold.

"Did you see that Darb?!" I just started to laugh.

"Told you it was a good floor Gethro." Darb cracked me up he never said much, that was his way but man I loved being around him.

What unfolded before us worked to our advantage as now we had the place to ourselves. We were getting sick of the fighting it was so stupid and it ruined our night time and time again. This was the norm, their lifestyle. Skins crews, the mentality they brought the violent side to their world of who has the best crew. Who is the hardest one amongst us? Really? Who gives a shit! We had all left that world behind us. We had a venue, all be it in their strange world, the only thing was the records. We had no music but this would now change.

After that night the management changed their policy, banning a lot of people even asking us about Northern and if we knew any DJs. For us it was a milestone, we took hold of the dance floor from that night and we never gave it back. The Ship evolved, moving away from its disco image and started to turn to more Northern, later promoting live Soul acts. Johnny Johnson and the Bandwagon to name one of the few. Just as important The Cats had something The Ship never would, atmosphere that was plain to see. Getting the best of both places was to our advantage and it would be awhile before we would find the perfect answer. Two very different venues, one had something the other definitely did not.

Chapter 19

CATS ON A WEDNESDAY NIGHT

"You got to pay the price"

The Catacombs were on twice a week but for all we cared it could have been on every night of the week. With DJs Blue Max, Alan Smith and Pep and the sounds they were spinning it really was that good. Records made their way to The Cats from The Wheel and Torch both of which had now closed down. Some from other clubs around the country, others were simply broken by the DJs at The Cats as Northern Soul exploded totally underground.

For years Graham Warr had been going to the States before others were doing it, supplying The Cats with endless records. We had been going for a few months now and it was the only place you could hear the latest Northern sounds but you had to be one of two things. Know someone inside or be streetwise. It wasn't a bad club in any way but being streetwise definitely helped and to us we thought we were.

The older crowd from The Torch ran The Cats, all Wolvo Soul boys and when they were all together they made me feel uneasy. Although we had respect for them it was clear from the start we still hadn't earned theirs. We already knew a few people inside, open from eight till two on Saturday and midnight on a Wednesday. It always closed too early for us and tonight we were running late. There was no record bar at The Catacombs, everyone here came to dance. Who played this first or that, we didn't give a shit. Bob Relf's "Blowing My Mind To Pieces" greeting us and that's exactly how we felt. We hadn't heard these records, many were still new to us and tonight was no different.

The rippled walls dripping with soul, shining with condensation, hand clapping in the background voices echoing from the floor. The Cats full with Soulies from around the Midlands: Shrewsbury, Bridgnorth, Newport, Dudley, Stoke, Cheltenham, Gloucester, and Kidderminster. This was the strength of The Cats and the music it was playing, new faces coming in every week, tonight a younger crowd. Along with Punna, Squeak, and Mulley you now had more local lads. Pixie, Evo, my old mate Paul Walker, Kev Harrison, Mick McAuliffe, Colin Walters, Jamo Ray, Wevrly Pedro, Aston Caddy to name just a few. As they were our age we instantly became friends with all of them. With all the Soulies from around Wolvo attending on a Wednesday it really was a Midlands night. It wasn't heaving like on a Saturday and the atmosphere was just the same. Wednesdays became a favorite night for us, as dancers we now had room to move around the club.

I peered into the darkness at the skinny figure coming towards us "Eggy! Too much fucking light man!" Promptly unscrewing the light bulb to our left making The Cats even darker, "That's better!" A smile of satisfaction lighting his face.

"Eggy you stop that!" Helen, Pep's girl rushing from behind the counter, fighting with her footwear stumbling into darkness as Eggy made good his escape. Hands in a fluster, straightening her long skirt "Platforms!" A statement in her fashion, dressed as many girls did. Returning back to us standing by the bar, ignoring our imminent laughter.

"These shoes, I'll bloody kill him!" Turning with a smile, shaking her head in frustration but her tone didn't match the command.

"Gethro, and where's Kim?!" her voice demanding answers, looking straight at me.

"She had to stay in tonight but she will be here Saturday."

"She had better be and you look after her!" Her wagging finger of authority as ever in a playful way.

"I will Helen." Darb smiling at my predicament, she always told me off whenever we were apart. Kim was just sixteen and Helen and Kim had become good friends. Tall and slim with short hair parted to the side in one length, her drawn features and wide eyes always expressing an inquisitive nature. "I'll be dancing later so you two watch out!"

"We will Helen. See you on the floor later." We made our way forward, the soft light of the bar evaporating into darkness as we ventured into the tunnel of The Cats. Wayne Gibson "Under My Thumb" drifting towards us bouncing off the low ceiling, creeping along blackened walls. That haunting Northern beat making us move a little faster, pulling us towards the floor. Max's voice drowned out by hand claps, the noise of the floor growing louder feeling the atmosphere of a Wednesday night. The alcoves empty and bulb less now in total darkness, I smiled as we passed telling Darb, "Eggy had struck."

"Yea but what's he doing with all the bulbs Gethro?" I had no answer to that. We stood at the edge of the dance floor by the speakers, this was now our usual spot. A warm summer's breeze filtered across the packed dance floor, the open fire exit to our right adding more heat to the already crowded club. Standing in the open doorway the lone figure of Dave Priest, a character I had got to know, a path I would always avoid. The floor wasn't big by any means stretching the full width of the building and not that deep, being wider than it was long. Slightly raised running the full width of the dance floor a stage extended to the back of the room. Even this was narrow with a few tables and benches scattered along the back wall.

The blacked out walls and low ceiling gave you the feeling of standing in an underground cave. Silhouettes of the Soulies melting into the darkness, distant figures at the back of the stage. Soul badges and colored tops, bright white of the dancers caught in the haze of fluorescents spinners holding the floor. I knew as we developed this dance floor would be a challenge especially for me and Darb.

On Wednesday we had room to practice but most of all this is where we learned to dance to get ready for the tight floor of a Saturday. The masters of this were Squeak, Mulley, and Punna. They would dance, holding the middle of the floor stepping to the side giving each other room. Sometimes dropping back to let the other dancer do a spin or certain move. We picked up on this right away. By watching people you learned certain tricks and moves.

Along with footwork, drop-backs, spins, and style little things, small details would catch your eye. How to move your hands either putting them on your hips as you spun or wrapping them around you sometimes throwing them above your head as you spun out. Most the spinners we saw at this time were spinning on the ball of their feet using their second foot to maintain their balance. All dancing in similar styles with little footwork some just cross stepping one leg behind the other. A slight twist of the foot stretching their arms before powering into spins. This to me was easy, helping you keep your balance in the slowness of your feet. A simple trick, one I noticed Punna use was to ease your foot out as you slowed down, this gave a little style to the move. Even then to spin at real speed required skill coupled with perfect balance and Squeak really was the master of this. No matter how many times I danced by him I could never match his speed.

We always danced in leather soled shoes although later we carried different soled shoes to match certain floors. Spinning really was that important to us, a really fast spinner always stood out on a floor. We used talc to help us spin faster, too much and you went on your arse. Whenever this happened to me I would try to turn it into a move, sometimes getting away with it.

I was eighteen years old and had the reflexes of a cat but not always to Jimmy's taunts and laughter, no mercy from any of our group. Not enough talc and you had no power for your spins, you had to have just the right amount to push off as you turned into your move. A critical mix that would come with experience crucial to your dancing and moves. The Cats was especially hard to gauge as with all the condensation in certain areas it was just like dancing on ice. With every record we improved our dancing. We learned to fit records at a certain part, timing your spin to fit a sax or specific beat, a long intro or vocal. Unlike at The Ship we had the latest sounds to practice so we could fit in the moves to the Northern records at exactly the right place. Mix it up and put your stamp on what you had seen other dancers do.

There are no set steps to Northern, no one style of dancing. It's whatever you as an individual want to do, your interpretation how you feel inside. Anyone could get out there and dance but to me it went a lot deeper than that. You didn't just go up and start copying someone that was trying to take the piss, and could get you blown right off the floor. Slowly, you integrated their moves into your footwork, this is what we did at The Ship.

In the end on The Cats' floor we were slowly being given room but nothing was just given. On a Saturday in the crowd of dancers like everyone else we had to earn every inch of floor. Our footwork demanded room to move out in a semi-circle of fast, twisting feet. This was our own individual style then fit in splits, drop-backs and spins the challenge to flow in one movement. We always studied the dance floor, looking for answers getting better coming with time and I mean time. We had spent months and months practicing to us nothing else mattered. Three basic moves we had to get right to perfection, but putting it together was still elusive. It all had to be done at speed! On a Saturday it was virtually impossible as with the crowd on the dance floor only perfection would do.

Moves we had seen on Saturday we now could mix in on Wednesdays. To us it was all about timing, this was to be the hardest part. You had to become part of the record, feel the singer's emotion, and belong to every note. Timing to the record demanded perfection, the exact set of moves at exactly the right time done in sequence and at speed and differently to each individual record. This would make you stand out on the floor as a dancer and what I as an individual was trying to achieve. The basics of our dancing footwork, spins, splits, and drop-backs but in time we would take these moves to a much higher level.

I alone had been on the dance floor well over a year now as we hammered our bodies in the pursuit of perfection our youth the only protection we had. The Catacombs became the breeding ground for a lot of good dancers from Wolvo that would show up on the Northern scene for many years to come.

"Gethro put the tape decks here." Darb found a small space on the table at the side of the speakers and we set up the mics, placing them along with others getting ready to record the night. No other clubs in Wolvo had these records so we taped them. This helped us to get to know the tunes. This was underground Soul, copies of certain records were exchanged between the DJs. Many you couldn't buy in the shops. As for us we had no interest in collecting records, neither the money, all we wanted to do was dance. We were learning fast, you don't leave the cassette decks by themselves.

"Remember last Saturday, Darb?"

"Yea, I know." We started to laugh it was funny though.

I came off the dance floor and looked at the table. Some guy was watching the dancers holding a mic to the speakers, only problem no tape deck on the end.

"Gethro." Darb nudged me. "Can't wait to hear that tape!"

"It's ok. It's called there's nothing else to say by the invisibles."

As I said, "streetwise," it was all part of the game. Just keep your eyes open it was a dark in The Cats and things disappeared, it's just the way it was. We often danced in this area for that very reason, all they had cost me was a house brick not a mark on them and we were proud of our new cassettes.

What you heard on a Wednesday wasn't exactly what you heard on a Saturday. The Cats closed at midnight so Pep and Max only had four hours to play as many records as they could. Cramming in stuff from their endless supply, mixing it up with sounds from The Torch and Wheel. Some we now knew but not all. Sometimes new stuff, just brilliant music to dance to came from nowhere and tonight was no different.

Max's voice in a gentler tone compared to Pep, filling the floor moving it in one direction - full. The dance floor swaying to the strong vocals and Northern beats, a mass of clapping hands in time to the record. The soul of the dancers, a bond with the DJ that connects as one on the floor. The powerful voice of Duke Browner "Crying Over You" adding to the atmosphere, our love of Soul music shared feelings of the night.

"Darb, there's Venton." He was in full swing, dancing by Robbo and I made my way across to the far side of the room. With the looks of Sammy Davis Jr. and a smile that could light up a sky, Venton was a character not only that he could dance. We often danced side by side joining each other on the floor with fast, sliding feet and that infamous Robbo style. He was the same age as me we had nothing but respect for each other. We went way back to my days with Conroy and always shook hands with our hearts. Although he knocked around with the older guys, we were close and trusted him and he always had our backs. Dressed in a suit jacket and Fred Perry parallels with Solatios he always looked smart. We threw our arms around each other as only close friends do, "What's up man?"

"Seen Jimmy, Vent?" My eyes scanning the crowd.

"He was here a minute ago, saw you and Kim dancing last Saturday. Getting good man." A smile between us, recognition from a dancer.

"You know me Vent, just trying to keep up with you and Robbo." Both of us starting to laugh, "Love to dance man."

"Always, Gethro."

"Later, Vent." We shook hands, crossing in the Northern style. Robbo nodded, the epitome of cool, afro styled hair that of a gangster's. His bearded face flashing smiles of gold, he too feeling the heat of the club. I looked around, noticing Jimmy and I made my way around the floor passing the fire exit to the back of the stage.

"Gethro, what's up?"

"Jimmy, where you been man? We waited for you." His muscular frame shining in the light of fluorescence, a yellow headband stretched and dark. The looks of an aborigine, his smiling face dripping with sweat.

"Come on, check this out." Leading him through dancers to Darb setting the tapes upon the table.

"Gethro, you bad man!" Jimmy's smile, the wicked eyes saying it all.

"What? ITT man?!"

"Nice Gethro. How much?"

"Cheap." A surge of accomplishment, my lips breaking to a smile.

"How cheap?" Jimmy inquisitively pressing the subject.

"Well, the batteries cost more than the tape decks!" I started to smile.

"Darb what we going to do with this guy?!"

"I don't know Jimmy." a slight pause, Darb shrugging his shoulders the look between us. "He's going for the record player next week."

"Yea I'm looking for a special house brick." All of us bursting into laughter, my face of innocence totally opposite to his. He knew we had been window shopping last week.

"You bad man!"

"I know Jimmy but we needed some tape decks!" My hands raised still pleading my case "I know I'm bad Jimmy, it's just the way I am." A little saying we had both of us laughing as we always did.

Jimmy was a typical example of how to dance in The Cats and knew he didn't fit into our style of dancing. The Cats' floor was always full but tonight you had room to work it, so Jimmy followed Venton and Robbos example. They were the masters of this, especially to "Psychedelic Soul", The Cats' anthem and "I'm Standing" by Rufus Lumley no one could touch them. Fast, sliding footwork shuffling your feet with little hand movement. Moving the whole of your body to the beats, keeping both feet together sliding along the edge of the floor. Dancing in a tight space, sometimes just shuffling on the spot with no sideways movement at all. Venton showed me the third style of dancing, one I had often practiced with Conroy no spins, no drop-backs just raw footwork. I got it, so did Jimmy. He watched and learned the footwork over time then put his own stamp on it. Adding steps and dummy moves as he showed us his unique style of dancing to Little

Carl Carlton "Competition Ain't Nothin'" a sound now igniting the floor. Jimmy, really fast on his feet, lighting up the floor with his energy that smooth style of footwork not many dancers could do.

Four of us spreading out to create the room we needed, the atmosphere pulling us onto the floor. The younger crowd giving us room, a respect shared between us now it was our turn to dance. We had started to link our moves together, the answer had come out of the blue. The leg break, that's what we called it. A simple move of kicking your leg out in front of you. We had seen someone kick out, drop to bent knees and then come up spinning. We just adapted it from this move. I would dance with my arms constantly moving, drifting around the floor. Then deliberately hold my left hand in front of me, kick up high at speed with my right foot and touch my hand. As my foot descended I would then drop, carry on through and throw myself into the splits. From there twist my body turning into a drop-back, push with my hands, rising from the floor crossing my legs as I did.

As I moved with momentum now I would power into a spin. We could do this at speed as the kick just flowed with our footwork instantly connecting all three moves. We still hadn't perfected it but at last we had made that vital link. This also helped with our spinning, as by doing the same fast feet move, kick high, drop down, hand on the floor with my leg bent to the side. Then in one movement push up with your hand at the same time crossing my feet and turn into a spin you gained momentum, it just flowed. The key it had to all be done at speed and the move would start a sequence of moves. I did a spin into a drop-back, even spin dropping straight into the splits.

It had taken me months to learn but now I could do the splits both ways, side to side or straight on. As we linked the moves together and moved out on the floor not everyone was impressed with our new style of dancing. Telling us it was just acrobatics and had no place on a Northern floor. Gladys Knight & The Pips "Just Walk In My Shoes" the lyrics making me smile, so many tried but so few around us could now match our style of dancing. One straight from our hearts that now just flowed to our feet. The floor holding us to fast footwork, joining spinners in the darkness as we all battled for the floor. The Cats alive to the sound of Northern, so many dancers with different styles, the younger crowd moving together all of us as one.

We were a new generation of Soulies and that's exactly how we felt. Some people accepted us, others didn't. In time as we made a name for ourselves, even they would have to remove the label, one of being a Div. Over the past months we had made our mark in The Cats as we started to pound the dance floor, some of the Wolvo boys watching from a distance. Not only did we show them moves they had seen and done at The Wheel and Torch but also new moves we could now do. As we taught ourselves to dance we didn't know it but we were making enemies along the way. In the end, one night it would all explode and they would make their move.

The music as good as ever, the driving intro of "I Can't Hold On" by Lorraine Chandler echoing around the club. More records hitting the floor, a vinyl avalanche that never stopped. Freddie Chavez "They'll Never Know Why", Bobby Garrett "My Little Girl", Johnny Wyatt "This Thing Called Love", The Superlatives "I Still Love You" the voice of Max setting the floor on fire, the pounding beats of Wombat "I'm Getting On Life", Earl Jackson "Soul Self Satisfaction", Herb Ward "Honest To Goodness", Jackie Lee "Oh My Darlin'", The Mob "Open The Door To Your Heart", Lou Johnson "Unsatisfied", Dottie Cambridge "Cry Your Eyes Out", Devonnes "I'm Gonna Pick Up My Toys (And Go Home)", The Tomangoes "I Really Love You", Fred Hughes "Baby Boy", and Eula Cooper "Let Our Love Grow Higher". The tempo increasing all around us the low ceiling capturing the heat of the dance floor.

A gentle cross breeze from both open fire exits the only air we had. Even this didn't help as the heat in the club intensified with every record. A constant shower of condensation, our bodies forever at boiling point, the floor slowly cooking us alive. "What Shall I Do" by Frankie & The Classicals, music unique to The Catacombs driving the atmosphere higher. Pixie, Canny, Milligan, Evo, Paul, Knave, and Wolfy smiles of recognition between us, Soul brothers from The Octopus, young faces in the crowd. Our youth shared together, all of us trapped in the moment that we thought would last forever. The yellow light of the dance floor shimmering in the darkness holding us all in a musical trance. Glancing at the tape decks Winston as always on guard, feelings of happiness engulfed me now at last I had these sounds. Leaving the decks we made our way across the floor. Working our way through dances, a nod of recognition, passing handshakes, a mutual respect from us. Soaking in The Cats' atmosphere, joining Soulies now on the stage. Finding more room in this area we now looked down on the crowded floor. Soft lights of the DJ's booth, turntables as ever in motion Max and Pep surrounded with boxes, tables full of tunes. The purple glow of the fluorescent dance floor, white flashes of the spinners, images of the dancers so different from the stage, Helen approaching the floor.

She had her own moves and a really unusual style of dancing for a girl. With a crossing footwork and I had never seen girls do this, drop-backs in perfect time to the music. Her slim frame drifting along perfectly to The

Salvadors "Stick By Me, Baby" one of her favorite records. The dance floor looking smaller from the raised stage, there was no light in this area a few benches scattered along the wall. I stopped to talk to Julie Allen giving her a hug, a soul sister we knew well.

"Look at these shoes Gethro, Ravels." Showing me her new platform wedges, twisting her foot held out with pride. Kim had the same addiction, adding to my confusion.

"I never understood girls and shoes."

"Where's Kim?" She asked.

"Couldn't make it, she'll be here Saturday."

"Ok, send her my love."

As we danced my old mates Rusty and Twenty Nine Crew caught my eye at the back of the room. I had told them about The Cats when we had seen them at The Ship. It was here that I made the first of two mistakes in The Cats and both involved a fight. One would work out to my advantage, the other would cost me dearly.

A new crew member had been taking the piss out of my dancing at every chance he could get. Once again I caught him and it was getting on my nerves, he just kept on and on. I had asked him to stop time and time again even warning him, but no he wouldn't listen! So I decided to end it as I went over into the darkness and with no warning just hit him square in the face. I had learned well from my black eye from Paul, "Hit first, talk later." Darb and Jimmy saw what happened and came rushing over, now standing by my side.

"What's up Gethro, you ok?!" Darb asked.

"Fuck him! I warned him enough times. I told him to stop taking the piss!" Pointing at the guy crouched over, now holding his face blood streaming through his fingers.

"Leave it Gethro!" Rusty standing between us as I tried to explain. I was eighteen, I demanded respect. If you didn't give it back I would hammer it into you! I know it was wrong, I had snapped but it would come back and haunt me later. It happened that fast and being dark at the back of the stage no one saw a thing. I felt sorry for Rusty, they were with him but I had changed. I didn't take crap from Divs and although I felt bad I wasn't sorry for what I had just done. I didn't want it to come to this, there is only so much you will take but I had forgotten the golden rule. I was a Soul boy, I was with no crew. They were but this was a Northern club and that skinhead shit didn't work in here, it was the other way around. As I walked away I would pay my price later.

"Gethro, you got to tell me when you do shit like that!" Darb's voice in annoyance.

"Gethro!" Jimmy started to laugh, rolling his eyes, his hands now on my shoulder.

"I know Jimmy, I know." I started to laugh too but I felt good they had been by my side in a flash and instantly had my back. We left the stage as if nothing had happened, joining Winston standing by the cassette decks. "What's up man?"

"Gethro just lost his head with some guy at the back of the stage" Darb replied.

"You ok Gethro" Winston frowning in confusion.

"Yea Winst, it was nothing. Come on, let's dance that what we came for!" We all hit the floor together rejoining the crowd of dancers, a wave to Helen. She hadn't seen a thing. I had witnessed a couple of fights in The Cats but they had been well hidden and over pretty quickly. The bouncers usually stayed by the main door with Helen and although would occasionally walk around on a Wednesday, on Saturday this was virtually impossible to do. With the crowd and in the darkness of the club they didn't see everything.

This was a Wolvo club with a Midland base and a brilliant atmosphere. Everyone knew each other but if you crossed someone you had better watch out! As I said it was useful to know people inside, especially if you turned up with gear (drugs) and thought you could knock it out in this club, you were mistaken. There were unwritten rules, hence the fights. I saw a few people get turned over and relieved of their gear, especially on a Saturday night inside and outside of the club. We watched and learned fast who not to cross but most of all who really ran the club.

We were inquisitive at the start but wanted nothing to do with gear, our attitude then was simple. If you needed gear to dance then you couldn't dance. To me you were cheating. We danced with energy and passion our bodies paid a price at the end of the night but we danced from our hearts. All we needed was the music, but I noticed especially on a Saturday Soulies on gear stayed on the floor longer. Dancing with more energy and enthusiasm from the start of the night to the finish and we just couldn't keep up with them. We were accepted, everyone was friendly but we weren't in their exclusive group.

The Cats was a good club with a tight crowd and fairly clean for a couple of reasons and this played to the club's advantage. The older Wolvo boys knew why The Torch had closed. The drug squad closed it down, no matter what was going around, that's the truth! They knew the Wolvo drug squad only needed a few good busts and they could do the same to The Cats. So all the gear went right underground. Also the times the club closed, too early at two on a Saturday and midnight on a Wednesday. With regards to Wednesday, why would you get smashed when it closed at midnight? And you had to be at work in a couple of hours, there was no point. Also if you got caught by the bouncers in The Cats with gear they would have kicked the shit out of you. They were big guys. So it didn't matter who you thought you were, you would get it and believe me they knew how to read the club. Saturday was different and the best night for atmosphere.

It just felt more intense and let's get something straight. Sure there was gear in The Cats, I'm not going to lie! We weren't blind and knew what was going on around us. If I saw something, I would look away. The odd handshake, a slight of hand bit of money changing hands it was all part of the scene. The older crowd were people we just didn't mess with or most of all trust. That exclusive club were tight, us being on the outside was just going to be easy money. A new load of Divs to rip off, we hadn't got a clue what was good and what was crap. I had never seen drugs and couldn't tell you the difference between a headache tablet and a bluey. The nearest we came to taking gear was to swallow a couple of codeine and rub some liniment on our legs. We had no interest at all but I knew one thing.

I didn't trust the older crowd as far as I could throw them. Still just like prohibition, if something is banned then that adds to the excitement. Curiosity takes over and you want in. For me I was frightened what it might do to me, it was our choice not to take gear and we turned our backs on it. We were still accepted and had great nights our attitude would change later but at the start no way. Didn't need it, didn't want it. Also my attitude was this, if you took gear I would go out of my way to dance against you. I got blown off the floor a few times but I learned your moves and would be right back next week. These were early times for this Soul Boy, my attitude would change later as we moved deeper onto the Northern Scene. The drug scene I would get heavily involved with but at the moment knew nothing about. For now we were on the outside looking in, albeit with curiosity at an underground scene fueled with amphetamines and driven by music we so dearly loved.

Chapter 20

RUMPY'S SATURDAY

This Saturday seemed no different from any other as I made my way to Rumpy's, the café we had made our second home. Just up from Ruby Red Records it was the ideal meeting place for the morning and I had already picked up my copy of Blues and Soul. The sun was shining, the summer had arrived. I would see Kim later and that always made me feel good and to top it off we had The Cats tonight.

With my black patch pocket blazer and yellow Slazenger top riding the outside collar, twenty four inch parallels and polished brogues I felt immaculate. I always took pride in my appearance but today I felt really special, my new trousers had finally arrived! Rusty had told me about Jacksons, the tailors', a while ago and after Darb's encounter at The Ship I had took matters into my own hands. My trousers were tailor made, you couldn't buy them anywhere. I was different and felt individual and that's exactly the way I wanted to be. Not only were my trousers fashionable, they were a loose fit ideal for dancing and I couldn't wait to show Darb.

We always met here on a Saturday, collecting my tea I took the window seat. Street life passing me by oblivious to my surroundings I relaxed in the mid-day sun. As I thumbed through my copy of Blues and Soul, a page caught my attention. There in bold letters, THE VA-VA BOLTON Friday nights ALL NIGHT SOUL SESSION from Eight till Eight featuring a list of artists and records they played. Wally Cox, Kenny Bernard, Shawn Robinson, The Jive Five, Linda Jones, The Volcanoes and more. Some of which I recognized from The Cats and I immediately wanted to go.

"Gethro!"

"Darb, you made me jump man! Hey, look at this!" I thrust the magazine across the table as he sat down.

"He drinks tea Diane, you know how he likes it. Shaken not stirred." Blowing the young waitress a kiss as I always did.

"Kim will kill you if she catches you Gethro!" Darb smiling at my openness.

"Hey, you know me. Just never mind that. Look all night soul from eight till eight." a serious tone to my voice.

"Yea, but it's in Bolton. How do we get there?"

"I think I got it covered. My mate at tech, Giddy."

"Who?" Darb raising his eyes brows in confusion.

"Giddy Patel, my mate. He just passed his test and wants to drive everywhere, he will take us won't cost us a thing."

"Why not?" Darb's expressions ever changing, an inquisitive look upon his face.

"Easy, I help him do some of his test pieces at college. That way he gets his welding projects done, ready for his finals and we go to Va-Va." I nodded my head in satisfaction smiling at the simplicity of my plan.

"Nice one man!" His boarding smile confirming he was cottoning on to my master plan.

"Good eh! Anyway Darb, I am sick of hearing about The Torch!" We missed it and that went deep. I would never get to wear that badge as I never went but I wish we had. Like The Cats it was a special club etched in the memories of those who went. We had the upmost respect for the people who danced there and the music they brought to the scene as most of the sounds we loved were from there. It was definitely a magic club and we had just missed out but it was getting old, as that's all we ever heard from the older crowd was, "Yea, but you should have gone to The Torch!!"

"I don't want to miss this, it's an all-nighter and look they have a badge." I knew I had him hooked, Darb loved badges just like me. All we had was The Cats badge but the design just didn't live up to the name of the club. A black fist with "Keep the Faith The Catacombs" with a couple of yellow circles around the edge. The Va-Va badge would get us some respect and make a statement, give us some history and show Soulies we travelled to all-nighters. Darb placing his tea to the side, both of us pausing in silence smiling at the distraction of Diane as she made a hip swaying retreat.

"You in or out?" My voice defiant.

"Come on Gethro, you don't need to ask that!"

"Sorry mate." Knowing straight away I should have known better. "It's just that I'm excited man. It's our first all-nighter!"

"What about Kim?"

"No way Darb, she looks too young and I don't want to go all the way up there to be turned away at the door."

"Yea but she's not going to like that. I don't want to be in your shoes when you tell her. I think we should all go."

"Well, it's my problem." Darb sensing the annoyance in my voice as I looked at my watch.

"Where's Jimmy and Winst, Darb?"

"Said they would see us in The Octopus. Look at the records Gethro, same as The Cats."

"I know, so we got the floor man. Wonder how big the floor is?"

"Maybe Ric Tic's been Gethro?"

"We'll check him out, he may be in The Octopus later. Come on drink your tea."

"Hold on man, there's some more stuff."

"Well get your own copy."

"Fuck you Gethro!" as we burst out laughing I had forgotten all about my trousers. "Hey, check these out!" Jumping up, shoving my hands in the pockets to show the double pleated front of my chalk stripes. The waistband had six buttons set in rows of three with dummy buttons on one side.

"Gethro, that waistband's neat man."

"Three inch." A smile between us Darb leaning forward, feeling the cloth. I could tell he was impressed.

"Jacksons?"

"Yea no one's got a pair of these, pale blue chalk stripes picked the cloth myself. Look at this (bending to my knees) see loose fit. Had him add an inch to the inside leg custom made for dancing mate. Ideal for doing the splits!" Trying not to crease them as I sat down, my face beaming with pride.

"Mine in yet?"

"No, Colin said about two weeks. He's waiting for some reinforced cotton." A cold look exchanged between us.

"You're never gonna let me live that down?"

"I will in time." Both of us breaking to laughter sharing the joke as we always did. Already we were striving to be individual and going to unusual lengths. Nothing to do with fashion everything to do with being different, to stand out in a crowd. In time we would take this even further. Anyway, if we we're going to Va-Va we wanted to look like Soul Boys.

"You got a sports bag Gethro?"

"No." I replied.

"Well you need one. How you going to carry your stuff?" This all-nighter was getting expensive. All of a sudden we needed spare shirts, different shoes, in case the floor was shit, talc, towel, and spare vests. Both of us took things seriously and we were going with one reason in mind, to show them the boys from The Cats could dance. This was to be our first all-nighter, our chance to get out on a different floor. We were both pretty good dancers now and couldn't wait. This was it but our day had only just begun.

We left Rumpy's passing Ruby Reds record shop to cut through The Mander Centre, a few skins were scattered around leaning on the side rail. Faded rolled up Levis, their cherry red boots, Harrington's and short sleeved check button-downs, a statement to their crew. Now we were worlds apart. We had changed, we felt different, we were Soul boys and they knew better than to try and roll us. We passed them by, a simple nod a sign of respect people that we knew remnants of our past.

It was useful knowing faces of the town it's the way it worked as me and Darb were tight and always had each other's backs. The football season hadn't started yet so at least the town would be quiet or as quiet as a Saturday could be. In the summer's sun life felt good finding happiness in our youth. Darb was my best mate but weren't like brothers at all, to us we were much closer than that.

To say The Octopus had picked up was an understatement, this now was the place for Soulies to meet as Swoz filled it with Northern Soul. Some original records, some pressings that were beginning to filter out of The Cats. It had been going for a while now, sixteen months and although slow at the start this was now the bar you would find anyone in Wolvo connected to Northern Soul. We had been there at the beginning and seen it grow and knew almost everyone in there as most of The Cats crowd now used it. We stood on the top steps watching dancers trying to spot Jimmy and Winston. Swoz on the decks, my eyes stinging adjusting to the darkness of the smoke filled room. The dance floor full as Soulies warmed up for The Cats tonight, some practicing moves others milling around the hub of noise hardly heard above the sound system.

"Your round Gethro!" Darb waving his hand towards the bar.

"No way. I brought the last one at The Ship. Ok, spoof!" Placing coins in my hand as always Darb guessed wrong. "See justice!" I had to smile as Darb left to fight his way to the bar, he knew it was useless to argue and anyway I would buy the next round.

Descending into the room I made my way through the crowd, it seemed fuller than usual. Pixie, Jamo, Paddy, Muff, and Cash young Soulies greeting me with handshakes as they always did. Slowly a bond was forming with the younger crowd, it's as if we knew we weren't totally accepted yet but we belonged on the scene just as much as anyone else. The label of being a Div was getting old. Slowly, we were forming new friendships keeping our distance from the older crowd. "Jimmy!" you couldn't miss him, the sheer size of his muscular build. He easily stood out in any crowd Winston bearing the brunt of his teasing laughter.

"Gethro! What's up man?" A beaming smile as we greeted each other. "Where's Darb?" I pointed to the bar. Eager to tell him about Va-Va I pulled the copy of Blues and Soul from my pocket. Jimmy took the piss out of my new trousers right away.

"What's up with that waistband man?! Gethro, you look like a bull fighter." Sticking his fingers on his head imitating a bull to the amusement of Winston bursting out laughing, he also taking the piss.

"No I don't!" I never thought of that, but I wasn't going to show him he had got to me. "Anyway, I haven't seen any bull fighters with double pleated parallels!" But I too had to laugh. "Stop messing around Jimmy!" Changing the subject as fast as I could thrusting the magazine towards him. "Look at this." Showing him the ad for Va-Va.

"Gethro, why you want to go all the way to Bolton when you have the same sounds at The Cats?"

"It's an all-nighter Jimmy look eight till eight."

"Yea I know," scanning the page as he held it in the light, "but the records man, they are the same."

"Some are different. You want to come?"

"No, I'm sticking with The Cats man.

I turned to Winston, "how about you?"

"No Gethro, I'm staying with Jimmy." Both of them definite.

"Ok, well I asked." Shrugging my shoulders, trying not to hide my disappointment. "Me and Darb are going," trying to get his interest one more time.

"When?" Jimmy asked.

"As soon as I can get the lift sorted." I wanted Jimmy to come but wasn't going to beg him. It was his choice. Darb returning with our drinks placing them off to the side. "What's up?"

"Just you and me Darb. Jimmy and Winston aren't coming."

"Ok. Well, I'm coming." We shook hands.

"Done deal, just me and you Darb." He smiled.

"Always was Gethro. You know that now give me that Blues and Soul." As I passed him the magazine I noticed Rusty walking towards me with some strangers at his side. I still felt bad about The Cats, it had been awhile now and I wanted to put my side of the story. I nudged Darb as they approached, "Watch my back."

"I got it Gethro." Jimmy clocked my look, Winston nodded I smiled at my instant protection we were ready if it came on top. I was expecting the worst as one of the new comers stepped forward.

"You Gethro?!" There was an uneasy silence as I tried to read his face, thoughts of, "here we go" entering my head. "Yea, I'm Gethro."

"My name's Jake. You know my brother?"

"Who?"

"Colin."

"I never knew he had a brother."

"Yea I'm the youngest."

"Gethro, tell him about your last bull fight." Jimmy chipped in as we all started to laugh to the puzzled look of Jake. We all introduced ourselves, Rusty turning away as I tried to speak not even saying a word, leaving Jake standing by my side.

That day we didn't know it, but we had just made a special friend and one we would all get to know well. I knew his brother Colin from my days with Twenty Nine Crew and walking around the park. With shoulder length blonde hair and the frame of Bruce Lee, Jake idolized his mentor and was built the same way. To the bone, there was no meat on him at all. Obsessed with martial arts and fitness Jake had a bouncy personality and a ton of energy to match and just loved to dance.

From that day Jake stayed with us, coming to The Cats on the nights we went, always dancing in our little group following our routine of dancing on the floors around the town. The French Duck on a Thursday with a small dance floor downstairs, Cats on Saturday and Wednesday even on a Friday when it was free, The Ship, Pink Elephant, The Octopus. Every night we would be dancing somewhere, showing that same drive for perfection we all had setting a bond with us right away.

I never crossed Jake and he never crossed me, we had a friendship from the heart built on trust and he showed this to me many times. Later creating and perfecting original moves that he shared selflessly with us as he put his own mark to his unique style of dancing. He too would leave a footprint on the dance floors of the Northern Soul scene. Jake would stay with us for six years, dancing side by side as we all became inseparable with a friendship that stood the test of time. There were now six of us, but to us he was simply "Jako" the final piece of the puzzle had finally arrived. He had a few ideas to improve on our dancing, one which he shared with us straight away.

Chapter 21

WOLVO BOXING - EARLY AUGUST 1973

"Left, left, right"

The first was Wolverhampton Armature Boxing, the reason for this was simple. To get us fitter to improve on our dancing and to me it seemed like a good idea at the time so why not? I had brought a new sports bag, bright orange with Puma in black letters on the side and wanted to use it before Va-Va. In my track suit bottoms and colored vest I looked just like a fitness fanatic as I waited outside the old red brick building for Darb and Jako to arrive.

For us there wasn't much happening on a Monday and anyway it was a beautiful summer's evening, what could possibly go wrong? Jako was already a member and had told us all we would do was training but for some reason I was nervous. I had never been to a gym. The three of us entered through the arched double doors and up a wide staircase, Jako leading the way. At the top on the left a single black door WAB in white letters shouts and noise greeting us as we entered through half open the door.

The room was large with a tarnished feel to it along the windowed wall two boxing rings extended the full length of the room. A slight breeze from the tilted windows made the heat in the gym bearable. On the opposite side of the room tattered posters adorned mirrored walls. Corners lifting to ropes skipping in rhythm to a flurry of bouncing feet the constant click of ticking on a battered wooden floor. Huge leather bags swung on cobwebbed rafters. Boxers pounding them, cracked wrinkled pendulums swinging in motion to every punch.

"Left, left, right! Come on put some power into it!" The trainer glanced in our direction stepping away from a boxer, immediately coming towards us. A chubby man short in stature graying hair pushed back revealing sweaty wrinkled features. A bubbled nose of a drinker flat and twisted from too many blows to the face. His prying eyes passing straight through me.

"These your mate's Jake? "His voice in a raspy, throaty tone.

"Yes Mr. George. This is Gethro and Darb."

"Well get changed and take them on your usual run then come see me, ok?"

"Ok Mr. George!"

As we dropped our bags on the wooden bench in the changing room, a strange feeling hit my stomach brought on by the stench of liniment and sweat. I really didn't want to be here, the place had the smell of violence but by now there was no turning back.

"How far we got to run Jako?" I asked trying not to feel like a wimp.

"Just three miles to warm up, then we do the fun stuff." Jako smiling at our predicament.

"What stuff?!" Darb asked abruptly, obviously feeling the same as me. Jako ignoring his question, "come on, its ok and at least we'll all get fit."

Jako was fit and it showed sprinting away as we left the gym, me and Darb speeding up to stay at his side. Finally we slowed to a softer pace the warmth of the summer's evening making our run pleasant. Trotting together all three of us side by side Jako shadow boxing along the way. "Gethro, you two still going to Va-Va?"

"Yea, you want to come?"

"Can't at the moment, got no money. When you going?"

"Couple of weeks." I had done some of the projects with Giddy at Tech which I attended three weeks on, three off we had one more to finish this week then we could go. Giddy said he's ready anytime. Darb told me today.

"Nice one man."

We stopped at the halfway point, all of us fighting for breathe stripping to our shorts hoping to make our run cooler on the way back. The run had been easy at the start but in the heat of the summer's night we were now covered in sweat. Our skinny frames reflecting our age like three bald chickens on the loose there was no meat on any one of us. "Jako you need some of Kim's cooking."

"No I don't Gethro. I'm fit." Taking a karate, stance sucking his stomach in and holding his breath before bursting to a smile. "Why, what's she got?"

"He only eats Chinese food Gethro. Remember Bruce lee? Look at your ribs Jako." Darb turning to me, "got any chopsticks, I could play a tune on them!" All of us bursting into laughter. Jako breaking into a sequence of hand movements as if fighting some invisible opponent, finishing in a round house kick impressing us with his moves.

"Come on you two!" We sprinted away, a little faster now keeping in perfect time matching each other stride for stride. We soon returned to the gym catching our breath and the attention of Mr. George who came over to us straight away. A towel draped over his shoulder, the voice of authority looking at me.

"Right shadow boxing and skipping." Throwing us a rope clapping his hands. "Come on, let's go! Jab, jab, move! Jab, jab, move!" He watched us take turns dancing in front of the mirror the others skipping on the mat. "Get your knees up! Twelve o'clock, four o'clock. Come on Jake move your feet! Paying attention to us all, scrutinizing our every move before leaving us to attend to other boxers nearby. By now Darb and I were feeling it, this session was taking its toll. We took a breather to look around the crowded gym, watching bouts unfolding around us.

"Thought you said we didn't have to box Jako?" Darb asked, arms folded in defiance as I stood by his side.

"We don't." We watched as one guy battering another boxer around the ring, two fights and they hadn't gone past the first round as he tore people up. My sixth sense kicking into overdrive as the trainer looked straight at us "right, who's next?!" Mr. George shouted to complete silence, "come on a volunteer or I'll pick someone!"

My arm shot up. Why? I don't know why, but I had put my arm up! I hadn't come to box, I hated bullies I know but to me this wasn't the place it was full of them! It was one of the bravest things I have ever done as Jako and Darb looked at me as if I had gone mental. Their faces in complete surprise. Thoughts ran through my mind, why to show off? To be brave why? I had no answer, really I didn't.

A lamb about to be slaughtered, I climbed into the ring to get laced up looking over to them for support. Then back to this gorilla who was about to tear my head off on the far side of the ring. The trainer checked my gloves to me, they weren't big enough I could see around them!

"Right three rounds with a standing count of eight!" We touched gloves in the center of the ring and I immediately jumped back to a right cross that would of took my head off. I had to move fast and keep moving or I was dead meat, I knew that! I had boxed a little at school and maybe this was behind my decision, but from where I stood now it didn't seem like a good idea to me!

As we boxed the first two rounds were brilliant as the guy chased me all over the ring. I just stayed on my feet dancing away, throwing left jabs catching him off balance. Turning away from his windmill of punches trying not to annoy him as best I could. I could see anger in his face, frustration boiling over as once again he punched thin air. In the third round I turned to Darb and Jako smiling away even giving them a wave staying behind my left. They encouraged me cheering me on never seeing the right that I turned into as I came bouncing off the ropes.

They both winced as the punch went through me I felt my knees buckle, a creak in my neck, a punch that shook me to the core. The trainer stepped in with my standing count his lips in slow motion, numbers ringing in my ears. I looked over to Darb who could hardly stand up putting his hand on Jako's shoulder as they both collapsed in laughter. The only thing I kept saying to myself was "you didn't go down! You didn't go down!" Shaking my head, clearing my mind after my standing count the round couldn't come to an end fast enough as I really showed them how to dance. The final bell sounded and I jumped down from the ring. They came over still laughing at my mistake in my defense I replied, "Hey I never went down!"

"No Gethro, we'll give you that. You never went down." The pair of them bursting into laughter once more. Darb telling me, "wait till Jimmy hears this!"

"Gethro you ok?" Jako biting his tongue trying to hold his composure, breaking to a smile before bursting out laughing again "You got to duck Gethro!" Hardly heard above the ringing in my ears as I asked, "Jako what next?"

"You're shouting Gethro!"

"No I'm not?!"

"You are." Darb fighting his laughter.

"Am I?!" Thinking to myself, the things I do for dancing banging my head to clear my ears. Knowing full well the laughs on me and Jimmy would show no mercy. He will really take the piss!

Chapter 22

THE SHIP - PAYBACK

What goes around comes around, it had been a while now and I had forgot all about The Cats. I never saw the punch coming as I left the dance floor of The Ship on that Tuesday night. We had arrived early and I had forgotten the golden rule, "hit one of us, you hit us all." As I jumped back my fists clenched ready to face one of the new members from Rusty's crew.

Darb instantly standing at my side. "You ok Gethro?!"

"Yea fuckin cheap shot wanker!" Some of The Parkfield rushing over from the far side of the room, Gary also standing with me just wanting one excuse to join in. Everyone frozen in time waiting for me to make the next move and I couldn't do it.

These were my mates from way back and I wasn't going to fight with them. That day in the park they had stood by me when I met Kim. Backing me up in the past, always standing by my side. We had many happy times together, our memories locked in time. All that was hurt was my pride and the fact I hadn't seen it coming as he ran past me.

I felt lost, empty inside. I turned away catching Rusty's stare. His face showing the same expression of pain at a friendship that spanned years now lost forever "From that night we never spoke again." I picked up my crombie and walked away never looking back with Kim by my side neither one of us saying a word. I suppose I brought it on myself. I felt really sad that it had ended like this all because some wanker wouldn't stop taking the piss!

I looked at Darb, he too could see the hurt in my eyes. "Gethro you ok?"

"Yea I'm ok." Nodding, my hand feeling the slight bruise on the side of my head.

"I know they are your old mates but you don't need them anymore." His voice full of resentment placing his hand on my shoulder wanting my revenge.

"That's what I told you!" We both smiled.

My mind was set, I had to leave this world of mindless violence. I didn't belong here, I hated it. From now on I would pick my friends they won't pick me I had learned my lesson the hard way. "I'm getting away from this fucking crap!" my voice now full of anger "I'm seeing Giddy tomorrow and its Va-Va Friday. I got to get away from these Divs and this skinhead shit Darb!"

"You're not going to have them outside?"

"No I can't do it mate. I just can't. They can say what they want call me a shit out I really don't care mate." My face cracking into a smile, "and anyway, I never went down!" We all burst out laughing.

'Yea, I know Gethro two shots in two days," but I knew he understood I had nothing to prove." Only to myself and a mirror. We didn't know it at the time but this night turned out to be a wicked twist of fate. "Destiny had just played her hand."

Chapter 23

VA-VA BOLTON

"Going to a Go-Go"

In these days it was one thing to have mates who were black and most of mine were, but it was a no-no if he was a Pakie. Giddish was, yet he had every right to be in this country. He was born here and was as English as you and me. He loved the things we did, he spoke like a Black Country kid and was a real good friend of mine from college. Yet these were dangerous times if you were a Pakistani. I had seen Pakie bashing firsthand from my days as a Skinhead and felt nothing but shame and disgrace.

An old guy had come out the pub a little drunk and was standing to the side as a bunch of us came down the road. Something was said and the next thing, "Get the Pakie bastard!" He was being kicked around on the pavement like a rag doll. Eventually his limp body falling motionless into the gutter. His head crashing onto the curb, a silent thud bursting into a pool of blood. I stood transfixed, staring at his twisted body. Rivers of blood from the back of his head flowing along cobbled canals slowly trickling towards the drain. He had done nothing wrong, he was a Pakistani that's all that was needed.

This was the early seventies and Giddish had every reason to be scared. He knew his colour was a problem as I explained and tried to cross the divide we had created, telling him not all people were like that. The image stayed with me as I reassured him. If he gave us a lift to Bolton and it came on top me and Darb would go down fighting by his side.

"Are you sure he got the directions right Gethro?" Darb's voice growing anxious as he peered through the windows of Rumpy's, the café we had made our home. The old clock on the wall showing seven thirty we had been here awhile now empty tea cups marking our time.

"I told him straight down the Dudley road and he would run right into us, just look for a dark green escort. He'll be here." Shuffling in my seat trying to hide the fact I too felt exactly the same way. Staying relaxed fingering through the old copy of Blues and Soul I had brought, folding the corner of the ad for Va-Va before moving to the next page. I glanced up acknowledging Darb's inquisitive stare as he turned to me once more.

"What did Kim say when you told her she can't come?"

"She was pissed off and cried. I felt like a right bastard but what could I do Darb, really?"

"I know Gethro, better you than me." Shaking his head I knew he understood my dilemma, he never pried.

"I told her she can come the next time after we've checked it out. In the end she seemed ok with that."

"That's fair."

"What shoes you brought?" I asked changing the subject as fast as I could.

"Leather and rubber, in case it's slippery."

"Me too should work. Got any talc?"

"Here he is!"

"At last! I felt a sigh of relief rattling the table of cups as I hastily grabbed my bag. "See you tomorrow Jim." Bidding my farewell. Darb at the open door his face in a beaming smile, "that's a nice car man!"

"Told you Escort GT, the dog's bollocks." We ran to Giddy parked in the bus stop at the side of the road. Tapping the roof of the car with excitement I opened the door.

"Giddy, how you doing man?" The cool air greeting me as I jumped into the front seat, "this is my mate Darb." Turning around only to see Darb smiling in the back seat.

"Gethro, we can't travel in this?!"

"Why not? What's up?"

"He's an Albion fan." Darb pointing to the sticker across the back window. "Fuck Jeff Astle! Fuck Wolves!" Giddy's reply drowned in our laughter.

"Do you know where Bolton is Giddy?" I asked.

"Yea, straight down the M6."

"Near enough, we'll find Va-Va from there," showing him the folded add with the address Great Moor Street Bolton. "You got the cassette Darb?"

"You don't need it," Giddy pointing to the tape deck built into the dash. "No 8-track here mate." His face glowing with pride.

"Nice one man." Darb even more impressed.

I dug into my bag pulling out a tape from The Cats. "Here Giddy put this on," throwing my bag on to the back seat with Darb. Pep's voice coming across the speakers loud then louder, Giddy adjusting the volume filling the car with Northern records from The Cats.

"Which way out of here Gethro?"

"Turn left at this light, then second light turn right, just follow it straight down and keep going till you hit signs for the M6. It's about seven miles," pointing to the first set of lights, a screech of tires as we sped away.

"Look at the legs on that! She'd keep your ears warm. No! Not you Giddy, you're driving." Our laughter filling the car, "anyway bet she supports Wolves, won't have anything to do with an Albion fan."

"Fuck you Gethro!"

"How you doing darling?!" I yelled through the open window, Darb turning in a spiral on the back seat trying to get one last look. "Gethro she flicked the v."

"No she didn't, she waved."

"She flicked the v man."

"Yea at you Darb." More laughter between us, our banter wrapped in the excitement of the night. We moved through the town eventually mixing with the holiday traffic of August heading along the M6 north.

"What's the top end on this Giddy?" I asked.

"Don't know never floored it but I keep it at about a hundred." I glanced at the speedo relaxing in my seat, suddenly Va-Va didn't seem all that far away. We sped down the M6 on that Friday night never seeing a cop, nothing passing us as we idly chatted away Northern sounds filling the car. Earl Wright "Thumb A Ride", Jackie Wilson "Nothing But Blue Skies", The Temptations "Ain't Too Proud To Beg", and Gloria Jones "Tainted Love" as we purred our way to Bolton the miles just faded away.

"Giddy, what music you into?"

"Oh Motown. You know, Diana Ross, Four tops stuff like that."

"Nice one mate, that's Soul but this is different. This is pure Soul, Northern Soul."

"Never heard of it."

"Come around with us, you soon will!" Darb shouting above Saxie Russell as we turned together to sing, "...let me psychedelic soul you!..." A slight harmony in our voices, our wagging fingers directed at Giddy laughing all the time.

"Darb, I never knew Pep DJ'd at Va-Va. Ric Tic told me and Alan Day.

So that explains the sounds from The Cats but I wonder who this other guy is, Richard Searling, I've never heard of him."

"Nor me Darb. Well it's on from 8 till 8 so he will be on at some time in the night."

"Gethro remember Ric Tic kept on about some guy from The Torch. A little guy called Martin Ellis, said he is a brilliant DJ brings energy to the dexks plays a lot of fast stuff.

"What till eight in the morning?!" Giddy's voice in surprise.

"Yea all night."

"You never told me that Gethro!"

"Oh I forgot. Yea it's on all night," to more laughter "Hey look Bolton can't be far now Darb." A sign passing us by.

The feeling of adrenaline raced through me, now we will see who can dance! We had been gaining respect around Wolvo as dancers with fast footwork especially to "Looky Looky" by The O'Jays, a record I would always burn the floor to whenever it was played at The Ship. Also, at The Cats our little group were beginning to stand out. All we needed now was a dance floor. To us it was all about dancing, expressing yourself on a floor if you stood out so be it just dance! Nothing else really mattered.

"Come on in Giddy. No one is going to fuck with you, this is a Northern Club."

"No I'm not coming in mate. I'll be here when you come out, I'll sleep in the car."

"Gethro he won't come, let's go! Look at the queue we'll never get in if you don't hurry. Come on man!" Darb getting pissed off turning to walk away as I tried once more.

"Look Giddy."

"No!" His voice definite, in a no means no tone.

"We got your back." My words pointless he wouldn't come. I felt sad as I left him to sleep in the car, they had won Giddy unable to overcome his fear. Nothing I could say would make him change his mind but deep inside I understood. I ran to catch Darb already in the queue surrounded by Soulies trying to get into the club.

"Lot of cops round here Gethro, wonder what's going on?"

"Yea I noticed as I came over. They're searching some of the cars, pulling people out. They got dogs, must be drug squad."

We had never seen squad in action and were fascinated watching the night unfold before us as we stood silently in the queue. There was gear in this crowd we could tell straight away the wide eyed expressions of the Soulies around us reminded me of The Cats on a Saturday night. Their constant chit chatting about the night and records to come, their voices in jumbled conversations lips constantly in motion startled looks of searching eyes. "Darb we must be the only straights in this queue mate."

"I know." Both of us breaking to a smile.

I felt nervous as we got nearer the neon sign, the bright letters Va-Va Night Club, the noise in the queue quieter. Bouncers standing by an open door checking people as they went in. My stomach turning over, the noise of the club in the background adding to the excitement, images building in my head. Our first all-nighter, the bouncer waving us through. This is it! At last!

We entered down the steep stairs to "What Shall I Do" by Frankie and the Classicals, the haunting melody pulling us into the darkness as we descended into the club. At the bottom the only light from a kiosk, we paid in ignoring the cloak room on our left moving along a short corridor. I pushed the double doors open with my bag, the club spreading out in front of us as we both stopped dead, looking in disbelief.

"What the fuck Gethro? It's a disco!" We both burst out laughing as I whispered in silent echo "A fuckin disco man!"

Everywhere there was plush carpeting, black seating with tables set in curved alcoves to our left and right. Back panels edged with chrome railings reaching to the ceiling. Through a gap in the alcoves bright colored lights illuminated a tiny circular dance floor, enough for four people.

"That's not a dance floor is it?"

"No way Darb, it can't be?" Straining my eyes in the darkness to see if it was real.

"Come on no standing at the bottom of the stairs and no bags in the club!" The bouncer moving us along pissing me off with his no nonsense manner.

"Come on Gethro the dance floors got to be this way." Turning to our right we fought our way through the sea of people crowding around a bar and on past more alcoves towards the back of the club. The Gems "I'll Be There", the tinny notes, their skipping voices crystal clear pushing us along with the flow of the crowd. We eased our way into the darkness towards the sea of clapping hands and colored lights drawing us deeper into the club. The place packed out with Soulies, a mixed crowd of all ages. Soaking vests adorned with soul badges bodies moving in all directions. Smiling, wide-eyed expressions, jawing faces dripping with sweat. A politeness in their tone, a friendliness adding to the atmosphere, an excitement to the night. I had never been amongst so many smashed Soulies, it felt cool as if we belonged. I wanted to be like them to feel that same high and become a part of their night. "A Lil Lovin' Sometimes" the powerful voice of Alexander Patton competing with the DJ, our voices hardly heard in the crowd.

"Gethro, there a lot of gear in here man!"

"I know everyone's off their fuckin heads mate! What do you think?"

"It's up to you. If you do some remember me."

"I will, it's our first all-nighter. I say let's do it!" My answer was all we needed and I knew he felt the same way.

"You bad man."

"I know Darb and you wait till I tell Jimmy!" As I caught his smiling face that look between us said it all. "Darb seen anybody from The Cats yet?"

"Not yet."

"We need some faces and bad. The Wolvo crowd's in here somewhere." The voice of the DJ screaming through the speakers causing the crowd to surge forwards. James Bounty "Prove Yourself A Lady" more sounds we recognized moving us together into the darkness, deeper into the crowd. Suddenly our night crashed around us. There surrounded by alcoves, illuminated in brilliant yellow light, the smallest dance floor we had ever seen. All around the edges colored panels of perplex reds and yellows lined the dance floor and to top it off, some stupid Wanker had decided to make the floor out of tiles! This was nothing like we expected and nothing like The Cats!

"This can't be the main floor man?!" We looked around another bar behind us returning our gaze back to the floor.

"Darb it is, it's the only floor!" Shaking my head in disappointment "That's fucked it!"

We dropped our bags never saying a word. Our hearts just sank to the floor, my head spinning. This wasn't happening, it's not supposed to be like this. The DJ announcing the next record, a small figure from a glass lined pit. Cheering and clapping all around us the odd whistles from the crowd. "From the legendary Torch Stoke. The one and only Mr. Eddie Parkerrr!"

"Look Darb, it's that little guy Ric Tic told us about from The Torch. That must be Martin Ellis!"

We could tell straight away why this guy was special, a DJ with a dancer's drive and energy blasting out "Love You Baby" filling the floor to capacity, carpeting around the edges dancers where they stood. We instantly fell in love with his fumbling style, he just seemed as if he was one of us. Driving the beats harder taking the crowd with him sweeping them along as he yelled down the mic. A face drenched in atmosphere, darting hands fighting glasses forever sliding from his face. His slim frame bent over the turntables, a face of concentration queuing his latest find.

Memories of The Torch, constant clapping from the dancer's one on one with the DJ pure vinyl hitting the floor! The Velvet Satins "Nothing Can Compare To You", Danny White "Cracked Up Over You", Sequins "A Case Of Love", The Fuller Brothers "Time's A Wasting", The Triumphs "Walkin' The Duck", Bobby Freeman "I'll Never Fall In Love Again", and Dobie Gray "Out On The Floor". We stood and watched as he worked the decks, a mass of vinyl energy scattered records to be put away. Roy Hamilton "Cracking Up Over You", the dancers transfixed anywhere you could find bodies moved with little room to dance.

The circular floor packed to capacity, yet in the bright yellow lights one dancer stood out straight away. A tall skinny guy with black cords, a soaked red vest edged in black dark and stained, a testimony to his dancing. In the center the black fist of a soul club, he could spin at lightning speed. Fighting to keep his balance as he spun off in different directions apologizing to whoever he hit but he could spin! We could see the floor was killing him, sometimes crashing into panels that lined the edge of the floor. We watched studying the competition.

"Gethro put any more than twenty people on that floor and it's packed."

"Yea well, let's get rid of these bags and hit the floor. That leaves eighteen of us mate, come on!"

Set around the alcoves the floor reflecting in colored full lights of Perspex everywhere, glistening with chrome this place just didn't feel right. We waited at the edge of the floor under the bright yellow lights, I instantly felt like a moth. Nerves turning in my stomach I felt uneasy but we had come to dance there was no turning back. In the center of our blue vests our badges worn with pride to us we were representing our club, The Catacombs and Wolvo. It was a feeling we had whenever we hit a floor. We looked smart in our matching vests and parallels, two Soul brothers from The Cats.

Thoughts running through my mind pushing all others aside, a confidence, a belief now we will show them how Wolvo boys dance. "Last record from me before I hand over to Richard, another classic from The Torch, one of our Anthems! Thanks for being a brilliant crowd! You know I love you!

"Cause You're Mine" by The Vibrations!" Martin Ellis, his voice lost in the atmosphere drowned by cheers thundering handclaps of admiration from the crowd. It was all we needed as we took the floor together breaking to an arc of fast footwork. We exploded onto the floor. It was clear right away it gave you nothing. Every move we did drop-backs fighting for room on that floor, splits in the tightness of other dancers was a challenge and hard to do.

We tried to make space for one another Darb stepping back in the same way we did at The Cats. Our shoes getting caught in the tiles, the uneven surface killing us adding frustration to all of our moves. Again we had all this energy yet we couldn't express ourselves to the music we loved. Changing to slower footwork and twisting feet, another style we had perfected. Adjusting to the floor, toning down our moves no splits or drop-backs holding on to what little room we had.

We moved out amongst the dancers, the spinner colliding into us but apologizing right away. His name was Shawn, a local lad from Bolton and was one of the best spinners on the scene at the time. Spinning like a top in a blur of speed, unraveling his arms as he came out of a spin dropping them by his side. Easily hitting fifteen spins to do that on a tiled floor was brilliant but this guy was spinning on one leg! Sometimes on his heel on this floor it was a move I couldn't come close to and one I definitely couldn't match. His style so different from Squeak, I had never seen anyone spin like that. Striking up a friendship we immediately gave him a dancer's respect.

All around us the crowd really friendly if you bumped into someone you held up your hand no matter how many times it was just accepted. There was no attitude here, only smiling faces. Dancers with passion and energy their love of the music all that mattered. In the tightness of the crowd we were welcomed, lost in the heat of the dancers I felt as one and knew we belonged. Shawn we would meet many times in the future, he was the first Soulie we had made friends with outside of The Catacombs crowd. As we all danced together there was a bond of admiration at our different styles but we just couldn't move. That night Va-Va's floor belonged to the Bolton lads and at the forefront was Shawn. They were all good dancers but in a small way we too had made our mark. This was an all-nighter, it had been a long journey for us but now we had finally arrived. The floor more packed than ever, a crowd standing around us, strangers to our table, smiling faces of searching expressions intense conversations at our side.

We danced in a small area we had made our own, adding talc to improve the floor. Now at last we could start to put some moves together. A leg break into a spin, Darb bursting into laughter at frustration written all over my face. All of us as one with the music mixing with other Soulies, the atmosphere unique as the night. The Charades "The Key To My Happiness", Jerry Cook "I Hurt On The Other Side", The Tempos "(Countdown) Here I Come", Shawn Robinson "My Dear Heart", Maxine Brown "One In A Million", Linda Jones "I Just Can't Live My Life", The Blossoms "That's When The Tears Start", Art Freeman "Slippin' Around With You", The Fuzz "I'm So Glad", The Shirelles "Last Minute Miracle", The Adventurers "Easy Baby", Wally Cox "This Man", and Gloria Jones "Tainted Love keeping the floor alive, driving the tempo higher to clapping hands at every record. By now we too were soaked in emotion shared friendships of the night. In the bright lights of the dance floor we relaxed in our dancing more sounds from The Cats filling the crowded floor.

Suddenly I felt a tight grip on my shoulder as someone pushed me off to the side, "what the?!" I turned around, an older guy was dancing beside me and I immediately felt intimidated by his arrogance. He had obviously been watching us and wanted to show us what he could do but with that attitude no way. "He was going to have to earn his piece of floor!" Wearing a waistcoat, white dress shirt with black suit trousers. To me he looked like a bouncer and totally out of place. He started to clear an area on the packed floor. His style was more graceful and artistic, catching his icy glare as we danced side by side. I could tell right away he didn't like me, the feeling went both ways I didn't like him either. At the end of the record I came off the floor, I wanted to watch his style of dancing it really was that different to mine. He was obviously old school and I wanted to learn more.

"Who the fuck's that Gethro?!" Darb at the edge of the floor standing by my side with the same question I had.

"I haven't got a clue mate. Who cares?" My pride still dented, changing the subject, "This new DJ's playing some good sounds man."

"It's that guy Richard Searling, the one we talked about. Look he's in that pit."

Richard keeping the atmosphere holding the crowd on the floor with sounds we had heard but not all. Our attention now focused on the dancer who had took command of the floor. Marsha Gee "Baby, I Need You, P. P. Arnold "Everything's Gonna Be Alright", Paula Parfitt "Love Is Wonderful", The Poppies "There's A Pain In My Heart", Towanda Barnes "You Don't Mean It" his intensity for the music flowing onto the floor.

"I don't know who that guy is Darb but you got to give it to him, for an old guy he can dance." He had that drifting style we had seen so many times from The Torch boys but he danced with more grace to define his moves. Jumping in the air to land in a spin which I had never seen anyone do before, using his arms to express his movements flowing to the music. Clapping his hands in a face of passion at exactly the right time and place to records he obviously knew. Even he struggled, we could see the floor was killing him as he too spun off fighting to hold his balance. As a dancer I felt his pain.

"Look at the way he goes into a spin Darb, jumping up crossing his legs then into a spin when he lands keeping a figure four as he spins out. I like that style and his footwork, it's different."

"Yea I know. It's more like Kim's he's got that skipping style."

"You clocked it, me too but the way he jumps into a spin wait till we show Jako, he'll freak! Kim's gonna love it here Darb and Jako if he can get the room."

"That's the problem Gethro. If they can get the room."

"If we don't get it we'll make it!" We were impressed and watched, we would practice later. I learned a lot from that night. Studying his technique, especially his hand movements which I had never seen anyone do before. This alone adding another dimension to the dancing one I had never even thought of and definitely impressed me the most.

"Come on Gethro, we've watched long enough. Let's hit the floor man, let's show him what we can do!"

"You Hit Me (Right Where It Hurt Me)" by Alice Clark blasting all around us, the sound system crystal clear cries of, "what a tune!" between us putting us back amongst the dancers we rejoined the crowded floor. He immediately stopped dancing as if he had proved his point. As we passed our eyes locked for a brief moment. The face of a dancer I would come to know well.

I was impressed but I would practice and he too would come to know mine. It was obvious we weren't liked by some of the older crowd. We had respect but if they gave us none then we didn't give a shit and they would not get ours. The days of backing down were now over. We were the young upstarts, new faces to the scene, a new generation so be it but we weren't going away. Little did we know very soon we would meet on a much bigger floor and next time there would be no excuses. Two of us from The Catacombs would dance on an open floor and neither one of us would give an inch.

Timothy Wilson "Love Is Like An Itching In My Heart", Kenny Bernard "What Love Brings", Jo Armstead "I Feel An Urge Coming On", Jimmy Bee "Wanting You", The Drifters "You Gotta Pay Your Dues", The Younghearts "A Little Togetherness", and George Carrow "Angel Baby (You Don't Even Love Me)" more sound we knew and loved. As we turned up the energy I could feel eyes burning into me, I knew we were being watched.

We were different, more athletic in our approach combining fast feet to the music, it blended well but we danced nowhere near to what we could do. The odd splits and drop-back, no combinations, held back by the floor. There was little we could do but by now we didn't care. Just being in a different club amongst all the new faces, this place had an atmosphere all of its own and the sounds to us were bang on. We left the floor to get a drink, descending into the darkness a world of chrome and polish full of bodies and carpet dancers. In the crowd there was little room, Soulies stopping to chat strangers we never knew their accents making us laugh.

"First time someone called me duck Gethro."

"I know and "Pall" do I look like a tin of dog meat? Their accents are right out there, Northern mate but they are really friendly, some of the girls."

Darb interrupted, "Don't start Gethro!"

"Just sayin'!" Darb bursting to a smile as he always did.

Both of us saturated from the heat in the club and just being out on the floor. We wandered around laughing at the antics of what we saw in the dimness of the alcoves. Couples entangled in the darkness the girls with skirts riding high.

"Jammy bastard, look at her now. She's nice man." nudging Darb my face brightened to a smile.

"I couldn't do that mate, well I could but not in the open like that." He too now smiling at what we had seen.

"Yea I know, bit too open for me but in the dark you can have some fun man."

"It's a bit much though, seems out of place to me Gethro. I mean it's all about the music man not the women."

"Yea I know what you mean. Wonder if all the all-nighters are like this?

Imagining the fun that would bring?"

"No I don't think so, the bouncers will jump on it." Both of us smiling at the openness of what was going on in the shadows around us. I felt a little jealous as we made our way back to the floor passing more Soulies we turned straight into Big Willie, at last a face from The Cats.

"Man, you two made it!"

"Told you we would come." I replied shaking hands, our faces glowing with pride. Big Willie was as big a name as you could get and knew everyone on the scene. If he spoke to you it meant something, he was a real cool guy. Tall, well over six foot six his hair in the helmet of a space man full of the afro style. The slim features of his drawn face complemented his tall skinny frame. An open friendly personality, he always wore a smile.

We had nothing but respect for him from that first day we met in The Cats. Straight away he introduced us to some of the Bolton lads who were standing near an alcove. Brent, Hank, Robbie, Budgie, Tall Martin well over six feet and Titch just above his waist the smallest standing at his side. Their wide eyes and darting expressions making me smile. I knew right away they were all smashed. Commenting on our Cats badges and wanting to know where we're from we instantly felt accepted by their friendliness and open nature.

"Anyone know who that guy was dancing earlier, the one in the waistcoat?" I asked turning to the group around me, inquisitive to put a name to the face.

"Yea that's Booper from The Wheel, one of the best dancers on the scene." Brent replied.

"So that's why he came and danced by us Gethro. Well at least we pissed him off so he must think we're good." Me and Darb feeling a sense of satisfaction at what had transpired.

"This DJ playing the tunes, is he the resident? Where's he from lads?"

"Richard Searling always comes up with new sounds, Pall local lad from Bolton top DJ round here Gethro." Tall Martin's accent making us smile.

"I saw you spinning earlier with Shawn Martin, you're pretty good dancers mate."

"Shawn's a good lad Gethro." Darb nodding in agreement, both of us suitably impressed. "Floors shit but you get used to it." To me I couldn't see how.

"How'd you get here?" Brent asked turning to us taking a swig of his Coke.

"In style man, Escort GT." Darb's voice coming from behind me before I could give a reply.

"Tell him he had better sleep in it. Cars like that disappear round here." He smiled in a friendly warning.

"It's ok Brent. We got it covered." I burst out laughing at Darb's comment, neither one of us saying a word.

"Hey up! Lot of squad in here man." Brent watching a bouncer scanning the club, I could sense his uneasiness. "You two be careful!"

"We will. Cheers Brent." I almost asked them about gear but held back feeling embarrassed at my lack of knowledge and not wanting to feel like a Div.

"Willie, where's Ric Tic?"

"He's over there Gethro with some of the Wolvo lads." Willie pointing to the alcoves at the far side of the room.

"Tell him we'll come over later, got to dance, you know us." Our goodbyes in words of "Keep the faith." An instant bond in our friendship, words of encouragement at our dancing, parting hands in the Northern style. The atmosphere all around us, a shared feeling of togetherness we moved forward on through the all-nighter deeper into the Northern crowd.

"Darb, nice people man. See their eyes, their pupils were like dinner plates. They were massive, did you understand them?"

"Hardly a word at times, it's their accents Gethro."

"I know." We started laughing. "I mean if gear does that to you, I don't know man. They talked fast and mumbled a lot."

"I know gear must do that but we saw them earlier and they were pretty good dancers Gethro."

"Yea there's that side to it!" "Just Like The Weather" by Nolan Chance, the beats driving us together, the smile on our faces to echoes of "hear it man" as we dropped back into the sea of clapping hands and dancers, held there by the DJ defying the piece of shit floor. Sam & Kitty "I've Got Something Good", Rocky Roberts and The Airedales "Just Because Of You", Father's Angels "Bok To Bach", Diane Brooks "In My Heart", The Jive Five "You're A Puzzle", The Sapphires "The Slow Fizz", Carl Douglas "Serving A Sentence Of Life", Rose Batiste "Hit & Run", and Lee Andrews & the Hearts "Never The Less" the atmosphere intensifying into a sea of passion as the night went on and on. Then suddenly a voice full of emotion causing us to turn and look at the DJ. His face showing resentment and anguish, a quiver in his voice as he announced.

"This is the last record for the night. I'm, I'm sorry the club will be closing. I am deeply sorry, there will be no all-nighter."

"What! What'd he say?! Did he say it's closing Darb? What the fuck? No way man!"

An explosion of noise and boos in the darkness, angry shouts filling the crowded club. Lynne Randell "Stranger In My Arms" filtering onto the dance floor, faint words echoing from Soulies surrounding us. We danced the night as we had started to finish out on the floor "Hey don't look away look in my eyes no not above me", slowly voices of defiance rising from the crowd. Our hearts heavy with sadness reflecting the mood of the club, feelings we could not control.

Hand claps of dissent resentment from the dancers this was our music, a togetherness, a brotherhood from the floor. Shawn, Martin, Titch, and Brent, the Bolton lads, Darb and Booper, all of us packed the floor a bond in our dancing. The words louder, our hearts feeling the emotion tears from some of the dancers, the significance of the night. "...all I see could be true who are you making me cry now stranger stranger...", voices all around us, the words crystal clear lingering then gradually fading away. The record ending to slow hand claps then a silence from the floor. A shared look of disgust Darb and me wrapped in the sentiment of our surroundings.

We found ourselves standing amongst a group of Soulies. In the light we felt naked all around us a sea of dejected faces. Some held our stare, expressions written with anguish, others feeling as we did angry and depressed at our night that had been lost. The bouncers wasting little time moving Soulies to the stairs at the far end of the club.

"Come on, the night's over. Everybody out! Come on move along!" loud voices telling everyone to leave.

"Gethro this ain't right man." Darb's face as mine, in disbelief.

"Our first all-nighter Darb. Our first fuckin all-nighter and this bollocks!"

"The badge Gethro! We never got the badge!"

"Shit!"

We turned around to face a crowd milling around a bar illuminated in the light at the far end. I noticed a commotion. "Quick Darb over here. Get a badge!" I raced over, lost in a jostling crowd of people, a bouncer selling badges. I dived forward thrusting our money barely reaching his outstretched hand. Turning away I held our prize, we had been to Va-Va. "Look at this Darb!" My face in sheer delight, there in my hand I held two badges. In the center set against a red background the white letters Va-Va, around the edge a blue circle more white letters in capitals All-Night Soul Bolton.

We instantly felt special, it made a statement, it gave us history we had danced on that floor. Now we felt better our first real soul badge one we had travelled for. We would wear it with pride! All had not been lost, at last we had got rid of the label, we had arrived. "Now call me a fuckin Div!" "We did it together Darb, you and me." He turned to me with that smile of his, crossing our hands in a hug, the bond of our friendship.

"I know Gethro. It's always was going to be just you and me."

The club in semidarkness we gathered our bags, joining other Soulies moving towards the door. The atmosphere so different now the magic of the night over slipping away in an instant, but we would never forget we had been there. Pausing by the door to look into the club once more I kissed my finger pointing to the dance floor. Two Soul brothers, a shared smile between us silent thoughts saying good bye. We turned away moving along the corridor climbing the stairs with other stragglers. Feeling the coolness of morning air we ventured around mingling with the crowds outside.

It felt strange talking to Soulies from all over the country, two years ago we had been fighting on the terraces at the matches. Now we had been mixing in a club feeling nothing but the friendship of total strangers. That was the power of the music and the scene before us pushing all barriers and boundaries aside. A different scene opposite to street life, slowly sucking away at the skinhead revolution. Here only a love of music and an expression in our hearts that we wanted to dance. Last Tuesday now seemed so far away from this new world we had discovered. We had never heard the records played anywhere but The Cats. Va-Va did that to me and

Darb, opening the doors to a new scene and the underground network of clubs that were playing just Northern Soul. Once again the drug squad had played a hand closing The Torch and now outside Va-Va searching and harassing the crowd. As we stood and watched anger welled up inside me. I had an instant hatred for them and their authority as they dismantled the friendship that was before us.

"What's up with that wanka! I mean they're just picking on anybody!" Darb's voice showing the anger I felt inside.

"Yea I know we got to go, I feel like steaming some bastard!" We had to leave, I knew we would get in trouble if we stayed. We wandered around past crowded coaches of Soulies to find Giddy fast asleep, oblivious to it all.

"What's going on? I thought you said it was all night."

"It was Giddy, till these wankers showed up," pointing to the cops as we left the car park flashing lights in every direction getting a second look as we drove away.

"The cops up here don't mess about Gethro."

"Yea I know Darb." We turned to watch everything happening around us, passing cars pulled over open searches at the side of the road.

Little did they know, their efforts were worthless. What started so long ago as a tiny ripple at The Wheel, The Pink Flamingo, Beachcomber, Nottingham, The Torch and other clubs before it had gained momentum growing stronger all the time. Now in the distance a massive tidal wave was about to hit them and they never saw it coming. As many drug squads of the seventies were unprepared for the storm called Northern Soul.

We sped down the M6, the cassette now turned down low the only sound the slight murmur of Darb fast asleep in the back seat. I glanced at Giddy a face of concentration his hands locked tightly to the wheel. Our adventure now over I had time to reflect in the stillness of the car. The headlights pushing us forward into the darkness, the bright lights of the dashboard bringing back memories of so long ago.

Rivers of thoughts, my childhood and the orphanage came flooding into my mind, to be pushed back to the dark place they had come from. Too painful even now to reflect upon, happiness that was not there. What had brought them to me, was it the friendship I had just left behind? The feeling of belonging to a family, of the togetherness that must bring? I was a stranger trapped in my own mind. Love? What is love? An emotion, a feeling I would find hard to understand. Was I capable of love? Love for Kim? Love for my parents? What parents? The bastards who left me in the orphanage, not even leaving their names or the two strangers I shared my life with. I lived with them, there was no bond between us only the constant arguments and comments about Kim.

Feelings of anger rising inside fueled by words that had been said. Who were they to tell me how to run my life when they had accomplished so little with theirs?! I paid rent, I was a boarder a stranger in the confines of that concrete shoebox, one that they called a home. I despised them as they gave me nothing but emptiness. No memories of a childhood, no pictures on the wall! This was my real world, one I had created and now I had Kim who loved me so dearly yet I was incapable of giving love in return. I didn't understand it. To love someone, did it mean you cared about them? That you thought of them all the time?

I had feelings for Kim, I felt a glow of pride when I was with her deep inside sometimes to feel so happy and loved but always to return to a loneliness, a shadow that would never leave my side. Had the sexual abuse of the foster home twisted my mind, affecting my emotions forever? A tear trickled down my face at my despair. Why won't you leave me alone? I felt dirty, tarnished, I just took what I wanted from girls. Always to return to cheating and lying, to destroy everything around me, to close the window to my heart. Was this how I protected myself, by taking revenge? The rejection of a mother and the sexual abuse had affected me deeply, holding me back from the love I felt inside. I was unable to give my heart to anyone as it was something that had been abused and destroyed. Love was a stranger to me, a faceless figure in my dreams someone to be kept at a distance in a feeling of mistrust. One I would never get to know as always in the past she had only ever shown me pain. Yet Kim with her pure love saw something deep within me and was determined to hold onto what she had found. I felt different from other people finding strength in loneliness, of a need for no one. A feeling that I was never really alone. Now my friends were the family I never had. A carousel of thoughts constantly turning, relentlessly

"Gethro, you're quiet mate. What's up?!"

"Oh nothing Giddy, just thinking." I leaned forward to turn the cassette up. "This is a good tune Giddy. Hey, got our finals coming up next year. Been a long time mate."

"Four years Gethro."

"I know and you still can't weld!"

"Fuck you mate!"

"No you can, just got to learn how to set your amps. You're as good as me mate, it's all about setting the rig." We had come a long way me and Giddy both of us were good at our trade. It meant everything to me, I had to pass that exam I had to set myself up for life.

"What's, what's going on? Where are we?"

"Just outside Wolvo. You slept all the way. Man, you're ugly when you wake up Darb." He rubbed his eyes, molding his face back to recondition. I waited in anticipation for the reply I knew was coming my way.

"Better than being like you Gethro. You're ugly all the time." Our laughter filling the car.

"It's not far now Darb."

"You be in The Octopus later?"

"Don't know, depends on Kim. I have to see her when we get back."

"Oh yea? Well if not I'll catch you in The Cats tonight. Don't forget your badge."

"I won't, don't worry. That's why I am seeing Kim, I want her to sew my badge on. She's brilliant at sewing."

"I bet she is."

"I said sewing Darb."

"Really?"

"Really?" As we laughed at my embarrassment, Darb knew me better than anyone as my mind wandered back to the alcoves I knew I would be late for The Cats. Little did I know my life was about to change. Dancing would lead me to new heights I never dreamed of and friendships beyond my dreams.

Chapter 24

TOO LATE

"No, he jumped up landed with his legs crossed then powered into a spin in one move, honest and he kept a figure four. Tell him Darb." My voice hardly heard above the music and atmosphere of The Cats of a typical Saturday night.

"What was he just a spinner or what Gethro?"

"No he had some good moves Jako, but this one we got to crack. The guy could spin with style."

"Show me again." Jako watched intently as they stood to the side of the speakers, the only room we had as I tried to show him the move once more. Moving out onto the floor twisting my feet mixing my footwork, copying the graceful style I had seen. A flick of hands turning into an arc before the jump, stopping with my legs crossed to emphasize my point. My hands outstretched parallel to my shoulders, a slight bend at the knees as once more I jumped into the spin.

"See his feet and arms when he landed Jako?"

"I got it man." Darb pointing to me as I ended up amongst other dancers. It felt strange spinning with my hands on hips and elbows out, once again I had lost control. Jimmy and Winston laughing at my efforts. Darb and Jako in deep conversation, Jako's legs crossed imitating my move.

My hands held up apologizing to dancers around me, embarrassment in their smiles. "I'll get it. You'll see!" Looking at Jimmy in my defense, but I too had to laugh. It was a feeble effort, I now knew the move had to flow in one movement turning the split second on landing was the key.

This would not only give you the speed but also help with balance. "Now you have a go Jako." My voice enthusiastic as he waited eagerly for a gap to appear in the floor. I smiled at our little group, out of all of us he was the best spinner. Sometimes hitting double figure spins but like all spinners he wanted to go faster, his mind intoxicated with speed. Knowing only too well from watching me that how you turned into this move was critical.

We could all spin but this was a completely different style one none of us had ever seen. I stood to the side joining Darb, wrapping my arms around Kim. A feeling of pride engulfed me, at times she made me so happy. Our lips in silent whispers, "I love you" written thoughts in our hearts.

"Quick Kim dive in here!" Winston handing his space a smile between them, she slid from my arms to the crowded floor. Kim had an air about her even at this early age she easily stood out in the club. She always dressed to dance and tonight was no different. Her skirt with length and matching V-neck top perfect for the heat of the club. The platforms replaced with canvas shoes, ones she called her "grannies," ideal for the unforgiving floor. She glided along effortlessly in front of our little band.

I too felt a glow of satisfaction at what we had achieved. We had moved up in stature amongst the younger crowd, people were beginning to mention our name. Va-Va did that for me and Darb, it put us in the lime light with the younger crowd. We moved in the direction I wanted to go built on two things, recognition for our dancing and respect from the floor. We had got off our arses and travelled out of The Cats finding a much bigger scene and tonight more than ever I felt on top of our game.

With our matching colored vests and the badges from Va-Va Darb and me felt special. Up till now only The Torch boys had travelled, we had been to an all-nighter none of the younger crowd had. Last night put us with history, our badge giving us instant fame. We belonged on this floor an area we had earned, one we had made our own. The mood in the club of togetherness steaming bodies saturated with atmosphere typical of a Saturday night.

Once again in the oven of The Catacombs our bodies being boiled alive.

Heat in the club unbearable, draining what energy I had. Showers of sweat from spinners in the dim lights of the dance floor, one at lightning speed. A blurred figure of emotion, a chimney brush of hair Squeaks spins dominating the floor. The Cats packed to capacity, music of the DJs and dancers in a class of their own. Jako nodded, a smile between us not really the place to practice we both knew what we had to achieve. Our move attracting attention young Soulies crossing the floor. Canny, Knave, Jamo, Bin Man, and Woolfy working the space around us trying to give us more room. Now the floor didn't seem as small we stood watching Jako hit some really good spins.

"Maybe he needs more talc Gethro?" Darb grabbing the talc off the speaker his face with a wicked grin.

"Yea definitely mate." A devious smile between us a quick sprinkle just in front of me before Jako had time to see.

"You nearly had it Jako, try once more!" I edged him on we just had to do it, our faces in anticipation of what was about to come. Jako turning on landing crashing into dancers, a bowling ball out of control to our laughter and sounds of, "You bastards!" Throwing my arms around him upon his eventual return. "Sorry Jako! I couldn't help it!"

"Gethro, I owe you one!" He too caught up in our laughter, he knew the joke was on him. I wished he had been with us last night then we could have taken them all on. Even now I knew as individuals we were good but as a group we would be unbeatable on the floors to come. Although still a little raw we were getting better and better every week. Jako was our spinner, faster than me but I too would practice and besides I had ideas of my own.

Booper had opened my eyes to a new style of dancing, one I wanted to pursue. On a Saturday it was tight, yet on the floor we were now being given room that's the respect we had earned for our dancing. Kim once again hitting the floor showing she wasn't just a pretty face in our little band, but a dancer who could hold her own. I had shown her earlier that afternoon how I had seen Booper's hand movements. Sometimes reaching from his waist the arc into a spin moves that had impressed me the most.

We often practiced at her home, now as I watched my student she never missed a beat. The flowing style of a natural dancer only one with really fast feet. Her expressions to the music were different. She danced totally immersed in the record her long skirt only adding to her movement. That of a floating skipping style, one she had made her very own. I looked at

Jimmy whose face as mine was beaming with pride.

"She's good man." Wiping his face of sweat, he too had just come off the floor. "You taught her well Gethro."

"I showed her the basics but really she taught herself Jimmy. She picks things up fast man. I can't keep up with her look at her feet, that's fast! Wait till Booper sees her." Jimmy slapping my shoulder his face as always in smiles.

"Tellin' you man, she'll blow you off the floor one day!"

"What! No way, no way Jimmy I can't have that! No way man, I'll I never live it down!" We laughed together at this scenario that's the way we were.

There was no leader here, we were all individuals that fed off one another. We helped each other with that inner rivalry with one goal to dance and be the best. In our group we respected one another for what you could do, what you brought to the floor. Who you were, not who you thought you were. That was the relationship we had. Sure we wanted to beat each other but it was never that important to us. Most of the time it was about friendship that youthful bond of being together. We were all young kids riding the wave of Northern Soul. We had no history, we were making our own. I was determined to take the styles of dancing we had seen to a new level by mixing all the moves together to create a new style of my own. To do this you had to more than just feel this music, every record had to own your feet. This was crystal clear as we watched Kim pour her heart out, once more stealing the floor.

Deep inside I knew this wasn't going to do for us with the style of dancing I wanted to pursue. The stark reality of what lay before me. We had already out grown this floor. The Cats on a Wednesday, The Ship, The Octopus and The Duck all the places we practiced for what. If we can't bring it all together there was no point. In my heart I knew we needed a bigger venue and I was going to find one. A dance floor we could explode on, one that would give us more room. Va-Va had opened that door to all-nighters and I was determined to step through it with Kim.

Little did I know how close we were and how big that door would be. My attitude about gear had changed as I had watched that car park unfold last night, "Cops who are they to tell me what I can and can't do?!" I had eaten rules every day with my porridge in the orphanage, words of defiance echoing around in my head. This was my life, I would do what I wanted no one was going to tell me what to do! Gear was another world to explore, one we had backed away from full of rules to be broken. "You should not do this," only made things worse for me. The more rules that made it illegal only added to the quest to become a part of it and the exclusive club that it was. I looked at dancers smashed around me once again, more than ever I wanted to be a part of their world. Their faces of excitement and energy their bond of togetherness reminding me of last night. How did they feel? What was it like? What do I need to take? But most of all, who has some?

Leaving Kim with Darb and Jako I wandered alone to get my answers. Through the crowd into the darkness music of the night behind me I moved deeper into the club.

"Gethro!"

"Pixie!" Another young Soulie from The Octopus, new faces to The Cats. A fiery little character from Wolvo with a heart as straight as a die, crossing hands in the Northern style our handshake turning to hugs.

"Heard about you going to Va-Va. What's it like?"

"Brilliant crowd Pix but the floors shit! Too small, Richard Searling and Martin Ellis DJ'd, the sounds were bang on though."

"How'd you get there? On your Scrott?"

"No way," the thought of that making me smile, "my mate Giddy give us a lift. Darb came as well, any way I'm selling it if you know anyone."

"Why what's up?"

"Nothing, need a car mate if I'm going to all-nighters. Got to pass my test, I need a set of wheels. Anyway look around, how many scooter boys in here Pix?" Pointing to the dance floor as if to emphasize my point. "We're Soul boys, man we're different! We don't ride scrotts anymore, we just steal cars." Both of us starting to laugh.

"Yea I know what you mean, lot of people dumping their scrotts. I'll ask around mate. Forty quid?"

"Yea if you know anyone, forty five you take a deal. Hey Pix talking about deals, anyone got any gear?"

"I haven't but I heard there's some Filon about." His voice now lower in tone.

"What they like?"

"Smooth man." My heart missed a beat. Was I really this close? "What they look like?"

"Little orange tablets, look like tic tacs. Be careful, you know what it's like in here man."

"Cheers Pix. Who's got em?" Eagerness in my question.

"You know the score Gethro, no names." His face breaking to a weary smile, "just keep going that way," pointing to the back of the stage. Parting in a handshake, our grip the bond of our trust. "Later."

"Later man."

We had made quite a network of friends, especially amongst the younger crowd. They too were beginning to make a mark, creating a new scene of their own. The scene was a grapevine as ever news travelled fast, albeit underground but it travelled. I was surprised it was easy to spot Soulies who were smashed tonight, it was much harder to find the ones that weren't. The place was kicking with conversations all of them wrapped in gear. Ever inquisitive I soon found out why.

There had been a rumor that a local chemist had gone down and by the feel from the floor the atmosphere they created there was more gear than usual in the club. I made my way to the back of the stage stopping to chat with other Soulies around me, following the trail of names. A figure I instantly recognized even in the subdued light his nervousness and darting expressions told me right away he was smashed. I burst out laughing, "Ronnie!" Our smiles the depth of our friendship we crossed hands in the Northern style.

I had known Ronnie awhile and trusted him. He was one of the lads from Stoke, a Torch boy about our age. A really good dancer he too knew the score with The Catacombs, the unwritten rules as he hung out at the back of the club. One night he had felt the full force of the older crowd and remembered it only too well. After being kicked about on the pavement outside and politely relieved of his gear. The Northern Scene wasn't just nicey nicey, at times you had to watch your back!

"Ronnie how you doing man? What you up to, you're usually on the floor?"

"Nice one Gethro. You go to Va-Va last night?" Ignoring my question pointing to my badge. "I heard it got busted."

"It did, we watched em outside. Fuckin wankers they came from everywhere." I lowered my voice to those around us. "Hey talking about squad, anyone got any gear? I could do with some I'm knackered from last night." He looked around yet in the darkness we were invisible. I felt safe amongst the younger crowd, the perfect place to do a deal.

"I got some dex and a few filon but I sold out of the blueys man, Fuckin SKF! They went fast!" His voice quieter now causing me to lean forward.

"Ronnie it's like a shop with you man." A sense of anticipation came over me, for some reason I started to laugh. "I mean watch yourself in here, you know what it's like. How much for the dex?"

"I've only got eighteen left, give me three quid." I smiled as I gave him the money, my eyes darting in every direction constantly looking for bouncers and unwanted figures in the crowd. Ronnie's face in twisted expressions counting so hard to do. The small yellow tablets filling the cup of my hands.

"Nice one man!" Inquisitive I tried to look at one.

"Gethro not here. Go to the bogs!"

"Sorry mate!" Placing them gently into my pocket, a feeling of energy and happiness came over me. I counted the tablets one more time. Sifting them through my fingers the little flat tablets hard to the touch. At last I had some drugs right here in my hand. I felt uneasy, nervous yet excited, now I just wanted to get smashed.

I was at the door of their exclusive club. There was no one behind me here saying, "Hey, you have to buy these drugs!" In the darkness of the club I had found Ronnie, I had tracked him down so who's the pusher here? It's a load of bollocks! I had made my decision, it's my fuckin life and I will do whatever I want. It's my choice, I came to him it's entirely up to you, in the world of Northern Soul, no one pushes drugs! And to me "push" was a dirty word. It's just supply and demand! If you wanted gear you had to find it and it wasn't always that easy. I had got lucky this time but I had a feeling even then this would not be the last time.

"Ronnie, we're all by the speakers man, come over."

"I will Gethro. I'll be over later."

"Nice one." We parted in the Northern style, my smile as wide as the dance floor as I made my way back through the crowd. I felt strange as if everyone knew, yet in the darkness surely no one could have seen a thing. Our little band at the side of the dance floor Kim chatting to Jimmy, laughing as I approached. The heat of the crowd unbearable, Winston and Jako hitting some spins. A lovers' embrace between us drawing Kim closer to me a whispered excitement in my voice.

"I just got some gear," my voice quivered in emotion thoughts of what that would bring, "I just got some dex." Kim's smile an expression full of mischief, one of total surprise. Soft hands drawing me near her eyes searching mine for answers to the trust she had to give.

Uttering very softly, "Then let's go and take some dex lover." In that simple sentence she tore down all the barriers we had put around us. As we walked away from the dance floor we left the past behind. I knew now more than ever no matter what I did she would always be by my side. In the soft light of the alcove we sat on the edge of a table. Our bodies steaming with heat smiles of affection between us watching the night go by. A face full of simplicity, trust in those steel blue eyes the look of "butter wouldn't melt in my mouth." I knew now she had a wild side, one I had not seen. Swallowing our tablets together we would come up at the same time. We looked at one another and kissed just like any couple but I knew in my heart we weren't.

"Darb, come here!" Catching him just as he passed the alcove waving my hand I called him inside.

"What's up?"

"I just got some dex. Six a quid." My voice lower, now a smile of achievement crossing my face.

"Who off?"

"I love you man but I can't tell. Let's say these are good, do you want em? We've have had ours, it's up to you."

"You had some Kim?"

"Of course I have, whatever you do I'm going to do." Adding in a playful way "I can't let you two have all the fun Darb." Betraying a wicked smile his look of surprise making us laugh.

"How many you taking?"

"Just six. You know we don't want to get too smashed, anyway it'll pick you up a bit. Help get over last night."

"Nice one man." I slid them into his hand, passing him my Coke. "Guess I won't need a drink now."

"Fuck off Darb. That's mine."

"Ours!" Kim's chipping into our laughter. "Told you if I found some."

"Nice one Gethro. I'm gonna get a Coke. I'll see you later."

"Get three. We'll be back on the floor."

It felt good to be on the wrong side of the law, a payback for Va-Va. A feeling I would become used to. Little did I know the journey I had just begun. We rejoined the other dancers Ronnie talking to Jimmy making me glance at his sideward look.

"Gethro, you're bad man!"

"I know Jimmy." He could read me like a book. I smiled at their closeness, he too wasn't the only one who could read.

I felt guilty after all the speeches I had made as if I had let people who had listened and myself down. We were dead against drugs but times change and the way I was feeling right now drove any guilt away. Very slowly a strange feeling, a surge of energy rose up from inside me. Intensified by the heat around me flowing through my body yet I knew I could contain it. The feeling wasn't running away with me, I was in total control my senses were sharper. I looked at Kim her eyes clearer, bigger, brighter, her face full of enthusiasm for the music. We constantly chatted watching dancers from the side of the floor.

"Kim, are my eyes big?"

"Yes." An inquisitive expression on her face as she stared into my eyes.

"Are mine?"

"Yours look really big. Your pupils are massive lover, there's no blue left at all. You look smashed!" Smiles bringing us closer together, our eyes locked to say, "I love you."

The night and gear taking over, sweeping us onto the floor. Pep's voice screaming down the mic, driving the atmosphere playing with the crowd. As requested "Too Late" by Larry Williams & Johnny Guitar Watson, pure vinyl from The Torch. The notes felt clearer, sharper, my feet felt lighter and my balance at first sluggish became totally under control. Now that move wasn't so hard. I jumped up crossing my legs and in one movement powering into a spin my feet never moved from the spot now they were glued to the floor. Coming out of the spin with my hands on hips to the smiles of Darb and Jako. Clapping hands with other dancers feeling elated.

I felt that bond of happiness of belonging on this floor. Looking around at other Soulies, the younger crowd with those same wide eyed expressions. So this was what it was all about, being straight didn't appeal to me so much anymore. We had made it to that exclusive club now I had all my answers. I liked being smashed, this new feeling as it put me right where I wanted to be, on a dance floor with energy to burn.

We all danced with more intensity joining the mood of the night. Our little band in a world of our own, our friendship like never before. Wanting the night to last, one that should never end. The music drove me to a high I never dreamed of, the atmosphere all around us Kim dancing right by my side. Our hearts as one on the dance floor feeling it would last forever in the sea of arms and clapping hands. Dancers soaked in happiness drenched in emotion all of us wanting more. Held in the music of The Catacombs the night as always slipped through our fingers, ending too soon.

Chapter 25

ANYTHING YOU WANT, ANYWAY YOU WANT IT

Wolvo was a strange place on a Saturday, the town center ignited in running battles and sporadic violence echoing around the town. Only last season Tottenham fans had decided to invade The Octopus to be met with a barrage of bottles and glasses as we drove them out the door. Feeling the full force of Soulies as we showed them we too could steam.

Caught in the middle of two bars the exchange spilling into the street cops trying to control the fighting. "Nowhere to run, nowhere to hide." I hope it doesn't happen this year, the memory still fresh in my mind. They had intruded on us, we wanted nothing to do with this football shit all we wanted was to be left alone.

It was safe to walk around on a Saturday if Wolves were playing away but at home it was entirely different matter. Wolves were in the first division, The North Bank had a big following, a massive army of Skins. If you turned the wrong corner you easily got caught up in the fights of opposing fans.

Feeling aloof to all of this mayhem was us after Va-Va nothing felt the same, it just didn't! Fashion was pulling in all directions Northern had really started to take off. The Octopus, a shining light, an island of soul. To us the only pure Northern bar in the town. Now, more than ever there were divisions in the town, we were Soulies, they were skins and now we were a million miles apart. The pointed umbrellas, Dr. Martens, the ever pressed crombie crews held no interest to us. Fashion was a joke and the music in the charts what! "Ballroom Blitz" by The Sweet, maybe for the masses but not for this Soul boy! Gone were the Ben Sherman's, Levis and loafers.

My wardrobe had changed but it wasn't for the sake of fashion. We wanted our own clothes and one thing that dominated our choice now, loose fit, freedom to move. No ball splitting Levis or Stay Press, our trousers were twenty four inch parallels, twin pleats always tailor made. A bomber jacket and our most precious things, dancing shoes and a vest. The wardrobe of a Soul boy everything else didn't matter. We had changed deep inside belonging to another world but now one sentence dominated the conversation.

The younger crowd started to make their mark from the dance floor of The Catacombs that bond now carried to the streets. The Octopus, The Duck, The George, and The Tavern a greeting of three words wherever we went, "keep the faith." We always greeted each other with a handshake of crossed hands it was our connection and link to the Northern Scene. The significance of this was twofold. One it meant you were into the music of the Soul scene but just as important to us it meant you were into gear. A secret handshake in a way as we met up in bars and discos scattered around the town.

A new drug culture grew up in Wolvo fueled by the younger crowd. Right under the noses of the drug squad and they hadn't got a clue. It meant you were different and that's exactly how you felt in an underground scene dominated by music, dancing and if you could get them drugs.

My attitude about gear had changed, I felt no shame it was a part of the night. I had tried to score gear on a few occasions since our last time in The Cats, each time I got ripped off! I just didn't get it, was it me did I have Div written across my head? I don't know! It's as if we the younger crowd was there for the taking and with the little knowledge we had in the respect of gear we were. This didn't go unnoticed by me and one thing it did was it drove the younger crowd closer together. We looked out for one another and started to build our own scene within the scene, one with our own set of rules.

We learned the hard way of who we could trust, not all the older crowd was like this but to some we were still just Divs. It really pissed me off! It wasn't about the money or the drugs, it was respect we just didn't do that to one another. We were a family there were rules and now more than ever I distanced myself from the older crowd and decided to go my own way. If you crossed me now you would only do it once. I learned from the street not everyone was your friend but most of all who your real enemy was and just by observation how the drug squad worked.

The drug squad were really helpful and quite naive in their approach. As soon as a chemist went down they would flood like unwanted sewer rats sniffing in all the bars. With their suits and had to be had waistcoats, short back and sides, brill creamed haircuts. Like bouncers at an anorexic convention they easily stood out in the crowd. All they needed was a blue light on their heads they really were that easy to spot. They were just too old to go undercover, there's no way they could penetrate the Northern Scene. Their time spent looking for junkies, anyone from the street they needed information informants their only way.

I would get to know my enemy well as they appeared around the town. I knew they were just doing their job, problem was it clashed with my youth. We the young crowd were easily able to spot, them every new Soulie was another set of eyes. Within minutes of walking into a bar I would know what bars they had been to. What they were driving? How many of them? And most importantly, their names? I would always watch for a while then leave, often clocking their surveillance cars parked right opposite The George. I never understood their obsession with British Leyland made vehicles, hence the Austin Princesses, Maxis, and Triumph Dolomites always with two men in the car.

I learned from keeping my eyes open but also from others mistakes I became invisible, a faceless figure in a crowded bar. This learning curve had an influence on me for the future and laid the rules, my rules of how one day I would deal drugs. There was only one problem I hadn't got any and no idea where to find them, my efforts had been fruitless. The squad's methods had obviously worked, Ronnie had now disappeared. We the younger crowd would in time have a huge influence on the drug scene in Wolvo but for now we were just learning the game.

My life at the moment was stagnant. Blues and Soul showing us there were other venues across the country. The Mojo, Sheffield Room at the top, Wigan, Leeds Central, an all-nighter that ran on a Friday, but there was no way I was going anywhere near Leeds! One of the main venues on the scene was the Highland Room at the Blackpool Mecca. Toney Jebb and Les Cokell, two good DJs. Ric Tic had told me about had put it on the map. This had been running a while now but it wasn't an all-nighter, like The Cats it also closed at two. I felt trapped with no transport and little money it seemed best to just stay at The Cats.

We had the records and always had a good time but I was restless and frustrated. It wasn't good enough for me and the dancing was tearing me apart. I couldn't express myself the way I wanted, held back by that tight floor. Yet my love for the music was stronger than ever. I had to escape out of Wolvo, but how? And go where? Basically I hadn't got a clue. Then on September the 23rd a new club called Wigan Casino opened that would change the scene forever. There wasn't much of a fanfare, it was just another club set in the north of England in a little mining town called Wigan. We had seen it advertised in Blues and Soul for a couple of weeks now with a postal application for membership on the bottom of the page.

I smiled when I first saw it. I mean the only thing I remembered about Wigan's claim to fame was George Formby and his ukulele from the music hall days. It held no interest to our little group with a DJ we had never heard of and a list of records that were played at The Cats.

No mention of the dance floor but one thing caught my attention. It was an all-nighter but only open from two till eight which seemed strange to me. That was a long way to go for just six hours and this put me off at first.

The Cats was in full swing at this time, one of the top clubs in the country discovering sounds that other clubs followed. The atmosphere was electric and the nights always packed out. I couldn't blame Jimmy Darb and Jako, why travel? We had one of the best clubs around right on our doorstep but Wigan played in the back of my mind. This was different. An all-nighter, I still felt cheated after Va-Va even if they weren't coming I had made my decision, if I had to I would go it alone and let destiny lead the way.

Chapter 26

OUR FIRST CONTACT WITH WIGAN CASINO

"Watch out!" I grabbed Kim's arm pulling her to the side as a coach eased into the bus stop. "Sorry lover, you ok?" I smiled, Kim's face a little brighter than it had been five seconds ago.

"Whew! I never saw him!" Waving her hand catching what breath she had left.

"I know. That was close, the wanker never signaled I thought he was going straight on."

A couple disembarked to be left standing on the pavement, sport bags at their feet. Windows full of young people the coach pulling away to waved hands and shouts of goodbye. It was Sunday morning, we approached faces I recognized from The Cats. Ever inquisitive I wondered where they have been. His tall figure lost in a long leather coat belt drawn tightly around his waist. Matted, curly hair revealed a face of fear. Wide eyes darting in every direction. Cracked, bleeding lips chewing frantically adding redness to his twitching mouth. His drawn features and sunken cheeks resembled that of a faceless skull.

I squeezed Kim's hand feeling the tenseness of her body, she like me was in total shock. A girl stood at his side her open leather coat revealing the sexless figure of a surfboard, a flat bosomless chest. Their arms interlocking white knuckled hands gripping him tightly, her features devoid of any beauty. Flashing eyes deep and searching never holding my attention for a moment. As we neared he too avoiding eye contact I could see they were off their heads.

"Dave how you doing man? Where you been?" He muttered two words.

"Wigan Casino." His face in constant movement, eyes in a glassy stare.

"What that new place, the one in Blues and Soul?" I could sense his awkwardness avoiding his gaze at every chance I could get. "What's it like?" My voice inquisitive, I had to know more.

"You got to go Gethro. It's fuckin brilliant, you got to go man." His voice mumbling, rambling in tone.

"How'd you get there?"

"On the Cheltenham Coach."

"I never knew one was running? When's the next one?"

"I don't know but Wigan's on every week man, you gotta go."

"What's the music like?"

"Brilliant man, same as The Cats." I could tell my questions were getting on his nerves but I persisted, I wanted to know more.

"Was there many people there?"

"Not really, the place was empty."

"What's the dance floor like?" His attention gone his eyes darting from object to object. The girl growing impatient nervously pulling on his arm, a renewed eagerness to get away.

"See me in The Cats man, I got to go we got to catch our bus!"

As they turned and left we stood in total disbelief I felt sad at what we had just seen. I turned to Kim I could see in her eyes she felt the same way. "You will never see me like that, never! That's too much gear!"

My voice in anger at myself and them, "I mean there's no need to get that smashed and they wonder why they get busted, fuckin idiots! You only had to look at them! Drugs are recreational you treat them with respect. You use drugs they don't use you!"

"Stupid idiots!" Kim shook her head and looked at me a flame of rage a depth of sadness in her eyes, "did you see the girl, she was a mess! Why? I mean you only need enough to last the night and dance, lover not that much surly?"

"I know that was over the top, that's just stupid, anyway the luck I've been having trying to score gear we'll never be like them." Causing her to smile, I too had to laugh easing the tension between us deflating the anger of our mood.

It shook me up, I am glad we met them it's as if it were a sign, a warning and we never forgot that moment. This was a dangerous game we were playing. Jako, Darb, Winston, and Jimmy treated Kim like a sister. If anything ever happened to her I knew I would feel the fullness of their revenge. We weren't going to back away from the drug scene, but if you went too far there was a deadly price to pay.

I vowed to myself there and then no would ever see us like that! Remorse came over me, I looked at Kim her beauty was second to none a reflection of innocence and youth. She was sixteen years old and possessed all the beauty of a young woman who would one day flower to a rose. Steel blue eyes of an angel drawing me forward to the softness of passionate lips.

She was giving her life to me and wanting me in hers. The responsibility was mine, I had to treasure and look after her as I knew the path I would take was full of recklessness and self-destruction. Everything normal didn't exist in my new world. All she ever wanted was to be by my side, to walk that same path and would take nothing less. I had cheated on her with other girls pushing her away not trusting her love, yet she saw something within me and refused to let me go. The strength of her love so deep I had just begun to realize the jewel I held in my hand. As we made our way to Rumpy's I put my arm around her drawing her closer to protect her from all we had just seen. For a brief moment I felt different, a warm glow of togetherness of belonging to a person the happiness that can bring. I liked this new feeling, is this how love really felt?

"Come on lover, let's get a cup of tea that always makes things better! I'll even buy you a cake!" Kim pulling away from my arm, stopping me in my tracks. "Wow, what's up?!"

"This time I'm coming. You promised!"

"Let's have some tea first." Softening my voice, wanting to calm her down. Those steel blue eyes on fire making me feel uneasy, reading my mind like a book.

"NO!" Her face red with anger, tears welled up in her eyes "You said I would come to the next all-nighter! You promised! You said!"

I knew right away I wasn't going to be able to talk her out of it. I had seen that face before! If I went to Wigan Casino, Kim would be by my side. She was coming no matter what! My problem how would we get there? And next, who else would come? I soon got my answers, no one. Everyone was staying at The Cats. The Cheltenham coach wasn't running and we hadn't got any money for the train. So we would have to thumb it, just me and Kim.

Chapter 27

WE WERE MADE FOR EACH OTHER

"You got the memberships Kim?" They had come that day, just in time for us to go tonight. Two small red cards on the front inscrolled letters Wigan Casino Soul Club. We had immediately printed our names and signed them next to the address of the club inside.

"Give them to me lover, that way we won't lose them."

"And what's that supposed to mean?!" Man she was in a sharp mood! I brushed it aside, must be the rain.

We had caught the bus out of town as far as we could go. Now in the darkness we had started our journey along Stafford Road heading on foot towards the M6 North. The rain only light, winter just around the corner a bite of coldness to the night air. I held my sports bag already feeling the cold and cursed, I had everything but my gloves.

We had walked a small distance always putting our thumbs out to the sound of an approaching car. My heart skipping a beat then dropping as they passed us by the sound of the engine fading into the distance, a strange stillness returning to the night.

"We'll get a lift, you'll see next one. I bet you a million pounds."

Kim smiled at my words, her face full of optimism written in adventure she hadn't a care in the world. Wrapped in a fur coat the collar making her headless "You'll scare them away walking like that!" I loved her she always made me laugh. My crombie collar turned up fighting the wind sweeping relentlessly across open fields. We wandered down the road, it had been a while now.

"I love you. You know that don't you!" She turned around her face caught in the headlights of an approaching car. Suddenly the engine dropped its revs, pulling to the side, the window wound down.

"Where you going?" An old gentleman asked.

"Wigan."

"Well I can't give you a lift that far but I can help you on your way. I am passing the M6, will that do?"

"Yes. Cheers mate!"

"Come on jump in." It was then that I looked at the car, an old Jaguar Mark Two I had never seen one this close up. Four interior lights illuminating the inside of the car. The wooden dashboard ablaze in colour clocks and dials neatly set out in rows the overwhelming smell of leather, we instantly sunk in our seats melting in the warmth of the car.

I glanced at Kim in the back seat surrounded in luxury, the looks of a film star her coat of elegance making me smile. We pulled away at speed and tore into the darkness on the front the mascot of a jaguar leaping fearlessly into the night. Wipers crisscrossing, fighting endless rain, I began to wander about my decision. When was it ever going to stop?

"It's a bad night to be out. What's your name?"

"Geoffrey and this is my girlfriend Kim, and yours."

"I'm Sid."

"Have you had the car long?" I asked politely.

"Oh about five years."

"It's beautiful."

"I just love old jags, they don't make them like this anymore." Sid patting the steering wheel with affection as we chatted about the car. He reminded me of someone's dad, a carefree wrinkled expression his head of graying hair. I could see the sign as we approached Gaily Island to the slowing of the car.

"Well thank you Sid. Thanks."

As we disembarked I stood and watched motionless as he drove away "Kim, I'm going to have one of those one day. Now that's what I call a car!"

"I know you will, I have faith in you. That's why I love you."

We turned and made our way to the top of the slip road. Standing for what seemed like hours we snuggled together cursing the rain. The odd car always to speed by our thumbs, chasing shadows long fingers stepping into the night.

"Come on, this is no good!" I started to walk down the slip road.

"No, you can't do that!"

"Yes I can!" By now I had stood long enough, "look its better than just standing in the freezing cold, let's do something!" As we approached the M6 a lorry pulled to the side, my heart lifted and I ran to open the door.

"Quick get in, you'll get me nicked if there's any cops about!"

I grabbed Kim waist lifting her unceremoniously in it to the cab following directly behind her I dived into the front seat quickly slamming the door. I felt elated, at last we were moving again our spirits lifted we chatted to the driver about his life and being on the road. Soon pulling into Knutsford services once again to say goodbye.

"Come on, let's get some tea." That's one thing she was getting used to. She smiled, it was my answer to everything. We relaxed in the heat of the canteen. Kim it's not far now.

"Oh I know we'll make it, I just know." Her enthusiasm was good, she never looked on the down side of anything but I knew we still had a way to go. It was getting late, reluctantly we had to move.

"Come on lover, we got to keep going it'll be opening soon."

"I'm coming don't rush me!" Forgetting the golden rule we ventured back into the mist of cold air. Once again to stand at the slip road, thumbs out cars passing us by. An old van strutted towards us, then suddenly screeched to a halt.

"Where you going?" A voice asked in a Northern accent.

"Wigan."

"And us. Come on, jump in!" As we ran to the open backdoors my heart missed a beat. Now at last we would make it, my adrenaline went through the roof. Once again we set off on our journey, the excitement of the night, the adventure of it all. We turned off the M6 and drove to the center of Wigan, their endless questions getting on my nerves.

"Do they sell beer?"

"No I don't think so, just soft drinks."

"What's the music?"

"Northern Soul."

"What's that?" Our answers baffled them they could see no point of us going to the club especially one that didn't sell beer. We pulled to a halt and jumped out the back of the van, slamming the doors as you do to a vehicle of age.

"Thanks mate, nice one." They pulled away to a crescendo of crunching gears, billows of smoke surrounding us brake lights disappearing into the night. There was no queue yet loads of cars a few people hanging around outside. Above our heads a half lit sign declared Casino Club in red scroll letters. The old white awning stretching the full length of the brick building, it looked like an old Victorian warehouse. I smiled, at least we had found the right place. We stood at the entrance of a white stone arched doorway the faint sound of music drawing our attention. I gave Kim a hug lifting her off the pavement turning around in a circle holding her tightly like never before. I could feel the excitement in her eyes.

"We made it lover. We made it!"

Her voice in a whispered happiness, "I love you." I felt so happy my hand in a sweeping arc my queen in a curtsy stepping through the yellow light of the wide open doorway climbing the stairs for the very first time. At the top a grey haired lady stood behind a battered counter looking totally out of place. She looked like someone's grandmother and dressed as old people do. Her gentle features and sparkling eyes revealed a face of no nonsense. She asked politely in a Northern accent.

"Can I see your memberships please?" We handed our cards, I took a deep breath. We were this close we had to get in. Kim looked so young for the age limit of eighteen.

"That's seventy five pence each please." Adding in a mischievous voice, "You're not going to make the lass pay for herself are you?" I blushed I could feel my face glowing on fire as I fumbled in my pockets for money, my nerves totally on edge. The redness of my face glowing brighter only adding to her teasing smile. We turned to the right, ascending two flights of stairs on through a set of black doors leading to a short dimly lit passageway. The muted sound of music in front of us, the DJ's voice getting louder. I looked at Kim her face glowing with pride a shared smile as I pushed the black double doors open The Jades "I'm Where It's At" their voices in perfect harmony a wall of sound echoing around the club.

We couldn't believe our eyes, the music lost in the vastness, the expanse of the open room. We were standing at the back of an old Victorian dance hall with all the elegance of times gone by. An enormous dance floor lay before us, the biggest I had ever seen. Along the walls pink art deco globes a softness of light in all directions melting on a polished wooden floor. Feelings of happiness flowed through me, this was better than my wildest dreams! We made our way forward trying to take in what was unfolding before us cutting through tables and seating along the sides. I couldn't take my eyes off the dance floor, I was totally blown away.

"Look at that floor Kim. It's massive!" Kim sensing the excitement in my voice.

"Come on I want to dance. This is our night!" Grabbing my hand I smiled at her eagerness pulling me towards the floor. The room reaped with age peeling walls of painted plaster, mosaics of chipped paintwork. The hardness of worn carpet adding stickiness to my feet on through the crowd past tables of Coke bottles we stumbled on sports bags that littered the floor.

"Mind lover, careful!" Darkness around the edges of the dance floor easing our way past Soulies, some sitting at tables others standing along the sides. Their tops displaying soul badges in acknowledge of their clubs.

"Kim look!" Square mirrored columns surrounded the dance floor. Our smiling faces of adolescence speckled reflections as we passed them by.

"Come on lover. Over here, there's a spare table." A perfect spot we were at the center of a huge dance floor. Dropping my sports bag unbuttoned coats thrown on the backs of chairs. "Wait till the lads hear about this place lover. They won't believe me, no way will they believe me!"

"I know I can't wait to see Jako on this floor, especially the way he dances. At least he won't bump into me anymore!" Her face breaking to a mischievous smile.

She looked so beautiful her long cream colored skirt, her white sleeveless top caught in the florescent light of the dance floor, an hour glass figure of beauty and youth. A feeling of pride engulfed me, she really was a beautiful girl her gentle face lifting my heart. I wrapped my arms around her holding her close, I wanted to share this moment I wanted her by my side. Feeling so lucky at the gift I had been given as I held her in my arms squeezing her tightly "I love you," this wasn't a dream.

Lifting my eyes we stood in amazement at our surroundings, this building was really old. Above us a balcony encircled the enormous dance floor, a perfect view on all three sides. Gold ornate looping scrollwork giving the room magnificence grandeur from the past. A huge chandelier reflected light on a polished wooden dance floor stretching the full length and breadth of the room. Ultraviolet lights hung from a domed ceiling flashes of white illuminating dancers below.

Groups of Soulies scattered here and there some spinning, others doing drop-backs to the music. Girls in loose dresses, long pleated skirts and white ankle socks danced with their shadows in the openness of an empty floor. Around the edges other Soulies stood chatting, some adding talc as they tested the floor. To our left a stage raised above the dance floor extending the full width of the room. An old black piano pushed to the corner, a remnant of the past. Curtains cascaded to the wooden floor with banks of speakers on either side a few Soulies sat along the front of the stage. To the right surrounded in dim lights a DJ I had never heard of, his name Russ Winstanley. Little did we know he was changing the face of Northern Soul forever. History was being made in front of our eyes.

"Thanks for bringing me lover."

"I promised Kim and anyway I wasn't going to argue, not with that temper of yours." The gentle smile between us, two teenagers falling in love telling me at last I was forgiven for Va-Va. Darb was right he said it would take a while.

We had come a long way from our first meeting in the park, now we stood in The Casino the world seemed at our feet. This was an all-nighter, a special place it had a feeling all of its own. Now we would leave our mark on the dance floor! "Gotta put my vest on Kim!" My voice upbeat rummaging through our bag the vest buried amongst spare shoes, towels, and talc. I changed at the side of the floor. The Va-Va badge from last month, my Cats badge in the center. The clubs I had been to, what history I had worn with pride. The white edging of my blue vest caught in fluorescents. "Such a poser." I smiled, not really. We were the new generation of Soulies, I wanted to stand out on the floor. It was all on me and Kim now, I missed our little group and wished that they had come. The excitement building inside me. I had three styles of footwork and couldn't wait to dance on this floor.

I knew no one, a stranger I ventured forward twisting my feet leather shoes searching for feelings testing the floor for talc. Checking my balance gently turning into a spin dragging my foot, reading the surface. Drifting around the floor watching other dancers around me pretending I couldn't dance. I did this on purpose it's just the way I was.

I wanted to draw competition to see what other dancers could do. I knew straight away we had found a good spot there was no ridges. From the lightness of my feet this floor felt perfectly flat. Glancing at Kim her face smiling with confidence gained from the dance floors we had been on she knew what I was about to do. The Catacombs, The Octopus, The Ship all the times we had practiced we had been dancing eighteen months I had waited a long time for this. Now all the moves would come together to show them at last what we could do.

We had our floor, even better an audience a few Soulies gathering along the side. For the first time on a Northern floor I had all I ever wanted only this time I had room to move! The voice of Hoagy Lands "The Next In Line" my heart burst erupting inside a record straight from The Torch. "...Whose gonna be..." a soulful voice pleading with emotion his harmonious voice so pure, melodic beats echoing all around us. The record drove us forward together dancing on a floor of Soul.

Stepping footwork in a diamond formation matching steps side by side nothing but space around us. Floating arms, drifting footwork, hand movements I had made my own. Moving out on the floor our footwork a style so unusual, twisting and turning into the beats. Feeling smoothness I couldn't believe it on the vastness of Wigan's floor it just made you want to dance. Expressing to the music, feelings held within me.

Kim dancing at my side her feet in love with the music hands at her side reaching to join as one. A transcending of happiness and music shared feelings held deeply in our hearts. I smiled checking the floor around me a burst of fast footwork the foundation of my dancing floating along the side of the floor. No one could come near it as I changed freely to my different styles.

A dancer's voice inside me, "come on let's turn it on." Kicking high, touching my hand sweeping one handed into a sideways splits. Legs perfectly in line lower than ever twisting my feet to a drop-back, hands at my side. My back arched pushing with my ankles rising in one movement gaining momentum hands reaching out. A dip of my shoulder finding my balance one foot touching the floor spinning on the ball of my shoe, arms at my side turning at speed. Dropping again a single flowing move landing one handed into straight splits. Turning my body into a drop-back, pushing with my hands rising once more. Crossing my legs spinning in the opposite direction, hands on hips, elbows tucked out at my side. Breaking out to fast drifting footwork all my moves done with precision at speed.

A smoothness in my dancing that only comes from being out on a floor. I could feel we were being watched so I deliberately pushed myself, I wanted to make a statement right here on this floor. A good dancer always attracts attention like flashes of light they just draw your eyes as you wait for them to do certain moves. Punishing my body we loved the adulation, both of us tore into our dancing a wall of blank faces watching our every move. Changing to fast stepping footwork half turns in the opposite direction dragging my foot once more in a spiral. My arms reaching out in an arc hands feeling the music, a dummy spin into fast footwork holding back waiting for the chorus, timing to all of my moves. More spins in both directions increasing in speed as I gauged the floor.

Dancing giving me everything emotions flowed through me I pounded my body to the music. "…I I I wouldn't want any any any other way the next in line…" so pure, so passionate his voice crystal clear my every move done with affection suddenly my heart broken. I could feel the atmosphere, the love, the happiness of other dancers around me a small crowd at the side of the floor. An explosion of grief welled up inside me full of memories locked away.

That journey I had taken from the orphanage through all the pain I had endured came to me on that dance floor. Dancing, releasing the pain in an expression of my emotions through my feet. I felt connected as one with the dance floor feeling the sorrow of love with the singers. The emptiness of my lost childhood crashed around me rivers of tears I could not control. I danced till the end of the record, leaving the floor wiping my eyes trying to hide my emotions, my head lowered in shame. Kim stopped dancing rushing to my side a puzzled look not saying a word. Holding me as a mother, her arms as if to protect me she could see the pain I felt inside. My voice trembling in whispered tears.

"This is where I belong Kim. This is my home." It had been a long journey for me, I felt connected as if from that very first step this was where I needed to be. Turning away I searched in our bag feeling embarrassed at my loss of control. Grabbing a towel burying my face in anger, rubbing my eyes burning with sweat and tears.

"Snap out of it! How could you and in front of Kim, you fuckin wanka?! It's a sign of weakness, you never cry in front of a girl!"

She knelt beside me, hands on my shoulders her face inquisitive, a gentleness to all of her words. "What's the matter lover?"

"Nothing Kim. Nothing." My eyes welling in tears, slamming the door to my heart once more, her affections pushed away. The taunting voice laughing inside me, the little boy a distant figure standing alone in the orphanage. "No mother's love for you." My heart in so much pain, a childhood devoid of happiness how could I ever understand love? Yet it had just surrounded me.

"I'm ok Kim. Just, just being stupid. I'm ok lover, honest."

"Hey come on let's dance. You promised!" Kim's voice giving me comfort, helping me gather my emotions. Once more memories that tore me apart invisible scars no one sees. Replaced with a smile, a new face of togetherness we ventured back out on to the floor.

A nod of respect from dancers around me I waited for the challenge of another dancer yet no one crossed the floor. We had obviously made our mark. We were from The Catacombs, the name of our club spoke for itself! In this club and on this floor the vastness of the room records just opened your heart. The Velours "I'm Gonna Change" one of many records we loved from The Cats. Dean Courtney "I'll Always Need You", The Coasters "Crazy Baby", Bunny Sigler "Girl Don't Make Me Wait Too Long", Wingate's Love-in Strings "Let's Have A Love-in", Darrell Banks "Angel Baby (Don't You Leave Me)", Eddie Foster "I Never Knew", Chubby Checker "You Just Don't Know (What You Do To Me)", Sandi Shelton "You're Gonna Make Me Love You", Freddie Chavez "They'll Never Know Why", The Impressions "You've Been Cheatin'", and April Stevens "Wanting You". The night full of Va-Va, The Wheel, The Torch pure Northern filling The Casino.

You had to express yourself to the music, you never wanted to leave the floor. In the protection of our youth, we gave our dancing everything we had. Both of us standing breathless reaching for a towel wiping our faces, our aching bodies covered in sweat. Stealing a Coke from our table, taking a swig I passed the bottle to Kim.

"Come on lover, we need a drink!"

"Hey mate, where's the cloak room?" Two Soulies near us pointing upstairs to the back of the room.

"What's your name?" One asked.

"Gethro and this is Kim. What's yours?"

"They call me Billy Back and this is Waka." Billy pointing to his chubby friend standing at his side.

"Can you watch our bag mate? We'll be back in a minute."

"Sure leave it with us," His instant reply, "where you two from?"

"Wolvo, The Cats."

"We're from Wigan. Nice dancing man."

"Cheers mate, we won't be long." As we shook hands there was an instant bond that all-nighters bring. There was a trust on the scene and it carried to the casino. I knew our bag would be ok. I felt proud at the recognition for our style of dancing.

We left with our coats moving along the edge of the dance floor, Soulies crowded around the front of the stage. In the brightness of fluorescents dancers stood out in the crowd. I smiled as we stopped to watch, looking for moves I hadn't seen before. Scanning for faces I might recognize, anyone from Va-Va or The Cats.

To our left a staircase led up to the balcony, standing at the bottom in the darkness bouncers catching my eye. Watching the entrance to the men's toilets obviously on the lookout for drugs. Reminding me of The Cats on a Saturday it was always good to know where they were. Soulies passing us on a wide staircase locked in intense conversations startled expressions from being smashed. Drinks in hands descending into darkness, eager faces rushing back to the floor.

"Kim look at this!" The balcony a magnet drawing us forward unveiling the floor below. The majestic design more beautiful than anything I had ever seen. Gilded crests of sweeping flowers flowing ribbons of cream and gold. The top rail of worn mahogany ending on the opposite side of the room. Chained fluorescents hung from the domed ceiling cascading on dancers below. Pink sconces lined the walls, their delicate glow of light creating a gentle ambiance surrounding the room. Directly across from us another wide staircase, couples descending out of site to mingle below reappearing at the front of the stage.

A few Soulies seated at tables, others out on the floor, florescent shapes in an explosion of movement. The intensity of the dancers swallowed in the vastness of the room. My eyes following Soulies darting figures as they crossed the floor. The odd drop-back catching my attention the night slowly coming to life. We stood watching the dance floor saturated in the beauty of movement, mesmerized by dancers below. I smiled with satisfaction, we had been practicing for a while now it showed. We flowed, there was no jerkiness to any of our moves with our footwork we danced in a different style. From what I had seen up to now there were four basic moves, everyone putting their own stamp on them creating their own individual style.

Spinning, Tall Martin and Shawn from Va-Va, Booper the graceful master and Matchy from The Wheel and Torch and the fastest of them all, Squeak. He had mastered the move on the tight floor of The Catacombs and for sheer speed I had seen no equal. Backdrops, a move from The Wheel and Torch that a few of the dancers below me could do. Splits, not many dancers did this, those that could only in one direction and usually bent one leg. Me doing the splits both ways from spins got us noticed it had taken three months to master that combination not only to do just one move. My footwork I had taken from Smokey and others, learned on the dance floor of The Cats adding steps to make it unique. Arms and hand expressions from Booper I now spun both ways but could only master the jump and spin in one direction. Dropping into a drop-back allowed me to cross my legs to rise and spin the other way. Like any good dancer I had stolen all their moves to create a new style of my own. I couldn't wait till all six of us hit this floor together, I knew what we could do.

"We're going to take this floor Kim."

"I know we will." She smiled and knew exactly what I meant.

Talk's cheap, it was up to us if we wanted this floor we would have to earn it the hard way. Like in any Northern club we would have to take them all on to prove we're the best. From up here I could see Wigan had a few good dancers, little did I know I was about to be blown off the floor. My eyes following the art deco wall sconces, darkness melting to light a mirrored bar illuminating the far end of the room.

"The cloak room must be over there Kim."

"I hope so, this coats heavy."

"It can't be, it's not real fur." Causing her to smile. "Here, give it to me. Come on, let's get rid of these coats." Passing other couples along the side of the balcony, strangers we didn't know stopped us introducing themselves. We chatted, feeling the warmth of their friendliness in accents I found hard to follow. Penny and Kerr who hitched from Scotland, a friendship sealed in one night. On his vest the badge of the Pendulum Manchester beside The Twisted Wheel. Mona and Lisa from Nottingham, a friend who for years would always dance by my side.

Friendships cemented in time, ones that all-nighters bring. Alan from Sheffield, miners, electricians, shop assistants, factory workers, ordinary working class kids. Their warmth reminding me of Va-Va my face in a constant smile as we exchanged names, everyone we met the wide-eyed expression of being smashed. Eventually we found the cloak room behind a set of black double doors at the far end of the bar. A steep flight of stairs led to a small room at the top. Behind the counter a tall skinny guy my age collected our coats, his ball of afro hair making me smile.

"How much for our coats mate?" I asked reaching into my pocket.

"That's ten pence each please. Hey, where you from?"

"Wolvo, The Catacombs." We shook in crossing hands introducing ourselves. His name was Scatty with a cheeky smile he asked.

"Want any gear? I've got some chalkies, ten a quid."

"What they like?" I had never heard of them.

"They're ok. Just a bit hard on your stomach. You'll be ok with a Coke, it'll mix em up." I looked into his eyes, we both started to laugh he just had that cheeky expression. I knew it was a face I could trust.

"Give me twenty, Scat." Whispering to Kim, "we'll take seven each and see how it goes." I looked around feeling apprehensive at our openness.

"It's ok, there's no bouncers up here. Just watch yourself down by the side of the bar. You'll be alright with ten each trust me that'll get you smashed!"

THEY DANCED ALL NIGHT

It seemed like a lot to me, I felt nervous. I had never taken so many drugs my mind fighting my conscience, a desire to feel the high they would bring.

"We may as well lover. Everybody else is smashed." Kim's face enlightened with excitement. The smile once again showing me I had an equal, her wild side that never held back. Money and drugs exchanged in the slip of a hand, the oval white tablets filling my pocket. Kim scanning the stairs little miss innocent as always watching my back.

"Cheers Scatty, nice one man." The grin on my face saying it all. "Come on lover we need a Coke."

It was like that at Wigan, so easy from our very first night there was gear in the club. As with any other club you knew the score if you got caught you were dead meat. In The Casino we had a huge advantage just from the pure size of the club. With the darkness around the dance floor and other areas hidden away the bouncers couldn't be everywhere.

Even then I was learning fast, you could deal just keep your eyes open be street wise and you would be ok. It was part of the scene, gear adding to the atmosphere the excitement. We didn't care tonight was our night, we would deal with tomorrow when it comes!

Descending the steep stairs we made our way towards the bar. A mirrored wall of crystal, reflections a softness of light igniting the room. The grandeur of old mahogany The Casino showing her age. On our right a wide arched stair case descending back towards the main room. All around us the echoing sound of Northern. Grabbing our Cokes we settled at a table to watch the dancers below. My mindset was simple, we had twenty so take seven each see how you felt, use them with respect. I didn't know how I would feel I had never taken chalkies.

The memory of last week still fresh in my mind, the couple we had met, the sign we had been given. His cracked bleeding lips a vision that wouldn't go away the voice in my head telling me, "stay in control." I wanted energy to dance, to push my body on the dance floor not to just take drugs to get smashed. Kim's innocent expression making me smile as we took our chalkies.

"One two three," counting them out, "six seven." My partner in crime making me laugh. I took mine, seven tablets at once filling my mouth, forcing them down for a second time.

"Man they taste bad!" My face expressive of the fact. "They taste like shit!"

"When have you tasted shit lover? Is there something we need to talk about?" Kim's face bursting into laughter at my twisted expressions at her side.

I knew one thing, drugs were expensive. If I was going to take them I would have to deal my own. We sat watching the dance floor, I noticed the blur of a dancer, a style I instantly recognized someone spinning at the front of the stage. "Kim it's my mate Shawn from Bolton. The spinner I was telling you about, he's on the floor!" A sense of pride came over me, a face I recognized from Va-Va our friendship made that night.

"Come on lover this way." We made our way around the edge of the balcony passing a few Soulies seated at tables watching dancers below. The glow of wall lights guiding us to a wide staircase we descend into semi darkness joining a small crowd at the side of the floor. "Kim, there's the girl's toilets." Not a single bouncer to be seen. I smiled a useful observation. So they think girls don't deal drugs?

We stood to the right of the stage a new energy on the dance floor all around us faces of gear. My eyes locked on Shawn, his figure caught in the fluorescents other dancers watching him spin. Hands in the air arms tight in a skater with no ice. A spinning body on one leg at speeds I couldn't match, a face of pure emotion his dancing holding the floor. At the end of the record he stopped dancing moving towards the stage "Shawn!" Immediately he turned around a red and black vest clinging to his body, the badge of Va-Va in the center. Matted hair a face of pure adrenaline, his shining figure soaked in sweat. "Shaw want this?" Stepping forward I offering my Coke.

"Cheers Gethro." A breathless voice as we shook hands. So, he remembered me. I felt proud, once again I was making a name.

"Where's your mate, the one with glasses?"

"Darb. Oh he couldn't make it but he'll be here next time and my mates Jako, Winston, and Jimmy wait till you see them dance."

"They all from Cats?"

"Yea."

"What's that place like?"

"It's brilliant Shawn. Lot of good dancers, you should come mate the atmospheres unreal and the floors bigger than Va-Va." I couldn't help it my face breaking into a smile, "nice spinning man."

"Thanks Gethro, see you got your Va-Va badge." Once more we shook in crossing hands.

"Yea I know that was a special night! Shawn, this is my girlfriend Kim." He also introduced a pretty girl her name was Angie, immediately she chatted with Kim.

"Dance by us Gethro, floors perfect!" That's all we needed, placing our Cokes on the stage waiting for our moment to move out on the floor. As we stood together I glanced at the DJ, giving him my instant respect the same guy working the decks holding the floor with dancers. I felt proud to be standing by Shawn, Kim too, I could see it her face smiling with pleasure from being at the front of the stage.

Fixed gazes from the balcony onlookers watching our every move. In the emptiness of the club we hit the floor together Martha Reeves and the Vandellas "One Way Out" pounding Northern beats filling The Casino. A surge of adrenaline flowed through me sweat streaming down my face. My heart racing an express train in the distance feeling the instant rush of gear. A new energy making me more aggressive turning faster, I tried to spin to keep up with Shawn. Slowing my footwork gauging my balance, arms in an arc feeling the music clapping hands at the end of a spin.

Forgetting all my other moves the gear taking over my mind locked in on spinning. His wide stepping footwork a floating style so different from mine. Both spinning at the same time getting faster closer to speeds that I wanted Shawn out lasting me every time. Dropping into splits at full speed pounding the dance floor, the music pushing me harder. The sensation of being high creeping through my body all of us giving our hearts. The respect for one another that only competition can bring. The intensity of our dancing fueled by amphetamines both of us holding the floor. The record fading out to our laugher I put my arms around him, our bodies interlocking covered in sweat. Shaking hands a statement to our dancing a mutual admiration for the way we could dance.

"Nice spinning Shawn, man you're fast! I'll catch you up one day"

"I know you will Gethro." Smiled competitive affection between us. Memories that last forever, two Soul brothers on a dance floor, the bond of all-nighters that dancing brings. One thing I noticed about Shawn he had a certain flow to his footwork enhanced by his cords. His feet flowed with the movement of cloth I looked at my sweat stained parallels.

In the future I would dance in cords and mine would be a lot wider than that. A slight adjustment we made to our clothing with massive dividends out on the floor. The night coming alive other Soulies picking up on the atmosphere we had created, the energy we brought to the floor. The Sounds of Lane "Tracks To Your Mind", Johnny Sayles "I Can't Get Enough (Of Your Love)", Billy Joe Royal "Heart's Desire", The Furys "I'm Satisfied With You", Thelma Houston "Baby Mine", and The Contours "Just A Little Misunderstanding". The DJ amping up the floor Kim's body dripping in sweat, the wide eyes of pleasure from being smashed. The driving style of her footwork matching record after record her skirt flowing in a spiral of movement showing other girls she too could spin.

The music pushing me to new limits, dancing and drugs driving me higher to a barrier that knew no pain. Paul Anka "I Can't Help Loving You", The Belles "Don't Pretend", Jeanette Williams "Something's Got A Hold On Me", Creation "I Got The Fever", Levi Jackson "This Beautiful Day", Just Brothers "Sliced Tomatoes", Rubin Parker "You've Been Away", Bobby Paris "Per-So-Nal-Ly", and Contours "Baby Hit And Run". Bouncing Northern beats igniting the dance floor, sweat streaming down our faces the atmosphere building in momentum dancers fueled by drugs.

The crowd growing larger, more Soulies joining the floor others stopping to watch. We had all the room we wanted coupled with endless energy to burn. Everything balanced, being smashed felt unbelievable like a dream come true but this was reality! Man this felt so good! My senses on fire the gear racing through me held by the competition of Wigan's floor soaked in the adrenaline of being high. An instant feeling, a connection with other dancers all of us totally lost in the moment of happiness the one to one of being smashed. My heart pounding, our bodies streaming in sweat, dancing in the atmosphere of fluorescents at the front of the stage.

"Shawn, who else is here from Bolton?"

"All the lads from Va-Va Gethro. Brent, Titch, Hank, Bub, Dave, Budgie, Big Roger, Colin, and Tall Martin few car loads. Hey want some gear? I can put the word out I think they got some chalkies and blueys, ten a quid.

"We're ok thanks Shawn. Hey mate we're dancing over there." I pointed across the floor. "Tell them to come over." We shook hands and parted, our handshake rapped in hugs to words of, "Keep the faith."

We left moving back to our spot crossing the floor at the front of the stage. Making our way through a maze of dancers, Soulies stopping us to chat. Exchanged names, new friendships born in the moment always bound in three words "got any gear?" I looked around the whole place an ants' nest of movement The Casino slowly coming to life. Moving through dancers I felt good in this new atmosphere of togetherness, the mutual feeling of being high. Not a single straight face amongst them on this floor that was so alive, who would ever want to be straight?!

"The bag's still there Kim, told you not to worry."

"Well I do. That's what girls do, worry."

"Gethro you're back!"

"Cheers Billy. Sorry we got sidetracked mate."

"It's like that in here. Hey Gethro, want some gear? I know someone with some filon, ten a quid if you want some.

"No Billy, we had some chalkies we're ok mate. Thanks anyway."

"Well if you know someone let me know." I pointed to where we had been dancing. "Lot of people we passed by the stage Billy just been asking about gear."

"Ok no problem."

"Hold on. Lover where's your address book? Billy, what's your phone number?" I turned to get my first name. I could see an opportunity. I knew that when this club picked up there would be a lot of people looking for gear. Tonight there seemed more people selling it! All I needed was some good contacts and I couldn't be in a better place. To me it was simple, if I was going to deal drugs they weren't going to be from Wolvo. I wanted my own set of friends, new faces out of the area that no one knew. Only problem I had, I didn't know anything about gear. Yet the answer was all around me.

We moved back on the floor, I turned into a spin it felt a little stiffer, unresponsive "Kim we need some talc lover, this floors gone tight." As I reached into our bag Waka came rushing over standing at my side.

"No don't put that on floor!" He looked at me his voice emphatic.

"Why not? We need talc to spin." I persisted, twisting my foot showing him the unresponsive floor.

"You'll spoil Billy's move."

"What move?"

"Show him Billy." Waka smiling as Billy ventured out on the floor. Three steps of slow footwork then a quick look over his shoulder. Bang! A perfect back flip. It looked brilliant, I couldn't believe my eyes.

"What a fuckin move! Do that again!" Spellbound by what I had just seen.

Once more he moved to an open space again the move done to perfection.

"That's Billy Back!" I burst out laughing, in that one move he had just blown me off the floor! It was a move I couldn't come near to, let alone match. He completely changed my approach to dancing, the style I had been trying to pursue. Straight away I could see if you put moves like backflips and handsprings together to the footwork I already had, the endless dimensions you could bring. If I could only make it all fit together I would be unbeatable on an open floor. With all the room we had at Wigan with our free style of dancing we had the perfect floor! "Billy, that's brilliant man."

"It's just something I picked up at school." He shyly replied.

"Can you teach me that?" Kim arching her back, looking over her shoulder imitating his stance.

"Not with that skirt on!" Waka's reply drowned in our laughter.

"What's this floor made of Billy?" Once more I gestured to the empty floor.

"Maple I think. Yea maple. It's what they call a sprung floor Gethro the best you can get."

"It's a brilliant floor to dance on, it bounces." I pointed to the stage, "and that DJ who is he?"

"Russ, he DJs at the Rugby club and British Legion. He's well known round here."

"He's played some good sounds mate. I mean it's hard to keep this floor alive, it's so big."

I dusted talc in front of us, once more stepping on to the floor. Too slippy. Grabbing a Coke from our table tipping a little onto the carpet, gently twisting my feet. The wetness of shoes adjusting to talc drifting in a semi-circle of footwork reworking the floor. An old trick, it really was that important grip, timing, and balance were everything to me. You had to get the floor to respond once again I started to wind into my spins. Suddenly I stopped dancing.

"Gethro! Kim!" Laney and Nesta stumbling along the side of the dance floor two soul girls we knew from The Cats. Dropping their bags to hugs of excitement all of us speaking at once. I could see from their wide smiling faces both of them were smashed. The togetherness of a friendship born in The Catacombs now at the side of Wigan's floor. They too had hitched from Wolvo after first going to The Cats that was the power of this music. The girls just as devoted as any Soul brother. In no time at all dancing by Kim. Expressing with their feet, their love of the music feelings deeply held in their hearts. All three of them stealing the floor to squeals of delight from Laney, Nesta had been here last week.

Leaving the girls I moved back to the floor, feeling the effects of the gear all I wanted to do was dance. Glancing over to the far side of the room my heart lifted I couldn't believe my eyes. Booper spinning in the right hand corner at the front of the stage. A group of dancers around him, the Manchester connection had now obviously arrived. Flashes of white a dress shirt caught in fluorescents an audience off to his side. Shawn from Bolton in the center of the stage both of them in a battle, spinning like tops.

Booper's footwork a lot faster, nothing but space around him showing all the moves he had perfected that graceful style from The Wheel and Torch. Stripping at the side of the dance floor waistcoat and shirt now gone, he too wearing a blue vest. I ventured forward to the opposite corner being given room at the front of the stage. Thoughts crossing my mind, all the moves I had been denied at Va-Va there was a large gap and I stepped forwards. Knowing full well he had to see me I relaxed in the style of my dancing, adjusting my footwork from slow to fast.

Playing to my strength for now holding back on my moves watching what he would do. The surface felt rippled, uneven on the left hand side of the stage spins turning to drop-backs rising to opposite spins. Matching the record to perfection never taking my eyes off him. Blending my hand movements to copy his technique my mindset was simple, gear did that to you. It made you concentrate as you strived for perfection you became locked into your moves. Tonight I just wanted to show the far side of the dance floor, "you're not the only one who can jump and spin." I was becoming a match for anyone on a floor but to me this was personal.

How do you beat a good spinner? Easy, use your advantage no one else could spin both ways. I knew how to work the floor, a lesson I had learned in The Cats. I played to the crowd, dancing in bursts my footwork attracting attention blending an athletic approach to my moves. On this floor to me with all the room you had it wasn't just about spinning and footwork, his style of dancing so different from mine. I stopped for a drink at the front of the stage glancing across, he had to have seen me. Once again no one crossed the floor. Thoughts of next week flooded to my mind of Jako, Darb and Jimmy I wanted revenge for Va-Va. If they came I knew exactly where we would dance!

"Gethro!" A voice startled me, another face I instantly recognized. "Gonk, how did you get here man?!" Our faces bursting in smiles.

"Muff's van. We came straight from The Cats, we picked up Laney and Nesta."

"I know, they're dancing with Kim."

"Pete's here and Chris, Ross, Popeye, Trebor, Julie, Alien loads of us. Big Willie, half The Cats is here man!" His face alight with gear, his bouncy personality always making me laugh.

"Can we have a lift back with you Gonk?"

"Yea, you're only a skinny bastard. We'll squeeze you in somewhere." I breathed a sigh of relief, I just didn't fancy hitching back.

"Any of the lads here Jako or Darb?" I asked more in hope than anything else.

"No but they were in The Cats" A voice behind me, I turned around two guys stepped forward both a little taller than me. Gonk introduced us. "This is Dave and Irish." The dark haired one held out his hand, he didn't wear any Soul badges? We shook hands as Soul brothers do.

"I had seen them in The Cats dancing by Squeak. They had caught my attention two really fast spinners." That night they had stolen the floor. Not an easy job in The Catacombs, I gave them my instant respect.

"Irish, where you from?"

"Howard Mallet Cambridge, that's our club. Tony Dellar the DJ Gethro. He's a really good kid."

"That's a long way to travel man." Immediately I was impressed.

"We called into The Cats on the way up."

"Was it packed?"

"Yea, you could hardly move."

"I know. That's why I came up here!" Both of us starting to laugh.

"Gethro we got a few back street blueys if you want some. We dropped a load off in The Cats earlier." Irish smiled, "Saw your mates, the one with blond hair he's a really good spinner."

"That's Jako, my mate. Brilliant dancer, I'm going to get them to come up here. This floor is gonna blow them away."

"Irish I'm going to see if Matchy wants any gear." Dave and Gonk leaving us at the side of the floor.

"How do you know Gonk, Irish?"

"We knew him from The Torch and we met up again last month at Leeds Central. You would like it there Gethro, bit small but a great crowd."

Two clubs I had never been to, one I had sadly missed. Irish like so many Soulies around me, Wigan full of faces from the Torch.

"Can you get blueys regular?"

"No problem, we can get them to order."

"What every week?" I was surprised, was it really that easy? Irish wiping his brow lowering his voice.

"You got to remember Gethro, were from Cambridge. It's full of post graduate drop outs, chemists looking for work. There's loads of gear about. Here try these." Dropping three pale blue tablets in the palm of my hand.

"Cheers mate!" I smiled at his openness.

"Anytime Gethro, me and Dave just want to see you dance!" Both of us laughing at the craziness of our situation, a friendship built on dancing fueled inevitably with drugs. Grabbing my Coke, swallowing the blueys our conversation turning to Booper igniting the side of the floor.

"I saw him dancing in The Torch and little Matchy. You know Gethro there's loads of good dancers out there, he's not the only one you've got to beat."

"I know but I'm just going to dance if they take me on, then that's different." My confidence sky high at what I had discovered. The thought making me smile at the competitions to come.

"Hey what do you think of this floor Irish?"

"It's brilliant Gethro but there's no atmosphere. It's as if the place is too big for itself."

"I know exactly what you mean mate. It's empty it's nothing like The Cats still the music's good though. Come on! Let's rip some floor!"

The competitiveness of Wigan's floor, plain to see the challenge of other dancers especially from The Wheel and Torch. I began to gauge the night spending my time with Irish his presence pushing me in my dancing. Irish spinning in his unique style arms pulled into his chest, long winding legs powering into spins a really relaxed spinner with a fast, deceiving style. He too occasionally spinning to a drop-back to finalize the end of a spin his moves getting us noticed, the Manchester Lads watching from the far side of the floor.

Tonight I was still learning, Billy had shown me I wasn't the most athletic dancer. Irish had just proved I wasn't the fastest spinner or the only one doing a certain move. Squeak, Irish, Shawn, and Booper could all blow me off but they only spun one way. Me spinning both ways fit right into the way I wanted to dance. The other difference, I danced in a sequence of combinations linking all of my moves together. I couldn't be the best at everything that was impossible but I did everything well, a neatness to all of my moves and ones I did excel at only I could do.

Dancers connect with each other there's just instantaneous bond of affection. I felt proud to be with Irish on the same floor just as we had at The Cats. We danced to record after record losing ourselves to the night, a few hours later we parted. Crossing our hands with our hearts in the friendship of Northern another dancer I would get to know well. I made my way back to Kim passing Soulies along the edge of the floor. Nodded looks from onlookers, pats on the back. I smiled and chatted Soulies wanting my name we had made an impression at the front of the stage.

It was clear from the start Wigan's floor was territorial and would come down to a contest between the Northern lads and other dancers from around the country. Leading the way for the Midlands would be The Catacombs with remnants from The Torch. To me we had danced for The Catacombs it's just the way I felt. The Northern lads had made a statement, to them this was their floor. Their best dancers would grace The Casino, the floor would become a battleground. A pedigree of lads from The

Wheel, Va-Va Bolton, Mecca, Blackpool, Leeds Central, and The Pendulum Manchester other Northern clubs around the country.

There was no bitterness between us we all just wanted one thing, this dance floor. It really was as simple as that! If you wanted a particular spot you had to earn it and that's exactly what I wanted, the challenge of other dancers to see who's the best. Straight away I knew it would take a brilliant dancer to move freely around the casino but with my idea and on this floor? Driven on by Jako and Darb my dancing would go to another level with moves that I would discover and no one else could do.

I started to check different areas out, I wanted to read this floor moving around with Kim passing the crowd from Wolvo we made our way to the back of the room. Above us the beautiful domed ceiling, the ornate circular balcony lined with mirrored columns my eyes drifting back to the floor. Wherever I looked large areas of polished dance floor reflections of light around me. All the room I could ever want, dancing alone with Kim we shared our time together the last records coming too soon. My feet searching the floor finding answers to all my questions, the one I had longed for finally answered. At last I had found a home.

Chapter 28

WHAT GOES UP, COMES DOWN

"What do you want to drink Gethro? You ok, you still looked smashed."

"I know, get me a Guinness and Vimto Darb. I feel higher than a pilot's bollocks, it'll help me come down off these chalkies."

"What they like?"

"My stomachs killing me other than that, well just look at us!"

He started to laugh, "Kim what do you want?"

"Britvic and lemonade please Darb."

"Now now lover, no moaning you know what goes up comes down!" Kim's face bursting to smiles to roars of laughter around our table my face reddened in shame. We had gone to The Ship, we always did on a Sunday night. I looked around the lounge, Skins crowding around the bar hammering pints of lager. Their cheers drowning with others lost in the smoke filled room. They looked odd to me in their denim jackets, boots and bracers our worlds so far apart. Oblivious to the surrounding our little group in the corner. The odd smell of Brut from Winston drifting in the air, a noisy bar behind us our tabletop full of drinks.

"Look I know The Cats is brill but you haven't got room, not to dance the way I want to."

"Yea but we make our own room man." Jimmy's eyes flashing in anger leaning forward trying to make his point.

"You don't have to at Wigan. The floor is massive and the sounds are the same as The Cats, honest Kim tell them, will you?" Feeling rough as a bear's arse, frustration in my voice I really hadn't got time for this. I knew if I stepped back they would listen to Kim.

"Look loads of people turned up from The Cats, in the end we had the whole side of the floor."

"Any girls Kim?" Winston smiling stroking his chin as if to emphasize his good looks.

"Loads Winst."

"I'm coming!" Once more our laughter surrounding the table Kim holding their attention.

"We danced all night the place is so beautiful just being out on the dance floor it's magical, it's unreal." Turning to Jimmy her eyes locking on his as if to emphasize her point. "Jimmy, Wigan Casino is nothing like The Cats." Their searching faces listening intently, their interest captured Kim's voice in a softer tone.

"Yea but look at you two. You're bad Gethro! I thought you weren't taking gear." Jimmy wagging his finger, a smile directed at me!

"What? Ok so we took some gear, everybody was smashed. Fuck it, it's an all-nighter it's different. You haven't been, we have! We needed energy, its record after record for six hours nonstop man we never came off the floor!"

"I hear you Gethro!" Darb handing our drinks now sitting at my side. "How big is this floor then?!"

"Darb, it's twice the size of The Civic at least, may be three." I knew I was exaggerating, must be the gear the thought making me smile.

"That's a big floor man." His eye brows rising in a look of surprise.

"It can't be that big!"

"That's my point Jako. It is and guess who was there?"

"Who?"

"Shawn."

"That kid from Va-Va, the one who can spin faster than Jako?!" Darb grinning, winding Jako up in an instant faster than he could ever spin.

"No way, I'm the fastest next to Squeak!" Jako pleading his point.

"So easy man! So easy!" Jimmy and Winston bursting to laughter teasing him even more.

"Well Jako he can spin even on the floor at Va-Va he was fast." I rubbed it in, now I had his attention. "Some good dancers but it's the place. It's an old dance hall with a balcony and everything. You can get lost, it's that big."

"Was there many people?"

'Well there was Jimmy, but it looked empty it's just so big."

"If it's empty and there's no atmosphere then why go?"

"Jako it's the floor. Trust me man, whenever have I let you down? Come on it's the floor! It's brilliant. Look here's my membership."

"Let's have a look." Darb now holding the red card. "This one from the ad in Blues and Soul?"

"Yea, if you post off for it this week you can collect it on the night at the club upstairs."

"What, before you go in?"

"Yea between 12 and 1:30."

"Well that'll work. Come on this is an all-nighter man, it's different from The Cats." Darb now backing me up, showing me he wanted to come.

"Darb, it's the same crowd at Va-Va. They were brilliant, we met loads of new people real friendly and some good dancers, Irish and Dave from Cambridge.

"Who?" The two guys we saw in The Cats, spinning remember?

"Oh those two."

"Good spinners Jako. I know you think you are good dancers then prove it!"

"We know we are good dancers Gethro, we don't have to prove anything."

"Yea in The Cats you are Jako. Look you can't stay in The Cats forever let's get out there and show them who we are! What we can do! This is our floor its wide open man, we need to take this floor."

"How Gethro?" Jimmy chatting to Kim now turning his attention to me.

"Let's say we all have the same colored vests and dance together like we always do."

"No one will beat us." Darb's face lighting with a smile, relishing the contest to come.

"Not on an open floor they won't, what I can't do you can Jako. You're our best spinner, you're a good dancer. Come on, I need you with us."

"I know what you mean Gethro. I could hardly dance Saturday night in The Cats, it was that packed. We missed you man." Darb, like me needed room it was our style.

"Come on even if you go once, let's all hit this all-nighter and see how good we really are remember Va-Va Darb? He was there."

"Who?" Jako now listening to every word drawing closer as I spoke.

"Booper."

"The one that pushed us off the floor."

"Yea and his mates. Darb remember what the Bolton lads told us. He's from The Wheel, one of the best dancers to come out of there. He won the first competition at The Torch."

"Never heard of him till Va-Va, Gethro."

"Nor me, I know we can beat them they dance on the far side by the front of the stage. They think they own that piece of floor."

"We'll see Gethro from what I saw at Va-Va if we get any room we can beat them."

"They ain't seen nothing yet! Wait till they meet The Cats!"

"I know Jako, that's all I'm trying to say."

"This I got too see." Winston breaking to a smile his voice alight with excitement, as ever stroking his chin.

"What moves they got?"

"Nothing we can't match Jako and anyway we want to learn new moves. Come on let's take The Cats floor to Wigan, we'll have all the room we want and we can let it rip." Now driving my point home there was no need unlike before, now I knew they would come.

"I'm with you Gethro." Darb turning to me as we crossed hands, our faces full of smiles.

"Nice one man." 'Always' the bond of our affection for dancing, stronger than ever.

"Well if you're going I'm coming, it's our first all-nighter together Gethro." Jako shaking my hand, the love we had for each other Soul brothers written in our hearts.

"And what about me!" Kim scolding them at her lack of attention.

"You know we all love you Kim. You come everywhere, you're our mascot." Winston giving her a hug, our laughter lost in the room.

"I'm coming, let's burn some floor man! You're right, The Cats is getting too small. Gethro, you bad man." Jimmy's wagging his finger his face broadening in that wicked smile.

"Hey one kid from Wigan danced by me did a brilliant move it was the only move he could do, a back flip."

"Fuckin hell, on the dance floor?!"

"Yea Darb but he hadn't got any footwork there's some good dancers it's not going to be easy."

"Was there much gear in there?"

"Loads mate, everyone was smashed they either had some or wanted some I was surprised."

"What about us?"

"Well I told you, I'm not doing all-nighters without gear Jako it's just not the same."

"Yea Gethro, but how do we get some?"

"Easy I made some contacts up there, don't worry about gear I got it covered."

"What's up there?"

"Mostly chalkies, filon, backstreet blueys, dex, loads of stuff from what I could see Jako. Some of the lads from The Cats had some blueys."

"Ronnie said there's a coach in two weeks outside The Cats coming up from Cheltenham."

"We'll catch that then Darb, was he there Saturday? I thought he would have come to Wigan?"

"Said he's going to wait for that coach Gethro."

"Well he'll have some gear even Jimmy knows that!" Pointing my finger to their laughter. Jimmy's eyes widened in anger the playful expression he always had.

"You bad Gethro man!" Trying to strangle me I struggled to get free of his grip.

"I saw you in The Cats Jimmy, don't give me that no gear crap!" Our laughter erupting in the corner, "look I'll always be a Cats' boy but when that coach pulls up I'm going to Wigan."

"We are going to Wigan!" Kim's face in a look of defiance.

"Gethro I wouldn't go there." Darb laughing at my uneasiness.

"Sorry lover I meant we!"

"Tell him Kim! Tell him! Jimmy now after revenge."

"It's too smoky in here I gotta move come on lover." We made our way into the main room to dance on the far side of the floor. I felt happier at last they were going to come, one nagging problem. I was glad it was in two weeks, from my little escapades just lately I was now stone broke. I needed money but in the back of my mind I had an idea and would soon take care of that. Knave and Wolfy had shown up, a few faces from The Octopus new friends entering our inner circle dancing by our side.

This was my crew I smiled one with no name just Wolvo Soulies killing the floor. The Ship had evolved the disco chart shit being replaced with Motown and Soul now it had become a real Soul night. The bouncers watching our dancing the night dedicated to Northern Swoz bringing records to help Jamo working the decks.

Over the next few weeks our dancing was more intense as we practiced on the floors we had made our second home. Every night of the week on a dance floor pushing ourselves to perfection. Our minds focused on one thing to beat The Manchester Connection before they took the floor. Jako and Darb were good dancers and to us it was our strength.

Ever since Jako joined our little band he showed he was an individual. One who danced his own way. He never tried to copy the footwork of me and Darb that fast twisting style. His was wider stepping and bouncy as if he stepped into the beats. He was by us regarded as one of Wolvo's best dancers and one I was glad to have by my side. He could dance, his moves flowed often done slightly slower but perfectly in time to the music. Splits he was a master of the straight splits always straight legged and low down. Drop-backs with a spring he could spin into at lightening speeds.

At times just now and again he would hit one and would spin with his arms in different positions. Sometimes on his hips other times pulled into his chest. That's the thing about him, he could do it all but always in his own way. "The Joker" by The Milestones featuring Butch Baker was made for Jako, a record he loved to dance to. The bouncing mistimed beats fit his style to perfection. We all struggled to dance to it to get into the awkward rhythm but not Jako. To us he was the joker of the pack that wild card that would steal a floor. Once again Jako blew me away with his latest move, one that he invented full of his individual style. I had never seen it before, he would move around with stepping footwork kicking high then go down to bent knees. Jumping up in one move clapping his hands between his legs straight splits full on in midair. Landing legs together dropping to bent knees rising into a spin the move fit his style of footwork and a move none of us could do.

I just couldn't get it to fit my footwork all of us tried it but he was the master of this move. Right away leaping to shoulder heights, ones we couldn't reach. It was a move I would pick up on later but Jako started this move. Darb, Jako and me all of us danced with a spring an athletic feel to our moves. In a competition it would be hard to say who would win. Jako wasn't just a spinner he could dance that was plain for all to see as we hit the floor in The Cats that night and watched his latest move.

"No room man, too crowded!" His face in frustration as he came off the floor.

"I know you nearly kicked her up the arse Jako."

"Who Gethro?"

"Her!" I pointed just in front of me his puzzled look catching my gaze.

"The one in the white top?"

"Yea!"

"Well that's a nice arse if I am going to kick one that's the one I would pick Jako." Darb bursting out laughing as he too came off the floor.

"What time's this coach?"

"Ronnie said midnight Darb." Glancing at my watch fifteen minutes the excitement gathering between us the night about to unfold "Hey did the lads get some gear off him, there must be loads about I got some dex for ten a quid."

"And us I haven't took em yet though, thought I would wait for the coach."

"Yea I know what you mean Darb; I don't want to be smashed with nowhere to go. Anyway, if we need some more I can get some up there."

"Nice one man, another all-nighter Gethro."

"I know Darb but this time we can dance." I felt a twinge of sadness The Cats was brilliant but to me we had outgrown our club. It had given us so much introducing us to the Northern scene but as I watched the crowded floor with Kim by my side. Unable to dance the way I wanted "I knew we had made the right choice."

"Gethro, come on the Cheltenham Coach is outside!" Ronnie easing through the crowd towards the exit acknowledging friends along the way. There was just a few of us, it was plain to see not everyone was impressed with this new club called Wigan Casino.

"And where you all going?" Helen holding our coats teasing as she always did.

"Wigan, we went the other week me and Kim."

"I heard about that Pep might be up later said he wants to check it out, where will you be?"

"We'll be on the left hand side as you walk in Helen you'll find us."

"Ok, you look after her. Kim you tell me if he doesn't!" Handing our coats, the look of a headmistress our friendship bound in smiles.

"I will Helen, see you up there!"

A fifty-three seat coach parked outside, the dimness of interior lights showing empty seats. I was surprised, the coach only half full? We made our way towards the back the warmth of my surroundings so different from our journey last week. The hiss of the doors closing I wiped the side window, a few figures left standing on the pavement as we slowly pulled away. The excitement already building inside me at last we were on our way. The organizer collected our fare, Jimmy instantly giving him stick refusing to pay the outlandish price of a quid! Never showing any mercy to endless laughter from our little group.

We played our cassettes to idle the time, records we had taped from The Cats. All around us in the darkness of the interior the constant chatter of Soulies. Odd words caught in muted conversations always about records and gear. Jimmy keeping us entertained.

"Winston don't dance by me man, you dance like a girl." A tennis match of insults. Winston enjoying the playful barrage giving as good as he got. The journey moving along much quicker the night unfolding before us passing the time I went through our bag. The contents more or less the same as Va-Va only now Kim had moved in. Double checking small towel although we used beer cloths now as they took up less room. Spare shoes mine and Kim's, spare tops cassette deck and batteries and most important talc. Kim loved our big sports bag she had nothing to carry it was all in there even the address book with the names from the previous week.

Ronnie's voice just above a whisper coming from the back of the coach. "Lads take your gear before Knutsford I heard you sometimes get a few squad up here." I looked at the flat yellow tablets sitting in the palm of my hand. On the back SK and F in capital letters my face breaking to a smile, I wondered what they are for. I knew we would be ok, a line I walked very carefully with Kim. We had taken them before we had learned the hard way. They were smooth in the respect you came up and down gently so different from chalkies the other week. Passing ten to Kim her wild side now on display.

"You taking all of them Kim?"

"Of course I am. We always take the same." Jimmy making her smile laughing at her openness, exchanging the drink between them the feelings of guilt now gone.

"Our first all-nighter together man."

"I know Jimmy. You wait till you see this place." The excitement building between us I couldn't wait to get back on that floor. We had all started to take gear now it was just accepted between us. I thought nothing of it, to me it was just the normal thing to do. We knew if we were going to do all-nighters the only way to go was drugs.

We were young, we answered to no one but our conscience and I didn't have one. Drugs gave you energy, kept you awake, you felt more at one with the music as you stepped into another world. It's not as if we were alone the whole scene was alive with gear. It's just a feeling inside your body coming alive with amphetamines, your senses on fire the energy that they bring.

Reveling in each other's company a new door of friendship opening drawing us all closer together. We watched each other like brothers and knew exactly how far we could go. The lads all buzzing with excitement we slowly came up on our gear by the time we got to Wigan we were "flying high." All of us intoxicated with stimulants the wide-eyed feelings from being smashed. A feeling of happiness, excitement, energy, a bond of togetherness opening our hearts to the special friendship we all had. We pulled to a halt behind another coach unloading outside The Casino. Stepping down I buttoned my crombie, feeling the chill of autumn air. I felt strange here we were about to start our night and everyone else was in bed!

Chapter 29

OUT ON THE FLOOR

"What the fuck Gethro?!" I couldn't believe my eyes. Darb by my side Jako chewing frantically each of us holding our sports bags staring in disbelief. Massed on the pavement outside, a queue four deep stretching the full length of the building. Soulies packed together yelling and moaning coming from the front. The weight of a bouncer arms across the open doorway his heavy frame pushing backwards against the mass, another at his side.

"Anyone waiting for memberships come to the front, you have to have a card to get in! Stop pushing or you won't get in! Keep to the side, don't block the pavement!" His voice lost in the noise murmurs and shouts of the swaying crowd. Soulies bags at their side many in long leathers and bomber jackets small groups moving in and out of the queue. More cars filled the car parks surrounded with Soulies, record boxes in hands darting here and there. All around us deals unfolding you could feel the energy of the night.

"I thought you said it wasn't crowded?!"

"It's not Darb, wait till you get inside."

"That looks like a big queue to me Gethro."

"Probably five hundred people, you'll easily lose them inside." Bursting with pride I pointed to the upper windows, "look how big that building is man!" Blazing in light two levels of The Casino's windows casting shadows on the awning below.

"We'll see you in there Gethro, left hand side towards the stage."

"Yea Darb you'll find us."

Jako pacing around swinging his sports bag growing impatient. Look at the time! Come on lads let's get these memberships! Come on! We gotta go!"

"Jako's gonna dance on the pavement man!" Jimmy bursting to laughter, Darb and Winston laughing at his side.

"See you in there it's through that door Jako, tell the bouncer about your memberships!" They turned and disappeared to the front of The Casino we made our way towards the back of the queue. I smiled may be The Cats hadn't come but not everyone felt the same way. Occasionally catching a whisper, a pointed finger as we passed people by. So they remembered us that's good, it's exactly what I wanted, recognition and after tonight we would get even more.

"Hey up! Gethro Kim! Quick jump in here!" Mona and Lisa making space for us we nearly passed them by. We dived in besides them no one moaned it was just accepted, Wigan was like that. After all it was only a queue. We joined in conversations with strangers, a warmth of friendship all around us from people we didn't know. Chatting away feeling the vibrancy of other Soulies, the mutual sensation of being high. Strangers we met felt like brothers and sisters as if we had known them all our life. It was clear this was a special crowd, all-nighters have an atmosphere so different from a club. I could feel the gear had kicked in now all I wanted to do was dance. We neared the yellow light of the open arched doorway.

"Memberships only or you won't get in!" The bouncer pushing against me, my sports bag trapped in the crowd. A tap on my shoulder yanking my bag through the open doorway as we surged forward with the Nottingham lads. At the top of the stairs the same old lady collected our money, her name was Hilda a bouncer stood at her side, "Memberships please. That's seventy five pence." A smile as she returned our cards. Surely she couldn't remember our faces? Not out of so many from last week?

Following the flow of the crowd, mounting the stairs all of us chatting away we hurried along a passageway pushing the black double doors open. Once again the beauty of The Casino exploded before our eyes. The atmosphere of the all-nighter surrounding us we ventured forward to regain our spot. A buzz along the sides of the dance floor open sports bags filling table tops.

The smell of Brut growing stronger. Soulies with brightened expressions changing at the sides of the floor. All around us quickened steps of new comer's friends in shouts of delight. Friendships bound in handshakes, hugs at the sides of the floor. The bond of our music Northern Soul filling The Casino a few distant figures out on the floor.

"Come on Kim." Dropping our bag and coats at an empty table we were back in the center of the room. I looked around The Casino. It truly was a magical place, it wasn't full but it wasn't empty either, the night starting to come alive. A pace to our surroundings a bustle along the sides of the floor. The gentle hum of conversations, Soulies settling at tables oblivious I rummaged through our bag. Kim soaking in the atmosphere looking for friends from the previous week.

"Can you see Billy and Waka, Kim?"

"No not yet. Why?"

"Good! Quick let's get this out before he comes." Sprinkling talc in an arc out on the dance floor dusting a wide circle turning to Kim my smiles of satisfaction. "That should do it. I don't want him doing that move by me!" She burst out laughing at my antics, she didn't know how serious I was! "Help me set this tape deck up lover." I pulled the cassette from our bag placing it on the table, searching for the mic.

Kim smiling shaking her head, "Everything's there lover." Her voice trying to calm me down. My heart racing, I could feel the dex fighting a dryness, a strange taste in the back of my mouth licking my lips everything done in a hurry. Already starting to sweat I found the towel to wipe my face.

"You know I love you."

"Really Gethro! I never thought you cared!" Spinning around to see Jimmy with the biggest smile I had ever seen. Winston, Darb, and Jako looking around The Casino, their faces in disbelief, dropping their coats and bags at our table.

"This place is unreal man. Look at it, the floor its fuckin massive!"

"My exact words Darb. I told you it's unreal!"

Jako bursting forward, twisting his feet moving out on the empty floor. "Hey it comes with talc already on it Gethro!" Testing the floor turning gently into a spin. Shrugging my shoulders I glanced at Kim standing with Jimmy and Winston now laughing neither of us saying a word. We looked different from Soulies around us. The uniform of Soul boys, our baggy trousers and matching vests standing out.

The red and white illuminated in fluorescents, the black fist of The Catacombs you could see we had come to dance. Jako attracting attention, pointed fingers the nudge of an elbow more Soulies filling tables, his dancing catching there eye. Bouncing wide stepping footwork his slim figure illuminated in the purple of bright light. Clapping hands, dropping down to bent knees, coming up powering into a spin. Legs held tight together a spinning top of illuming light. Easily one of his fastest, breaking out to wide stepping footwork flowing into his moves.

My heart bursting with pride at the way he could dance, the moves he was going to bring. I joined him feeling the smoothness of the floor this really was a brilliant spot. Interconnecting steps of fast twisting feet, my hands feeling the music arms floating at my side. A slight dip of the shoulder hands reaching out jumping up crossing my legs. A snap to my moves, an aggression twisting in midair. Hands on hips, arms in a diamond a blur of speed clapping hands ending the spin. The gear racing through my body, feeling the heat of an adrenaline high. Jako exploring the floor, Darb dancing at my side wrapped up in the emotion now bringing his moves. Dropping to straight splits, rising from a drop-back his feet rolling into fast, stepping, footwork.

Darb and I were Soul brothers we always danced side by side feeding off one another just as we always did. All of our styles individual immediately given space by Soulies around us who stood to the side and watched. A glow of pride engulfed me, our little crew had finally arrived.

From that very first time on Wigan's dance floor we were always given room. Dancers just opened up around us they could see we loved to dance. As I connected with the gear deep inside I felt as if I was dancing for them. There was an instant respect on Wigan's floor if you bumped into someone you were the first to hold up your hand to say sorry.

The same as in any Northern club, there was never any attitude on a Northern floor, only an inner rivalry between dancers till you became friends. I didn't try to blow people off I just danced but if you took me on then I would rise to the challenge even now not many dancers tried.

Jimmy started to show the moves he had brought from The Cats another style of dancing so different from any of us. Fast shuffling footwork he glided along the edge of the floor. His feet moving as one as if tied together, he never broke into the stepping footwork of our style. Kim and

Winston at his side their faces full of laughter.

All of us joining as one the smiles of pleasure between us that dancing together brings. Jako joining me in a contest of spinning Darb counting us down both of us hitting spins at the same time. The feelings of gear kicking in even more, a surge of energy racing inside my body, fighting an aggression that wanted to dance at a pace, show them what I could do to tear into the floor. My mind racing in thoughts I came off the floor.

"What's up Gethro?" Darb at my side. I don't want to give too much away, I want to take the Manchester lads on. We can work the floor later. Come on, let's put these coats up, grabbing our coats as I turned away from the floor. "Be back in a minute lover. Come on, I want you to meet Scatty."

"Who?"

"My mate from last week, the one with the chalkies." We paused by the left hand side of the stage a staircase behind us dancers catching our attention. "Look see how he does the splits, I haven't seen any one do it like us Darb straight legs all the way down."

"Yea I know but look how long it took us to learn that Gethro." The standards of our dancing satisfaction glowing in our smiles.

"Come on he's up here. Wait till you see this floor from the balcony man!" We climbed the stairs together a low top collecting a second look the smiling face of a young girl returning our playful smiles.

"Did you see her Gethro?"

"I know she should be a pirate with a chest like that!" We burst out laughing Darb's face changing to a stern expression.

"Gethro she was looking at me!"

"Well I was looking at her tits. Lot of girls in here man!"

"I know." Our laughter breaking to smiles, "I could get into a lot of trouble Darb."

"You can't I can."

"No I can as well, just can't get caught!"

"You and the girls Gethro, you're bad man!"

"I was born that way Darb, you know that!" Our faces full of mischief. "Hey check this out!" Below us the dance floor starting to fill, more Soulies streaming into the club. All around the edges people bonding together, groups from corner to corner. Stacking bags underneath tables, the side of the floor a honeycomb of movement, others crisscrossing the floor.

We looked around at other dancers our little group instantly stood out. Kim skipping along the side, her skirt of white in a whirl of movement illuminated in lights. At her side Jimmy and Winston now dancing, their twisting fast shuffling footwork lightness to their feet. Jimmy's muscular frame shining in sweat, a towel looped to his trousers the occasional wipe of his face. Jako's spinning getting faster, a flick of blond hair at the end of a spin. His darkened vest a patchwork covered in sweat jumping up clapping hands turning in motion. A face locked in concentration, spins at lightning speed. Flashes of white from his spinning easily standing out on the floor. Our gaze wandering the room I could see Darb was blown away his whispered voice beside me. "This is unreal man. Look at it."

The Casino was reminiscent of a beautiful woman, her blemishes hidden in darkness. Shadows of the night her makeup, she came alive at night. Northern all around us the place had its own atmosphere, it wasn't like The Cats or Va-Va this was a much grander scale. The odd handclaps from dancers below us I pointed across to the far side of the floor.

"See over there that's where Booper dances with his mates."

"Where?" Darb's face in an expression of mixed confusion.

"By the front see that girl by the stage in the yellow top in that corner down there." My face breaking to a smile, "that's where we are going to dance later."

"You'll never forget will you?"

I shook my head. "No, you know me better than anyone. You know I never forget."

"I know, we weren't ready for that man."

"And they won't be ready for us either." The thought of that making us laugh. "Anyway Darb, we're gonna put Wolvo on the map by taking this club." His face now in a look of surprise.

"And how you going to do that?"

"Easy, take the dance floor. When you got that people are attracted to you."

"Why's that?" His face alight with attention made worse by the looks of the gear.

"You're smashed. They want to know what you're on. They want to be on the same high then you can start to run gear." My hands gesturing to the dance floor smiles of satisfaction in my plan. "It's got to work like that and tonight we take our first step mate. We got to beat the best dancers in here, we got to take this floor."

"Seems like you got it all worked out."

"I have I want us to be the best mate and we will!"

"Big ideas Gethro."

"Yea I know. You think we can do it Darb?"

"To be honest mate with you, I don't know we just might." I put my arm around him as we shook hands our bond deeper than ever, a brother I never had a grin on our faces.

"Give me a year, you'll see."

"Only a year." We started laughing at my little speech, what a load of bollocks! I wondered if it was the gear. I seemed to be talking a lot, maybe drugs make you like that?

"Gethro! Darb!" A Northern accent we recognized, both of us turning around. "How you doing pal?!" Our faces bursting to smiles. Brent standing with his mates, their expressions wearing the mask of Soul boys wide eyed and totally blocked! We greeted one another with handshakes. Titch, Mart, and Big Roger the hug of our friendship the bond from that night at Va-Va but now we were on the same high.

"Lads want some chalkies, ten a quid?"

"We're ok Brent, we had some dex." I started to smile turning to Darb "I told you there's loads of gear up here. Brent's mates have got it all!" We all started laughing.

"There's loads of gear in here tonight, it's the only way man. Fuck being straight!" Brent's carefree attitude making us laugh even more.

"What's in the boxes? Gear?"

"No! Few records Gethro, we always bring a few to swap or sell. We're waiting for Russ's hatch to open at three." Brent gesturing to a serving hatch behind him a poster on the side of the wall. "Richard's on later, Russ gave him a spot it's his second week."

"Nice one Brent, he's a good DJ held the floor at Va-Va." I remember his spot well. "Seen Shawn or big Willie?"

"No not yet but they'll be in here somewhere." As we looked over the side of the balcony I pointed to the floor below.

"Brent see that girl in the braided skirt? That's Kim, my girlfriend, next to her the big guy with the yellow headband, that's Jimmy."

"Who's the guy spinning?" Tall Martin leaning over the balcony.

"That's Jako our mate. We all came from The Cats." My voice full of pride at their dancing below us.

"Looks like you got some competition Mart, he's a good spinner." Titch smiled, his turn of phrase saying it all.

"Hey Gethro we might have some filon and blueys later, we're waiting for more of the lads to come in."

"Well you know where we'll be Brent, come over." As we shook in crossing hands and parted in our friendship an inner glow came over me. It felt good to be on the scene Darb gazing over the balcony.

"You weren't kidding Gethro. This is like Va-Va only out of control."

"I know I guarantee everyone you meet is the same as us. It's one big block up man! You wait till it picks up." I could see Darb was impressed by his new found surroundings. We made our way forward passing a small kiosk on the wall, a list of the latest pressings they held no interest to us. Following the flow of the balcony caught in the light of the bar a few tables with record collectors. A couple of Soulies scouring boxes, clutching their latest finds. We entered the black doors at the side of the bar ascending the steep stairs.

"Scatty what's up man? This is Darb my best mate from Wolvo, all of us have come this week!" Dropping our coats with others on the counter the mountain piled high.

"Hey up mate, how you doing? Name's Scatty." His tall frame leaning across the counter wide eyed slim features, a face bursting in smiles. We introduced ourselves with a handshake my face beaming with pride. Two girls stood at his side looking at us with inquisitive expressions, obviously smiling at our accents. "This is Diane and Lynn, they're taking over from coats, Gethro."

"Scatty said you're a good dancer." Lynn's attention now focused on me.

"I'm ok it's not just me, we can all dance. We're from the floor of The Cats."

"Hey want same as last week Gethro?"

"No Scat were ok." Passing the money for our coats.

"Watch them two Gethro, they'll have your trousers off in a minute." Scat laughing as he turned away.

"Scat! Take no notice of him he just wants what he can't have!" She lowered her voice, her face now in a smile, "they have pass outs if you get a bit tired from dancing. Come and get me we'll go for a walk." Her eyes locking into mine a smiling face full of mischief. I felt a rush of adrenaline, my eyes searching her body at the pleasure that would bring.

"If I go outside with you it won't be for a walk!" Both of us laughing at my openness.

"That's even better." Her face lighting with a smile not in the least bit shy.

"Gethro!"

"I know Darb but I can't help it." My hand gestured towards her. "She's a pretty girl man!"

"Come and see me later." A persistence now in her smile I began to blush.

"I can't. I've got my girl."

"Shame."

"Told you to watch out Gethro!"

"Get lost Scat!"

"Later Scat!" We turned away descending the stairs.

"You're bad Gethro!"

"I know Darb but that's on a plate."

"What about Kim?"

"You know I love Kim but that's not love its well, you know, and they are two different things! I'm eighteen man I'm going to screw anything that comes my way. When I'm dead at least I'll die with a fuckin smile!" We bursting out laughing in the closeness of our friendship, my hands on his shoulder. "We'll keep that one to ourselves!"

"I know what you mean Gethro, she was putting it out there man."

"Like I told you lot of girls in here and it seems these Northern girls don't mess about."

"Come on let's get back before you get in trouble man!"

"And you she had a mate, I saw her giving you the eye."

"When?"

"Just, didn't you see her?"

"Was she?"

"Yea."

"I like this club."

"Me too, come on! Let's get back on the floor." As we made our way forward, I stopped by the kiosk. "Darb tell Kim I'll be in the Nott's corner."

"Gethro!" Darb turning, smiling at me a look of cross examination. "No honest. I'll see you later."

"Later man." We never judged each other, that's how close we were.

I had a problem. I was broke after paying in, then two quid on the coach, two quid gear and my board I had fifty pence in my pocket. My wages of an apprentice to last the rest of the week my pride would never allow me to ask a girl for money.

Now it was time to put my idea into action. Glancing over the balcony I could see all the pieces in place. Buzzing from the feelings of gear my senses felt sharper even more than the people around me. My mind racing making decisions, thoughts turning in my head at lightning speed. Sure I wanted to dance but first I had to make some money, this would be the gateway to my dancing.

I knew exactly what I had to do, hustle and good for me I was a natural at it. I moved across to the far side of the balcony pulling a chair by the side of Irish greeting in crossing hands our conversation soon turning to gear.

"We only just got in Gethro. I've got a load of blueys to knock out, know anybody?"

"How many you got?"

"Four hundred."

"Fuckin hell Irish, you don't mess about! What do you want for a hundred?" I wasn't interested in running backwards and forwards all night, not for someone else. "To be straight Irish, I need to make some money." For some reason I felt in my pocket, I still had fifty pence! I was just being honest both of us racing with adrenaline, our expressions intent sharing that same high.

"I paid a fiver for hundred. Just give me seven quid."

"Thanks Irish. Thanks mate!" My voice full of sincerity responding to his smiling face. I had just learned my first lesson, always sweeten the deal give someone a margin of profit and they would always work for you. No bouncers around the room I reached into the open sports bag taking the bag of pills to my pocket. "Nice one Man!" I couldn't believe it, I had never held so many tablets. I smiled my senses on fire, a confidence about me I felt I belonged in this new world. We parted in a handshake a shared look between us one of absolute trust.

I moved along the balcony watching dancers below me, descending the wide staircase my heart racing with excitement. Once again no bouncers by the girl's toilets. The DJ queuing the latest record The Righteous Brothers Band "Rat Race" Northern filling The Casino, pounding beats driving me forward. Submerging in the atmosphere of the all-nighter I moved along the side of the floor. All around me the hum of conversations Mona approached his face alight with energy that comes from being out on the floor. Grabbing a Coke we sat at a table renewing our conversation from earlier.

"Still want any gear Mona?"

"What you got? There's some dex and filon about." His face lifting in anticipation, beads of sweat trickling from his forehead dripping from his chin.

"I know but I've got some double strength blueys, a new batch. Just got them from my mate help me knock them out I'll give you some for free."

"How much?"

"Eight a quid." I upped my price and took a gamble. Straight away I was hustling by selling dearer, I gave the impression they were stronger. By coming up with a load of bollocks I was giving you a deal. I knew Irish's blueys were strong, they were the reason I couldn't come down in The Ship. I smiled at the scenario, eight of them would blow your head off!

"I'll be back in a minute with the money, get me forty." We parted in a handshake the strength of his grip his heart no lectures spoken between us. I knew he was as crazy as me. Now how the hell am I going to do this?! I had a problem, the only place I could count them would be in the men's toilets. I made my way through dancers feeling nervous as if under a spotlight crossing the floor heading straight to a pack of suited U-boats. Bouncers in the darkness guarding the entrance to the men's toilets.

My mind fighting anxiety the bulge of pills in my pocket. Fighting my nerves keeping calm pushing the door open fixed eyes not saying a word. Remnants of the early disco scattered around me, toilet paper littered the floor. Cigarette butts, blocked urinals, yellow canals of stale piss lining the walls. I leaned into a sink, the scum of old porcelain, cool water refreshing my face. I felt like I wanted to throw up the place had a smell all of its own. A row of single black doors behind me, I dived into a half open stall.

Locking the door grabbing hold of the bag so that's how they do it. A polythene bank bag, why hadn't I thought of that?! A piece of toilet paper in my lap dropping forty blueys in the tissue for Mona. A calamity of nerves, hands shaking, tingling in my fingers, the slightest sound making me nervous, everything done at speed. I had to get out of here, flushing the toilet making my exit.

A sigh of relief on leaving, the bouncers not even there. I made my way back across the dance floor sitting down at the same table. My heart pounding racing thoughts crossing my mind. I had made mistake after mistake, "what a fuckin armature!" I knew that wasn't going to work for me. Too many open chances and for what? No reason! Finding comfort in the darkness there's no way the bouncers can see me. A hive of activity all around me Soulies in verbal led conversations others out on the floor.

I instantly felt relaxed now I had my answer. I had a good view of the balcony and all around me, I would deal at the side of the floor. I waited patiently watching dancers, their moves pissing me off. I wanted to get back on the floor, I couldn't what if this lot came out of my pocket? There would be a rugby scrum out on the floor. I smiled at the thought, how would I tell Irish? You always think the worst. Mona returning to our table. Shaking hands we exchanged money.

"Sorry Mona, I had to put them in bog paper."

"Hey up don't care what you wrap em in, so long we all get smashed!" Handing over the gear both of us burst out laughing, his face in a squinting grin.

"I've got some more if you know anybody "

"Gethro I'll be back in a minute. Give me another forty."

"Why move? I counted the pills, dropping them into an empty cigarette packet that's how easy it was. In the darkness of our table, turmoil around me no one could see a thing. The dex making me talkative chatting with the Nottingham crowd I started to learn about gear. Bombers, black and whites, green and clears, red and browns I knew nothing about these drugs. My education wrapped in jumbled verbal conversations, Soulies telling me what they had taken others wishing they had. I felt comfortable in my new surroundings the blueys just disappeared. My attitude was simple I didn't give a shit was I the only one selling drugs in here? Oh really! Just me?!

"Thanks for helping me out Mona." Dropping the spare blueys in the palm of his hand.

"Pass Coke Gethro." His profit gone in one swallow, his face bursting to a smile he seemed more than happy with that. Money didn't interest Mona but our friendship did. We began to verbal about gear I would be Mona's student as he taught me all he knew. Not only the best gear to take but the different strengths of caps and pills. I had made a special friend, "the perfect right hand man." Mona knew a lot of people tonight, I had made contact with the Sheffield and Nottingham crowds.

I felt the money in my pocket, well that's Irish covered. In less than one hour I had made half a week's wages. My first deal. I felt elated, I had just doubled my money, not really, I had started with none. "Later Mona." We parted shaking hands, a Soul brother who would enter my inner circle. Lessons learned from the past, I picked my friends they didn't pick me. My methods in dealing needed fine tuning but something had caught my eye. I now knew exactly how to deal in The Casino and Kim would play a big hand in this. Biggest problem for me, I had been gone from the dance floor too long. The night slipping away, still no Booper, I began to wonder if he'll come.

Working my way through dancers, three spinners catching my attention at the center of the stage. Shawn, Titch, and Tall Martin, they too had footwork similar to Jako more in a wide stepping style. The Bolton lads from Va-Va shining bodies, colored vests twisting in motion spraying sweat on dancers around them feeling the heat of the floor. To their side Dave and Irish locked in a contest of spinning, the competition tonight a reminder.

If you want a piece of this floor you had better bring your best game. Such was the quality of Wigan's dancers they didn't just come from The Wheel and The Torch. Darb rising from a drop-back, Jako spinning at his side Winston burst into smiles "Gethro look at Kim man!" A whirling figure of speed skirt swirling in motion. Kim's face soaked in the atmosphere a free spirit connecting out on the floor. A leg break into a spin, fast feet skipping in a line, hands turning in circles drifting effortlessly at her side. The Incredibles "There's Nothing Else To Say" Northern filling The Casino, surrounding us in Soul. Taking a swig of Coke I relaxed with Winston at the side of the floor. Our bond stronger than ever this was our youth, the most precious time of our life. Tonight was our night! We shared our dancing together.

At last, I was where I belonged. For the first time in numbers The Cats' floor had started to move. Stouport, Cheltenham, Gloucester, Paul and Pete from Kidderminster mates of Ronnie's from Stoke mixing in with Wolvo. Kim dancing with Julie, Allen, Helen, Nesta, and Laney all Midland Soul girls on the left-hand side. As soon as I hit the floor I could feel the effects of gear, my energy levels to the max. Joining a new generation of Soulies surrounded by a much younger crowd. Our dancing increasing in tempo one big family, our friendship bound in Soul. Feeling the magic of the night a sensation of dancers around me I just knew this club was special, one that would forever remain in my heart. Record after record holding us on the floor claps and spins from dancers, a feeling of one to one.

The atmosphere fueled with amphetamines, a bond with the music driving us into the beats Mel Williams "Can It Be Me", Sheila Anthony 'Livin' In Love", Jimmy Conwell "To Much", Garnet Mimms "Looking For You",

The Dynamics "Yes, I Love You Baby", The Capitols "Ain't That Terrible", Little Anthony And The Imperials "Gonna Fix You Good", The Detroit Shakers "Help Me Find My Way", Jeanette Williams "All Of A Sudden", The Sherrys "Put Your Arms Around Me", Jackie Day "Before It's Too Late", and Bobby Garrett "I Can't Get Away" suddenly a dancer catching my eye. Directly opposite, towards the front stage the unmistakable dance moves of Booper. My heart exploded, at last he had finally arrived!

"Come on Darb, no, not that way. Come on, let's have the crack with Jako. I want to watch Booper from the balcony." Leaving the floor we made our way to the wide staircase behind us rising two at a time.

A perfect view to their corner, a small crowd gathering at the side of the floor. Booper playing to the audience, the looks of a bouncer taking to the floor stripping from his dress shirt and waistcoat meticulously folding his clothes. As ever the showman an open briefcase to his side. Dancing in a blue vest and black parallels, to me he looked really old! Wigan's floor suited Booper's style in the respect to his footwork and spinning I could see he needed room. Straight away I knew why he made his choice to dance on the right-hand side of the floor. There was hardly any foot traffic coming and going from the girl's toilets so different from the men's on the opposite side of the floor. Freedom to express yourself uninterrupted. Vital to a dancer as you wound into your moves out on the open floor. He wasn't the fastest spinner out there but he was more graceful, I had to give him that.

"He's still good Gethro."

"I know Darb, he's got class man!" We watched him dance his flowing hand movements, arms in an arc a discipline to all of his moves. The crowd getting larger he really was that good to watch. The style of a dancer is his uniqueness it's the little touches as he connects his moves to the music. Booper, to me, was a master of this, an arrogance to his dancing he definitely thought he was the best. I studied him more closely looking for weakness both of us silently weighing up the opposition at the battle about to unfold.

By his side two other dancers, a fast spinner with a similar style. The other I had never seen before a dancer small in stature one with really quick feet. We stood watching them work the floor they tended to lean back when they danced, their footwork in a skipping style.

Little did we know we were about to see one of the most definitive dance moves to ever hit the Northern scene. The small guy dropping to bent knees, a figure four he spun his outside leg crossing under his body a Russian Cossack turning on the spot. On his yellow vest the badge of The Wheel, white skinners alight in fluorescents a spinning top rising from the dance floor, "a light bulb about to explode."

This one move defined the style of Northern dancing for years and years to come. I had just been blown off the floor before I got on it by another move I couldn't do! "Did you see that Darb! What a fuckin move, how did he do that?!"

"We need Jako, Gethro!" Both of us started laughing, spellbound by a brilliant move. We made our way around the balcony never taking our eyes off the floor. Shawn and Tall Martin spinning like tops, a mass of twisting bodies Dave and Irish below us the back of the room totally empty. We watched the small guy again he dropped into a leg spin, no one else was doing this move his dancing in a class of its own.

"Come on I've seen enough! Let's get down there!"

"That's Booper's corner Gethro."

"No it's not. This is a free floor it's anybody's corner no one owns this floor. Like I told you I'll dance where ever I want! Fuck them!" Darb sharing in my anger, a belief my confidence infectious.

"I'm with you man! Let's do it!"

We made our way forward, descending the wide staircase coming out at the front of the stage. A buzz in the crowd all around us dancers illuminated in fluorescents the atmosphere of the all-nighter drawing us to the floor. Working our way through crowded tables, Mona at the side of the floor his thumb gesturing to the dance floor.

"Hey up! Gethro you gonna dance against this lot?!"

"Too right we are mate. We're gonna introduce them to The Cats! We're the best dancers in here!" Mona's eyes shining with gear his face beaming with smiles. "This is my best mate Darb, Mona the one I told you about." Crossing handshakes as we watched introductions at the side of the floor.

My dream had finally come true, now we would make our statement this time on a much bigger floor. To our right Booper's corner a large area around him his dancing style commanding the floor. A record we loved filling The Casino the driving beats an unmistakable sound "Seven Days Too Long" by Chuck Wood one of our favorite records, we couldn't ask for more.

"Hear it man?! Hear it?! Darb's waving hand a face bursting to smiles both of us feeling the rush of gear. Hitting the floor together as always side by side Soulies around us parted giving us instant room. A tidal wave erupting in the right-hand corner as we unleashed our interpretation of how we dance to Soul! Exploding into the footwork we had perfected gliding effortlessly along the side of the floor. My arms stretching, reaching feeling the pure Soul of the record the fast pounding beats. Breaking out into a semi-circle of cross stepping footwork three styles combining to one. Half turns into dummy spins, side steps of movement in different directions spreading out across the floor.

The foundation of our dancing footwork! Footwork! Footwork! I knew they couldn't match. A quality to our dancing everything done with precision little touches we had learned from Booper connecting all of our moves. Breaking into combinations to match the record we knew had been played at The Cats. The crowd intensifying, onlookers in surprise Soulies lining the dance floor others leaning over the balcony.

Booper instantly recognized us, my heart racing. At last we had got the competition we wanted more vinyl hitting the floor Laura Lee "To Win Your Heart" and Mary Wells "Can't You See (You're Losing Me)" blasting my rush into overdrive! Bob Wilson Sounds "Strings A GoGo", Billy Butler "Right Track", and The Vel-Vets "I Got To Find Me Somebody". This was pure Northern! This is what made us dance! Both of us tearing into the dance floor my arms in an arc hands locked together, whoa! "I got to find me somebody!" Whoa! Spins to the chorus self-expression from the heart a freedom to dance that held no bounds.

Two DJs watching the dance floor the atmosphere of the all-nighter rising in a crescendo feeling the buzz of the crowd. More dancers joining the Manchester corner they knew we were a challenge. Some deliberately crossing in front of us to break our momentum, others trying to box us in. Booper's spins intensifying in speed an aggression to his dancing clapping hands at the end of spins. His grace and style full of passion hand expressions in time to the music, skipping drifting footwork. Jumping up, spinning in midair, sweat spraying across the dance floor turning on landing a perfect figure four. His back arched, a grinning face pointed fingers in my direction willing me to challenge his moves. Hands in constant movement his unique style dominating their corner. I moved closer, the icy stare glaring at me a face of anger streaming in sweat.

Relishing the contest a passion welling inside of me this time I wasn't going away. I had something to prove, my look of defiance the young upstart willing him to bring it on. Now I deliberately matched him step for step my footwork flowing in style easily equal to his.

Booper grinning with other dancers joining him, there's no way he would walk off a floor. The leg spinner standing to the side I knew what he was doing watching our dancing, a cat waiting to pounce.

Darb like me rising to the challenge breaking to smiles at the moves we were about to unleash. Old and new styles clashed, this was a straight contest The Catacombs against The Wheel! The DJ looking over, riding the wave of energy one on one with the dancers, a smile of recognition, a connection with the floor. Bob Brady "More, More, More Of Your Love", The Artistics "Hope We Have", and The Monitors "Share A Little Love With Me" more records dear to my heart driving me in my dancing. A flood of vinyl holding us on the floor Earl Grant "Hide Nor Hair", The Ad Libs "Nothing Worse Than Being Alone", The Fi-Dels "Try A Little Harder", and Johnnie Taylor "Friday Night".

The small guy stepping forward straight away showing his footwork, twisting feet moving along the edge of the floor. Kicking high, dropping to a leg spin, a helicopter rotating in movement spinning out on the floor. Rising this time to fast footwork, clapping hands turning into spins. Hands tucked to his chest neatness in his dancing a move we had to match. Claps of recognition from Booper, a contemptuous smirk and nods to fellow dancers he thought he had us beat. Turning to a drop-back I came up spinning the opposite way, hands in the air in defiance a move he couldn't do. I wanted to piss him off, wipe that grin off his face!

My head spinning blurred faces on the balcony watching our every move. Crowded tables around us pointed fingers, shouts from the crowd. I loved the competition, a battle out on the floor a target on my back now I just wanted more. Heat welling up inside my body exploding on the inside sweat streaming down my face. A pounding heart driving me forward, drugs pushing me in my dancing. Wigan's floor playing to our advantage all the space we needed. We gave no respect to The Wheel boys this was a fight for the floor! Catching Jako in the corner of my eye a face of concentration clapping hands now at my side. Coming out of a half turn a shoe at the side of my head his wiry frame covered in sweat.

"Come on Gethro let's burn this floor man!" A burst of smiles between us full splits in midair. "Our joker had just arrived!" Smoky And The Fabulous Blades "Jerk, Baby Jerk" a record that tore us apart! Three of us coming together hardly a break in the music.

"Let's let them have it. Come on Darb! Jako! Let it rip man!" Quick exchanges between us, a glow of pride engulfed me now I knew we could beat them as we unleashed our moves. Sequences deliberately held back at Va-Va now flooding onto the floor. Spinning straight into the splits, multiple drop-backs to spins at lightning speed, we had no equal more Northern hitting the floor: Marvin Holmes And Justice "You Better Keep Her", The Hesitations "I'm Not Built That Way", The Platters "Sweet Sweet Lovin'", The Showmen "Our Love Will Grow", and Dee Dee Sharp "What Kind Of Lady".

Coupled with our youth our stamina second to none we were born to dance on this floor. The pure speed of our moves in combinations tearing the floor apart. Sweat spraying across the dance floor all of us locked in the competition, the corner alight in fluorescents my arms in an arc at the end of spins. Hands held high pointing to the balcony dropping one handed to sideways splits.

Cockiness in my dancing anger welling inside me, I had to beat that leg spinner! I had to match that move! Rising at speed crossing my legs in midair landing one legged my spins tearing into the floor. The surge of gear racing through me the spinner trying to match my move.

Jako laughing at our madness dropping to sideways splits, his chin nearly touching the floor. Coming up from a drop-back hammering into a spin a whirling upright figure of speed. Hands tucked into his sides straight into a drop-back never taking his eyes off the leg spinner.

Booper's face intense, other dancers around us launching to more spins. This was a Northern floor, an open contest not one of us giving an inch! Three of us breaking out in an arc deliberately pushing towards their corner, multiple drop-back combinations new moves now hitting the floor. Drop-backs done in a circle my feet barely leaving the floor. Pushing with my ankles shoes in perfect position turning on the spot, knees kissing the floor. A new move I had practiced rising up with no help from my hands. A touch of the heel. My feet a flurry of movement bending my legs at the knees a slight pause in my dancing. Legs held tightly together stopping and starting the next move. Turning on one foot, arms outstretched reaching feeling dipping my shoulder hammering to more spins.

Darb's footwork like mine fast twisting feet a circle of movement leaning forwards burning into the floor. Jako grinning I knew that look on his face.

Nottingham Soulies joining us, Mona dancing in front of us three of us going into overdrive, more records hitting the floor. Morris Chestnut "Too

Darn Soulful", Reparata & the Delrons "Panic", and Danny Wagner "I Lost A True Love" all of us laughing, smiling, our minds lost in the moment dancers on a crowded floor. Jako's spins faster now a nod of appreciation a respect we instantly had.

My heart bursting with satisfaction, still we had more moves Soul Brothers Six "Thank You Baby For Loving Me" cries of "what a tune!" Between us our footwork faster, twisting turning leather shoes responding to talc and the freedom of the floor. A mass of energy a record that let us open our hearts snapping up-tempo beats, fast floating footwork playing to our strengths. Clapping hands faces soaked in emotion feeding off each other the drugs pushing us higher.

The black fist of The Catacombs, our matching vests soaked in adrenaline, shining bodies burning in sweat. Jako turning from a move I looked across Jimmy now joining us flawless shuffling footwork Winston by his side. Gleaming figures of light moving in time to the record pounding beats driving them along the edge of the floor.

Kim at my side, arms floating effortlessly fast skipping footwork drifting in and out of dancers. A leg break to a bent knee a rising spinning top. Little Joe Cook "I'm Falling In Love With You Baby", The Sweet Things "I'm In A World Of Trouble", Johnny Moore "Walk Like A Man", Lou Ragland "I Travel Alone", and Bobby Hebb "Love Love Love" a record that brought me to my knees made me so happy inside. More and more sounds from The Cats.

Conversations lost in the moment, shared drinks at the side of the floor. None of us giving an inch, smiles of recognition willing each other to retake to the floor. Record after record, the atmosphere fueled with amphetamines driven by music, a timeless spell a magical power of music of love of togetherness.

Laughing, feeling the friendship of other dancers around us our youth, our age the bond only all-nighters bring. Still the battle raged on dancers interchanging constantly rejoining the floor, none of us backing down. Jako's uniqueness for all to see. Clapping hands, a leg break, dropping turning faster arms at his side, a stern face locked into his moves. A rag doll of blond hair standing on end, "a chimney brush in a two footed spin." He too showing unusual footwork perfection, dropping to bent knees, rising twisting to full splits in midair.

Along the side a large crowd had gathered. Onlookers in a gaze of amazement watching his latest moves. What a dancer, my heart bursting inside at my Soul brother the bond we had the moves that he could do. A nod of respect from the leg spinner acknowledging a dancer's full flight in midair. The glaring face of Booper, our eyes clashed turning away leaving the floor his steaming body soaked in sweat. Slamming his Coke on the table, grabbing a towel wiping his face. A look of disbelief, the sheer pace of our dancing finally tearing him apart.

Booper had a weakness, his age, he was easily giving us ten years. To us he looked old as if he belonged to another generation he took us on, that was the caliber of his dancing. Had he been our age I doubt the outcome would have been the same. That's how good he was, he had been on the floor for years. Such was his arrogance he was determined to go down fighting, a dancer I disliked but one I respected and admired.

Booper was the leader of his dancing generation deep inside I was determined to lead mine. We had to pull out all of the stops and we did. We proved it in our dancing, at last we had made our statement. If you want to beat us you had to bring more than just footwork and spins, our dancing went a lot deeper than that! Sure they could do certain moves we couldn't do but so could we. It had been a close contest who won I don't know but we had arrived and it was clear for all to see.

There was an age gap and it showed on the floor, they were remnants from The Torch and The Wheel. Both clubs had played their part in the development of our dancing but we were the new wave of dancers and our styles were now miles apart.

Our average age was seventeen, we were younger, fitter, more agile. The sequences of our moves coupled with the athletic approach mixed into our dancing out on an open floor we had no equal. Unlike other younger dancers we had fast footwork that complemented and matched our moves. Wigan's dance floor dictated these kinds of moves. Due to its pure size a new style of dancing would eventually evolve. I wasn't bothered about the leg spinner, I knew Jako would take care of that. He could watch someone dance and within one night he would be able to do their moves. That was the strength of his dancing, I knew The Joker would crack that move!

We moved into their corner now dancing in front of them taking revenge for Va-Va with sequences they couldn't do. All of us coming closer together our footwork killing the floor The Drifters "You Gotta Pay Your Dues", Jerry Williams "If You Ask Me", Doni Burdick "Bari Track", The 5th Dimension "Train, Keep On Movin'", Tony Clarke "Landslide", Milton Wright And The Terra Shirma Strings "The Gallop", and Clifford Curry "I Can't Get Hold Of Myself" endless music driving us on and on and on.

The night this time so different from Va-Va, still we had energy to burn Willie Mitchell "The Champion Part 1" a record full of our beats, feelings so deep inside now I became one to one. The lazy sax climbing the walls, pounding Northern beats, a Casino anthem, the floor bouncing flowing in an expression of pure love of Soul music. Rivalries pushed aside, faces locked in ecstasy sisters and brothers out on the floor. Jeanette White "Music" driving us wild the power of this record. Her voice totally igniting the dancers, an inferno of burning passion willing me to dance more and more. My body soaked, feeling the gear, heart pounding, alarm bells ringing in my head. An express train out of control drenched in emotion of what had just happened, finally I came off the floor. Collapsing in Winston's arms his muscular frame lifting me off the floor holding me tightly our bodies covered in sweat.

"That was brilliant Gethro man! Brilliant! You pissed them off!"

"I know we did, I meant to fuck it!" Hardly able to speak, my body breathless, slumped over blood roaring in my ears sweat streaming from my face. Fighting for air, catching my breath my voice in a whisper. "We're from Wolvo man!"

"Hey up Gethro that was brilliant! You were dancing that fast, shadow couldn't keep up with ya. Good gear eh!" Mona hugging me, eyes like dinner plates his beaming smiles sharing the moment riding our adrenaline high.

Feeling the thirst of dancing, my head spinning in a cocktail of chemicals grabbing a Coke and catching my breath. Slowly I ventured forwards joining the leg spinner, people watching at the side of the floor. Hand claps, small groups of Soulies surrounding us, driving the atmosphere a constant noise from the floor. Everyone still out there, Jako making me smile spinning against other dancers faster than anyone they could bring. Inquisitiveness got the best of me, I had to put a face to that move.

"What's your name mate?" The leg spinner turned around, twisted curly black hair a sharpness to his features, he too looked much older than us.

"Chrissie, I'm from Preston." Smiling he gestured to the dance floor, "Where the fuck you lot from!"

"The Cats Wolvo."

"Ah! So that's where you learned to dance!" We used to go to Torch up that way, never made it to Cats though." His Northern ascent profound, as always making me smile.

"My name's Gethro. That's a brilliant move you've got mate!" He started grinning, tapping his badge.

"It's just a move from The Wheel." We shook hands, a true Soul brother, another dancer who would impact my dancing gaining my instant respect. Darb and Jako now leaving the floor laughter between them, recognition at what we had done. Jimmy and Winston at my side.

"Shit! I hadn't paid Irish, he'll think I've ripped him off! Lad's I'm going back to the Wolvo corner." We made our way weaving through dances across to the Wolvo side. Soon finding Irish at the left of the stage instantly throwing our arms around each other, as always a dancer's respect. He too soaked in emotion, the adrenaline and atmosphere of the all-nighter, competitions held on the floor. Our faces in the mirrored columns so different from before, paying for the blueys we chatted for a while.

"That was some competition Gethro. We've been dancing with the Bolton lads nearly came over to help, some brilliant dancing mate! I told you he was the one to beat!"

"Yea but you never told me about the little guy! Both of us laughing. Hey thanks Irish." Our friendship stronger than ever, smiling as we parted to words of "keep the faith."

I looked across the dance floor pausing for a brief moment. Would Booper ever try to push us off a floor again? Time would tell. Deep down I didn't feel like we had won anything except maybe the hearts of the younger crowd. A few things stuck in my mind I had learned a lot from our encounter.

If you are going to stand out as a dancer dress bright and I mean bright. More important than that, if you have a move that only you can do use it sparingly. That one move had dominated the floor, no one else but he could do it. I wanted that move bad. This was the missing link to a whole set of new moves and I could see it straight away but he had made a mistake. Jako dropping to a leg spin in front of me, not the same smoothness but he had the basics of that move! I stood to the side watching intently.

"Look at Jako Darb. He's unreal."

"I know he's a brilliant dancer Gethro. We'll be dancing against him one day,"

"Well I'm the best dancer Darb!"

"No you're not, it's me!"

"No I'm the best!"

"No I am Gethro!"

"I'm the best!" Jako standing beside me, our smiles in faceless expressions all of us burst into laughter. Dancing against each other that will never happen, the scenario that would bring. As we stood and watched other dancers at our side introduced themselves. A small guy was spinning to our left his snapping style and countless tries went unnoticed as he turned into numerous spins. When he stopped I went over to speak.

"Got any talc mate?"

"Yea it's in the bag over there, help yourself?"

"Nice spinning mate. What's your name?"

"Booky, I'm from Wigan."

"I'm Gethro. This is Darb and Jako were from Wolvo." Such was the bond of The Casino all of us shaking hands, little did I know the friend we had just made. Sprinkling talc in the area in front of us another dancing partner friendship made at the side of the floor. Big Willie, Badger, Ric Tic, Brent, Shawn, Dave, Irish, Billy Back, Waka, Mona and many more, a constant flow of our friends joining us throughout the night.

The friendliness of The Casino, the atmosphere it created our only love was Northern and dancing. Friendships that would span a lifetime in the uniqueness of an underground scene. The night slowly fading away, slipping through our fingers as we gave our hearts out on the floor dancing with more passion than ever before.

All of us captured in the moment, there wasn't any competition anymore. Jimmy Radcliffe "Long After Tonight Is All Over" filling the casino, the balcony now empty the warmth of togetherness from dancer's handclaps all around me. A feeling of belonging to this moment our little band out on the floor. Dean Parrish "I'm On My Way" ending our night in handclaps, our hearts sinking back to reality the night over.

Arms wrapped around each other like brothers and sisters, friends coming over to say goodbye. We didn't care about the future we lived for now, this moment. A youth that never wore a watch, a timeless hand that thought our lives would last forever.

We rode the wave of Northern till it hit the shore eight years later. That's the way we all were. This was our adolescence, our time, the most precious time in our life and we all climbed on board the atmosphere of Wigan Casino. Windowed shafts of light cascading onto the empty dance floor, the cloak of darkness melting before me. A developing Polaroid picture resting in the palm of my hand, reflections of our youth smiling back at me. Memories lasting forever, faces of youth locked in time.

Chapter 30

THERE'S NO STOPPING US NOW

The bubbles in my tea cup reminding me of my life, a concaving spiral spinning round and round. The smell of cooking bacon filling the air, shouts of orders drown in a clatter of crockery. Rumpy's crowded with customers, the clutter of shopping at tables a typical Saturday afternoon. Darb and I sat, bemused at the antics on the opposite side of the table. Jimmy, Jako, and Winston in a constant battle, "Jimmy stop pushing!" The table rattling with tea cups Winston's croaking body squeezed in the middle, all of them fighting for room. Jako's head bent, a face of concentration drooling over his martial arts magazine.

"Look at this Winst, no one can kick like that!" Stabbing the table with his finger owahhhh! A muted cry between them, another picture of their mentor, their master Bruce Lee. I couldn't idolize anyone, their infatuation making me smile.

"You left The Cats early?"

"I know Jimmy, Kim's on a curfew." Shrugging my shoulders, sipping my tea, I don't know why. I dropped her off then bumped into Carol." Jako looking up from his mentor.

"Who the one with big ti?"

"Smile Jako! Yea two big smiles." Laughter filling our table, the young waitress placing sandwiches to correct orders. Brown and red sauce crossing between us, a silence for a brief moment.

"You bad Gethro!"

"I know Jimmy." Looks of forgiveness and mischief between us one girl I loved, the other I didn't. I felt no guilt, a dog forever chasing his tail.

"Hey I found this new club. Its ten pence to get in and loads of girls walk around half naked." Suddenly all eyes in my direction even Darb turning to my side. I knew I had them, Winston the first to crack.

"Where?"

"The swimming baths." All of us laughing at Winston's face of confusion, grinning in embarrassment stroking his chin.

"Well I found a better place than that." Jako finally joining us from the land of Bruce Lee curiosity. Getting the better of me I had to ask.

"What place?"

"Next to my class, I looked the other day, loads of girls doing gymnastics."

"What?! Where?! Now he really had my attention."

"Next to my martial arts class in Wallsall." I couldn't believe my luck, exactly what I wanted a gymnastics club.

"When's it on?"

"Tuesdays and Thursdays."

"I'm coming." Before I could ask I had my answer from Darb. Jimmy leaning across the table, passing me a fiver.

"That's for the bomber jacket Gethro, we're quits."

"Nice one Jimmy." Now I could get my sheep's skin secondhand but who cares. To me I would be a lot warmer and anyway the bomber jacket was miles too big.

"You going to Ruby Reds record shop? I want a copy of Bobby Hebb."

Jimmy had started to collect records even I had now, started to take an interest with one golden rule. If I danced to it I would buy it but labels and fancy prices held no interest to me. We always popped in there on our way to The Octopus, after all Pep also had a shop but we had morals "we didn't like to steal records from Pep."

Mike the middle aged proprietor looking nervously from the counter as we entered the shop. A really nice guy who would play anything for us. Lists of Northern pressing mixed with the latest imports surrounding us. Some of our favorites Rubin Parker "You've Been Away", Mel Williams "Can It Be Me", Mitch Ryder "Breakout", and Rufus Lumley "I'm Standing" today we behaved ourselves, but it wasn't always the case. The records reminding me of Billy Back and our first night at Wigan, gymnastics was the answer now I could work on Billy Back's move.

Three of us marched into the gymnasium with our sports bags, I smiled at what lay before me Jako was bang on, the place packed with young girls. To me I was in heaven, gymnastics right easy, "what could possibly go wrong?" The gym a hive of activity girls of all ages free falling, tumbling on the mats others forming a line. The lead one running, springing onto a vaulting horse arms held high, a perfect landing on mats. We stood at the back watching a young girl disappear in the roof lights bouncing on trampoline. Some older girls doing bridges, I started to smile.

"Come on lads, concentrate." All of us burst out laughing at the site before our eyes as we changed at the side of the floor. After introductions we joined a small group loosening up, stretching was easy. All of us were supple, our dancing dictated that. The first moves we did were arrow springs. A short run diving onto your hands with a turn and twist with your legs in midair. Landing on my feet was easy, I immediately thought of a drop-back following through turning this to a really simple move. As usual playing to the girls I began to show off, the young trainer coming over.

"So you think you're a dancer?" Holding me close his face in red annoyance. "No one disrupts my class, you obviously don't know me?! I want you to do some stretching." Darb and Jako joining us at the vaulting horse. "You, what's your name?"

"Darb sir."

"Stand on his feet." My arms stretched backwards, my body in an arc the trainer applying pressure from the opposite side. Darb and Jako laughing at my predicament. "Gethro, man!" My body being torn apart before their very eyes. After that, I took things seriously. Gymnastics helped us stretch, become even more supple as they bent us in every direction. One exercise we would do was walk down a wall backwards. Do a bridge against the wall and move down and touch your ankles. Over the weeks we attended classes Darb and I devoted our time to our dancing. In the end, paying a heavy price in discovering many new moves. One we concentrated on was the handspring and my mate learned this one the hardest way. First, we would practice front somersaults on a trampoline.

"That's it stay with it, right up higher lean forward hands in and over. Good, next!" Arnold the trainer watching attentively at my effort, Darb and Jako by his side "next."

"Come on Darb, you got this mate!" I egged him on higher and higher, suddenly a rag doll twisting in slow motion totally out of control landing legs apart in the springs grabbing with both hands. Rising to the scream of a banshee, then dropping to scream even louder a second time. The legs of an octopus, a line of tentacles two perfect rows of blood blisters bleeding on either leg. Finally we released him, his face grimacing in pain. Jako and I couldn't stop laughing, a right pair of bastards. "Wait till Jimmy hears about this! A payback for me being in the ring!"

Deep down I felt sorry for my mate, the things we do for dancing! Over the weeks we learned three basic moves, the arrow spring, front somersault, and handspring. I took to gymnastics like a duck to water always with one thing in mind. How can I link this to our dancing? Time would give me the answers. In the end, I too would pay a heavy price, tweaking a cartridge, my dancing over. Darb and I watching from the sidelines an ending to the year we least expected. Spending our time watching Kim, Jako, Jimmy, and Winston dancing on the floors around Wolvo, most of our time now devoted to The Cats.

Chapter 31

THE DIARY OF A SOUL BOY (ONE THAT DOESN'T LIE)

I always rubbed my feet together, even Kim stated the fact it's as if I danced in my sleep. They never stopped. The crackle of radio Luxemburg filling my bedroom "Behind A Painted Smile" by The Isley Brothers drifting in and out over the air waves. Sitting at my desk my thoughts drifting aimlessly with the music.

My concrete jungle of tenement building wrapped in the folds of darkness. The evening rain reflecting a yellow glow of streetlights, the snake of empty roads. A desolate miserable night. Wow, glad I'm not out there! It was now early April, what had happened to the weeks and months. Time had flown on by. I was nearing the end of college, the finals to my welding exams only months away.

Four years I had pursed my goal, this homework so boring "The Theory of Welding". Who gives a shit? Enough for tonight, pushing the book aside replacing it with a diary. Flicking through the pages I smiled at the heading "The diary of a soul boy 1974, one that doesn't lie" my private thoughts and emotions. I had kept my first new year's resolution, I had written it in every day. My list was endless, the wants of a teenager to self-achieve, I had set the bar high. New cords, take driving lessons, pass my test, pass my exams, go to more Northern all-nighters, buy Kim a ring, and improve on my dancing. A time capsule of memories drawn to the pages I began to read my notes.

We had started the year with Major Lance on January the 1st at Top of the world, a club in Stafford. What a joke, the venue full of Divs Major Lance igniting the crowd with a few of his classics, "Ain't No Soul (In These Old Shoes)", "Investigate", and "You Don't Want Me No More". All through the day there had been fighting, local Skins not liking the fact that Wolvo were on their patch. The territorial bullshit still the norm, ending in more fights at the end of the night. Soulies from The Cats and Stoke battling it out against Skins. The crowds at the all-dayer so different from all-nighters, Northern still very much an underground scene. Not only unrest at the all-dayer, the mood of the country of rebellion with the working class backing the miners working to rule. The winter of discontent, the news had called it, the Heath government in turmoil. Power rationing to commercial users, factories limited to three days a week.

A work force thrown into part-time, the television closing down at ten thirty. The paper walls of my shoebox, a silence in the opposite room. I smiled now they were really in trouble, they would have to talk to each other. A marriage born of convenience, devoid of happiness and love. Working construction I had been the only one of our little band doing five days and more so we pooled our money to make it to venues. My injury over, we had kept our momentum on the dance floors. In January alone we had done three all-dayers and two all-nighters. All listed meticulously in the back of my diary with artists, dates, and times.

On the 13th of January we had returned to The Casino. On from two till eight, all of us coming away disappointed. Kim's purse being stolen, rip-offs in the venue rubbing salt into our wounds. The sounds were terrible, new DJs filling the lineup showing their obsession with labels. The club lacking in atmosphere dancers staring at a half empty floor. That night they held semifinals of the first dancing competition, all of us dismayed at the quality of the dancing. Watching, wishing I had entered. Wigan Casino a relatively new club, slowly emerging on the Northern scene.

The best all-nighter had been right on our doorstep. Held at The Catacombs on the 26th of January on from eight till six, the atmosphere electric and the place packed to the rafters. The youth of Wolvo feeling the buzz of Northern, the club itself an icon on the Northern scene. Nothing could compare to The Catacombs, the sounds and atmosphere unique to the venue but again we struggled to dance. Once more I scored some gear, again I got ripped off. When would I ever learn? I had broken my rule, only deal with people you can take out, what a wanker! The insult of The Torch boys going deep so they still classed us as being Divs yet I kept coming back for more! Even now anger welling up inside me, just wait, every dog has his day and I would have mine!

I'll show you bastards how to deal drugs. I now started to take painkillers, we could buy them across the counter. Too many caused internal bleeding, a mere side effect to an adolescent, and "in my mind they gave me a buzz." Finances dictating everything, the three day week killing pay packets. We stayed local, going to all-dayers at Top Rank Suite Hanley on the 20th and Tiffany's New Castle under Lyme on the 27th. A mini bus taking us to the all-dayer, a trip I organized. The smartness of Tiffany's impressing me, the dance floor shaped like a lagoon with palm trees around the edge. A far cry from The Catacombs' all-nighter and the atmosphere of the previous night.

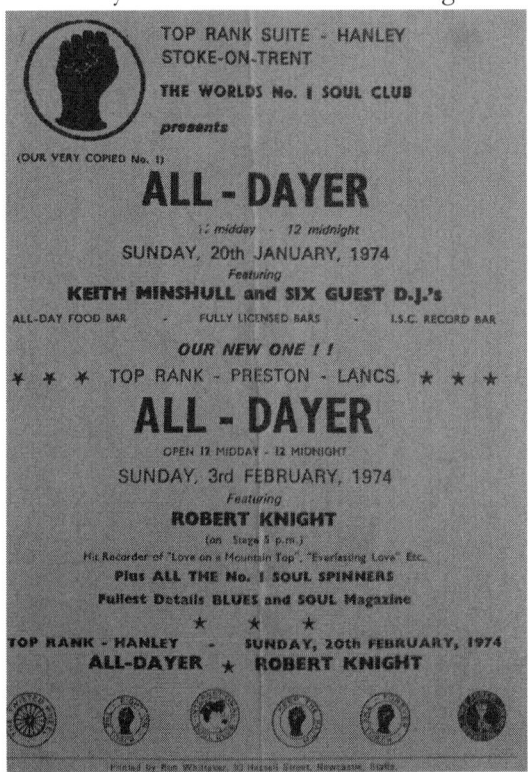

Twice I had clashed with Booper at all-dayers, dancing myself to a standstill, the painkillers doing their work. Each time I felt I had been the victor, to me by his attitude he felt the same way. Regarding my New Year's resolution I decided to push myself even harder in my dancing and put my ideas into action. Cats six times, even on a Friday when it was free and totally empty. Octopus three Saturdays, Ship five visits. This had been our schedule we were totally dedicated to our dancing.

Besides gymnastics, another area I concentrated on was the leg spinner. The move had fascinated me. At The Ship with the help of Jako I fine-tuned this move. To me, there were two different types of dancers, upright spinners who were obsessed with beating each other for speed and low level, the style we had. A mixture of acrobatics and spins. Linking the two together had been a problem, we were close but now I had another key. The leg spin was too awkward for me, passing your leg around and around without the jerkiness of a hop was hard. With just one modification it would lead to so many new moves.

I would kick out, touch my hand at height, drop down, right leg bent at three o'clock, my left hand touching the floor. By bringing my right leg anticlockwise just as my legs crossed I would spring them apart. One leg stopped at nine o'clock the other at three o'clock, then follow through by dipping my head. I was now in a sideways splits.

Another modification in this position was by leaning back, twisting my body and pushing my knees together, both hands at my side now I was in a drop-back. Sometimes as I came to six o'clock with my right leg, I would throw my left leg out and bring them together and stop. Now I could bring my legs through into a drop-back, not only this, if I wanted I could bring one leg through into straight splits. I treated the dance floor as a pummel horse, sometimes letting my legs rotate together with my hands constantly moving ending in drop-backs or splits.

This was the caliber of my dancing, at low level often linking the moves to opposite spins. To improve my suppleness I had an answer. I had been practicing at work, often to be found at odd moments of embarrassment, kicking the tops of door frames with either foot. My efforts drawing attention even leading to bets, free-standing, straight kick, or no jump. This was all natural to me, my heart and soul lived to be on a dance floor. Dancing was an art and the floor was my canvas a spirit deep inside me, one of self-expression, the individual I wanted to be.

Another area I worked on was my spinning. Again I had learned from practicing if you dragged your foot you could push and make the spin last longer. That wasn't my style, to me, you were cheating. One foot, the other crossed and hit it in midair landing on one foot, now that's a spinner. Shawn from Bolton and Booper the masters of that style.

My ultimate goal was double figure spins, either way in one hit. Over and over I practiced even getting Darb and Jako to count me down. Slowly, subtle changes would come to me. I could jump and spin or stand free, style the key to speed was what I wanted. By jumping up crossing my legs on landing, Booper had the same move. Now instead of my arms at three and nine which allowed me to turn with ease into a spin and drop-back, I changed to twelve and nine. My right hand reaching out then pulling back to my body feeing the air around me. At exactly the right moment launching into the spin, this gave me power as I twisted from the hips on landing.

Timing and balance critical, changing my hands led to an increase in speed. That's what made you stand out on a floor. We were miles in front of our game, but the best was yet to come.

What a month! We had even been to the football match to see Wolves beat Norwich, to seal a place at Wembley. Northern is Northern but this is your team, dancing on the terraces before The Cats all-nighter. The gold and black of the North Bank alive with many of The Cats crowd. I had stayed true to my goals, now taking driving lessons even more, so I had never missed a day from work or college. Not letting the Northern scene interfere with my trade my stepping stone to freedom. From there I could leave this time bomb they called a home.

Chapter 32

FEBUARY 1974

Once again the month started well, I was now an Improver, receiving a rise and back pay. Now at last I could get my cords, money I had spent before it touched the ground. We had returned to the dance floors with a vengeance. Two all-nighters, two all-dayers with twenty-two venues in between The Cats, Octopus, Ship, Duck, and Civic the last one bringing back memories of a point we had made on the 8th.

Still grinning at the page, I reflected on the night in February, the first time in Wolvo Kim and I had left our footprints' on a dance floor. Every Friday The Civic held discos, the venue full of Cats' Soulies but also other elements of Wolvo street life. Two crews from the town dominating the venue, Temple Street and The West Park. The large floor attracting us like a magnet, giving us a chance to practice arrow springs and handsprings. Although neither fit our dancing at this time, we drew unwanted attention.

Kim and I had been pushed into the dancing competition, four couples at our side. Looks of arrogance greeting us, Kim nervously looking at our opponents across the stage. Below us the lads nudging each other. "Come on Kim!" "Gethro, burn it!" Shouts of encouragement from many of the younger Cats crowd. Paul Gambochine, a radio DJ queuing the record. Harold Melvin & The Blue Notes "The Love I Lost" blasting from the speakers. We danced the only way we knew, pure Northern footwork and drop-backs now hitting the stage. Suddenly the music stopped, the DJ placing a bunch of records in our hands to cheering from the crowd.

Later, the night turning ugly some members of The West Park demanding our records. The lads and our friends from The Cats standing by me, one push or punch from a fight. At The Civic, The West Park had met a white boy who could dance and for some reason they didn't like that. On that same night they met one who could really fight. Kibble and his crew, all six of them taking them on. The night ending in running battles across the dance floor. The town still full of violence, not every venue was a Northern floor. Just Wolvo street life, being Wolvo. Darb and I chatting the next day as we walked on through the town.

"See Kibble last night, Gethro?"

"I know me and Kim got surrounded at the top of Board St. If it wasn't for Venton and Ralfie we would have been dead meat, man they were pissed off! Come on its empty!" Both of us turning into Jacksons by passing suited dummies in the foyer, one thing now on our minds.

"Gethro, Darb, what brings you two in here?" A young suited assistant greeting us.

"Colin, you old tart, we've come to be measured up for some cords."

"What's up with Karman Gear?"

"Fuck that! I wouldn't be seen dead in a pair of them, that's for the High Street. Anyway you're the man." The banter as always between us, I knew I was in for a rough ride. Colin throwing the material books for us to scour through.

"Right, who's first?"

"Go on Darb, I want to find the material."

"No. You first."

"No. You."

"Yea, but you know what he's like."

"I'll keep my eye on him mate." Colin grinning, wrapping his tape around his fingers, Darb's arms now high in the air.

"You stand like a duck Darb." Patting his rear, "nice arse."

"Gethro see!"

"Twenty-eight waist, you fat bastard. Keep still!" Colin kneeling by Darb as he measured his inside leg to a face held in fright.

Leaving them to their devices, a material had caught my eye. A sky blue needle cord, perfect for The Casino, it would stand out in the fluorescents. Looking up I shouted across, "What pockets you having Darb?"

"Three inch deep flap, three button fastening."

"Nice one man. What about the waistband."

"Three inch, three button."

"You said that already, you think I'm made of buttons?!" Colin blurting out by his knees. "Any turn ups Darb?"

"No Col, just straight parallels."

"How big?"

"Thirty inch."

"What, thirty inch parallels?! You sure?"

"Yea and mine." Colin rising, stretching his tape measure and laughing at our choice.

"Right. You're done."

"I got the material for mine mate." Darb coming over, "see if you can find anything."

"That's nice material man."

"Right, come on Gethro, you're next." Darb grinning at my dilemma.

"Thirty inch parallels. Why don't you just wear a skirt?" Colin laughing, holding the tape around my waist. "Twenty-six you skinny bastard." Tapping my legs apart, now kneeling beside me. "Come on upps!"

"Hey watch that!" Measuring my inside leg.

"Still want the inch off, like last time?"

"Course I do. These are for dancing." Looking at Darb's face of embarrassment.

"Hey do that to mine!" Remembering our night at The Ship.

"What's the waistband? You want three inch as well Gethro?"

"No inch and a half Col, with overlapping single button fasten."

Darb looking towards me confused, "What no buttons?"

"No, I want them to be different." Colin raising his eyes.

"Ok what else."

"Straight side pockets with nylon zips."

"What! Why?" Darb even more confused.

"Never mind, you'll see."

These were designed for dancing with handsprings and somersaults in mind. Not only that, also for dealing. Remembering Irish and the blueys nothing would come out of my pockets. I could deal and rip into the floor. Now I had really blown his mind, laughing at their faces, if only they knew why. "I want two adjustable sides zips on the waistband, one either side, three pleats at the front, and two back pockets with no button flaps."

"No flaps, that's different."

"I know Darb. I want loop fasteners."

"Hey Colin, I want some pleats."

"You can't. Not with flap pockets on the front mate."

"Guess we're gonna be different Gethro."

"We will, but what about the material?" Both of us falling in love with blue needle cord.

"Wait till we hit the floor in these Darb!" Both of us agreeing we had made the right choice. We wanted to be different, individual. If I was going to dance in cords they would be, to my own design.

My second pair of tailor made, so different from the first. Three pound deposit, five weeks to make them, they couldn't come soon enough. This was evident in The Casino on the 10th of February, that night we were swallowed up by dancers on the crowded floor. New faces filling The Casino, the etiquette of the dance floor changed, much more territorial. Booper and his mates exacting their revenge, blowing us off the floor. Deliberately boxing us in, unable to find room for our new moves we couldn't dance the way we wanted. Spending my time making new friends, contacts I would need later. The night belonged to Manchester, they had retaken the floor. I smiled at my writing. "A diary that doesn't lie."

It was simple, if we were going to make any impact at The Casino we have to go every week. A different story the next day at the Steam Machine Hanley all-dayer. Arriving early, changing our shoes from leather to rubber to compensate for the material of dance floor. We hit the empty venue with arrow springs into a drop-back, our moves from gymnastics starting to come together. Booper watching from the side line with Manchester dancers as we took our revenge. Squeak outstanding in his spins as Wolvo and Stoke dominated the floor.

Robert Knight the following week on the 17th of February at the Top Rank Hanley another all-dayer we attended. "Love On A Mountain Top" his latest hit. I wasn't into live acts, but even I had to admit he could sing. At this venue we picked up a flyer not believing our eyes. In March a Torch revival all-nighter. Not only that, in April a Soul festival to be held in Leeds both venues organized by The International Soul Club. The month of February ending at The Cats all-nighter on the 23rd, this time completely empty, no crowd, no atmosphere. The Civic Soul nights on a Friday coupled with The Casino having an impact on The Cats or maybe it was just Wolves? We had the floor to ourselves, again we practiced arrow springs and handsprings, Jako coming up with some brilliant new moves.

Chapter 33

MARCH 1974

The sands of youth slipping through my fingers, now trapped in these pages, day's events jumping out at me. On March 2nd I joined forty thousand Wolves' fans descending on London. A tidal wave of elation in a convoy of Gold and Black. Wolves in the League Cup final at Wembly, our opponents Manchester City favorites to win the game.

I had never been to the Capitol, we had arrived at ten thirty. Bit early for a pint, not really soaking in the atmosphere unique to a Cup Final. Fans mingling together we soon found our way to the nearest pub. I smiled at the name The Torch, now at last no one can ever say I hadn't been there. Pushing the door open a wall of sound greeting me, the crowded bar packed with City and Wolves. Scarves of Blue and White, others of Gold and Black, the bar a mass of denim and Skins.

All the fans in good humor, many old faces from The George and Exchange. Later the bar picking up on The Cup atmosphere, breaking out into singing contests. City's Songs of Sumerbee Marsh and Lee greeted with cries of John Richards and Dougan. The choirs of the Kipax and North Bank all of us ending in an alcohol fueled chorus, "We all fuckin hate Leeds!" The most hated team in the land. Suddenly windows shattered, glass flying in every direction rocks being thrown through windows a massive uproar in the bar. Chants of defiance outside, Cockneys spoiling for a fight trying to ruin our day. City and Wolves joining together I knew I would be safe following Kibble and his crew in a mad rush for the door. All of us pouring onto the street, Kibble in the middle of the mayhem steaming into Cockneys backed up by City and Wolves. Bringing back memories, a face that knew no fear!

All of us moving forward, a chanting mass towards the ground. My body tingling when I entered the stadium, there's something special about a Cup Final. The swaying of the crowds in their chanting, the brightness of green turf. A sea of golden shirts, the Blue and White of City, the tingling of the Manchester bell. The crowd roaring with excitement at a game played fair and square. Hibbitt scoring for Wolves, sending us all into hysteria. Bell equalizing for city, their fans in equal jubilation. The game played out on the wings, Richards scoring for Wolves! Setting the terraces alight in total ecstasy, the Wolves' fans going mental, bursting into song.

Forty thousand eyes now focused on the clock. Six minutes of pure anxiety, willing the fingers to move, chewing my nails, my knuckles in desperation. The final whistle drowned in an explosion of happiness, feelings of euphoria bursting deep inside me. Jumping, singing, dancing, joining the conga of the terraces "Eee hi adio Wolves had won The Cup!" The day ending at Piccadilly and Trafalgar fountains celebrations in the Capitol, once in a lifetime memories and parties into the night.

The miners work to rule over a general election been and gone. The normality of street life didn't matter to me. I didn't live in reality, my life was in a different world. Northern Soul sweeping through clubs. Twenty three Soul venues in Wolvo alone, this month local dance floors igniting our feet. Every Wednesday, The Cats full to the rafters, The Octopus crowds on a Saturday. Sunday and Tuesdays at The Ship packed with young Soulies, another vibrant floor. Everywhere the fever of Northern, yet still to the masses an underground scene.

Twice we had been to the Top Rank Handly, our visit this month to an all-dayer on the 17th of March to see Limmie & Family Cookin'. All of us now trying to be more individual in our dancing, again we arrived early. To make an entrance on the dance floor Jako would do a somersault, straight over no hands. At the same time to compete I would do an arrow spring into a drop-back. Our moves complementing each other, both of us rising up into spins. You had to have an empty floor to pull this off or get your timing down to perfection.

Many of the younger Cats crowd now coming to the venues trying to imitate our moves. Evo had a new move he copied from Bootlace, one of our friends, a well-known dancer from Stoke. If done right it looked good but it could have disastrous consequences. He would dance away with stepping footwork then dive on to his hands, holding his balance for a brief moment. Then as he lowered down, push back with bent arms and kick out with his legs, jumping back on to his feet.

As usual at all-dayers, Divs would be walking around the edge of the floor with trays of drinks. I watched in slow motion, the guy never saw him coming as Evo took the tray right out of his hands! Bottles and glasses spinning in midair, a tidal wave of liquid refreshment saturated a crowded table to shouts and squeals of fright. To us the same rule at all-nighters applied to all-dayers. We came to dance, we had no sympathy for them, and alcohol didn't belong on a Northern floor!

On the 23rd The Torch Revival All-Nighter from two till eight holding a special place in my heart. The name of the club a legend on the scene. Matchy, Booper, Smokey, Nero, and Cody names in muted conversations, two dance floors packed to capacity. Martin Ellis, Keith Minshull, Dave Evison, and Brian Rae, DJs igniting the dance floors the night full of records we loved. All of us dancing nonstop, the flame of The Torch burning brighter than ever. An atmosphere unique to the venue I would wear my revival badge with pride.

Many of our friends from Wigan reconnecting on the floor. Others we met that night, Mick and Polo from Worcester, Glenn Walker from Blackpool and many more. Our network of friends growing wider with every venue. . Two coaches would leave for Leeds from The Catacombs, we had already booked our seats. The next day we purchased our tickets, there's no way were going to miss The Leeds Soul Festival, we left nothing to chance. Two questions were on everyone's lips. "Have you got any gear?" and "Are you going to Leeds?" The Soul Festival gathering in momentum, the flyers now more descriptive. The biggest all-night Soul event ever, in bold letters, "SOUL FESTIVAL The Queens Hall Leeds, over seven thousand capacity" sending our imaginations wild! A dance floor I could only imagine, live Soul acts of who's who on from eight till eight.

```
QUEENS HALL — LEEDS                • Saturday, April 6th
(over 7000 capacity)                open 8.00 p.m. — 8 a.m.
2 minutes from main station.
"Everybody's coming to".... The country's first ever!!
            ALL-NIGHT SOUL FESTIVAL
            The full all USA line up now features"...
MAJOR LANCE                                        J.J. BARNES
            HEARTS OF SOUL
                            MEL AND TIM

                              ON STAGE 4.30
                                                ON STAGE 3.30 a.m.
              ON STAGE 1.00 a.m.
ON STAGE 2.30 a.m.
              PLUS "THE SUPER-SOUL-SPINNERS"
• KEITH MINSHULL • KEV. ROBERTS • HUNTER SMITH • ANDY HANLEY • RICK
          COOPER •COMPERE CHRIS WILLIAMS
  Advance Tickets £1.60 (over 4000 already sold) On the night £2.00 — guests £2.50  Still available from
                    head office and ticket agents
  You must have a current I.S.C. Membership card to be admitted to any of our events ... 10p plus S.A.E.
              "This is the soul event of all time" (our May one's even bigger)
  Blues & Soul — Black Music — Hot Buttered Soul Promotions • £25 I.S.C. Dancer of the Year
                              Competition
          "OUR ANNUAL BARBEQUE 'N' Splash is now being lined up!!
```

Now we started to make a mark as individuals, not only did we strive to be unique on the dance floor we wanted to stand out in the crowd. Square cut collared Fred Perry's, Slazenger tennis shirts, V-neck patch work jumpers, cheesecloth shirts of many designs. Pointed patterned shirts, as ever non-conformists, we dictated our own style, the lads as demanding as the girls. My cords had now arrived, thirty inch parallels of faded blue. Being distinctive made me feel good. If you were different you instantly stood out in a crowd. We weren't the only ones doing this, the scene was full of individuals like us all with their own ideas.

Kim like so many of the girls dressed different from the High Street norm. She would buy and alter old patterns to designs she liked, making her skirts and dresses with length, free flowing for dancing. Her blouses were V-neck short sleeved with turned back cuffs. Long dresses were fashionable, different cuts of V and square cut fronts with thin straps. Wide belts looped, fastening at the waist. Box and full pleated skirts from Chelsea Girl, long Macs and leathers. Big buttoned canvas trench coats from Wallis complemented with paisley scarves worn at the neck. Flat canvas sandals, granny's for dancing, Sasha cork platform wedges, low flat heeled loafers and brogues from Ravels. Graduated short bob style haircuts, girls carrying vanity cases covered with Soul badges.

The scene didn't have any set fashion but it definitely had individuals with their own style. To complement this even I had gone a stage further. I used to carry an orange Puma bag to all-nighters, I never put badges on my bag I didn't want to be like everyone else. To be different I had got some capital letters and put them on the side, spelling my name in an arc Gethro. I drew around them and peeled them off, then in matte black paint I went over the letters. Now I had my name on the side, identical to the Puma logo, totally original. Whenever I was asked where I got it, I gave various answers just like Ric Tic and his Cats badge. "Oh, you have to special order it. I had it made."

"Turn that bloody light off! Wasting electric!" The unmistakable voice of "growler" a nickname I had given my foster mother. My bedroom door flying open, angry fingers flicking the switch.

"It's ok, I've done my homework!" My voice as ever in a sarcastic reply. I hadn't, but what did they care? Closing my diary in darkness I relaxed upon the bed. My mind could only wonder, a venue that holds seven thousand, we would make our grand entrance on the dance floor at Leeds.

Chapter 34

LEEDS SOUL FESTIVAL APRIL 6th 1974

"It's darker than The Cats"

"How much further Gethro?"

"I don't know mate, I've never been this far up north." Darb throwing himself back in the seat in frustration the slight murmur of Jimmy sleeping at his side. The Marvelettes "Only Your Love Can Save Me", a Cats' tape drifting from the speakers, hardly heard above the constant chatter of voices. I glanced at my watch marking time. Nearly six thirty, we had left The Cats at four, surely it can't be that much further? The stuffiness of stale air, irritating my throat.

"Look at that Kim!" I love you written in the mist of the side window. Smiling, I wiped it away. The Manchester canal crossing a viaduct on the horizon. Rolling hills of English countryside, long shadows of tree-lined fields melting to a fading sun. Kim snuggling up beside me, resting her head on my shoulder. "We'll get there when we get there," her voice in a gentle sigh.

Two coaches had left from The Catacombs, this one full of the younger Cats crowd. Binman, Derm, Canny, Squeak, Milligan, Mulley, Punna, Knave, Syd, Eggy, Ray Weverly, the Jamo's and more.

"Gethro I heard you got some gear." Pixie joining us from the back of the coach.

"I have and I haven't Pix. Only painkillers." He smiled.

"How many?"

"Three hundred."

"Fuckin hell! That's a lot. What if they search you?"

"There's no way they can search seven-thousand of us, it'll be closed before we get in!" Both of us bursting to laughter, "I never thought of that?"

"I did. What you got?"

"Blueys and filon, ten a quid."

"Where from?"

"Gethro how many times?" both of us smiling at the stupidity of the question.

"Any spare?"

"Yea, how many you want?"

"Give us ten of each." Our deal hidden by Kim's lap and the back of a seat. We, the younger Cats' crowd, now dealt with each other, Pix moving on down the coach. Suddenly, something hit me. Pix didn't realize it but he had just given me a brilliant idea. "What could be so difficult in running a coach?" I read the flyer once more to idle the time. Little did I know what lay before me, the significance of this night? Major Lance, JJ Barnes, The Funky Sisters, Willie Henderson's Chicago All-Stars, and Mel and Tim live acts that would appear from eight till eight. Back to back terraced houses caught in streetlights, black slated roofs twisting along endless streets.

We spotted odd signposts for Leeds, the noise on the coach rising. "Pass the Coke lover." Holding the orange and blue tablets separately, taking five at a time. My body tingling with excitement at the vibe pills would bring. I smiled at my surroundings, the bottle passed between us, everyone dropping their gear. Time passing so slowly five minutes feeling like an hour, made worse by the oncoming rush of gear.

The infectious tone of our voices a testament to our arrival. We finally pulled to a halt outside a decrepit old building, we were in the center of

Leeds.

"Listen! We leave at nine, don't miss it!" The muffled voice from the organizer drowning in noise as we disembarked.

"What is this place?" My voice in a whisper.

"Queens Hall." Darb's brightened face in a smile, beside me pointing to the sign above our heads. A tall Victorian stone building, three stories of red faced brickwork encompassed the corner of two cobblestoned streets. To our left old tram lines glistening in streetlights, disappeared into a bricked, domed entrance. Repetitive arched windows swept in a curve at street level, stretching away into the distance. A huge crowd surrounding a narrow doorway, the swaying mass extending into darkness as far as the eye could see.

"Stop pushing! Get back!" Voices of bouncers fighting a crowd twenty deep, no semblance of organization, totally losing control.

"There's no way I'm joining that queue Gethro. Look at it!"

"I know. Come on Jako, stick with The Torch boys, and follow Robbo and Venton. Darb tell Jimmy keep together." Shouting and screaming surrounding us, we plunged into a sea of bodies all of us fighting for room.

"Management! Move over! Management coming through, I said move!" Robb's tall, hustling figure edging deeper into the crowd. Kim following in their wake, feeling our protection her face now in fear. The crush of the crowd unbearable, our momentum stopped feeling the pressure of bodies. Kim's feet off the ground, pushing, struggling for help, her arms trapped locked down at my side. Finally at the front, our bodies aching, fighting the surge of the crowd. Tidal waves of bodies bursting into a small foyer. Sweat streaming down our faces, all of us gasping for air.

At the side of two open doors, bouncers ripped our tickets. We ventured forwards instantly feeling the blast of ice cold night air. A wall of darkness greeting us, we entered a huge black hole. Strings of lights traversed upright columns revealing the vastness of the venue. Sporadic, industrial lights suspended from the domed ceiling casting silhouetted shades of yellow, filtered on crowds below. I smiled in the envelope of darkness, I would knock my painkillers out with ease. After all, no one could see what they were buying, I couldn't ask for more. The hum of voices reaching from the darkness, a muffled echo of Northern inaudible above the crowd.

"What the fuck is this place? It's darker than The Cats." Jako's voice behind me.

"I know, I can't see a thing. It's like being in The Cats with shades on man! Where's the dance floor?!" Jimmy laughing, searching for answers at my side.

"Must be over there, look by those two stages." Darb pointing directly in front of us, my eyes adjusting to light. In the distance a lighted area, a mass of motionless heads hugging the sides of two stages.

"Man, its dark in here!"

"Don't you dare let go of me! I'll never find you." Kim's voice full of anxiety, nervously clutching my arm.

"We got you Kim." Winston taking her other arm reassuring her. Barely able to see in front of us we stumbled on through the crowd. The faint sounds of Northern drawing us into the venue, a line of figures blocking our way.

"What the fuck's this?! Hold on, what's that?! Look tram lines! They're taking the piss!" My voice exasperated, in confused annoyance. Imbedded into the concrete, protruding steel rails disappearing under a make shift wooden dance floor no bigger than twelve foot square. Caught in the half-light Soulies huddled together, others lining the sides with bags at their feet. Faces I didn't recognize, long shadows crossing the floor.

"You got to be kidding me!" Darb bursting to laughter. "Gethro, Va-Va's floor was bigger than this!"

"Come on, this way man!" Jimmy's patience exhausted, working his way on through the crowd.

"Look there's a gap over there by the speakers. Must be another one of those floors." Jako now leading the way. Kim holding my arm for dear might in the carousel of twisting and turning. At least now we could hear the music. We ventured towards another group of Soulies standing in subdued light.

"This one looks slightly bigger." Encouragement in my voice, dropping our bags and coats at the side of a wooden dance floor.

"There's no way we can dance on this!" Winston arms crossing in defiance.

"Use what you got man. Come on let's dance!" Jako stepping forward, immediately launching into footwork ending in a somersault and spin. I gauged the floor, interlocking planks of wood at my feet. A handspring straight over landing in a drop-back in one flowing motion. Another move I had perfected from gymnastics, my time in the club paying off. Darb, Jimmy, and Kim laughing with Winston, all of us hitting the floor. A small crowd instantly coming towards us, I smiled as I watched them.

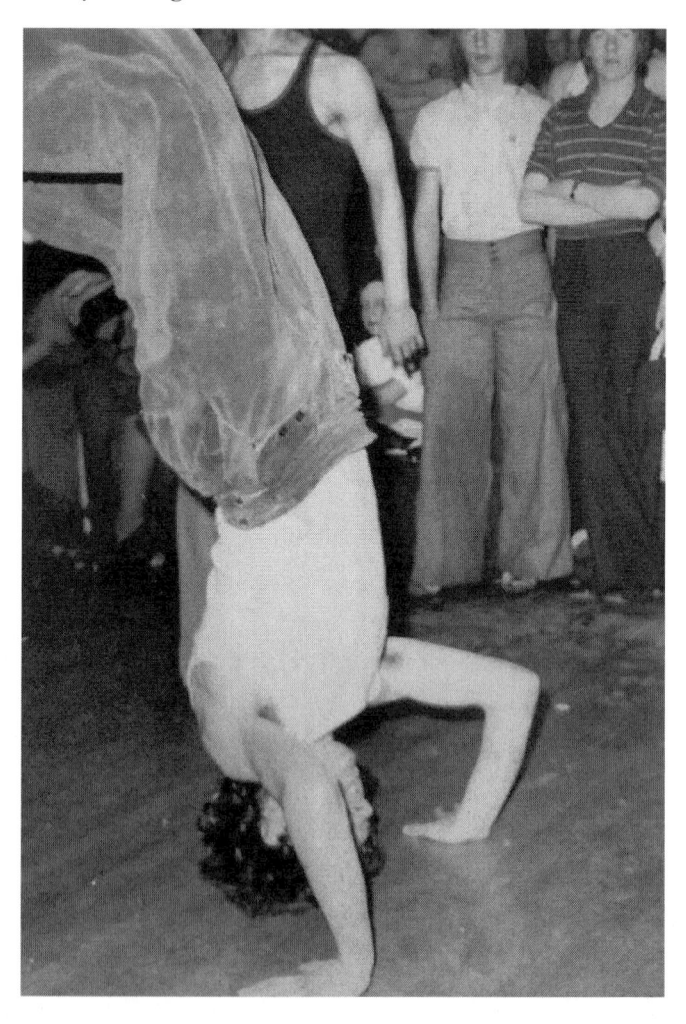

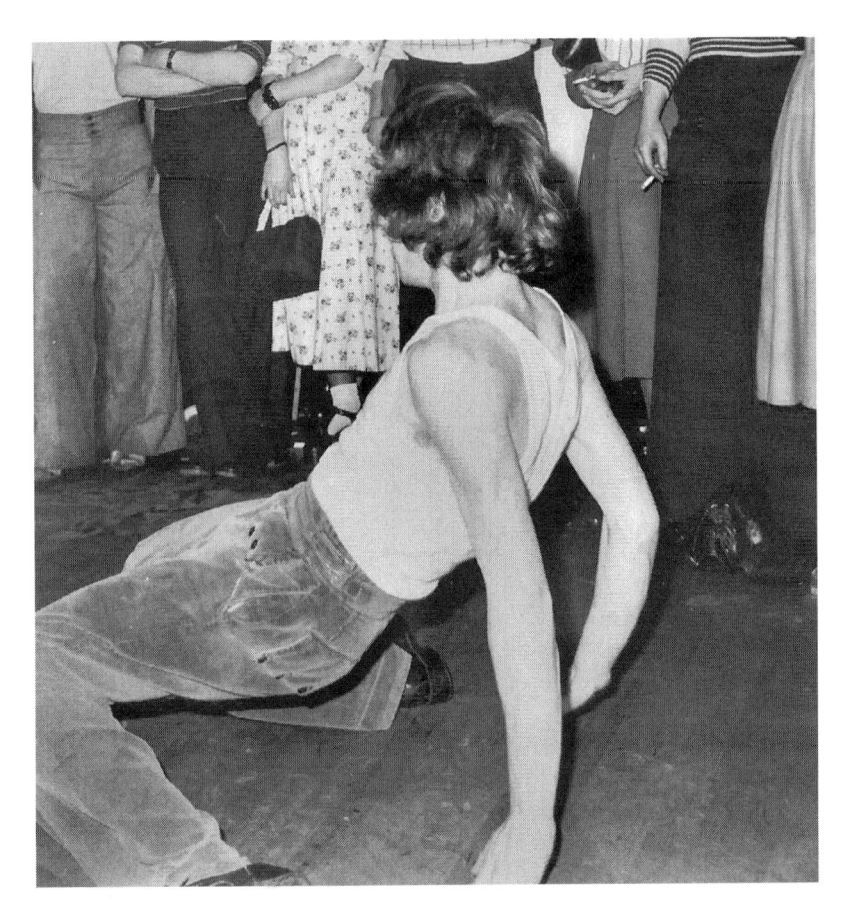

"We had made our grand entrance at Leeds." Our sky blue cords matching the blue and white of our vests bearing the Soul badges of our clubs. Va-Va, The Catacombs, The Casino, and Torch Revival. Herb Ward "Honest To Goodness", one of many records we knew and loved. With hardly room to move, the dance floor far too dangerous for me. My mind racing, stepping off the floor I started to dance.

"Gethro, what about the floor?"

"To small Winst. I'm not going to bother! I'm dancing right here. If I have to, I'll dance on the fuckin concrete!" The next record igniting my feet. Six of us starting to dance, the crowd backing away, our semi-circle growing wider.

"Hey up Gethro!" Mona and Nottingham Soulie's bursting from the crowd. A special bond locked in our greetings of pure friendship and love. Bags and coats abandoned on the dance floor, more of our friends joining us.

The Stoke lads, the Midland crowd, Soulies from Wigan, the night exploding to life. All eyes watching us, Jako playing with the crowd hitting the grove of his dancing ending in more spins. Stopping to talk to Mona, we chatted at the side of the floor.

"What you got?"

"Help me out Mo, I've got a load of bent chalkies to knock out."

"Good job its dark in here." Both of us started to grin. Why tell a lie when it's already told?

"No problem all you need to do is walk through the crowd. Everyone's looking for gear, just tell them their special strength. Come on, load up!" My zipped pockets working to perfection, painkillers in plastic bank bags, we ventured into the crowd. Unrecognizable faces appearing in the darkness, one word on everyone's lips.

"Hey what you got? Got any gear?" I couldn't believe my eyes, I had never met so many Soulies looking for drugs!

Faceless figures of black, the hum of Northern ascents frequent in our conversations. Deal after deal hidden in the safety of darkness, reveling in the sensation of my surroundings, the buzz of dealing driving me on. Tablets exchanged in minutes, crumpled bank notes from every direction. I made two weeks wages in less than a heartbeat. Mona as ever watchful, guarding my back.

"Now you got rid of them, I'll get us some real gear!" Our faces bursting in smiles, "Just you wait till you see what my mates bring in."

"Why what's he got? I know where there's some dex and filon."

"This is different mate, no one's ever had this come on!" Our voices infectious, upbeat in tone. We weaved our way across the venue the crowds ever larger. On-lookers ringed the temporary dance floor, now a mountain of bags and coats. Jako, arms tucked to his side spinning in a sea of talc, flowing into his footwork. I smiled at Kim and Darb's sweating figures, other Soulies dancing in the shadows trying to match their moves. "Gethro over here!" Mona constantly on the move, another Soulie small in stature stood at his side. Three of us exchanging greetings, bowed heads creating a wall of safety. "Show him Graham." The stranger extending the palm of his hand. In the center an open square of foil no bigger than a stick of chewing gum. The flatness of a fine white powder glistened in the flame of a cigarette lighter.

"What is it?" My voice inquisitive, I had never seen anything like this.

"Amphetamine sulfate mate. Here smell it." Mona lifting the foil, a strange smell of chemicals immediately hitting the back of my throat.

"Wow!"

"That's the dog's bollocks man. Crystal sulfate, you won't get any better than that!" Mona's face flickering with excitement. "Good eh?!"

"Graham how much is it?"

"Two quid Gethro. Here try it, this ones on me." A wet finger of bitterness igniting my mouth in a vile cocktail of chemicals. Both of them laughing at my expression of twisted disgust. One thing I realized straight away. Instead of bulging pockets of caps and pills if I had deals of amphetamine sulfate I could equal the effect of anything they could bring. After my encounter at Wigan I knew I had reached a red line. Sure I had made a little money, but the risks far too dangerous for me. Right here was my answer never thinking of the consequences, the normal life I would destroy. I had never heard of this drug before yet it would have an impact on my life and that of so many others. It would take no prisoners as it blazed a trail of a comet through the Northern scene.

I now brought every move in my dancing to that circle of onlookers, I felt all eyes on me. Our little group in a class of their own, challenging anyone to dance against us record after record. Jako, Kim, Darb, and Jimmy our unique styles clashing, my heart racing loving the adulation, timing all of my moves. The handspring done again and again into drop-backs rising to opposite spins. Pounding the concrete, splits in either direction sequences breaking into fast footwork. The circle ever wider clapping hands with renewed aggression suddenly my dancing over. In the distance a lone figure in white, Major Lance igniting the crowd. Soulies in a sea of passion arms held high distant voices singing with every note. A repeat of songs we had heard at Stafford. Kim wearing her fur coat we wandered aimlessly through the darkness, endless figures blocking our way.

"Gethro, Kim!" A voice I recognized shouting our name. Gonk stumbling stepping forward, "Fucking tram rails! Kim lends your coat?"

"What?"

"Your coat, can I borrow it?" His voice in a pleading expression, all of us bursting in laughter. "Kim go on, I'll look after it."

"You promise Gonk?" Her eyes searching for trust a playful sternness to her voice.

"I will Kim, honest. Lends it?" A perfect fit, his face lit up in smiles adjusting his old trilby to a tilt, the perfect Al Capone. Complementing Kim's fur coat he strutted away like a penguin vanishing out of sight. The night full of madness, friends off their faces we moved ever deeper towards the stages.

J.J. Barnes now in the spotlight, songs we knew so well. "Sweet Sherry" sang with affection "Real Humdinger", "Please Let Me In" words so meaningful, adding to the magic spell of the night. His sheer presence mesmerizing swaying crowds, the ambiance growing louder. "Our Love Is In The Pocket" handclaps in unison, shouts of acknowledgment, synchronized arms held high in the crowd.

Seven thousand Soulies in the venue, the largest gathering ever. We had never felt anything like this, the atmosphere rising with the night. Our hearts captured by the precious moment together wrapped in each other's arms. The night passing before us, Mel & Tim on the opposite stage. The acoustics destroying their harmonious voices, any semblance to the artists or records denied. "Starting All Over Again" drifting through the speakers "Backfield In Motion" swooning the massive crowds. More acts rotating between the stages Funky Sisters singing "Do It To It".

Rekindling memories of our first time in The Catacombs, haunting beats creeping along tunneled blacked out walls. It now seemed so long ago. Willie Henderson's Chicago All-Stars playing many Soul classics. Unable to dance we wandered throughout the venue watching various acts unfold.

Our names shouted in many directions, time shared in verb led reunions laughter with many lost friends. The venue nothing like I had expected, the loss of a dance floor playing heavy on our night, something we would never forgive.

Our semi-circle ever wider Soulies watching from the side lines. The filth of the floor making an impression, Jako's blackened face making me smile. The rush of sulfate held back by live acts hitting me like an express train, record after record our little group pounding the floor. Drop-backs, splits, and spins fast footwork driving my feet. A quick step added to a sequence leaping to splits, touching my toes in midair, landing in a drop-back. Jako bursting to laughter, he had never seen me do this move before. Darb, Kim, and Jimmy dancing in our circle, our night ending I watched from the side of the floor. I had never been to an all-nighter without a dance floor.

Moves I had perfected I struggled to accomplish at Leeds. Two massive welts the size of golf balls appearing on the inside of my knees. I could press them, they were full of fluid. Doing handsprings into a drop-back, I had paid a heavy price.

Every time I misgauged the move my knees hammered the concrete. The surface hard to gauge, it just wasn't the same as dancing on wood. Gonk returning Kim's coat the night ending in laughter and sadness. Parasites in the venue, a few bags stolen from behind us, typical of the Northern scene at this time. Our bodies battered from dancing, cords scuffed and filthy. All of us looking like miners, the night had been a disaster. We left our footprints on the concrete, never again returning to Leeds.

Chapter 35
THERE'S NOTHING ELSE TO SAY

After Leeds Soul Festival Wolvo changed. It's as if the younger Cats crowd had finally been to an all-nighter. They had travelled out of Wolvo and been immersed in the Northern scene. Their attitude was different, The Octopus and Cats became more packed, the dance floors more intense. A new openness now emerged between us, after all we had been hitting all-nighters for the last eight months and now they wanted in. The only problem was they, like me, had no respect for our youth and would do whatever they want.

Chemists would fall like dominoes as they embarked on a crime wave of Soul. Not even a week after Leeds, the first chemist went down. I had learned from The Cats, if you have some gear this could put an instant target on your back. Not only that, trouble would arrive from two directions. One from the squad, the other from rip-offs. It wasn't all lovey-dovey in the world of Northern Soul. At street level things could get really nasty and at times they did. I hadn't got time for glory boys, who did the chemists.

The golden rule had been broken, don't shit on your own door step and now heat arrived in numbers around the town. The drug squad were now a little sharper, but their routine followed the same old lines. Only problem was they started to harass The Torch boys and they knew nothing of what had gone down. Chemists demanded two things, first the balls to actually break in and at this time I hadn't got that. Secondly you had to control the supply of drugs that hit the streets. This was no more evident than when we walked into Whitchurch Bank Holiday all-dayer.

> **April 15th EASTER MONDAY**
> With Sam's Soul Sound + PEP +
> Colin Curtis
> Ian Levine + Neil Ruston +
> Russ & Guest D.J's
> The One and Only
> **ALL DAYER AT**
> **WHITCHURCH CIVIC CENTRE**
> *SPECIAL OFFER TO BLUES & SOUL READERS— TICKETS 50p (with s.a.e.)*
> **1 HIGH ST., WHITCHURCH SHROPSHIRE**

A wave of energy greeting us, reminiscent of an all-nighter. The floor packed with Soulies, others lining the sides. Pep, Colin Curtis, Ian Levine, Russ Winstanley, and Neil Ruston a DJ line up of all the top names.

The function room crowded with many of Wolvo's best dancers, faces from The Catacombs standing out in the crowd. Classic Northern blasting from the speakers, absorbed in my surrounding I stood to the side and watched. Spins and clapping from dancers, a vibrant dance floor that only comes from gear. Bin Man coming to join me, one of the younger Cats crowd. His piercing eyes and dilated pupils, the drawn features of a fruit monkey. Ever inquisitive he always made me laugh.

"What's up?"

"Oh nothing. Just resting from dancing, fucked my knees up at Leeds."

"You're not the only one, what a load of bollocks that was! Mind you Major and J. J. were good but no fuckin dance floor!" I smiled.

"Yeah but the flyers never said there was one, just a dancing competition."

"I know but I still feel ripped, it's the last time were going to any International Soul Clubs. That's how we all feel."

"Same here, we're done with them." My voice etherizing our disgust.

"You dropping any gear?"

"No, just a couple of painkillers."

"I heard about that. You still got some left over from Leeds?" Both of us laughing.

"Hey I did what I had to do man!" The palm of my hands pleading my innocence.

"Mind you, you weren't the only one doing it Gethro. You entering the dancing competition?"

"No. We won't dance against each other."

"Why not?"

"It's a pact we've got. It's just the way we feel."

"Same here, but I think Squeak's going in for it. He should piss it the way he spins."

"Well he's got some competition now!" My voice in a challenging tone, both of us turning to the doorway. Booper and his entourage, recognizable faces from The Casino strutting into the hall. His presence turning heads in recognition of his reputation, as one of the best spinners on the Northern scene. Booper weaving his way through dancers halting at the front of the stage. My old nemesis not letting me down, briefcase in hand, his arrogance for all to see.

"Booper's here!"

"I know Darb."

"Later Gethro." Bin Man drifting into the crowd.

"Now what? You gonna dance?" Darb's face in a look of apprehension.

"I've got no choice mate. There is no way we're giving him this floor." Reaching in my bag taking a swig of Coke, painkillers filling my hand. "Where's Jako?"

"With Kim at the front. Come on!" Darb working his way through Soulies we stood in a small crowd to the right of the stage. Booper now down to his waistcoat, already halfway through his habitual routine. As many times as I watched him he never let me down. The thing I hated was his arrogance, showing little respect for dancers around him he just took command of the floor. That was his style, one of intimidation. Jako's sweating figure coming to join us.

"Fuck him! He must be suffering from dementia. We blew him off in The Casino, someone said he's here for the competition." Anger in his voice, "Well I'm going in for it! I'll show him!" I looked at Darb.

"What about you?"

"I'm in Gethro."

"Well that's four of us then." Kim dancing as she always did, her style of skipping footwork standing out amongst the dancers, not giving Booper an inch. "Better let him know we're all here, come on!"

All of us hitting the floor, Jako now bringing his signature move, a somersault from a standing position landing to bent knees. A brilliant one flowing move, powering into a spin and drop-back. A look of disgust from Booper as he launched into a spin landing one legged, a perfect figure four. The graceful style he had perfected, hands as ever feeling the music, little touches he could do. Today, a real challenge, a dancer on top of his game. Now we would finally see who the best dancer was. Up till now our contests had never been officially judged. Not only that, we would find out who is the best dancer in our little group. A question we had steered away from, our pact now broken. I wondered, "Would we ever be the same again?"

I had to challenge him, only problem for me I couldn't dance the way I wanted. My moves of a handspring and splits impossible. The foundation of our new style of dancing, the athletic approach even my footwork denied. My legs buckling a strange feeling of lightness, a squelching from my knees. Kim and Darb in front of me, my legs not responding nothing but emptiness no feelings for the music. Other dancers from Wolvo joining us, my heart lifted Squeak and Punna, well known faces from The Catacombs, their spins at lightning speeds. Squeak easily the fastest spinner, Wolvo had brought its best dancers to this venue, they too showing little respect to the challengers up north.

Russ Winstanley announcing the competition, clearing the dance floor, contestants gathering in the center. My nerves racing Darb and Jako to my left and right excitement building in momentum. Booper pacing around, a boxer ready to fight, Chrissie from Preston, the leg spinner, waiting patiently. Other dancers I didn't recognize, they too had come to win this competition on our doorstep. Crowds lining the dance floor others standing on tables and chairs, our first real competition. Shouts of encouragement to dancers, Kim coming to my side.

"You know you shouldn't be dancing!" A lover's look of worried concern. Jerry Cook "I Hurt On The Other Side" the competition evolving in front of me. A new aggression from dancers, a Northern floor full of vengeance. Booper floating around, arms parallel at his shoulders demanding loads of room, a jump and spin snapping, skipping footwork. A lion in for the kill his face beaming in smiles his moves of precision done to perfection, blowing me off the floor. I had nothing to challenge him. Jako and Darb taking over a battle now raging in front of me. All of the moves we had perfected, Darb showing he too an accomplished dancer, Kim at his side.

The crowd cheering us on, Squeak spinning a blur of motionless footwork. Jako now holding the center stage clapping hands arms at his side spinning into a drop-back. Our little group fighting for recognition Darb and Jako flowing into their moves. Kim smiling, loving the competition pushing herself, driving into the beats a connection she had with the floor. My legs feeling like jelly, my footwork out of sync, I had nothing to give. Hardly a break, the second record Chubby Checker "You Just Don't Know" blasting from the speakers, not a beat missed Darb timing his feet in our floating style. A pride at my mate's dancing, holding his own with the best they could bring. The leg spinner bringing his move, Jako instantly copying it a look of defiance turning into straight splits. We would go down fighting none of us giving in. They too stepping up with the dancing, a neatness to their moves our footwork different, more refined.

Booper still dominating with his aggressive style, quicker steps added. One legged spins at exactly the right time to the record, a style you had to admire. Darb's little touches stolen from Booper more cheering from the crowd as he copied his moves. The last record upon us The Tomangoe's "I Really Love You", a record from The Torch now the advantage with no one. Room on the floor so tight dancers nearly clashing, none of us giving them room. The younger crowd now showing adulation, we were the new generation. Squeak and Punna Catacombs' dancers, untouchable hitting some of their fastest spins. Our faces saturated with sweat, breathless bent over hands on my knees my legs buckling, the record fading, the competition over.

Our faces in smiles, slaps on the back from Darb and Jako, hugs for Kim. She had been outstanding, I felt so proud of her, my face in nothing but smiles. We had given the competition our best shot. Booper standing by Russ chatting at the front of the stage, heated words between them, turning away in disgust. Russ announcing the crowd would decide, claps from fellow dancers in recognition of what we had given on the floor. Each of us stepping forward to receive our accolades, my heart broken a slight cheering from the crowd. Next Jako stepping forward, roars of appreciation, Darb and Kim in equal recognition, the competition had been tough. Two more girls stepping forward, Jane Keitley and Angie Lawrence the audible as equal. Squeak and Punna more cheering now, The Wheel dancers a murmur, odd handclaps from the crowd. The announcement finally made.

16
Whitchurch All-Dayer

I DON'T KNOW why but the Whitchurch All-Dayer of the northern Soul Club always seems to go extremely well — Tony Petherbridge pointed out that it was the first All-dayer of them all (and called a Soul Festival 12 months ago) — but whatever the reason everyone seems to enjoy them.

The latest one, at Easter, was the only thing that got me out of the house over Easter (even I have to have some time off) and Wes Marchant came along. Again this was one of those "do's" when the news isn't exactly thick on the ground 'cos I was too busy enjoying myself but we must give a mention to the dancing competition.

I personally feel that these competitions have got rather out of hand because no matter how the thing is judged there are always complaints. Anyway, first this year was **Graham Jackson**, aged 18, of Wolverhampton, second was **Paul Derby**, also aged 18 and also of Wolverhampton and there were three third places, **Kim Habbits** of Wolverhampton, **Jane Keitley** of Gloucester and **Angie Lawrence** of Rugeley. As I said earlier there always seems to be problems at these things no matter how they are judged and this year quite a few people pointed out the fact that most of the crowd at the front with the best view of the dancers were actually from Wolverhampton. (I should mention that the judging was by crowd reaction). All I can say is congratulations to everyone who took part — the Northern Dancers just have to be amongst the most accomplished dancers in the world! (And I mean World).

In first place Jako, Darb had been pushed to second, Kim placed in third with two other girls, all the questions had finally been answered. Jako was the best dancer, suddenly Booper standing on the stage holding the mic.

"You're all shite! We won that hands down! That's not dancing, just a gymnastics display! We're the best dancers! That's not Northern!" Shouts of resentment, drowning his voice booing from the crowd. Booper leaving the stage, glaring at Soulies around him, a face red with anger, frustration boiling over friends trying to calm him down. Russ spinning a sound to lighten the atmosphere. Darb, Jako, and Kim huddled around a reporter, their names would appear in Blues and Soul.

At last, the fame we had strived for, I felt elated yet sad. I had tried so hard to accomplish so much in my dancing. I wondered, would I ever get the recognition for the way I danced, for what I brought to the floor? Booper and his entourage storming out of the venue. I felt sorry for him, he had given everything in the competition. Both of us had lost. As I watched him go, thoughts of our previous battles filling my mind. He had taught me so much, without him I wouldn't be the dancer I was. Taking solace in the thought "all the competition proved was you entered a competition." It really was as simple as that.

Chapter 36

BEACHCOMBER, WOLVO, AND WIGAN

We now hammered the dance floors at various Soul venues. Our nucleus Wigan Casino, The Catacombs and The Ship packed every week. The music in our blood, the friendships we created, we were drawn together it's all we lived for.

Every Saturday a small crowd of us would catch the train to Wigan. The coaches had stopped picking up at The Cats. Rip-offs and scum finally given their answer, out of town Soulies sick of being rolled. Wolvo was a rough place if you were a stranger with no backup. We kept together, our bond even tighter the younger crowd watching each other's backs. We were regulars in The Casino, I knew many faces, my dancing always interrupted I had been given my answer.

All night the same questions, friends of friends a never ending stream of Soulies, always on the lookout for gear. I knew the opportunity was there, if you ask me enough times, then I will go out and find it. Chemists alone could never supply Wigan's floor, there was a void and I stepped right into it.

At Leeds I had made my first contact with a drug that would change my life forever, setting new guidelines of how to deal drugs. I would play by my rules, working alone. My contacts handpicked, not just for the good times, but to have each other's backs when hard times would follow. A pact, a band of brothers wrapped in an unbreakable chain of trust. I was sucked in by the chase, the thrill, I felt like a prohibitionist, us and them. I was the good guy, the squad were the bad guys, no one's going to tell me how to run my life. I was far too young to realize the dangerous circumstances and retribution my new world would deliver if I ever got caught.

It's strange, I wasn't even into drugs to make money, I just wanted everyone to feel what I felt. To be on that same high of happiness and one to one with the music, to feel the atmosphere of the night. To succeed in supplying gear, you need a constant supply. My connection made in Chesterfield, a small market town in Derbyshire. My directions to the letter, the Merry Monk a black and white beamed pub opposite a church with a twisted spire. I felt a little guilty at what I had done at Leeds but every dealer needs a float and I now knew there would be better days.

For me there was no turning back, I entered the dark side of Northern Soul. The game of cat and mouse had begun, the cat fast asleep. A wild horse in a gallop, with amphetamine sulfate I would enter full force as a dealer on the Northern scene. My first rule in place, always meet in the week, the bar totally empty Mona and Graham sitting at a small table in a room off to the side.

"Hey up Kim, Gethro!" Our greetings in crossing hands, Mona always made me smile. His lighthearted infectious attitude, giving Kim a hug, lifting her off the carpet with a gentle whisper in her ear. "Kim don't look in your pocket." The fur coat coming in handy. Graham going to the bar ordering our drinks, blocking the view of the bar maid, a well-rehearsed event operating before me. Money exchanged in the quickness of hands. I smiled, an ounce of sulfate, it really had been as simple as that. Spending little time in the bar our trip back to Wolvo in darkness, not even bothering to use a stash. That was the beauty of powder. Unlike caps and pills if it came on top, just pour it out of the window. "Good luck with finding that!"

I couldn't believe my eyes, a fluffiness to the mountain of white mirrored powder increased by a chopping blade. The slight rose of pink in texture, crystal shards glistening like diamonds, a strong smell of chemicals filling the air. The bitter taste of powder from the tip of my finger reminding me of our night at Leeds. Squares filled into deals, surely thirty was enough. A small amount set aside for our group. My second rule in place, always take what you sell, I didn't want to screw anyone up.

My gear stashed for up and coming nights. I ventured into The Octopus, Darb and Jimmy as always by my side. A typical Saturday afternoon, the bar full of Soulies all the customers I wanted, only one problem. None of my gear would be sold in Wolvo, why would I? I didn't want local attention.

The town still full of squad, trying to find answers to yet another chemist that had gone down. This time the assailants entering through the roof, their ingenuity making me smile. A builder's ladder put to good use, their methods seemed to have no bounds. Not only did they take the drugs. This time they took the DDA cabinet and that was taking the piss! This wasn't what I wanted, I admired them but the chemist bashers were getting on my nerves.

The Torch boys wising up, heated arguments between us of something we knew nothing about. Even if I did, I wouldn't tell that bunch of rip offs! Remember me, I'm just a Div! I had to give it to the lads, they were keeping it tight between them, but in the end I knew someone would crack. The problem with chemists, they were full of what we called fast and slow. The fast was never a problem, all-nighters took care of that. The slow was an entirely different matter, junkies would always over indulge leaving a trail.

I wasn't blind, I could read the streets. What broke my heart, one or two of my mates already experimenting with barbiturates to help them come down. This wasn't what Northern was about, our scene was take some gear stay awake and dance. That's all it ever was to me! I kept my distance, all of this mayhem gradually unfolding around me. I knew a train wreck when I saw one, the scene in Wolvo to me was out of control.

My advantage was huge, the drugs I had were manufactured. The only way you would draw heat was by your own stupidity. My gear would be sold in The Casino, sure I was taking risks but they were controlled by me.

To help eliminate these, unbeknownst to the management they had just given me a helping hand. A coffee bar annexed to The Casino called The Beachcomber opened from twelve till two. The inspiration had been to help alleviate the crowds of the all-nighter on the pavement outside. Timing is everything, as ever the opportunist I had other ideas.

To the right of Casino's main entrance, a narrow doorway lead to a sloping passageway. Total darkness echoing to the sound of Northern, you were in the very bowels of The Casino. Dripping pipes puddled in areas around the dance floor, the room felt damp and cold.

Two DJs in the center, spinning tunes the only light from the decks and a small coffee bar to the right. Murals of odd designs, easy rider adjourned black painted walls, crowds gathered in numbers girls with vanity cases and Soulies' bags at their sides. Huddled groups in conversation, others seated at tables, people milling around, not a bouncer in sight.

The passageway a dangerous place, unsavory characters waiting in the darkness. A few steps in the wrong direction odd Soulies pulled, beaten, and rolled. I hated the bastards but they never crossed us, we had somehow gained a reputation in The Casino. We were from Wolvo, we could handle ourselves with attitude if it came on top. In this environment I would lay my gear off, the last thing you wanted to do in The Beachcomber was to flash money. Payments made later in The Casino, crossing handshakes sealing deals.

Mrs. Woods as always would greet us with a wistful smile, the sparkling eyes of mischief. I'm sure she knew what I was up to, I felt she could read my mind. No matter how many times I walked into Wigan, you knew it was going to be a special night. The doorway opening up, another world, an underground scene, a generation of youth seeking a different direction. The golden age of Northern unfolding before my eyes, well over a thousand Soulies filling the club. Wigan had picked up in momentum, it had now arrived on the Northern scene. The heat of the club, a sledgehammer as you walked into a wall of sound. We always danced on the right hand side of the stage, everyone now had their areas.

Deals laid off to runners, sold in minutes, take six sell five, I never expected something for nothing. I had now created a buffer. I never met half the people I sold to, why would I weaken the chain? I now could dance uninterrupted, joining Soulies fighting for space on the crowded floor.

Record after record exclusive tracks of Northern all around me, Wigan now had an atmosphere all its own. The heat on the floor unbearable, a mist rising from dancers fueled by amphetamines, a never ending high. Drawing you, pulling you towards the dance floor, an invisible wall of energy I was now a part of the night. The face in the mirrored column, a smiling sweating reflection features drawn and alert. Staring, piercing eyes smashed on the outside but a mind in total control.

Our dancing style dominating the floor, handsprings, splits, and spins perfected at gymnastics we had no equal. Crowds, as ever, watching from the sides. We had room and we used it. Our style of dancing so different, many dancers trying to imitate us. The club dingy and tatty in appearance, a dump but our dump. One I had made my home. A family of Soul brothers and sisters connecting the best Northern dancers the scene had to offer, competitions played out on the floor.

The DJs playing out the same battle in a game of one-upmanship, "some of their egos out of control." Russ Winstanley, Richard Searling, Ian Fishwick, Kev Roberts, Dave Evison, Brian Rae, Ian Dewhurst, and John Vincent,

DJs changing every hour fueling the floor with their latest finds. For us as dancers the best of them all, small in stature standing miles above the prima donnas.

The one with the least amount of labels in his box, Martin Ellis. His spot always igniting the dance floor in a river of Soul. Taking control of the night, driving the dancers, his enthusiasm infectious every record introduced with passion screaming down the mic. The atmosphere sucking you in, rising slowly, increasing throughout the night. A simmering volcano ending in a thundering eruption, each DJ adding to the raging fire.

Wigan's floor now packed with dancers clapping to various records, a mass of arms and hands held high. Week after week the crowds growing larger sometimes I would move an ounce in deals, supply always outstripped by demand. Stay small keeping it tight no one ever tried to rip me off. Why would they? I was one of the few moving pink champagne, a name given to the sulfate that instantly sold itself. I used my eyes, my senses on fire.

The bouncers never scrutinized me or followed me around. I wasn't stupid I knew the rules, don't push drugs in our face and we won't rearrange yours. At odd times they would watch the dancing competitions evolving in front of them. If Wigan's bouncers had a trait, it was their weakness. They always made me smile with their obsession of finding chewing gum. They would come up and demand you spit it out as they rummaged through peoples bags. A dancer's nightmare, many times I had to dig it off my shoes, I hated it! Lucky for me the bouncers felt the same way. They seemed totally oblivious to the mayhem of drugs flying around them. The balcony and the men's toilets, their main areas, they left the dance floor alone.

The Casino now had many faces, at the back of the main room a record bar had opened. Vinyl detectives full of intensity, scouring endless boxes for the latest Northern sounds. Soulies, yes in their own right, but I never got it? Collect all the records you want, there was a dance floor come and express yourself, get out here and dance! No, take your records home and dance in your bedroom?

To us they were just Divs and that's how we saw them. They would buy some gear and off they went to verbal their heads off with their own little click. All around them the buzz of The Casino, a dance floor packed to capacity. Many of them spending their entire night in the record bar, one I could never understand. I had no patience for them, I lived on the dance floor feeling and breathing the heart of the night. The dance floor controlled by occupancy, this was our club DJs as ever, careful of playing new tunes. If we didn't like it we walked, the floor would empty just as fast as it had started to fill. Wigan's crowds demanding pounding Northern beats by dancers who gave their hearts to the music. Many DJs learned the hard way, labels can stay in your box.

Chapter 37

THE MECCA AND NORTHERN DIVIDE

"Moonlight, music and you"

There was a big following of Northern Soul in Wolvo due mainly to The Cats. Our club always packed, playing Wheel and Torch classics plus new ones Max and Pep had discovered. The Casino following the same format, their DJs also playing sounds unique to their boxes. The two clubs interconnecting DJs, trading records, feeding off one another playing fast up-tempo Northern that always filled a floor. It was well known on the scene if you had a venue playing Northern then dancers from Wolvo would soon arrive.

What had attracted us to The Mecca, a Tiffany's Night Club on the coast at Blackpool were articles we had read. Various Soul magazines heralding a new wave of dancers and a new direction in the music of Northern Soul. Tony Jebb and Les Cokell had played at the venue from nineteen sixty-eight and built it up as a Northern club. Their format of playing new discoveries and Torch sounds laying the foundation for the two new resident DJs Ian Levine and Colin Curtis. Although not an all-nighter, The Highland Room, a part of the venue closing at two, had caused divisions in the Northern scene.

Mostly fueled by Russ Winstanley and Ian Levine, the two main DJs from either club, The Mecca and Casino, their rivalry out of control. We as dancers hadn't got time for them or their bullshit! There was no us and them on the scene! To us Northern was Northern and that's all it really was. Ian after his guest appearance at Wigan, uttering the immortal words, "It'll never take off." Well Wigan had taken off! Being regulars in The Cats and Casino we were inquisitive about this new wave of Mecca dancers and like the Soul brothers we were, we wanted to take them on. After all in The Casino we challenged anyone to dance against us. Today would be even more special, two rooms would be open. This was an all-dayer, on from twelve till twelve. Junior Walker and Edwin Starr would be appearing live Junior's record at this time "I Ain't Going Nowhere" a massive tune on the Northern scene. I personally didn't like live acts, if I am going to see one then I don't dance, but if I am going to dance then I want tunes. To me they stopped the flow of a venue and completely killed a floor.

This weighing on my mind we entered through two double doors into the Blackpool Mecca. A drab looking building on the outside, three stories of 60s architecture, a typical concrete square structure of shapeless design. On the ground floor a bowling alley, a small kiosk collecting our money Soulies from Wolvo's coach forming a queue.

"Who the fuck is Andy Simpson Gethro?"

"I don't know Jako, Squeak knows him he's supposed to be a spinner.

They've got some good dancers up here, ever heard of Roy Ashworth or Rene Gelson?"

"Never heard of them Gethro."

"Well I saw their names in an old copy of Blues and Soul, Ric Tic knows them ask him."

Kim smiling at my side both of us exiting the escalator, a short corridor to our left. Another escalator rising in front of us the opulence of the venue unfolding before us. Shaded art deco lights cast gentle shadows of blues and yellows. White paneling reflecting the polished chrome of the escalator. Jimmy trailing his fingers along burgundy embossed papered walls, turning to me as we rose to the top.

"Look at this place man. This ain't no Wigan Casino!" Fifty of us now riding the escalators a buzz of excitement between us, we couldn't wait to hit this floor. Wolvo bringing its best dancers, our fastest spinners Squeak and Jako, I relished the contest to come. I must admit Squeak wasn't as competitive as us although he often danced by us. I just loved to see the shock on people's faces when they saw him spin!

"Mind the step lover." Kim stumbling as we disembarked along another short corridor.

"It must be up these stairs Gethro." Jako's excited voice leading the way, opening the door in front of us. The Highland Room in bright yellow letters clearly posted above a steel framed doorway. A venue that had caused tidal waves on the Northern scene.

"What a trek man!" Jimmy turning to me his face in disgust, more double doors at the end of a short foyer. We entered at the back of a large room. Two bars, a small one to our right hidden in semi-darkness another running the full length of the room. Beamed ceilings encased the bar area, crested shields and crossing swords mounted on tartan patterns walls. Plush carpeting of deep blues and reds, our surroundings lavish in Scottish décor. Seating and tables lining the bar, deco wall lights in every direction creating ambiance in secluded corners. Our entrance so different from The Casino, The Voices Of East Harlem "Cashing In" a record I didn't recognize Soulies, scattered throughout the room. A small stage in the center the back drop of trailing silver ribbons creating a modern disco image, it didn't feel like a Northern club. Ian Levine bent over a set of turn tables.

"Hey Gethro, he looks like Elvis!" Jako pointing to the stage.

"Go up and tell him. Ask him for his autograph man!" Jimmy laughing at our side.

Ian's chubby features, long dark sideburns and shaded glasses, uncanny resemblances making me smile. At his side a tall, long haired, skinny guy holding my gaze. Seating and tables to our left and right encompassed a large wooden dance floor. We headed in that direction, dropping our bags at the side of the floor.

"Man, this place is posh."

"I know Gethro, I've never been in a venue like this man. Better wipe your shoes Jako or the bouncers will kick you off the floor!" Jimmy making us laugh at Jako's face of confusion, our joker joining dancers heading towards the floor. The beats of the record hard to follow, a mellower Northern sound. Watching Jako adjust, I changed my shoes with Darb at the side of the floor. We had learned from the past always bring two pair of shoes. Tiffany's floors renowned for their polish and shine. Leathers weren't going to cut it on this floor, the way we danced one bad landing, a pulled muscle away. Ian looking up from the turn tables a smile of pleasure at the crowd now entering the room. Kim joining Jimmy and Winston, more Mecca dancers filling the floor. Their style of dancing very similar to Jimmy's. A fast, shuffling footwork of sideways movement, tight steps and twisting feet as they glided across the floor. The odd dancers breaking into spins, hands held out, elbows tucked in at their side.

Neatness not only in their dancing but the way they dressed. Tailored trousers, bowling shirts of various designs, sleeveless tops, pointed collared shirts, and short sleeved jumpers. The Tiffany's dress code of a tie dropped for all-dayers, I felt naked as I watched in my vest and sky blue cords. The girls their long skirts a tighter fit, short sleeved blouses and striped dresses, wide black belted fastening. Others dressed in brighter flamboyant flowered skirts, bright colors tops matching their paisley scarves.

More records I had never heard of now hitting the floor, The East Coast Connection "Summer In The Parks" a heavy brass section adding a fast tempo, the floor full of funky disco beats. Some of the dancers breaking out into fast sideways steps, then a forward and backward motion to their dancing. A creative skipping, one legged style, a shuffle to their footwork I had never seen. The floor had a funky feel with beats hard to follow and nothing like we had heard before.

"How we gonna dance to this man? Same as Jimmy and Kim. Remember Venton and Robbo?" Darb inquisitive at my side we ventured towards the floor. Back to our roots that style we had adopted so long ago stolen from The Catacombs. Fast twisting feet, the foundation of our dancing both of us laughing at our efforts, devoid of drop-backs and splits. The floor being slippy, I started to slide my feet like dancers around me.

I felt strange as I fought to climb on board the funky, intricate beats. Jimmy creating a stir, the floating shuffling footwork he had mastered now attracting attention, a dancer so big moving light on his feet. Kim adjusting her footwork, a natural dancer the skipping style slowed down. Feet moving in sideways steps, flowing arms drifting effortlessly at her side. Edie Walker "Good Guys", Bernard "Pretty" Purdy "Fickle Finger Of Fate", Richard "Popcorn" Wylie "Rosemary, What Happened", Lynn Varnado "Wash And Wear Love", and Joshie Jo Armstead "I Got The Vibes". Some of the records breaking in many directions, break beats in stops and starts throwing our dancing out of rhythm and sync. Levine queuing the next record, Pixie coming to join us Bin Man chatting to Darb and Jako laughing at the side of the floor.

"Gethro these sounds are fuckin shit!"

"I know Pix. He's gonna run out sooner or later" More records filling the room, "Who's the tall, skinny, hippy guy by Levine Pix?"

"That's Colin Curtis, he's supposed to be on later. He's a good DJ, used to DJ at The Torch and Levine."

"He couldn't have been there long if he played shit like this Pix!" A slight pause in our conversation, both of us watching the half empty floor.

"You drop any gear?"

"No, we never bother for all-dayers Pix. None of us have."

"I thought you looked normal." Both of us starting to smile, we didn't see the point the atmosphere so different from an all-nighter, so evident on the floor.

"What's that champagne you got?"

"How'd you know about that?" My voice annoyed at the trick question and the fact he knew.

"Oh just a whisper. Word travels man."

"I just get a little now and again Pix, you know the score."

"Well just watch your back, some wankers keep hitting the chemists." His face in a look of pure innocence.

"Yea those ladders come in handy Pix."

"I'm frightened of heights Gethro." Both of us grinning with laughter.

"Wish I knew who it was Pix. I've got the contacts, I would buy the lot and move it in one hit." Both of us starting to smile, we knew what we knew, our friendship as ever bound in trust.

The tingling of a telephone catching our attention, my heart lifted. Two voices arguing on a phone, a pounding driving beat blasting from the speakers. A sound we recognized from The Catacomb, pulling me to the floor Tony & Tyrone "Please Operator" the emotion bursting inside me, their voices crystal clear. All of us breaking in an arc, "this is how we dance in The Casino!" Squeak hitting a spin, igniting the floor with his speed. My face breaking to smiles, "at last a record!" Our footwork gauging the floor, the polished surface giving me a responsive feel my spins in opposite directions at speed. Darb at my side dropping straight into splits and dropbacks matching the record, fast, flowing, feet burning into the floor. Our corner alive with energy, a passion to dance to show what we can do.

Ian Levine smiling at our dancing watching from the turntables cuing his next record. He unleashed one of his best new sounds as if to show us the new face of Northern. A complete contrast to what we had just heard The Temprees "At Last", a record I had never heard of and one I instantly loved. Her pleading, soulful voice, the hypnotic jumbled beats sending the floor in a different direction.

Shuffling footwork, the Mecca's style of dancing not so different, we stayed with the tempo of the floor. Our sliding footwork, dummy spins to half turns, tighter steps matching the record to perfection. Dancers around us watching Northern is Northern, a dancer can adapt my attitude changing with every new found beat.

Suddenly a record that changed the scene forever, the epitome of the new direction of Northern "It Really Hurts Me Girl" by The Carstairs. The record unfamiliar to anything we had ever heard, it wasn't the disco crap of earlier. This was a tune you could dance to time and time again. If any one record impacted the scene at this time, this was it. A record that blew me away, the beats alone, soulful cries of "What a tune!" between us. All of us feeling the vibe of the floor Eloise Laws "Love Factory", James Fountain "Seven Day Lover", T. D. Valentine "Love Trap", Mickie Champion

"What Good Am I (Without You)", Johnny Williams "You're Something Kinda Mellow", Boby Franklin "The Ladies Choice", Ila Vann "You Made Me This Way", Van McCoy "Soul Improvisations", Doni Burdick "Bari Track", and The Detroit Executives "Cool Off". The beats now far too slow and funky for me.

At times it felt just like a disco, but this was a Northern floor, so different from The Casino. Tunes that divided a dance floor but not the scene, no one man had that much power no matter what he thought. The new face of Northern soul? No handclaps or hands in the air, no energy and drive from the dancers, not one ounce of atmosphere in the venue. The floor full of rare music but to us many of the records lacking in soul. The feeling deep inside, that spark of emotion that made you get up and make you stay on the floor. Our footwork slowed to a pace I couldn't handle. Darb and I sat at a table frustrated, listening to more new tunes. Jako coming to join us, a face of twisted disgust.

"This is shit man!" The master of the joker struggling with the new found beats.

"The last time I sat on my arse this long was when I went ice skating. I'm done, I'm going down stairs." Darb as ever making us laugh.

"That's Glenn isn't it? Hey mate!" My voice travelling to a Soulie standing near our table. Glenn Walker Foster from Blackpool, clutching a record box nervously in his hand.

"I thought I recognized you, what's up man?" Shyness in his nature, a young Soulie we met at The Torch Revival. Joining our table, seated introductions and Northern greetings of crossing hands.

"Hey Glenn, where's all the best dancers?"

"They all left ages ago Gethro. As soon as Tony Jebb stopped DJing none of them come here anymore."

"That's you sorted Jako. You'll have to dance against your shadow!" Laughter surrounding our table Jimmy and Kim coming to join us. "What sounds you got Glenn?"

"Just a few pressing Gethro."

"Let's have a look Glenn?" Darb holding the box as Jimmy looked over his shoulder.

"I can't handle this music anymore lover, I'm going downstairs!" Kim smiling, acknowledging the frustration in my voice. "Which way is it Glenn?"

"Come on, I'll show you. Soul Sam's on in the main room, all of us gathering our bags. I felt sad in a way but I knew in my heart the direction I would be going and there really was only one venue for me. Connoisseurs of music the Mecca crowd may be, but the Highland Room and The Casino different as night and day.

What divisions in the scene had The Mecca really created? When Northern up till now had been fast, hard, soulful tracks not disco funky beats. Ian Levine's reputation on the scene as we knew it was that of a spoilt, fat, bastard who had everything handed to him on a plate by rich parents. Yet none of it was true. Sure he had a plane ride to America but after that he was on his own and took every opportunity he had. Scouring junk shops, warehouses, and record shops to build up his vinyl collection. I didn't like him, I don't know why, maybe it was the rumors. After all he had everything I did not. His arrogance distasteful to many people, but I had to give him respect. In truth he owed no one a thing, he was a self-made guy. Ian and Colin Curtis would discover many new sounds and mold the scene the way they wanted it to go, the problem for them was Wigan's DJs would do the same.

Once again we entered The Highland Room corridor following Glenn down the stairs, the speed of our exit making me smile. Another corridor leading to a large open foyer, dropping our coats at separate cloak rooms we entered through double doors leading into the back of the main room Little Richard blasting from the speakers "I Don't Want To Discuss It", strong Northern beats greeting us, records full of Soul.

"Look at this place Gethro!" Glenn leading us forward, his face bursting with pride. All of us pausing, speechless at the bottom of a spiral staircase, the noise of a small bar serving drinks to our right. A large stage held center of the main room with a small DJs booth almost hidden by curtains. Soul Sam spinning sounds on the right hand side of the stage. Five thickset oak trees encircled a huge wooden dance floor, their twisting branches covered in flowering vines. A low ornate railing encompassed the dance floor, separating dancers from seating. Three other spiral staircases spaced around the room led to a modern Tyrolean balcony above the dance floor to end on the opposite side of the stage.

I had never been in a place as smart as this, the custom made disco felt so out of place playing Northern. The speckled light of a revolving disco ball, countless flickers of light encircling the darkened room. Chrome and polish reminiscent of Va-Va but this was on a much grander scale. "That stage revolves Gethro, you wait and see" Glenn leading us forward, finding spare tables and chairs we settled at the side of the floor. "I'll Never Fall In Love Again" by Bobby Freeman filling the room.

"These are our sounds man!" Darb and Jako bursting in smiles, their enthusiasm infectious joining other Wolvo Soulies along the edge of the floor. Jimmy and Winston faces intent, sat scouring Glenn's record box, pulling out one of his latest finds.

"How much for this Glenn?"

"You can have it for a quid Jimmy." I smiled, as ever teasing Jimmy.

"Jimmy, behave. Remember he's our mate."

"You bad Gethro man!"

"I'll watch him Gethro" Winston laughing, it's just the way we were.

"Come on Lover, let's get a drink." Kim holding my hand.

"Check the Bali Hal Bar out Gethro."

"Where's that?"

"Along that back wall." Glenn pointing directly across from us.

I wanted to see the dance floor from the top of the trees. Climbing the spiral staircase we headed in that direction, passing another bar on our left. Coffee and drinks, a food menu the smell of cooking hanging heavy in the air. Pausing on the balcony handrail we joined other couples, Divs, and holiday makers staring in our direction. My cords and vest the attire of the all-nighters, our dress code so different from theirs. The huge dance floor divided small areas alight with Soulies, other figures of motionless hand baggers and small groups filling the floor. Flowering trees reaching above our heads, a venue the opposite of Wigan's shabbiness and grandeur replaced with flamboyant decor and chrome.

"This is nothing like Wigan, Kim."

"You know what all-dayers are like. What do you expect lover?" Both of us laughing, the stares and pointed fingers not bothering us. We were from another world, an underground scene so different from theirs. Passing the lighting box, descending another spiral staircase we came out on the opposite end of the room. Both of us taken aback by our surroundings. Along the back wall deep blue murals of volcanic south island seas bordered Aztec patterned designs. Brightly painted totem poles and carved tribal masks' staring faces guarding the entrances to three open doorways.

Following Soulies we entered the Bali Hal bar. Above us the peaked roof adorned with numerous flowers, palm leaves, fishing nets, and shells. Bamboo walls forming a jungle stockade, the lavishness of our surrounding steeped in tropical island design. This venue like nothing we had ever been to.

A mixed crowd greeting us, well-known faces from the scene, all of us had come for Junior and Edwin. The momentum building inside lads from Stoke Crew and Nottingham, Wigan Soulies packing the room. Greetings of friends in crossing hands, that indescribable bond we had from all-nighters. What divisions on the Northern scene?

Kim working her way through the room, finding more friends. Sue Ready, Nesata and Laney, Paul and Pete from Kiddy, Polo from Worcester, and Ronnie from Stoke. All of us Soul brothers and sisters our time spent reminiscing of favorite records and previous nights at different venues blocked on gear. Collecting more drinks we reentered the main room. Larry Williams & Johnny Watson "A Quitter Never Wins" sounds from Wigan. A drunken scuffled by the doorway, bouncers showing no mercy, onlookers filling the room. We made our way around the dance floor. For all its ambience and chrome I just didn't feel right.

"I'm glad we never took any gear lover."

"Me too. This place is just full of Divs. Come on, let's show them how to dance!" Quickening our step, rejoining our little group it was time to hit this floor. My confidence boiling over, I'll give them something to point at! After all there is no bigger insult to a dancer than being blown off your own floor. Anger welling inside me our records filling the venue. The Jewels "We Got Togetherness" my feet exploding onto the floor. Jako and Darb joining us, Jimmy already out there with Winston bringing his moves.

My handspring into a drop-back just making the landing, coming up blasting into a spin. The polish of the floor helping with speed, our corner alight, full of energy, Northern dancers joining us. Onlookers on the balcony, Wolvo making a statement. It was time to take this floor R. Dean Taylor "Let's Go Somewhere" Jako and me buzzing off each other. Handsprings and somersaults, splits in unison both of us letting it rip. A friendly competition, my footwork flowing into backdrops.

Our matching vests and soul badges making a statement, "we're from all-nighters, this is how we dance!" The Show Stoppers "What Can A Man Do??", Sandra Phillips "World Without Sunshine", and Reparata & The Delrons "Panic". Squeak coming to join us laughing and joking between us, his multiple spins blowing us off the floor. Dean Parrish "Determination", Leon Haywood "Baby Reconsider", The Perigents "Love On The Rampage", The Soul Twins "Quick Change Artist", The Sons Of Moses "Soul Symphony", Robert Knight "Branded!", Billy Harner "Sally Sayin' Somethin'", more of our favorite tunes The Four Larks "Groovin' At The Go-Go", David And The Giants "Superlove", and Edwin Starr "Way Over There". The room plunging in darkness then cascading to bright yellow light.

Illuminated in the center of a revolving stage Edwin taking over the vocals, his backing band playing his tune. All of us stopped dancing, the room bursting to life Soulies surging to the front of the stage. Clapping and cheering the atmosphere exploding all around us, his charismatic figure moving across the stage. A singer captivating the audience, full of energy and emotion his melodic voice crystal clear. "Stop Her On Sight (S.O.S.)" now blasting from the speakers, my feet rolling to soulful Motown beats. Edwin's outstretched arm holding the mic to the crowd, a chorus of "stop her on sight" igniting the room. A tune full of memories, The Ship and Cavendish all of us dancing, records played in my bedroom now coming to life.

Kim falling into my arms both of us immersed in the happiness of our surroundings. A stolen kiss, dancing as a couple in the old days Jako and Darb laughing at our side. "Agent Double-O Soul" and "Twenty-Five Miles" Edwin pounding the Northern beats, sweating in the lights of the stage. A brilliant performer sounding exactly like his records, giving the audience his heart and soul. My opinion changing of live acts, applause from the crowd, hands in the air, cheering, the atmosphere intensified with every new tune. "You've Got My Soul On Fire", "Love Never Dies", "Girls Are Getting Prettier", "24 Hours (To Find My Baby)", "Time", "Headline News", "War" his next tune setting the room on fire. Edwin getting help from a few Soulies from the audience.

"Look, it's Julie Pender!" Kim pointing to her friend on the stage. "She's a good dancer." Her face glowing with pride. "Back Street", another Northern classic, all of us now dancing at the back of the room. Exactly what I had wanted, I couldn't just stand and listen to the artist, a live act so different from what we had seen at Leeds. "I Have Faith In You", the lights fading to reds and yellows, Edwin taking a bow roars of appreciation, Soulies showing their love of his music. Slow handclaps demanding an encore, the crowd wanting more. Edwin's rendition of "My Weakness Is You" his lone figure slowly fading in lights. Blown kisses, waves to the crowd, thundering applause echoing around the venue his spot ending far too soon.

"Wow! That was some show!"

"Brilliant Darb. I mean the guy just killed it."

"Gethro, he has to be one of the best we've seen so far."

"I know Jako. Class act man." All of us elated at what we had just seen.

"Thanks for bringing me lover." Kim holding me in her arms.

"Hey there's no way we go anywhere without you Kim. I love you." Her smile full of mischief, I knew that face.

"I'm going to find Julie and Bob, see if she will give me her autograph." A playful giggle, "see you later." A gentle kiss and she was gone.

I had to admit I was wrong, Edwin doing what no live acts we had seen so far had done. Taking the roof off with his songs, a venue perfect in a way but still full of Divs and drinkers, the crowds of all-dayers so opposite from us. Soul Sam spinning more tunes, our time spent out on the floor. After all, that's what we lived for, to dance. Our approach wasn't just gymnastics, intricate footwork had to match the records and flow in just one move. I had now taken Jako's move and improved on it. Still attending gymnastics twice a week sometimes on my own, it was here I learned even more moves.

Knowledge of the sounds played, being our strength as many were from The Catacombs and Wigan our timing now down to perfection. Jako and me doing somersaults and handsprings from a standing position, my difference of landing in a drop-back I turned to my advantage. I hadn't forgotten Whitchurch, now with a full recovery even on this floor I decided to unleash some of my new moves. From a drop-back position I could easily double it and go straight over into another. Sometimes breaking it up with a leg spin. What I did now was a game changer, I could land in a sideways splits turning this sequence into opposite spins. A move I didn't do very often but I had never seen anyone else on the scene do this move. Raising the bar in our dancing to heights only I could achieve.

Even Jako and Darb couldn't do moves that I now brought to the floor. I pushed myself to perfection, Mona as always cheering me on or dancing at my side. It wasn't to show off or blow people off a floor, it's the way I danced, it really was that simple. My attitude would get me in trouble later as I strived to be the best out on the floor.

All of us were now accomplished Northern dancers, a crowd always watching us lining the floor. I never felt paranoid or out of place, such was our ability and confidence we were completely at home in the spotlight out on the floor. John Miles "One Minute Every Hour" the floating beats perfected into our style of footwork, Towanda Barnes "You Don't Mean It" spins at lightning speed, Sandy Wynns "Love's Like Quicksand", Johnny Caswell "You Don't Love Me Anymore", Mel Britt "She'll Come Running Back", Jodi Mathis "Don't You Care Anymore" and The Dells "Run For Cover". Darb and I showing our strengths, adjusting our footwork to any Northern sound.

"Come on then Gethro, show me that move once more?" Jako laughing as he came over, standing at my side. The first handspring done to perfection, my back arched to gain momentum. Another handspring from a low position my legs opening as I landed in the splits. Turning this into a leg spin and drop-back rising into opposite spins. The speed of the move imperative, playing to the crowd infectious, a quick bow as I approached Jako.

"This floors too slippy man, I nearly didn't make it." My voice full of anguish, both of us laughing.

"I know, thought you was going on your arse then Gethro!"

"Won't be the first time Jako!" Our arms around each other, such was our closeness. We had a bond of affection like brothers.

"Come on, let's hit it!" Darb as ever wanting to hit the floor, dancers around him giving us room. No one trying to take us on, our moves dominating the venue, another floor we had taken. A nod of recognition between us, The Mecca floor ours. My heart bursting with pride listening to Billy Woods "Let Me Make You Happy", Danny Monday "Baby, Without You", and The Younghearts "Little Togetherness", my feet changing to the speedy tempo, a free flowing spirit matching the beats. Dummy steps, dropping to spins, we too showing our styles of dancing more and more of our tunes.

"The one and only Mr. Soul man himself, Junior Walkeeer!" Soul Sam screaming down the mic. The stage revolving, bursting in reds and yellows, filtered lights from the balcony the side stepping All-Stars turning into the room. A magnet drawing us across the floor, a gathering crowd at the front of the stage. Lights flashing to the backing beats of a brass section suddenly Jr. bursting from the curtains, dropping to bent knees sliding across the stage. His tonic suited figure leaning backwards, saxophone in his hands fingers dancing on keys.

"Only Junior could play a sax like that!" The unforgettable intro "I Ain't Going Nowhere" exploding from the speakers. The atmosphere going wild, cheering, whistling, hands in the air, endless faces of happiness the audience caught in the lights of the stage. Swaying figures of the backing band feeling the soul of his instrument. Cheeks inflated, note after note in perfect timing, a wave of recognition to the band. "I ain't going nowhere unless I go with you", his throaty voice igniting the room, Jr. on bent knees at the front of the stage. The power of a sax like nothing I had ever seen, his mastery as if connected as one with the instrument. His upright figure now center stage, holding my attention watching his every move. Neck inflamed, cheeks puffed up, a glistening golden sax blasting out his tunes.

Some we knew well "(I'm A) Road Runner", "Way Back Home", "Come See About Me", "Right On Brothers And Sisters", "Shotgun", "Take Me Girl, I'm Ready", "What Does It Take (To Win Your Love)", over an hour on stage more and more of his tunes. Jr. like Edwin, giving it all, an artist totally blowing me away mesmerizing the small audience of the all-dayer flooding the room in Soul. He too ending in an encore to cries between us, shouts of appreciation "Pucker Up Buttercup" and "How Sweet It Is (To Be Loved By You)". Sweat filtered notes, playing with the crowd he too fading in lights to roars of appreciation, his act over. Our smiling faces giving our reply, "best couple of quid I've ever spent Darb."

"And me Gethro." Both of us in acknowledgment of what we had just seen and heard.

"What times the coach leave outside Darb?"

"I'm sure he said twelve thirty."

"Good I've got something in my pocket for Kim." Darb's face breaking to a smile, a slight hesitancy as he leaned forward hand on my shoulder, his voice now lower almost to a whisper.

"Look Gethro we're close man, but not that close."

"What no! No! You don't understand, remember last week?!" My hands parting I could see his mind racing in paused silence, a nodded expression frowned burrows lining his face.

"Oh yea!"

"Well, just make sure they don't leave us." Kim chatting to Jimmy, laughing with Jako at our side. "Come on lover, let's go for a walk."

"You going?"

"Yea."

"Later man."

"Later." Collecting our coats, leaving The Mecca, venturing into the evening darkness. I wanted us to be alone to walk along the beach.

The full moon of a cloudless night, our long shadows stretching in front of us. Shoes in hand, feet sinking in foaming surf, rolling waves kissing our ankles I hadn't a care in the world. We had been through so much on our journey, she had been with me every step of the way. She felt like a mother, a sister, a lover, everything I could ask for always at my side. I felt nervous, in my pocket a simple ring. Pausing for a moment I nervously reached for her hand. "Kim close your eyes." Slipping the ring on the third finger, "you know you are my Bonnie." Kim smiled, looking deep into my eyes.

"You are my Clyde lover. I just want to be by your side."

"See I'm eternalized! That means I love you forever Kim!" Gentleness in our kiss, a longing so deep in my heart to give all of my unconditional love to her.

Why couldn't I just let go and return the love she so freely gave to me? My words full of meaning, but emptiness, my heart hollow inside. The sexual abuse, the darkened rooms had destroyed whatever love I had. "You dirty little boy!" Echoing in my head, my heart wasn't pure, it was abused and destroyed. The torture of a childhood memory that even at this very moment would not allow happiness to release and cleanse my pain. Why did I cry at the emotion, the connection of being loved? Tears and pain blocking the happiness I was to be denied. Locks without a combination, a timeless emotional key, would it control my life forever? Would it ever set my heart free?

Once more we walked hand in hand, the cool waves crashing in darkness two lovers on a desolate beach. The Blackpool Mecca, a special moment that lasts forever etched in your memory. I smiled, endless thoughts wandering in and out of my mind. Seeking sanctuary in reality, the winds of change before me, what divisions on the Northern scene?

Chapter 38

BLACK AND WHITE DIVIDE

"The winds of change"

"What that little slut?! You brought her a ring? Ha! Don't make me laugh." Sarcasm in her tone of voice, "thinks she's too good for us! Sticking her nose in the air, coming round here. Who does she think she is?!" My foster mother's vengeance full of venom turning to me with the hiss of a coiled snake. Her redden face twisted in anger, out to destroy every dream I held precious to run rampant through my world "You'll never be anything in your life! You or your mother!"

Staring straight at me, glaring eyes emphasizing her words, your mother! "You want to know what she really was, eh?! A worthless prostitute working the streets, you have nine brothers and sisters they want nothing to do with you!" I tried to hold back my emotions, not to respond. The avalanche of insults, her goading words demanding a response. Egging me on, probing at my anger held in check, teeth biting my tongue, words of endless abuse filling the kitchen. Her clenched fist holding a rolling pin, I had felt her violence as a child but not this time. Grabbing her hand forcing its release and throwing it aside.

"You mean nothing to me!" My body shaking in anger, tightened lips, sternness in my words.

"What! After all we have done for you?!" Her voice now screaming, "You ungrateful bastard!"

"What did you do?! Nothing! You've never shown me love, I was just a paycheck so you can gamble. That's all I ever was to you! Leave Kim alone, she has done nothing to you!" Releasing my anger, shouting at the top of voice.

"Get out! Go on! Get out and don't come back! We're sick of you coming and going whenever you want!" Yanking the front door open, pushing me, stabbing fingers pointing to the open door. "There's the door, get out!" Turning away I went to my bedroom throwing a few clothes into my puma bag. Her screaming words meaningless, hurting pains of anger, tears welling in my eyes. I wanted to smash the place to pieces, destroy all the memories of a childhood that had no dreams.

Our eyes clashing in a mirrored reflection. I brushed past taking hold of the open door, a hatred between us that had simmered far too long. The door slamming behind me spinning on my heels, two V's flicked in defiance "Fuck you! Fuck off out of my life! My bag swinging in midair as I reminisce at the corridor I had walked so many times, "goodbye concrete jungle. Fuck you and your shoebox!" A relief, nervousness excitement at what had just occurred. At last I was on my own!

"Cup of tea Jim, please." Rummaging in my pocket for change, Rumpy's almost empty the clatter of washing crockery and stale cigarette smoke filling the air.

"What you doing here, it's not Saturday?" My face breaking to a smile at his open inquisitiveness.

"Just been kicked out Jim."

"Ah! Sometimes it's for the best lad." A head of graying hair adding substance to his comment, the cup steaming in brown hot liquid.

"Cheers Jim." Taking my tea, finding a table I would wait for the afternoon paper, tossing my bag with vengeance to the empty window seat. My mind still racing at what had just happened. Now what Mr. Smart Arse? You're on your own now, what are you going to do? Where will you sleep tonight? My nerves starting to run away with me, visions of a park bench, a homeless tramp filling my mind. Hot sweet tea lifting my spirits, open fingers stroking my forehead. Stay calm, think comes on! You have a job, a trade I had even passed my finals. At last my dream came true. Sure, not the way I wanted but after all their hatred, "fuck them! I'll never go back!"

Don't worry, a strange feeling of calmness engulfing me as if Kim were by my side. What will she say? Would she be proud of me? Thoughts turning in my mind.

"Hey Gethro, what you doing here?!" Winston smiling coming towards my table. "Tea Jim please." A chirpiness to his voice, my heart lifted. Plonking himself in the opposite seat, "What's up man? You look worried."

"I am Winst. Just been kicked out." Winston stroking his chin, his searching eyes sharing my adolescent pain.

"Hey, come stay with me and Jimmy. We got a room in a house on Villa Street, landlord's a bit weird though." Winst shuffling uneasily.

"What do you mean bit weird?" My inquisitive look demanding more.

"Oh he just is. You'll be ok, just stay out the way. They use the house for parties on Saturday nights. Works perfect as we're always at Wigan."

"That's cool. What do you want? I'll chip in."

"No nothing! It'll be ok till you get on your feet. The room's locked, no one touches our stuff."

"You sure mate? Thanks Winst." A sense of relief in my voice at the weight lifted from my shoulders.

"Gethro I know you would do the same for me." I felt humbled at Winston's depth of friendship, the brothers that we were.

"Two bacon sarnies love." The waitress bringing more tea.

That night I moved into Winston and Jimmy's, both making me feel wanted. At least it was a home.

"What time you meeting Kim, Gethro?"

"She's coming straight to The Ship Jimmy, its Friday night man!" Excitement in my voice, all of us gathered at the top of the stairs Winston locking the door to our room. The front door flying open startling us, a Jamaican holding a crate of beer, another two guys behind him.

"Put it in der'e man." A stockier older guy pointing to an open door. "What!" His voice in a shrill. "Get that white boy out my house man! Ain't no white boy living here!" Rage in his words, widened eyes in anger, a pointed finger straight at me. Jimmy and Winston standing in front of me as if to protect me from his vengeance as he rose with others to the top of the stairs. "Blood clautt white shit! Why you with this white boy after the way they treat us man?!" Piercing eyes glaring at me.

"Look he'll be gone tomorrow, it's late. One night, that's all. Come on Randolph, just one night" Winston pleading my case, his face now turning to anger I had never seen before. Thoughts rushing to my mind, at least we've got the high ground.

"Get him out! Only white thing come this house is white pussy." A slight pause as he leaned on the banister glaring at me. "If him here tomorrow, you all out!"

"You want him out Randolph?" One of his friends draped in gold, spoiling for the fight.

"Winston I tell you man, I come tomorrow if him here I mash him up and you hear me boy! Hear me!"

"I hear you." Winston's voice in murmured defiance.

"Now get out!" All of us gingerly descending the stairs, his voice lost in directions of the oncoming party tomorrow.

"Fuckin hell Gethro, I never knew you was white boy!"

"Only on the outside Jimmy, you know the way I dance." All of bursting to laughter on the pavement outside. Our walk to The Ship almost in silence, all of us gathering our thoughts. I couldn't read minds but I could feel their pain. I didn't want to talk about what had just happened, the embarrassment of our color. Black, white, pink, who gives a shit?!

We never saw that in each other. There were no barriers with us but I knew in my heart Jimmy and Winston would have gone down by my side. Our night in The Ship subdued, I would find somewhere to live tomorrow but first I would go to the post office. I wanted a copy of my birth certificate, a niggling question gnawing at me. Up till now I had been denied an answer, I wanted to know my parent's names.

All of us rising early, after all I had caused enough problems, I felt saddened and guilty. Washed, clean and ready placing my bag by the open door.

"Gethro, you be in Rumpy's later?"

"Yea Winst, then The Octopus."

"Ok, see you in there. Try the New Hampton Rd. Gethro, there's loads of bed and breakfasts down there."

"Cheers mate. Hey, tell Kim I may be a bit late."

"We'll look after her Gethro, she's our sister." A smile between us our arms interlocking, Winston giving me a hug, our friendship stronger than ever. Their bigotry and intolerance would never destroy our friendship, we had no place for racism in our hearts.

"I'm coming with you man!"

"No, I'll be ok Jimmy."

"I said I'm coming with you man." Jimmy defiantly holding my bag of belongings.

"Well at least I'm ready for Wigan. Bit early but I'm ready." All of us starting to laugh.

The new Hampton Rd. a short walk from Winston's, crisscrossing a maze of side streets, our walk felt pleasant in the morning sun. Grimy bay windows of patchwork multi-colored curtains. Bed sitters dissecting old Victorian houses, I felt sad at their loss of grandeur. Their drabness a testament to landlords, who spend little or no money on repairs. Trimmed hedges of cul-de-sac side streets, parked cars hugging the pavements, the odd sign of bed and breakfasts. "Try this one Gethro?" A neatly manicured garden behind us we approached the leaded glass door. Vacancies, curtains twitching in the side window, our third try, maybe our luck will change?

"Can I help you?" A middle aged woman with the scrutiny of a detective staring into my eyes.

"Have you?" Her gaze darting past me.

"We're full!" The door abruptly closing, the window sign reversed. The whites more discreet of their distaste at the colour of a man's skin, the knife just as sharp whoever plunged it. The true face of Wolvo.

"It's no good man. You ain't going to find anything with me." Jimmy shuffling uneasily.

"Come on, one more."

"No Gethro! You see what I see."

"I'm sorry Jimmy." Shaking my head.

"Ain't you man, it's just the way it is." Our crossing hands as deep as our love for each other. We parted in the street, unable to turn around my eyes welling in tears. Heartbroken at the pain they had inflicted on my friend. My head bowed in shame, the colour of my skin an embarrassment to me. A reality of their hatred and mistrust. "Judge a man by his heart not the colour of his skin." Their generation lost in ignorance. Walking in a daze, moving on, changing my surroundings. Another crescent of Victorian houses, seeing a sign in a window I approached another door, this time alone.

"Have you any vacancies?"

"Yes we do actually. Its five pounds a week and eight with an evening meal." An elderly lady dusting her hands on an apron welcoming me to a carpeted hallway, wiping my feet as I did. The house was old, draped in Victorian décor the narrow hallway leading to different rooms. "This is where we serve breakfast and dinner." Waving me into a large dining room, a cuckoo clock in the hallway announcing our arrival. Three old men, our eyes locked in a searching gaze, I felt uneasy I shouldn't be here. "Introductions later, come with me I'll show you your room."

Her voice aloof, floating above repetitive chimes. Turning away moving swiftly up the stairs, pausing to push a door open we entered a small room. There was a bed, dressing table and wardrobe, none of them matched. A musty smell of old blankets, the landlady leaning forward, parting curtains and opening the window. Obliviously, explaining about times and clean sheets as if reading a script rehearsed from many visitors before me. "One week in advance." Spinning around to face me her hand in the flatness of a well-oiled palm. I pulled out all the money I had, taking it she smiled turning away. Sitting on the edge of the bed dropping my bag. A cloak of loneliness around my shoulders, a fear of my future. I had all these friends yet I had never felt so alone.

"You and your mouth, when will you ever learn?!" The noise of the bathroom breaking my thoughts, "come on Wigan tonight!" A different world calling me, collecting my receipt and key bag in hand I marched out the door. I smiled in her ramblings I didn't even catch her name.

Chapter 39

WHO ARE YOU

"Name please!" Passing my driver's license to the woman at the post office, a slight hesitation as she scribbled my name, hurriedly turning away. "I'll take a minute." I sat to the side waiting, excitement building inside me, nervousness in my stomach. I wonder who they were. What did they do? Where was I born? I was nineteen years old, finally I would get some answers. Just who the fuck are you?! No more heated nightmares, the turmoil of saturated dreams.

"Geoffrey Jones!" Taking the folded paper I returned to my seat. Certified Copy of an Entry of Birth, the bright red lettering jumping from the page. My date of birth, then Mary Jones, at last my mother's name. Even by holding a simple piece of paper I felt connected, it was all I had to hold on to. My mother was a journeyman file cutter, I didn't even know what one was. Maybe that's why I was good with my hands. Grasping at a word that would mean so much to me. My father's name and trade blank. Why did you leave me nothing? Why? Tears blurring my vision, my emotions fighting an inner battle of equal hatred for the both of them, bastards! Who are you? A question that would remain unanswered as I stared at my father's blank space. Ah well Jones'ey now you have the truth. I didn't even feel let down, after all what did you expect? Wiping my eyes I started to smile. Taking solace in my thoughts, whenever someone called me a bastard at least they are using my proper name. It's just you now, you have no roots you must create your own. The voices of my inner conscience giving me hope that in my dancing at least I would leave a legacy with my name.

Chapter 40

CENTER OF OUR UNIVERSE

Last night the same as many before it, to us there was only one venue and that was Wigan Casino. The center of our universe, nothing could compare to the nights there, the club now a giant on the Northern scene. The summer crowds ever larger, gear openly flowing in every direction. Week after week it's all any of us lived for, to be in that environment. To dance and feel the atmosphere of that floor. My dealing had now intensified, with drugs came money and with money came style. I could now afford new clothes.

A new film had just come out called *The Great Gatsby*, set around life in the twenties. I loved the images of this period and modeled myself on it. Waistcoats, collarless shirts, and tailored trousers, looking sharp meant everything to me. Crombies were still the fashion, even for us and I wanted to be different. Every one wore blue, I had one tailor-made, full length light brown to match my puma bag. I was becoming recognizable on the scene and that's exactly what I wanted. Strange for a dealer but this one was different, I felt aloof, untouchable. I was now a face, a permanent fixture in the crowd. With my methods of dealing working like clockwork, laying gear off always giving rewards. Flying under the radar, sure there were whispers in Wolvo but really no one knew about me.

I knew the score by dealing drugs I was playing roulette with a loaded gun.

Every time I pulled the trigger the chamber was empty but for how long? I didn't care, nothing could touch me, I was invincible everything I touched now turning to gold. With my new found freedom came a confidence, after all I answered to no one but my conscience. Being a dancer who stood out, girls would come to find me from every direction. Like I had promised I took every one that crossed the floor. Secret moments, youthful passions unleashed away from the heat of the club. Mrs. Woods giving me pass outs smiling at my demise. Hardly missed, such was the size of The Casino I would be back to dance in a little while. A dark side to my nature, a payback for the way I had been treated. Or was I just like my father? A cheating lying bastard taking what he wanted, living up to my image of his name.

My first few hours in The Casino always spent dealing on the right hand side of the floor. The beauty of powder over pills, spare deals easily stashed down by my bollocks. A simple safety pin and plastic bag retrieved with ease in the mayhem around me I was just another Soulie adjusting his cords. Deals laid off to Mona and others, Darb and Jimmy never far from my side. I didn't like taking risks, they had to be eliminated yet it was now I made one of my boldest moves.

Such was the following in Wolvo, I now organized coaches to The Casino. Following Pixie's idea, after all, every week at the train station our numbers had been growing, to me it was a simple move. Collecting deposits and names in The Cats and Octopus my fifty-three seat coach filling rapidly. A stream of new faces joining us every week. Problem for me, I attracted attention from two directions, rip-offs and squad were my enemies. Sure I had back-up but only to a certain degree. My coach leaving outside The Cats was far too easy a target, Soulies forever beaten and rolled. I felt a responsibility, this was my family they were all I had. These were my mates, I had to pit myself against the rip-offs and protect them. Not only that but from the drug squad. Outside The Cats we were a sitting duck, waiting to be busted.

I now took it underground, the only way you knew the ever changing pickup point was from me. By solving one problem I created another, unbeknownst to the driver my coach was always full of drugs. The younger Cats' crowd relentless in their crime wave of soul, chemist after chemist now going down. Drugs from their escapades openly flowing onto the coach. Many times our adrenaline high fueled with caps and pills of every description. Black bombers, their smaller sisters, black and whites minstrels that made you verbal your head off. Brown and clears, green and clears, red and browns, two tone pinks, filon, blueys and dex by the handful. Some weeks we had more drugs than Boots, a local chemist! Adding to this mix, I too openly moved my champagne.

Eliminating my problems by selling spare deals before we even got to The Casino. Drugs moving quickly in and out of my hands, possession is nine-tenths of the law. Never letting my guard down, to beat the squad I used a simple technique. I carried two envelopes, one with the money for the coach, the other full of deals.

By passing the deals wrapped in paper to the driver, he thought he was holding the money for the coach. I did this till we were out of Staffordshire, always know your enemy. Drug squads, as I was led to believe, could only operate in their own county, Wolvo squad weren't regional. Once out of Staffordshire I would swap the envelopes, telling the driver I had to add more money. He hadn't a clue as I moved down the coach collecting fares and selling deals. No one forced drugs on anyone, I wouldn't allow that. We had morals you weren't belittled, it was your choice.

As I returned to the front I would often smile, the driver holding the wheel the only one left who was straight. Events were running away with me, spinning out of my control on the coach I let anything fly. Breaking all of my rules drawing attention to myself, "never shit on your own doorstep" gone out the window. Such was my trust in the Soulies around me but very soon I would pay a heavy price.

With one problem solved, came another Knutsford Services squad always in the back of my mind. To eliminate this we stopped at Sandbach Services, never forgetting our days of thumbing to The Casino. My coach had an unwritten rule, no matter how packed we never drove past Soulies thumbing a lift. Such was the bond on the Northern scene, all of us one family, one destination. The Casino. Wolvo not only impacting the dance floor, but adding to the never ending supply of gear. Reputations built on trust, I never cut gear at this time. Repeat customers were the foundation of my enterprise, joining many others fueling our nights with gear. The club now holding over one thousand five hundred Soulies. The nights we all lived for, a weekly reality our meetings in Rumpy's on Sundays, now a regular matinee.

"Where's Kim?"

"Had to take her home Winst, mom's rules." Scuffing my chair as I joined our table. The loss of her presence irritated me, I wanted her by my side.

"What's your new bedsitter like?"

"Only been there a week mate. It seems ok, better than the bed and breakfast. At least I don't get strange looks anymore. How's chalky?" A nickname we had given his landlord.

"He's still the same." The smile between us acknowledging the improvement independence brings. Sipping my Lucozade mixed with orange juice I gazed out of the window. A different world from one we had just left behind. Shimmering cars caught in halted traffic, occupants cooking in summer's mid-day sun. Winston's and Jako's voices the mumbled noise of our table, Jimmy's laughter filling Rumpy's empty café. Still feeling the effects of gear, my thoughts drifting aimlessly over last night. Shirtless figures shining in sweat, darkened cords clinging to my body. Steaming nicotine mist of the dance floor, hair matted to my forehead, pounding heart beats hardly able to breathe. Fluency of feet releasing a handspring to a drop-back, fingers touching my shoes, full side splits in midair.

Condensation showering dancers, The Casino thundering in hand claps. A sea of rising hands, two thousand arms reaching to the domed ceiling. "Cochise" by Paul Humphrey echoing around The Casino, a sound we knew and loved. My body a well-oiled machine, fine-tuned with bombers and sulfate, a dancer on top of his game. Our fitness in muscle toned bodies, saturated in the sauna of Wigan's floor. All of us wanting more, tune after tune igniting our feet. Riding the rush of atmosphere, feeling the amphetamine high. Hands on hips between records, a Wigan lizard darting its tongue wetting dry lips. Jawing faces in verb led conversations, the haze of wide-eyed crowds lining the floor. Tilted heads of the balcony scrutinizing every dance move. Our shirtless, sweating bodies weaving through dancers Darb at my side, Soul girls crisscrossing the floor. Visions of Glenn's face not going away, arms held either side by scum. Rip-offs in The Casino Glenn Walker Foster, our friend instantly catching my eye.

"Wow, fuck off!" Placing my hand on his chest, his face in startled fear, halting his assailant's momentum in front of the stage. "Darb, get the lads."

"No Gethro, we're just talking!"

"Fuck off! You always talk to someone with a knife in their back?!" My voice full of anger, fist clenched about to unleash our brand of justice. I hated rip-offs, the taller one holding my glare releasing his grip, stepping backwards. "Glenn's with Carol, she's from Wolvo! That means he's with us, so fuckin leave him!"

"We don't want any trouble Gethro, Darb. Honest." Their voices patronizing, now standing by Glenn's side.

"Gethro! Gethro! You all right man?!" Jimmy's voice breaking my thoughts, the noise of Rumpy's growing louder. "You got to come down off this gear man!"

"I'm ok!" Shaking my head, clearing my mind. "I was just daydreaming. Those bombers are strong man!"

Jimmy rolling his eyes, "You bad Gethro!" Both of us laughing, Jimmy looking out for me, a playful concern of the brothers we were.

"I heard The Cats is closing." Darb getting my attention, polishing his glasses as he always did whenever he was being serious.

"When?"

"Next month."

"That's a load of bollocks, it's packed every week!" My voice in annoyance at the thought of losing our club.

"That's what Swoz said Gethro. He was talking to Pep." Darb readjusting his glasses, as if to emphasize his point.

"It's the Wigan coach Gethro!" Jako joining our conversation.

"No way man. Most of the coach don't even go to The Cats." Trying to relieve my guilt at the thought of what I may have done.

"Jako you're wrong. Swoz said its compulsory purchase order by the council. It's closing definitely next month, they're holding a last all-nighter from eight till eight."

"You sure Darb?"

"That's what Swoz said Gethro." Shrugging his shoulders, his spoon relentlessly stirring his teacup.

"Well, I'm not missing that!"

"Me neither Jako. No coach that night, we've got to finish in The Cats man. That's where we all started, that's our roots!"

"That's our club man, what we going to do?" Jako's glazed expression making me smile.

"Keep going to Wigan."

"Yea but what about in the week?"

"Keep practicing at The Ship and Civic Jako. There's nothing else we can do mate. If its closing, its closing." The loss still not sinking in, we owed so much to The Cats, what it had brought to the scene in Wolvo. I felt saddened by the thought of it all.

"Talking about The Ship Darb, Guinness, and Vimto I'll see you all later."

"Later Gethro."

"Later man." Rising, leaving Rumpy's I had a lot on my mind, I felt restless, uneasy, my sixth sense in overdrive. Something was wrong. I wanted to share my afternoon of new found freedom with Kim in my bedsitter. If I couldn't do that an old flame would have to do.

"I locked that fuckin door!" My voice in a mumbled expression, splintered wood beneath my feet in the hallway. Slowly, tapping the door open a cold chill running through me as I entered my darkened room. I had been turned over, nothing but devastation lay before my eyes. Tins of soup splattered across walls, the television on its side, screen kicked in. Wardrobe door open, my clothes slashed, shredded to pieces, scattered rags around the room. Cassette and Cats tapes gone, bed turned over.

"This wasn't just a burglary, look at it!" Someone had been looking for something. I had been taken out trod on toes, someone close had wanted retribution, but who? Thoughts flooding from every direction, yet no one knew where I lived. It just didn't fit. I had let my guard down by putting myself about I had made a bad mistake. Trying to stay calm, think!

First, I had to find somewhere new to live. Next, find the bastards who had done this, vengeance racing through my mind. With no insurance I had lost everything. Cops were useless, they would not solve this but we would. Streets are grapevines, I soon my got my answers. Unbeknownst to me the last occupant was a heroin dealer who had just been sent to prison, his customers exacting their revenge. I hated smack heads before, now I hated them with a passion.

Junkies had no place in my world. Sure I dealt in drugs, but to prey on another's addiction you were a low life. You put a pound note before the life of a brother. The dirty side of dealing, to me you were a piece of shit! A trait that would never change, I hadn't got time for their pathetic nonsense. Addiction! Addiction to what?! It's all in your head, a rush is a rush, handle it! What goes up comes down. We used our drugs to dance, not mull around in some hazed stupor. To me they were wankers and now I had paid their price. Junkies and burglars, parasites preying on their own kind. A world I would rub shoulders with in the future as I moved into chemists. We were speed freaks, all-nighter boys, dancers our scene was clean. We were decent criminals, we hit chemists not the working class. The opposite of those who had preyed on me, my hatred of them and their needles knew no bounds..

Chapter 41

JUST A LITTLE MISUNDERSTANDING

Holding the door for Kim, the nostalgic graffiti covered wall greeting us as slowly we climbed the stairs. The Torch lives on, Northern Soul, keep on keeping on, a circled black fist The Twisted Wheel Manchester faded names of Soulies passing us by. Memories of two other lost clubs and now The Catacombs, I wondered how many more? Tapping the kiosk window my heart saddened by what lay around us, the loss of The Cats hitting home, playing heavily on my mind. The rasp of a sliding wood Helen's brightened face appearing in a flash.

"You're not coming in!" A mischievous pause as the side door opened. We entered The Cats, even on a summer's evening the club still dark inside.

"Have you got your tickets for tomorrow? Without it you won't get in." Helen's playful stare directed at me. "Kim can, you can't!" Both of them teasing at my predicament of a lost ticket.

"Of course I have, you two when you get together. Look at you," shaking my head at their laughter, "you're bad!"

I felt smart after work I had collected my new cords from Jacksons, in my brown full length crombie I felt unique, a Soul boy striding with style. Thirty inch bottle green parallels, my new dancing trousers I couldn't wait to try them out. Leaving the girls Jimmy Thomas "The Beautiful Night" echoing throughout The Cats, Northern beats as ever calling me. Passing Smokey and others by the bar a respectful nod between us as I ventured towards the floor. The uniqueness of the alcoves unfolding before me, the simplicity of arched painted brickwork. Black tables holding center of tunneled rooms. A gentle glow of yellow light suspended from the domed ceiling, how many times had I walked this path before? Feeling the emotion of my surroundings, the blacked out windows and painted walls reflecting haunting memories, a calmness in the club.

"Not many in tonight really for a Friday Darb."

"Yea I know, you would think with it closing tomorrow there would be more faces." The music echoing around us as only The Cats could, our little band in our corner. Winston and Jimmy by the speakers Jako out on the floor. Pep and Max working the decks "I'm On My Way" by Dean Parrish, a few dancers filling the floor.

"Remember when Helen pestered Pep to play this for the first time?"

"Yea five times in one night Gethro! Pep and Max discovered a lot of sound man."

"I know. Makes me laugh at Wigan sometimes with their new discoveries."

"Yea! I know what you mean." Both of us lost in the moment.

The summer's breeze of the open emergency exit drifting across the dance floor, a few dancers silhouetted on the stage. Not even Dave Priest in to guard the open door. Tonight quiet, tomorrow would be a different scenario The Cats coming alive for the last time. Many of our friends attending the loss of our club, going deep a one off venue like nothing on the scene. Still challenging the might of Wigan Casino our nights the past month packed to the rafters. Wednesday's always a special night.

"Is it just me or is it subdued in here tonight Darb?"

"Everyone's on a downer Gethro."

"Hey check these out." Hands thrust in the pockets of my cords, my face bursting with pride, Darb feeling the material.

"Nice one man! That color's brilliant."

"Similar to yours but bottle green mate. Wait till they fade, see this double side zips when I sweat just tighten the waistband." Darb smiling checking the pockets.

"Three inch button flap pockets front and back?"

"Yea but look at this stash pockets behind the adjusters."

"Nice cords Gethro."

"Cheers Jako." He too impressed, joining us from the floor grabbing a Coke, our table full of bottles and cassette tapes recording our voices with every new tune.

"Russ is on tomorrow, out of respect to The Cats."

"Fair do's that's a nice gesture Jako. Tell you what, you had better dance tonight."

"Why?"

"You won't move in here tomorrow. Come on I want to test these out." Thelma Lindsey "Prepared To Love You" a floor burner we knew and loved. All the room we wanted, my dancing more intense my attitude had changed. I would take anyone on who came into my space. I wanted to be the best, taking no prisoners my moves now impacting the floor. Smokey beside me, both of us in a friendly competition a drop-back to a handspring. Risky in The Cats, pulling off one of my best moves to a glaring face beside me. I had just made a big mistake, Smokey leaving the floor.

"He looked pissed off Gethro." Darb now at my side.

"Fuck him, I was just dancing." More of our tunes filling the floor, the night spent fine tuning our dancing our little band as close as brothers, Jako as always making us laugh.

"Kim can you sew my Cats badge on" His face full of apprehension at the answer.

"Of course I can Jako."

"Kim, have you got a long lost sister?"

"No."

"How about a cousin?"

"No." Kim's face breaking in shyness and laughter, his persistence that knew no bounds.

"How old's your mom?!" All of us bursting to laughter.

"Jako, you're bad man!" Jimmy booming hand slapping his back, still laughing, leaving to get Cokes as I ventured past the alcoves.

"Hey you, come here!" Smokey calling me towards the bar. "What's that all about earlier?" His voice angry.

"What Smoke?" I hadn't a clue what he was on about.

"You trying to blow me off the floor?!"

"I wasn't Smoke, you know that's the way we dance."

"That's not fuckin dancing!" His eyes glaring into mine, searching for fear.

"Then what the fuck is it?!" Raising my voice, equal to his for once, not backing down.

"Acrobatics. That's all you can do Gethro, just acrobatics." I had backed away before, this time sarcasm taking control.

"Tell you what, me and you on the floor just footwork. I'll blow you off the fuckin floor mate!" I too losing my temper, red hair leading to my short fuse! Turning away I never saw the punch coming as I was thrown sideward, instantly turning around.

"Come on you bastard!" Smoke coming at me with more punches. For some reason I smiled, at last he had my right name. No time to think, the second punch just missing my chin.

"Fuck it I steamed in!" Both of us trading punches suddenly on the ice of The Cat's floor we went down, Jimmy and Darb running to my side.

"Gethro what's up man?! You all right?!" Smokey rising with me from the floor, backing away from the three of us Helen coming between us.

"You two bloody grow up! Cut it out Smoke! I can't believe it, the only night we don't have a bouncer and you two start!"

"Hey he started it!"

"Stay here, you're fuckin dead Gethro! Just stay here, you got your back up,

I'll just get mine!" His glaring face quivering in anger, finger pointed directly at me. "Just wait! I'll be back! You just hit the wrong guy!" Turning away, leaving in uproar.

"What the fuck you doing man? What's that all that about?"

"Dancing Darb." My voice subdued now realizing what I had done.

Jimmy bursting in laughter. "You kidding me?! Dancing, you crazy man?!" Darb looking at my head.

"You got a few bumps Gethro."

"Yea well so has he!"

"What happened?" Kim rushing to my side her face in anxious concern.

"He's all right Kim!" Helen's angry voice scolding me, "Now you behave!"

"I never even started it lover, honest. Fuck him!"

"You just made a bad enemy Gethro, you know who he's gone to get, Pristy and that lot." Darb looking apprehensive.

"We got your back man." Jimmy reassuring me.

"No Jimmy, it's gone far enough. He must think I'm fuckin stupid if he thinks I'm waiting around here." Jako and Winston joining us.

"Gethro, what happened?"

"I just got into it with Smokey Winst."

"That's not a good idea man. You know his reputation."

"Yea I know. Well I won't be coming tomorrow, I'm going to Wigan. If he thinks I'm walking into his trap he's fucking mistaken, not with that lot behind him." The night in ruins I moved to the dance floor with Kim, "sorry lover." My voice full of remorse. She smiled, proud of the fact I had stood up for myself, she had seen it all before.

Kissing my finger I pointed to the floor, one last look around to say goodbye. Pep and Max giving me a wave from the DJ booth leaving the floor, passing the speakers and alcoves. The club I had loved so much and now this bullshit! "You and your fuckin mouth!" Ringing in my ears, when will I ever learn? The lads all saying goodbye.

"You be here tomorrow. You've got your tickets." Helen smiling, looking into my eyes and passing our coats.

"We'll see Helen." Total sadness engulfed me at what had occurred. "Take no notice of Smokey, he'll be all right when he calms down."

"Come on lover." My heart heavy with dejection, leaving The Cats passing graphite covered walls, pausing for the last time we too added our names.

CATACOMBS CLUB
TEMPLE STREET · WOLVERHAMPTON
SATURDAY 13th JULY 1974
Grand Last All-Nighter
FEATURING BRITAINS TOP SOUL SPINNERS
BLUE MAX · PEP
SOUL SAM · KEITH MINSHULL
ROSS FROM WIGAN · MICK FLELLO
BASIL
12 HOURS OF NON-STOP SOUNDS
8.00 pm. - 8.00 am.
Refreshments Available   Advance Tickets £1.00

"Well if we go to Wigan at least there'll be more room." Kim cheering me up, as always looking on the bright side. We would go to The Casino, even I broke into a smile. Let them bake in The Cats, in my heart I knew she was right.

"Hey up! Look at wa wa's on that!" Mona making me laugh, a girl spinning catching his attention, pretty girls the furthest thing from my mind. Breathless from dancing we stood at the side of the floor our shirtless bodies soaked in sweat. Martin Ellis our favorite DJ working the decks Billy Harner "What About The Music", Torch classics filling The Casino. Tonight all the room we wanted on the right hand side of the stage. Fluorescents light reflecting open spaces around us, I couldn't ask for more.

"Did you get rid of that gear Mona?"

"All gone mate, got anymore?"

"No I moved it, all I've got now is just personal for us." Mona breaking to a smile, not bothering to ask he knew my answer. It was the only way I could protect him and his desire to get even more blocked. I would have to hold on to his gear. Even without the crowd from Wolvo another night fueled with amphetamines, supply always outstripped by demand. The closure of The Cats having repercussions for the first time, The Casino's attendance impacted by another club. I loved an empty floor, it put an edge to my dancing. Set my spirit free to express how I felt deep inside, to bring on all of our best moves. Our corner as always alight with energy friendly competitions played between Soul brothers out on the floor.

"Gethro!" Ronnie from Stoke grabbing a table next to ours along the back wall, inquisitive as to why he was here I ventured over.

"I thought you were going to The Cats?"

"We went but its murder. You can't breathe or fuckin move, the place is that packed everyone's just standing around." My face breaking to laughter, so Kim was right.

"Was Smokey there?"

"Yea he was looking for you, told him I hadn't seen you. He looked pissed off!" I smiled so it wasn't over, I would have to watch my back in Wolvo. "Want some gear, I got some filon."

"No Ronnie I'm ok mate. You'll soon move them in here though, I'll send some people over." Pointing to the stage, "See the guy in the red vest, black hair, he's a good kid Sam from Kiddy, his mates over there are looking for gear.

"Gethro sit down for a minute. I got something I want to tell you."

Sitting at our table I watched Mona rip into the floor his style so similar to mine that floating footwork we had made our own.

My attention turning to Ronnie still rummaging in his bag. "What's up?" Finally he sat down, his voice quieter, subdued.

"You know I got busted last time I hit a chemist. I made some bad mistakes man." Resentment in the tone of his voice.

"Yea I heard about that, but if someone grasses you up you're screwed mate." I felt sympathetic, we had known each other a long time.

"Look, I got my eye on another one, only this time it's bigger." He paused, looking into my eyes for trust he knew was there "I want you to have the fast one hit I'll take what I want, you move all the gear."

I felt uneasy, after all even with the champagne I still considered myself small time. Wolvo was becoming a dangerous place for me, already I had stepped on toes. Sure I had connections but caps and pills created heat. Up till now I had stayed under the radar but this was different.

"Look I'll be dead straight Ronnie. What if it comes on top, does it end there? Can I trust you?!" Ronnie glaring at me, ignoring my comment "Look I got to say that!" My voice showing annoyance at the insult I had just made. "You know what I mean Ronnie, I got to be careful man Wolvo's crawling with squad."

"You've known me a long time Gethro, you know I don't grass!"

"Sorry man it wasn't supposed to be meant like that. When you thinking of turning it over?"

"Soon Gethro, definitely before Wigan's anniversary." I broke into a smile.

"Is it local?"

"The less you know the better Gethro." His glazed eyes locked on mine.

"Ronnie, for fucks sake be careful this time." Our handshake sealing the deal. "Me and you, that's it."

"Just us man. I'll phone you when I've hit it." Both of us laughing, our crossing hands the bond of friendship that would be put to the test. I felt nervous, uneasy. This time I was really crossing a line. My dark side taking over, maybe it was the thrill, the chase but I was in. To me the ultimate high was dealing in caps and pills, my senses would be put to the test as never before. There would be repercussions, little did I know the hornet's nest was about to explode. Already I had an idea. I needed a car, then I would move the gear.

"About the filon, how many you got?"

"Two hundred." I smiled they would be gone in no time, finding Sam by the stage one of many of my connections I sent him over.

The Casino starting to fill, the night coming alive Jackie Lee "Anything You

Want aka Any Way You Want It", Mona at my side both of us hitting the floor. Acrobatics, the insult still ringing in my head. I'll show you fuckin acrobatics, my footwork faster than ever every step matching the beats feeling the music deep inside. Stepping into the record dummy spins into twisting feet, arms pounding at my side floating through dancers. Kim joining us the floor bouncing to marching Northern beats, spins faster. Floating in an arc of footwork, arms reaching for more speed, elbows tucked to my sides. Footwork breaking effortlessly turning to Mona's gliding feet sweeping the floor, smiles of recognition to one of our favorite sounds.

Martin Ellis the energy of his voice infectious, driving the dancers Johnny Sayles "I Can't Get Enough (Of Your Love)", Patti Austin "Take Away The Pain Stain", The Steve Karmen Big Band featuring Jimmy Radcliffe "Breakaway", James Carr "That's What I Want To Know", Bobby Taylor "Oh, I've Been Bless'd", Eddie Floyd "Bring It On Home To Me", Ann Perry "That's The Way He Is", The Precisions "If This Is Love", and Duke Browner "Crying Over You". Arms in the air, hand claps in recognition of Martin Ellis mayhem of the night all around us. An avalanche of wide eyed faces feeling the vibe of amphetamines and the love of The Casino's floor. Tall Martin and Shawn from Bolton all the regulars, spinners at the front of the stage so many of our friends.

Suddenly my heart dropped. I stopped dancing, Smokey crossing the floor weaving his way through dancers coming towards me.

"Fuck me, now it's on!"

"Hey up what's up?" Mona at my side.

"Problem. Big fuckin problem."

"Me and you, in the bogs!" Smokey, his finger pointed at me, calling me to him. Matted hair, staring penetrating eyes the same expressive look of anger throwing his leather with others on the stage. I had backed away from fights before but this was personal, it was about dancing and this time I wasn't backing down. What courage I had drove me forward, at least I would go down fighting. After all the orphanage had taught me hard and fast but deep inside I didn't fancy my chances. His reputation around Wolvo scared the shit out of me my stomach endlessly turning over. I entered the toilets passing Smokey leaning on the sink. Turning to face me now I was trapped, already he had made a smart move.

"Where's your back up now, eh? Let's see you run your fuckin mouth!"

"Look you hit me Smoke, I never started it." My voice in a pleading defiance, suddenly the door bursting open.

"Gethro what's up?!" Mona brushing past Smokey, joining my side as more Chesterfield lads crowded around us. Soulies piling into the toilets to join us Boko and Derrick from Aldershot, Dave Wise lads from Newbury. Alan from Sheffield, Tom from Barnsley and others Steve and the lads from Wales. Friends from Wigan, Nottingham, and Bolton a crowd of staring faces all looking at me. An eerie silence Smokey surrounded, encircled, standing alone.

I never wanted it to turn out like this after all he was the one who introduced me to Northern. I felt sad at what was happening and after all, for what?! A stupid comment, a wrong word. Why? I knew Smokey's pride would never allow him to back down, even with these odds he would go down fighting. I had to do something and quick!

"Look Smoke, I'm sorry for what I said." My outstretched hand reaching to him, my voice full of sadness, remorse. Suddenly his face burst into a smile.

"Me too Gethro. I just lost it."

"I mean it Smoke, I'm sorry."

"Forget it Gethro." A look of friendship now replacing anger as the tension lifted we embraced and shook hands.

One thing dwelling on my mind, looking around I never realized the friendships I had built in The Casino. Even Smokey taken by surprise, he may rule in Wolvo but in The Casino it was a different scenario, this was now my domain. The friendships I had made touched my heart. All my Soul brothers had come to protect me, to stand by my side. Why? I didn't realize I was that special to them. A glow of pride engulfing me, a feeling so deep tears welling in my eyes, the emotional strain of what had occurred. The love of brothers, the family I never had, of belonging, people cared about me. I felt humbled by their presence what they were prepared to do for me, Smokey turning to leave.

"Thanks Mona for coming to help me."

"No one's touching you Gethro, not while I'm around!"

"I owe you mate, big style."

"No you don't. Anyway I had to come and help, I didn't want you losing our stash!" Both of us bursting to laughter, walking to the open door.

The beauty of The Casino, the night felt different a packed balcony, the hum of crowds, sweating figures caught in fluorescents, crowds lining the dance floor. Brut and nicotine smoke filling the air. More friends surrounding us to words of, "You ok?" Kim throwing her arms around me, a passionate kiss held in a melody "Just A Little Misunderstanding" by The Contours, Martin Ellis calling us back to the floor.

With the closure of The Cats we hardly missed a beat. We still had The Ship on Tuesday and Sunday, The Octopus and Wigan on Saturday nights. To fill in the week we now used a new venue on Wednesday and Friday, The 67 Club set in the red light district of Wolvo, along Pipers Row.

A predominantly black club with all the shades of racial tension from many of the older crowd. I don't know what it was but I had a bond with black people. My skin was white, so what? They were black I just didn't see any difference, they were exactly the same to me. Never knowing my parents was my answer as who was to say my father wasn't black? I never knew him and to me he could have easily of been, so where's your prejudice now.

Our first visit creating quite a stir, getting stares from every direction as Darb and I walked into the club. Two friends greeting us from across the dance floor surrounded by tables and chairs. A pool table and bar to the back of the room, the place reminding me of The Cats painted walls and dark inside. Me being the only white boy I instantly felt uneasy. It was time to hit the floor one of our mates requesting a tune. As we danced side by side tension lifted, these were my brothers but one thing stood out, this white boy could dance.

Northern did that, it bridged that gap took away racial tension and threw racism in the garbage right where it belonged! We were accepted, by now I could read any club and I knew you didn't go to the toilets alone. The cliental of older Jamaicans and odd prostitutes not the ideal climate for a Northern venue but to be fair they never bothered us. Max and Swoz began to DJ, from there running the venue under the flag of Intercity Soul Club. A few of The Cats' crowd started to use it but its main advantage to me, the drug squad wouldn't go near it. We had a safe haven and with Wolvo crawling with squad we were out of the spotlight once again.

Chapter 42

IN MORE WAYS THAN ONE

Ronnie bursting to laughter kicking the tires of my pride and joy. "You know it's a cop car!"

"No its not, it's a mini clubman estate!"

"Gethro it is. Look at that dot in the roof," yanking the passenger door open, "See look at that zip in the roof lining, that's where they turned the blue lights on."

Immediately I sprang to my defense. "Yea well, I wanted a cop car. After all I'll be in camouflage, the cops won't be looking for a cop car, will they? Just imagine the confusion of that!"

The salesman's words still ringing in my ears. "It's only been driven by virgins, used to belong to a nunnery." I had taken every word as gospel, with no parents to guide me or give me advice I had been wrapped around his finger.

"What a wanker!" Both of us laughing at my teal blue mini, not the Jag I wanted but I had to start somewhere. At least I now had a set of wheels. I called her my Gladys mk two.

My life had changed dramatically this past month, not only had I found somewhere new to live I had underestimated Kim, she had decided to move in. My philandering clipped at the wings, it's what I needed really. I was crashing through my life and although I felt I was in control, in truth in my personal life I wasn't. I needed Kim, she calmed me down, provided stability, made me think things through but even she possessed a contagious wild side. Lessons learned from the past no one knew where we lived, even the lads sworn to secrecy. Quietly tucked away we rented the top half of an old house near the town center, a self-contained flat in Haden Hill.

With the coach working like clockwork it evolved into a perfect front for running gear. Constantly moving the pickup point for now I had out thought the squad and my enemies. Every Saturday collecting names in The Octopus, now the main venue in Wolvo to connect with Northern Soul. Our little band mixing with Wolvo Soulies, the younger Casino crowd.

From there we would visit Ruby Red records. I soon realized I didn't need money to get what I wanted, my record collection now starting to emerge. Ruby Red, my supplier the young assistant only too eager to swap records for gear to me a win-win situation. Our Saturday afternoons spent listening to records with other Soulies, the assistant placing our selections to one side. Our timing impeccable, once the proprietor went for his dinner the transaction done in seconds. A deal of sulfate to him it was a three pound deal, to me a minimal amount of gear.

Everyone was happy, he would write it off as shoplifters and we would cut the gear. I felt no guilt, it wasn't stealing just a business exchange. This went on for a period of time till Mick the proprietor realized the cost of his dinner breaks and brought a packed lunch. That's the way Wolvo was, all of us would hustle in our own little way. Sure you could pay with money if you wanted, but gear went a long way.

Ronnie's chat in The Casino in the back of my mind, I now did the ground work for moving the gear I knew would be coming my way. Every spare moment we had spent driving, my intentions were simple. I needed stashes but within a short distance of where we lived. Ten minutes and we were in countryside. Meandering lanes, side roads to nowhere, all the time finding markers the odd boulders, desolate church graveyards, laybys with fallen trees. To succeed it required preparation, I was playing with my freedom and to me it now wasn't a game.

Wolvo was crawling with squad, The George and Duck their favorite haunts, many times I met their acquaintance. Often passing as I left the bar with deals on me, holding an open door. Such was the arrogance of my youth. We now had a new meeting place for the coach. Our Saturday evenings spent waiting in the Snooker Rooms directly opposite from them in The George. Why give them a name, a face? Staying out of the limelight, drifting around the town keeping a low profile. I knew they had informants, but so did we.

With my sulfate in Chesterfield temporarily out of production, the squad had made too many busts in the area, I now had a problem. All the customers I had built with no gear to supply them, my empire would fold like a deck of cards. Contacts made in The Casino, a friend of a friend, I now turned to Moss Side Manchester to score. The quantities bigger, the environment more dangerous, from now on I travelled alone.

An hour and a half drive north, ending in back streets. Mature trees in perfect unison, shaded streets of parked cars parallel to curtained bedsitters. Newspapered windows overlooking neglected gardens. Whalley Range Manchester, endless Edwardian houses shimmering in summer's heat. Pubs on crowded corners, tables and chairs scattered outside, drunks spilling onto pavements, life passing me by. The depravity of my surroundings sharpening my senses, rechecking the address for the last time. Nervously I ventured along the overgrown pathway. A small terrier charging towards me, his escape route through a half open door. Dancing, snapping at my ankles.

"Fuck off will ya?!" Kicks aimed at my tormentor.

"Spot, come here!" A figure appearing in the doorway.

"Hey mate. Which room's Rain's?"

"What you want her for?" A bearded youth in a holed jumper, a walking tramp blocking my way. I reached in my pocket, gently feeling my knife.

"That's between me and her mate!" Anger at the dog in my voice.

"Name's Rowdy." Nodding his head in the direction I must go. "Up the stairs, first door on the left. Watch what you catch man, we got better girls than her." I entered the filth of his home, one of countless others on the once elegant street.

Junkies staggering in the stench of a darkened tiled hallway, pausing in drug induced stupors. "Hey man I used." Mumbled ramblings, reminiscent of their previous life. Blaring radios and televisions of interconnecting rooms. Shouts and screaming behind a half open door, prostitutes fighting over a trick to buy their latest fix. A mahogany staircase leading to rooms full of the gutter, a cesspit of low life struggling for survival, living in the torment of addiction. My surroundings the stark reality of the destruction drugs can do.

A Jewish girl called Rain my final destination. Climbing the stairs I second guessed what I was doing here, gently tapping the door.

"You Gethro?" The softness of her voice relaxing my mood.

"Mickey said you would be coming. Come on in." The back of her head leading me into a blacked out room "What is it you want? You can have me for a price, I like young boys." She paused, spinning around leaning forwards stroking fingers touching my face. Her low top revealing the cone of breasts, slightly raised nipples of a pink bosomless chest. No girl had ever frightened me, but this was a woman with all the experience she could bring.

"He said you can sort me out." I laughed at my comment, gently halting her searching hand. Through the lace of her top I could see scabs on her frail arms, a shudder ran through me at the slight of her touch. Not a grain of beauty left in her features, her youth faded away to a wrinkled, shadowed face.

"Don't get me wrong, you're pretty but I came to buy some sulfate, not to fuck you. Business is business." Feeling the warmth of her breath as she turned away.

"What's that club you all go to?"

"Wigan Casino."

"That's it. Mickey told me about it, do you think they'll let me in?" Turning to me, hands caressing a curved figure, her drawn face breaking to a warming smile.

"Only if you sell me some sulfate."

"You are persistent Gethro. Are you like that with all the girls? I like that!" Reaching into cupboards, placing a bag of sulfate and scales on the table. "It's 29 grams on the ounce, I put one extra for petrol. I got a works, you can use or one of the junkies can test it if you like."

"No, I don't do needles. I just go on taste." Dipping my finger into the open bags the bitter taste making me shudder "I trust you. Mickey said you were good then that's ok with me." Passing the money, taking the bags of powder to my nose, the smell of chemicals familiar to me.

"Did you hear about the murder on the news?" Crossing her legs seated at the table, a slight quiver in her voice constantly scratching the heroin itch evident before my eyes. "Another prostitute cut to ribbons, they think it's a serial killer. That's two from round here."

"Doesn't that frighten you? I mean your job, your line of work?"

"Not me, I don't work the streets, not anymore." Her smile showing the gap of broken teeth. "I've got an idea, I want you to have something. A little present from me, someone left it and I'm sure you could use it." Rummaging in the bottom cupboard she pulled out a green and orange oil can placing it on the table, Castrol GTX liquid engineering, one gallon bold letters proclaiming the contents. Inquisitive I burst out laughing.

"What's that?!"

"The best stash you'll ever see. You have a lot to learn Gethro. See it's fake." Easing her nail along the bottom seam. "This place is crawling with cops, just throw it in the back of your car. I don't want you to get busted, a pretty boy like you, oh they would have some fun with you, wouldn't they?" Pausing as she pried the bottom open, "There look at that, perfect. Completely sealed."

"That's brilliant Rain. You sure?"

"Of course I am. A present from me to you, it may save your arse one day." She smiled, looking straight at me. "In more ways than one." Both of us bursting to laughter.

"Thanks Rain." I liked her, I felt sorry for her. A heroin addict, selling her body, what she had to do to survive. I wondered who would want her but really it was none of my concern.

Taking the can I stashed my gear with old newspaper, replacing the bottom. I felt more relaxed, a useful tool, one I would be putting to good use.

"Maybe we can fuck next time. I do love young boys." Rain smiling, looking into my eyes.

"Maybe Rain." Giving her a gentle kiss on the cheek, her words following me out of the doorway to my car.

It's from her I learned another trick of the trade, I had bought in bulk this time. Taking no chances that night, the gear cut into deals bagged and stashed, nothing kept in the house. Her soft voice and haunting words lingering in my mind as I drove to my drops, "it may save your arse one day."

Chapter 43

THE SHOEBOX

I now moved the coach to a permanent pick up point, Falkland Street Car Park, just a short distance from the town center. The advantage of this was simple strength in numbers, we could see squad or undesirables a mile away. Overcrowding on the coach every week, more Soulies added from pickup points along the way. Deals done in the open, everyone off their heads as I fought to collect coach fares and money from gear. Chaos all around me as we rode on a wave of total happiness. Sounds of Northern floating above the constant drone of voices, conversations of records, dancing, and gear, the atmosphere infectious.

The Casino now packed to the rafters every week, a swelling queue outside. On August 25th we had seen The Exciters, a band who had graced The Casino. They hadn't impressed me but their best was yet to come. All of us hanging around in The Beachcomber, now a permanent fixture open from midnight till two. Warming up, practicing dance moves, linking with Soul brothers and sisters till that magical time of two. A surge to the front of the queue, no one ever complained.

The dancing competition for the first anniversary now starting, all of us entering the heats, our pact now over. The rumor in Wolvo, Jako was Wolvo's best dancer. I had a point to prove, up till now I had never been placed in any competition. All of us were destined to clash, one name standing tall above all others, Kim. It wasn't a matter of who would beat Kim, more like who would Kim beat. She was an outstanding dancer with a unique free flowing style. "Telling you man, she will blow you off a floor one day." Jimmy's words from The Cats never forgotten.

Darb, Jako, Kim, all three had been placed at Whitchurch, beating both me and Booper. There wasn't a dancer in The Casino who didn't want to win Wigan's first anniversary, to wear that dancer's crown. The competition now raging full on, crowd's following their favorites. Tickets now going on sale, our nights spent on the dance floor in total ecstasy of our surroundings, the music and friends we loved.

My sulfate had gone in no time, but for some reason I had attracted unwanted attention from the drug squad. Wolvo had to have a grass. The beauty of my stashes put to the test, none more so then one day as I drove on an open road heading towards Manchester. Two cars appearing from nowhere, a brown Dolomite Sprint and just behind that a green Austin Princess two men in each car. Why didn't the Dolomite pass, the road's clear. A cold shudder ran through me, they must think I'm fuckin stupid, it's got to be squad! The Dolomite backing away, immediately I sprang into action.

Let's find out boys, come with me for a drive. I smiled, wankers! I knew I couldn't outrun the Dolomite but on backroads I could even the score. A quick unsignaled left turn to a country lane, I had nothing on me and most of all, nothing to lose. They had blown their cover now, let's see who follows. Third gear then fourth, I gunned it creating distance constantly checking my mirror, finally pulling into a farm entrance turning the car around. Not even two minutes "How about that?!" The Dolomite tearing past, screeching to a broadside and halting in a cloud of gravel and dirt. I pulled out racing full on into blind curves, "Well look who's coming here." The Austin Princess, I held center of the short straight, keeping my car steady. I just didn't think, my mentality consistent of my age, I didn't give a shit about anything. A split second of slow motion, over in a flash as they swerved into a ditch. Another car approaching, a blue Austin Maxi flicking the V's at two occupants as I passed them by.

My adrenaline through the roof, the biggest rush I had ever felt my laughter filling the car. "Fuckin wankers see that! Man that was funny!" My hatred of them knew no bounds, never second guessing my destination I carried on to Moss Side. This time returning in darkness, going directly to my stashes. Playing the game as it should be, using the cover of darkness to improve my chances and evasion. I was now on their radar but nothing would slow me down, I would self-destruct in my own way. My first encounter face to face. This time I had won but in my heart I knew this wasn't over.

Wolvo now a flaming inferno, everyone feeling the fever of Northern with just weeks to The Casino anniversary, tickets and gear in short supply. Little did I know I had the answer to both problems. At last, the phone call I had been waiting for. Beeps telling me it was from a call box, Ronnie breathless on the end of the line. As always, our conversation in code.

"I got the records you ordered, lot of demos man."

I couldn't help but smile he only went and did it! "How much for the whole collection?"

"One fifty."

"Lot of money man, those records had better be worth the hassle. I'll be over tonight." Our conversation short and brief, a pre-arranged drop. I felt nervous. That night I drove to the outskirts of Hanley Stoke returning with a shoebox full to the brim with caps and pills. I couldn't believe my eyes, I had never seen so much gear. Every type of speed in quantity, many I didn't know. With the help of a Mims I went through my haul, I hadn't got a clue what I was looking at. I only knew my gear from nicknames on the street. Red and browns, green and browns, blueys, green and clears. White and Blackbombers, black and whites, daps, ephedrine, filon, perellys, apisate, chalkies, sk+f, dex in two sizes brown and clears, green and grays, maroon and grays. Here I was in the thick of it, the pharmaceutical names meaningless to me.

Time was my biggest enemy, I had to move smart and fast. Using a phone box I called my contacts, a busy few nights as ever, my oil can put to good use. Gear laid off to Soul brothers, crossing hands, sealing deals payments made in the casino later. Squad always in the back of my mind. The gear moving itself, the smoothness of the operation proving I could deal under pressure. All I had now was personal, but I was being delusional thinking I had beaten the squad.

The next problem solved by a chance encounter, with repercussions that would last a lifetime, fate playing her hand. A normal Saturday morning in Wolvo with my copy of Blues and Soul I strolled to The Octopus to meet Darb. Pausing at my reflection as always the poser, I looked smart my new white Fred Perry a perfect match for my bottle green cords. Plain royals highly polished, a girl I recognized coming towards me. A regular from the coach. "Julie how you doing? Haven't seen you in a while?"

"Gethro, you must have been really smashed last week that's all I can say!" I leaned forward, kissing her cheek.

"You make me laugh, you're a fucking charmer!" The softness of youthful skin tender to my lips, a shared hug between us.

"Hey you know I love you." Both of us laughing.

"I don't know how Kim puts up with you!" Shaking her head, scolding me in a playful way.

"I've got a new job." Trying to change the subject, she knew me only too well. "I'm in the print room, I like it." An alarm bell rang in my head.

"What?" My eyes widening in interest, "Did you say print room? What you doing in there?" Not waiting for an answer I had to tell her of my idea. "Julie come with me, you might be able to help me." Cautiously, she crossed arms her smile full of infectious mischief, our shadows stretching in unison in the morning sun.

"Look I got a proposition, but first we got to have a cup of tea."

"Gethro, you certainly know how to pull the ladies." Sarcasm in her smile.

"You know me. Hey, I'll even buy you a bacon sarnie, come on Rumpy's is just around the corner." Passing Saturday shoppers soon arriving at Rumpy's we took our usual window seat. Diane the waitress smiling at what she thought was my new conquest, taking our order then leaving us to our devices.

"Julie, I need some help." My attention now on the task in hand.

"I knew there was a catch Gethro. What do you need?" Her voice softening, sympathetic to my oncoming problem.

"Can you print some of these?" Reaching in my pocket placing my anniversary ticket on the table, she burst into a smile. There in bold black letters, Wigan Casino Soul Club 1st Anniversary All-Nighter Saturday-Sunday two till ten September 21st. I started laughing at her enlightened expression.

"That's easy, how many do you want?"

For some reason "four hundred" just sprang from my lips. Ever the opportunist, why not? It's a long shot, worth a try. "It's just a number, if it's too many then that's ok."

Scrutinizing the ticket, feeling the context she looked closely then started laughing. Suddenly her expression changed.

"Now here's what I want. A good deal of sulf and a ticket Gethro." I couldn't believe my luck, I was in shock gathering my thoughts.

"Julie, you sure? I'll tell you what, I'll make it a gram of sulf, a ticket and a free coach ride to the anniversary." Her face breaking to smiles of instant pleasure.

"This is no problem Gethro." Holding the ticket between her thumbs. "When do you want them?"

"Soon as you can." I tried not to be pushy but in the back of my mind time was running out.

"Tuesday ok? I'll see the night shift on Monday, they'll print them before the morning run."

What a day! I was just blown away, a chance meeting and just like that! I could sell them in a heartbeat and would at one pound each. Screw them and their one pound-fifty, our time spent in the craziness of our youth. Me trying to get into her knickers and her fending off my charm.

Tuesday I collected the tickets, a perfect reproduction our night spent stamping numbers on the backs, Kim leveling the stacks to groups of fifty.

I had to move fast the anniversary was coming up soon. We made our way to Chesterfield the following night, Mona greeting us, a bear hug of affection his usual way.

"Hey up, let's have look." I handed the original and reproduction, trying to hold back my pride "what do you think?"

Mona scrutinizing both tickets, a short pause.

"They're spot on mate. Give me two hundred, I'll move em."

"Help me move them and I'll bring you some caps and pills for the anniversary, but don't forget to tell them to get in early. That way they won't realize they've been turned over till it's too late."

"No problem. Everyone's looking for them, I heard The Casino sold out."

"Not anymore!" Both of us laughing, our round trip completed before midnight. I still had places to go, more people to see. The clock to the anniversary ticking, now less than eleven days away.

Chapter 44

THE NIGHT OF THE ANNIVERSARY

"This will be a night to remember"

"What time's the coach Gethro?" Lorraine and Rachel checking their watches simultaneously, vanity cases at their sides. I smiled, the Thompson sisters a politeness from them, as always.

"It'll be here in a minute. I told him ten thirty." My voice optimistic, yet already I felt nervous. "Come on, don't let me down not tonight." Nagging voices clouding my thoughts. A veil of darkness descending upon the crowd, shouts of laughter surrounding me.

"Got any more tickets Gethro, Pix needs four?" Jako's distraction snapping my attention, Darb at my side. I pulled out the stack, only twenty left. Handing four to Jako, the rest I would move up there.

"They all gone, how many did you sell?" Darb's face in a curious smile.

"I moved a load last week, just a couple of hundred Darb." I never bothered mentioning Mona, for a second I wondered how he had got on.

"You be careful man."

"I will. Just watch my back in The Beachcomber."

"You know I got that, look at this crowd man. Must be over seventy here this week." His wandering gaze in a look of concern.

"If the money gets too much I want you and Jimmy to hold it for me ok? I'll drop three hundred on you."

"Yea no problem." A simple nod of reassurance between us, Darb polishing his glasses to idle the time.

"Where is he Darb? I can hear him."

"He's over there with Paul, Martin, Mossa, and Judy. Kim's with him, you know Jimmy he's always messing about."

"Where's this coach Gethro?" John Harper, another regular approaching. "Behind you! It's here mate!"

In the distance two headlights coming towards us, the unmistakable front of the coach. At last nagging voices evaporating, the pressure gone in an instant. I could now enjoy the night.

The Wolvo crowd surging forward to the hiss of opening doors. "After you." The odd pinch of a girl arse to squeals of laughter.

"Cut that out you two or you'll get a vanity sandwich!" Cash and Muff the culprits, shouts of innocence making me smile. More Soulies clambering on, window seats filling rapidly. As always I waited to be last on. Kim reaching in our bag for a Cats' tape passing it to the driver. "Put this on Mel."

"Another night of insanity Kim? I love these runs to the Casino." Melvin laughing, inserting the tape.

"Sit down, even if it's on your bag at least till we get out of Wolvo!" My voice hardly heard above the commotion.

"We only got half a seat Gethro, we aye payin full price!"

"Stop moaning, just sit down where you can!" "I Want It Back (Your Love)" by The Voice Box echoing throughout the interior. The door finally closing to dimming lights, we lunged forward to shouts of laughter and cheers. Kim chatting to other girls, leaning across the front seat, "we did it lover" a gentle kiss in passing, I moved on down the coach.

"Sit down for fucks sake! If we get stopped by the cops they'll empty the coach." The serious tone of my voice finally having effect "If you know anyone who wants tickets let me know! And don't forget to get in early!"

"Gethro you bad man! You'd sell your mother. You're a hustler!"

"I would if I knew her!" Jimmy laughing with Darb and Jako, crunched up three to a seat. The atmosphere rising, at last we were on our way. Tonight we were really pushing our luck. Sounds from The Cats crackling through speakers The Inspirations "Touch Me, Kiss Me, Hold Me", Cindy Scott "Time Can Change A Love", and Jackie Wilson "The Who Who Song", some our favorite tunes. The coach settling to shouts and laughter, records fighting to be heard in the melee, a background sound all of its own.

Time to relax at the front, Billy sitting with Kim idly chatting. I squeezing onto our seat I would collect the fares later. The dancing competition in the back of my mind by tomorrow there would be only one winner. Darb and Jako still in contention I had never beaten either but tonight I would bring all of my best moves. Last week Kim easily winning her heat, a fairy tale evolving before me. Would we be King and Queen of Wigan? Romantic thoughts drifting in and out of my mind. Headlights pushing us into darkness, The Casino our destination. A beacon of shining light, another world, our world drawing us forward deep into the night.

Placing my crombie on the back of the seat I took a deep breath, now the hard part. I wandered back along the aisle collecting coach fares. On the girls I would use my charm, my eyes could melt a heart I knew it and I used it the lads as always having other ideas.

"One pound fifty, you rip off Gethro! We aye even got a seat!"

"I know. I never promised you one, just a ride to Wigan. Come on you tight bastards, man it's like pulling teeth with you lot at times!"

"It was only a pound last week! We aye got no more money."

"Just give me two quid." My voice quieter letting things go when I needed. Muff and Cash paying me in change, laughing as they always did.

"We want a piss!"

"You kidding me Cash?! Look, I'm not stopping the coach at Keel too many squad!"

"Gethro we got to have a piss, we had too many beers in The George, honest. We'll piss out the door if we have to." Cash for once being serious, their faces in twisted agony. Muff double kneed holding his crouch, making me laugh I knew that pain.

"Ok come on." Moving back to the front three of them now standing by the open door screaming with steaming relief, I left them to it. Jimmy and Darb adding to my grief, Jako trying to sneak past.

"Jako come on you lot play the fuckin game here!" Muff coming back down the coach to roars of laughter, his trousers stained in urine.

"What happened?"

"He stood at the end!" All of us laughing, my night starting well. Pedro, Ritchie, Paul, Martin, Paddy, and Mary from Ashmore. Pixie, Mulligan, Bin Man, Lee, and Canny all the Busbury lads giving me stick. I really didn't give a shit, I was in the limelight with that came bullets from every direction. I just gave as good as I got. More girls Julie, Trudy, Jackie, Elaine, and Vicky Brown the coach packed to the rafters, our destination getting nearer. Northern blasting around us The Vogues "That's The Tune", Lorraine Chandler "I Can't Change", and Debbie Dean "Why Am I Lovin' You" our music from the floor of The Cats. Time lost in idle chatter I wandered up and down the coach.

"See the squad in The George Gethro?"

"No I didn't go in Pix, we stayed in The Snooker Rooms."

"Yea one had his arm in a sling, guy with a beard stood out a mile. Fuckin wankers!"

"He must be in camouflage Pix!" Our laughter with others filling the coach.

"What you got Gethro?"

"Few deals of sulf Pix, Brown and clears, filon and dex rest I'm saving for Mona, hear about the Bolton lads?" Pix leaning forwards as I lowered my voice, "Someone did a warehouse, took over a hundred thousand dex and stashed them on The Moors. Now they're slowly knocking them out, that's where all the dex are coming from in The Casino."

"We got bombers and red browns man." Ronnie's interruption making me smile, his handwork fueling the night. Gear dropped in open palms caps, pills, deals of sulf passed around freely. None of us really cared, to us this was our normality, the night as many before unfolding around me. I glanced at the coach clock already eleven-thirty.

"Knutford's coming up. Watch for squad, you know the score!" My voice traveling to the back of the coach. "Half hour so be quick, we need to get in there early!" We eased into the services, my eyes constantly scanning for cops. More coaches already here, next to us the Cheltenham coach. Sharon and Shawn, Dyke, Polo from Worcester. Sandy and Liz from Eversham plus Jerry, Mark and Gary, their coach packed to the rafters as ours. All of us wrapped up in the vibe of excitement. Crowds of Soulies filling the services, Northern tapes playing in the background long leathers the fashion, soul bags plastered in badges openly on display. I smiled no way, not on my bag running the gauntlet of squad never far from my mind. "Got any more tickets Gethro?"

"What you up to Jako?" I couldn't help but smile.

"I'm knocking them out for a quid fifty, everyone wants them just turning a coin man. Give me six more!"

"There's seven Jako." Spreading my hand, "Call it a fiver." Both of us laughing wrapped in our friendship that went way back. "Hey, I hope I don't draw you in a heat man."

"Me too Gethro. I want us in the final so we can show them how we dance, but really I don't care who wins so long as it's one of us." Our eyes locking in sincerity, both of us knowing in our hearts we were destined to clash.

"Me too mate." Nodding my head, our respect for each other as dancers went much deeper than words. The services a hive of activity, not a cop to be seen "Come on you wankers, we're waiting for you lot!" Stragglers returning to the coach, "Everybody on?" My voice barley heard in the mayhem of shouted replies.

"Ok Melv let's go!" Soulies caught in the headlights on the slip road, we screeched to a halt the door reopening, "Come on, we'll fit you in!" Caroline, Bridgett, Sue, Paddy, and Cody a crowd of faces we picked up regular. More playful insults from the back seat. At last we resumed our journey, traffic heavier than usual passing at speed.

I never liked taking my gear before Knutsford, grabbing a Coke I relaxed, envelopes switched earlier. Brown and clears, black and whites caps going down a lot easier than pills. Others joining me in a cocktail of amphetamines, all of us dropping our gear. Everything in moderation, sulf kept for later. Tonight I would be smashed, never forgetting our warning, that vision of so long ago. I knew my tolerance, how far I could push my body, a line I never crossed, relishing the feeling of dancing on the ultimate high. We had been doing this for a year now. Were we addicted to drugs? No, not really. We were addicted to the scene, the friendships of sisters and brothers, the love of a Soul family. The music that was my addiction, the gear just kept us awake!

"Look out, cops!" A flashing blue light igniting the coach interior, a cop car at our side, turmoil all around me.

"Fuck where they come from?!" Before I could even think or stand they sped by. "Man that was a rush Kim!" My face flushed with adrenaline.

"Seems you're not the only one lover!" Kim's words drowning in laughter and cheers Jackie Wilson "Nothing But Blue Skies" drifting through the speakers, harmonious melodies carrying us into the night.

Chapter 45

LOOKING FOR YOU

"Get out of the way!" Waving my hand at the windscreen darting figures caught in the headlights we eased forwards to unload in our usual spot. A swaying mass lining the pavement, Soulies queuing under the awning, others spilling into the road. Coach doors flying open shouts and screams of the crowd, screeching cars breaking the night.

"Stay out of the road! Get on the pavement, you need tickets to get in!" Three bouncers swamped in the light of the main entrance. I stood to the side of Melvin, my voice fighting above the din.

"Don't forget it's on till ten. Everyone back on the coach by eleven or I'll leave you!" Chewing smiles of wide-eyed excitement, disembarking shouts of exuberant laughter hitting the pavement.

"What time's the coach leave Gethro?" Playful banter that never stopped!

"Look at that crowd man! It's worse than Leeds! It's only twelve thirty." Darb beside me staring through the coach window. His face in a startled expression an owl peering into the darkness. "How many tickets you sold Gethro? Look at it!"

"I've never seen The Casino like this man, they maxed out!" Kim's laughter adding to my comment. "Hold this hundred for me Melv, put it with the coach fare, I'll sort it out tomorrow." Finally surrounded with empty seats grabbing our bags, we disembarked.

A freshness to the night air, the outside wall of The Casino silhouetted with parked cars. Interior lights flickering from opening doors, Northern breaking the odd silence, scurrying figures disappearing into the night.

"Look over there man!" Squad pulling occupants from a car in the corner, flashlights in hands. Darkness giving them protection, I felt a twinge of nerves my stashes loaded with gear.

"Come on, stick together Darb. If it comes on top we got to steam it! I'm not getting busted man!" My mindset was simple, I would rather be done for assault. "Let's get in The Beachcomber, it's safer than hanging around out here!" Winston, Jimmy and Jako adding protection, all of us melting in the crowds. Cars cruising past The Casino, Northern tunes drawing my attention, brake lights halting at Soulies. Crouched figures leaning through open windows, sports bags at their feet. Long leathered figures crisscrossing the road, girls' squeals of laughter, cassette tapes blaring in the distance Northern accents filling the night. Soulies patiently sat on the wall outside The Casino others gathering around the café. Our names shouted amongst the crowd, Soul brothers and sisters greeting us, words hurriedly spoken along the way.

Clarkie at The Beachcomber entrance, low life at his side, "Come on, pay up!" Another hustler from Manchester, one of many who roamed The Casino. "Come in! Come in!" Our hands touching in friendship and smiles, twenty pence demanded from punters we eased by. A nod of respect, our code quite simple, you don't mess with us and we won't fuck with you. A stream of Soulies entering The Beachcomber "I'm Getting' On Life" by Wombat, Northern drawing us through the darkness along a short passageway ending in steps.

In the light of the coffee bar two local DJs, Brian Rigby and Alan Cain working the decks. Soulies crowding the dance floor, Shawn from Bolton spinning, others dancing around him, twisting spiraling figures holding center of the pitch black room. Derrick, Alan, and Dave from Rotherham. Tom and Paul from Barnsley, car snatchers of the nicest kind, banter as always, characters we knew so well. Penny and Kerr from Scotland, wristbands matching his red and white vest adorned with badges the uniform of a Soul boy. Sisters and brothers greeting us from every direction, our night bursting to life. Booky from Wigan joining spinner's mural led walls reflecting in subdued light. Darkened shadows hunched on bleachers, trench coated girls in idle chatter, a hum of voices floating above

THEY DANCED ALL NIGHT

the music. Open record boxes labels and gear inspected in flickering light.

"They're brave with Clarkie about!" Darb's observations making me smile. Dealing and hustling, dampness adding to the atmosphere an underground scene about to explode beneath The Casino. Mingling with the crowds I soon found Mona and Lisa surrounded with Nottingham Soulies.

"Hey up, man you made it!" His brightened smile infectious, hugs and handshakes as we moved to a darkened corner.

"Here's three fifty-two off the tickets, others off caps and pills."

"Nice one man. You sold them all? I never thought you'd do that! Here!" Our exchange as promised, crossing hands sealing the deal "Hey take it easy right. Sell some, that's a lot of gear!"

"I'll be all right." So, I relented.

"Mona I know you. If you fuck yourself up, it's over I won't bring anymore!"

"Ok Gethro. What time's the dancing competition?" Mona grinning, deflecting the subject.

"I heard the semifinals is at four."

"Well I'll be smashed by then!" Our hugs of friendship, a Soul brother, his welfare my only concern.

"You know I love you man its well, just take it easy!" Pix, Bin Man and others joining us, our numbers growing at the side of the floor, the last few tickets sold in minutes. Deals of sulf stashed down my bollocks. "Come on Kim, it's getting late."

"You using a real ticket Gethro?"

"No way Darb. I want my original for a scrapbook, let's see how good these are!" After all, I only had four left. When I was smashed I didn't give a shit about my surroundings. I had a confidence that I could do anything and I did. Our little band fighting through the darkness, weaving past bags and Soulies Garnet Mimms "Looking For You" following us to the doorway. The noise of the crowd growing louder, our exit blocked by the queue, trapped hardly able to move. A mass of crushing, entangled bodies, screams and shouts of agony breaking the night. Conversations in speed, muffled replies inaudible my body surging with energy. I wanted to dance, pushing with others towards the entrance Kim in the cocoon of our circle. Bouncers linking arms, fighting the tidal wave of emotion, surges of movement inching towards the narrow entrance. Record boxes, vanity cases, sports bags adding to the blockade of crushing bodies damming the door.

"Stop pushing in! Hey you! Get to the back!" Pointed fingers from the doorway reflecting wide-eyed faces, drug induced Soulies pushing towards the light. Once more we stumbled into the foyer, the pressure of a champagne corked bottle released from the crowd. Twenty of us rushing the counter. Hilda bombarded with handheld tickets, a quick glimpse returning them with the anniversary badge and a coat ticket, not a second to spare. Harry Green, the head bouncer, to our right guarding the stairs open hands collecting the coat tickets discarding them in a bin as we passed by. Clever idea, so that's how they monitor the crowd. I couldn't believe my luck that was so easy. The excitement building inside me with every step, a rush of gear surging through me. Muffled music driving us forward, our pace increasing as we climbed the stairs, turning into a short corridor passing Mike Walker's office. The black double doors pushed open, we burst into The Casino. Northern blasting all around us, Larry Santos "You Got Me Where You Want Me" the heat and beauty of The Casino, as always, exploding before our eyes.

Tonight a queen in her jubilee, crowds lining the jewel of her golden balcony, arches of the dome ceiling her towering crown. The whole building had come alive. Wigan's territorial floor in evidence Blackburn and Bradford Soulies joining Wolvo on the left-hand side. Coats piled high, sports bags, and discarded vanity cases thrown under tables, dancers streaming out on the floor. Vinyl detectives clutching record boxes, quickened steps disappearing to the back of the room. Weaving our way through the crowd, my exuberance infectious.

"Did you see that Darb?! They worked like a fuckin charm man. So long as everyone gets in early they won't suss it till they run out of coat tickets!"

"Yea but that's when the shit hits the fan Gethro!"

"Yea but by then it'll be too late!" Little did I know the impact I would have on the night. Friends surrounding us as we reached our corner, shouts and laughter, greetings in triumphant hugs.

"We did it man!" Mona's face bursting in smiles. Derby, Chesterfield, and Nottingham Soulies claiming tables along the back wall. Across the far side of the dance floor Preston, Wigan and Bolton, Northern dancers we knew well, tables filling along the bottom of the stairs. Cambridge lads grabbing their usual spot, Irish and Dave at the front of the stage. The Casino filling rapidly, well over a thousand Soulies flooding into The Casino, a torrent of bodies in every direction, radiance to the night.

Immediately dropping our bags and coats we changed at the side of the floor. My Celtic top of green and white shimmering in fluorescents, Wigan's first all-nighter badge dead center, Catacombs, Va-Va, and Torch Revival our clubs on full display.

"That's a neat shirt Gethro."

"I know. Kim put my badges on last night, Kerr gave it me to match my bottle green cords. I saved it for the comp Darb! Look he even gave me a Celtic badge!"

"Gethro!" Boko and Derrick from Aldershot calling me, money exchanged for services rendered, Northern handshakes sealing deals. Pete from Hemell, Southampton and Cheltenham lads joining our corner, mayhem of the night simmering in an amphetamine high. Bouncers walking around as we hit the floor Billy Butler "Right Track" my heart bursting inside, happiness surging through me, at last all of us on the floor. Words ringing in my ears, "I've been trying to reach my goal too long to give up on my journey now". Hitting a spin in perfect timing, pausing I glanced at the stage.

Russ, did you ever feel as I felt at this moment really? Did you ever understand this floor that you and others had created, what it really meant to us? Sure you had to earn your place, your right to dance but the floor was much more than that! I had never seen any of you out on the floor standing where I stood now. Martin Ellis and Dave Evison, two DJs with dancer's hearts the exceptions at your side. Who really controlled this floor, us or you? You the DJs played the sounds, chose the tunes. We fed off one another, without you we had no music, without us you had no dancers. Who dictated the records the driving beats of The Casino? We did! Rambling thoughts filling my mind.

Russ igniting The Casino with Northern, my heart exploding with others around me, feeling the love of brothers and sisters, that's what this floor was really all about! Cries of what a tune! Bobby Garrett "My Little Girl", Marke Jackson "I'll Never Forget You", Jeanette Williams "All Of A Sudden", The Triumphs "I'm Coming To Your Rescue", Jackie Moore "Both Ends Against The Middle", Len Jewell "Bettin' On Love", The High Keys "Living A Lie", The Carmel Strings "I Hear A Symphony", Micky

Moonshine "Name It You Got It", Porgy And The Monarchs "My Heart Cries For You", Spiral Starecase "More Today Than Yesterday", Gary Lewis & The Playboys "My Heart's Symphony", R. Dean Taylor "There's a Ghost In My House", and The Belles "Don't Pretend" tunes from our scene filling Wigan's floor.

I didn't like dancing against anyone, blowing people off wasn't my game, but tonight was different the floor dividing before me.

I had a point to prove, the competition only hours away. For the past year we had graced many floors on the Northern scene. Rising to the challenge of every dancer we came up against, beating many of them on their own floor. Our style still unique, the complex footwork and moves flowing in an effortless, smooth style. Dancing was everything I lived for, every emotion I could feel released from the depth of my heart. Wolvo, the talk of The Casino, The Catacombs with six dancers in the semifinals, my nerves kicking into the music we loved. Darb and Jako out on the floor, hardly able to move the crowds ever deeper like nothing I had seen before. Burnley, Halifax and Hull on our side of the room, battles being played out on the floor. Scott's corner on the opposite side of the balcony. The Casino full to the rafters, a road map of towns and cities such was the power of the music we loved. All of us one, feeling undying respect for each other a love so strong our bond unbreakable, all we lived for this moment to be together out on this floor. "The Zoo (The Human Zoo)" by The Commodores another one of my tunes, I let my moves rip. Fuck it, I'm here to dance!

The floor exploding around me, a thousand clapping hands in the air, the atmosphere rising in a crescendo with every new record. Heat of the floor already unbearable, showers of condensation, invisible rain clouds dripping from the dome ceiling. Chewing, smiling faces streaming in sweat, clapping hands reaching in thunder all of us connecting as one, transfixed by our music. A swaying mass of bodies in constant movement I crossed the floor turning and twisting through dancers. Sweating shirtless figures, a never ending snake of Soulies flowing in and out of the toilets, not a bouncer in sight. Endless faces of vibrant expressions wide-eyed Soulies, greeting me friends from Wigan. Billy, Waka and Merv, Scatty at the bottom of the stairs.

"Hey up Mike Walker and Harry Green just pulled me. He thinks someone forged tickets, he's going mad told me to ask around."

"Yea I know Scat, seems a bit more crowded than usual." Both of us bursting in laughter, my face in a blank expression.

"Seen these?" Pulling a stack of badges out of his pocket the clicking fingers of a Stax sign, "he's looking for these as well."

"Scatty man you crack me up! Hey thanks for helping me out with the tickets."

"No problem. Now can you help me get rid of these?"

"Give us one, I'll send people over." Our crossing hands, a hug the depth of our friendship sealed in that first night.

"Later man." "Later Scat." Edging my way forward, ever deeper into the crowds, the heat unbearable Brut and Armani clouding sides of the floor. Mirrored columns streaming in misted reflections, dancers packing the front of the stage. Glowing deco lights of reds and yellows illuminating the back wall. Empty bottles, swamping smoldering ashtrays, spiraling smoke filling the air. Soulies clustering around tables, spare towels draped across chairs. Glazed eyes of dancers, darting tongues licking, hand claps at the end of records. Every movement halted by new conversations, dilated pupils turning to gear. Seconds turning to minutes, time slipping through my fingers every one sharing the night. Fighting my way along the dance floor, a small space, evolving gear surging, racing through me. Back to my roots, a tidal wave of memories, rejoining the floor of The Catacombs along the Wolvo side. That same place I had danced so long ago, a different dancer taking the floor now I felt I owned it.

What you do with records, I will do the same making the night come alive with my feet. Stanley Mitchell "Get It Baby" a record I knew by heart and loved. My body uncontrollable, the lazy beats pulling me forward to a forest of moving bodies lost in the mist of the floor. Al Wilson "Help Me", Andre Brasseur "The Kid", Little Richard "A Little Bit Of Something", Yvonne Baker "You Didn't Say A Word", Frank Beverly And The Butlers "If That's What You Wanted", Don Thomas "Come On Train", Patti & The Emblems "I'm Gonna Love You A Long, Long Time", Eddie Holman "Eddie's My Name", The Shalimars "Stop And Take A Look At Yourself", The Invitations "What's Wrong With Me Baby?", The Total Eclipse "6 O'Clock", Ed Crook "That's Alright", The Jelly Beans "You Don't Mean Me No Good", and The Malibus "Gee Baby, (I love you)" a record electrifying my feet, not even bothering to see who was DJing Soul pouring out of the speakers flooding onto the floor.

"Gethro! Gethro!" Mona fighting through the crowds, his expression of excited anguish breathless as he reached my side. "Hey up two bouncers looking for you, just been to our corner said Mike Walker wants you in his office!"

"Find Kim, tell her I'm ok. Here, keep this." Handing my pockets of money. "I'll deal with it later, tell Jim and Darb it's on top. Hey, see if you can move this badge. Scat's got them." My calmness suppressing his startled expression.

"You're not going are ya? They'll kick shit out of you!"

"Well I'm not running away all night, fuck it!" I felt safe in The Casino, there was a pact I would deny everything and grasses would never last long. Instinctively I looked towards the toilets, two bouncers now standing by the mirrored column.

"Later Mona."

"Be careful man!"

"Find Kim. Go on, I'll be ok." Crossing hands, parting our company. My mind set was simple, act dumb what proof had they got? Approaching the bouncers I took them by surprise. "Mike Walker's looking for me."

"You Gethro?"

"Yes." The bigger of the two stepping forward.

"Can you come with us please, Mike wants a word with you in his office." My first contact with Wigan's bouncers, their politeness and manners unaccustomed to people of their trade. Oblivious to my surroundings we ventured through the crowds to the back of The Casino. Soulies milling around the main doors parting as we entered the passageway.

"Coming through!" One of the bouncers holding the door to the manager's office. Mike Walker leaning on his desk, stepping forward as I entered the room. I had seen him many times in The Casino cajoling his bouncers by the main entrance, we had never met this close up. I stopped dead in my tracks! Jimmy and Darb standing against the back wall, three bouncers lining their sides. Our eyes met for a brief moment, I knew it was on top.

"I'm Mike Walker, manager of The Casino and you?" Extending his hand. His straight, combed hair and fresh faced features reminding me of Herman's Hermits, a pop band from the sixties. A youthful face showing none of the stress associated with a club like Wigan Casino. Dressed impeccably his black suit and matching dickey bow, a white dress shirt the attire of his trade. A mutual respect we firmly shook hands.

"I'm Gethro, I heard you wanted to see me?" My voice in a calming tone.

"Ahh so you're Gethro. It's always nice to put a name to a face. Your name's been mentioned a few times tonight." His smile breaking to a grin, an uneasy silence between us. I glanced at the clock on the back wall, my eyes avoiding his gaze. Four o'clock, nerves dancing in my stomach Mike turning to Darb and Jimmy the competition flashing into my mind. "We have a problem. These lads were acting suspiciously and they have quite a large amount of money on them. According to their story it belongs to you."

"That's correct Mike. I buy and sell records, I also run coaches to The Casino as I'm out on the dance floor I gave them my money to hold." Immediately I pulled out my empty side pockets to show I had nothing to hide, forgetting about the forged ticket and original in my back pocket. Darb and Jimmy shuffling, uneasily riding my bluff.

"And how much would that be?"

"Three hundred Mike." The truth to a fashion.

"Well I'm glad we cleared that little confusion up. Thanks for helping us sort it out." Mike stepping forward, holding the door I knew I hadn't fooled him for a minute. He was an old Wheel boy, an uneasy tension as we left the room.

"What the fuck man?! What happened I haven't even given you any money?!" My anger boiling over, "Come on give me a fuckin break here! That was close man, what you two been up to?!"

"You're not the only one who can hustle Gethro!" Jimmy bursting to laughter, his booming hand slapping my back.

"Man you two crack me up!"

"Look the semifinals already started!" Darb pointing to the stage, Kim illuminated in bright lights with other dancers fighting for space. A ballerina dancing to Northern, effortlessly gliding across the stage. Jako turning from a spin dropping out of sight, his red and white vest barely visible above the crowds.

"Come on we got to move man! We're gonna miss it! Darb quick, this way!" Onlookers blocking our way, Soulies packing the dance floor "I'm Gonna Pick Up My Toys (And Go Home)" by Devones. The record stopping, crowds surging forwards our momentum blocked, cheering and clapping surrounding us.

"The competition, we got to get to the competition. Darb, fuck man!" Frustration welling over me, a sea of heads and bodies jamming our way.

"Sorry Gethro. Sorry mate."

"Forget it Darb!" Weaving and pushing, easing to the front right-hand side of the stage. My eyes fixated, held by Kim, the dance floor standing room only. "Excuse me, sorry mate." Kim's soaked figure illuminated in bright yellow light, matted hair, her face streaming in sweat gracelessly stepping forward. Thundering roars cheering filling The Casino. Russ hoisting Kim's arm, she had eliminated Jako and won her place in the final! My heart bursting with pride. "Darb she just beat Jako man!"

"Gethro get up there!" Soulies near the front helping, parting our way.

"Go on Darb! Gethro! Show em how it's done!" Shouts of good luck the third semifinal starting we scrambled to steps at the side of the stage "I Need You" by Shane Martin filling The Casino.

"Quick come up here!" Jako greeting us from a corridor at the back of the stage, Kim beaming in smiles at his side. "She beat me man." His face bursting to laughter giving Kim a hug and a gentle kiss on the cheek. Brothers and sisters, our bond unbreakable, we had been here before. "Looks like you two in the last semi man." Jako turning to face us.

"Best dancer takes it all Darb." A smile of acknowledgment, we ventured forward through the curtain unfazed by the crowds.

The balcony deep in faces, onlookers in our direction shouts of encouragement from the floor. As far as the eye could see two thousand Soulies, motionless figures holding our gaze Russ standing by the decks, other dignitaries around him.

"You did it lover." Our hug of affection deeper than ever, my heart exploding in happiness now it's all on me. The third semifinal finishing, hardly time to think Sharon Dyke from Gloucester, a brilliant dancer from The Cats easily taking the heat.

"Last four contestants for the dancing competition." Russ calling us forward, immediately I could feel the stage floor uneven beneath my feet. Connie Clark "My Sugar Baby" a record we knew and loved, sports bags lining the front of the stage, room so tight. A large cake in the corner set on a table draped in gold, a single candle of flickering light. Soulies crowding the edges all of us fighting for room, I danced at the front by the speakers. My feet drifting in arched stepping footwork, gentle hands feeling the beats, body flowing in motion. Splits and drop-backs, spins in perfect combinations pacing myself, holding back on my best moves. Darb giving it all, our styles so similar, unique from other dancers my head lost to the music. The crowds oblivious, our dancing taking over, a belief in our hearts we were the best. A battle raging between us but my heart wasn't in it, this was my brother we had been through so much together, always side by side. I had to pull off one of my signature moves to finish this. Jumping high, touching my toes, landing in sideways splits a move I knew he couldn't do. Once more the record fading, breathless hugging each other we shook hands my heart racing with emotion. Kim at my side, a whispered, "You got this. I love you." Cheering and roars from the crowd at each dancer.

Russ approached raising my hand, The Casino erupting. We had made it to the final Jako and Darb hugging us in a dancing circle. We had to finish our dream, this was our moment, three dancers from the Midlands in the final.

Mike Walker stepping forward, a break in the competition, now holding the focused attention of the crowd. Calling out the raffle numbers on the back of tickets, contestants collecting their prizes. Each time I held my breath looking at Kim, "please don't let it happen." A whisper in her ear. My worst fear unfolding, two contestants coming to claim a prize. A commotion on the stage, Mike Walker making an announcement.

"It appears someone printed a large number of tickets. We the management, are sorry for the subsequent overcrowding. If anyone has any information regarding these forgeries, could they please come to my office? I can assure you we printed one thousand five hundred tickets only, we're very sorry for the inconvenience. To help reduce the congestion we will be opening another room upstairs." Mike pointing to his right. "At the top of the stairs two double doors will be open. There is another dance floor in this room, Brian Rigby and Alan Cain will be playing records. Please feel free to dance in there. We are sorry the raffle is now closed! Our eyes clashed for a brief moment, I knew in my heart I had blown my cover, my face breaking to a smile of cockiness. Good luck with the grasses in your office! You've got no chance in The Casino, there was a bond not even you could break that! Little did I know history was just made in the opening of a room that would later become Mr. M's. Russ announcing the judges for the competition Andy Peebles, Frank Elson, and Dave McAleer from Pye records. The finalists would dance in twos, Darb now at my side.

"Gethro, at least you got more room now. I would hate you to do a handspring into that cake."

"He may as well Darb, no one's going to eat it!" Jako easing the tension, all of us bursting to laughter. Kim stepping forward, she would dance against Steve Cesar from Leeds, the winner of his heat. I had never seen him dance but he came over a brother with class introductions and best wishes. "Good luck Kim."

"Thanks Steve, same to you." Words shared genuinely between them. Once more the competition starting, this time Kim showing her talent as a dancer who had no equal. Terrible Tom "We Were Made For Each Other" blasting from the speakers. Cesar showing why he was held in esteem, turning effortlessly into spellbinding spins. His footwork, a stepping style similar to us but his dancing devoid of drop-backs and floor work. Kim matching him step for step, that unmistakable drifting style she had mastered. Arms floating at her side back and forth as her body moved one direction then the other in perfect sequence to the beats and rhythm. She too dropping to leg breaks and spins, her granny sandal flying past the DJ, unfazed she kept dancing.

"Come on Kim!" Darb and Jako willing her on "Come on lover!" Our voice's hoarse from screaming words of encouragement lost in the noise of the crowd. The fast up-tempo beats driving Cesar, he knew he had a legitimate challenge pulling off one of his fastest spins. His wiry frame standing perfect, a blurring figure, his reputation as a fast spinner for all to see. Smoothness in his moves, flowing in motion, an arc to his footwork, a dancer you had to respect.

The contest closing, roars of appreciation ringing The Casino, the first part of the final ending to more cheers from the crowd. All of us shaking hands Kim and Cesar breathless, there was no malice we were Soul brothers and sisters. This was a contest with a difference, this was Wigan Casino and I wanted that crown.

My thoughts now on dancing, what moves can I bring to the floor to end this. Jimmy words from The Cats ringing in my ears. "I'm telling you man, Kim will blow you off a floor one day." Sharon stepping forward, a hug between us, we knew each other well. Russ queuing the next record, waving us forward. Everything I had tried to achieve now put to the test in these three minutes. All the times we had practiced, my nerves evaporating before me. Norman Johnson & The Showmen "Our Love Will Grow" hitting the decks, I couldn't ask for a better sound, snapping soulful beats their voices lifting The Casino.

My footwork in our rolling style, a straight line breaking out to an arc of crossing twisting steps. Another half turn, outside leg sweeping the edge of the stage, turning working my way into space. Jako rolling his arms, willing me to pull off one of my defining moves, the handspring from a low position. Jumping up, touching my toes one flowing move landing in a drop-back, no hesitation straight over back arched landing in another. Roars of approval from the crowd! Stop starts in my footwork, bent knees, a touch of the heel my signal for a combination of moves, adding more fluency to my feet. Hands reaching in an arc as Booper had taught me, opposite spins at speed dropping to one handed splits. My leg now in rotation, sequences in bursts to match the chorus, his voice so clear. Feelings inside of me exploding with every beat, emotion I could not control. Connecting my heart in an expression of pure love and passion of all I had tried to achieve, using everything I had learned from dancers before me. I had to prove I was the best. Gear pushing my body, steps of fast intricate footwork twisting in flashes of speed. Hands reaching, feeling their harmonious voices a blur of the crowd below me, this is for you. My heart crying on the inside, cheering driving me on, "don't you cry! Keep a telling you! Keep a telling you", words of the singer filling my head. Sharon moving to space, avoiding each other.

I had seen her dance in The Cats holding her own against many dancers. She too turning with speed to spins and footwork. Arms in an arc, both of us side by side roars from the crowd. Touching my hand, a leg break and jump remember how to beat a spinner? Cesar in the back of my mind. A twist of the hips, dipping my shoulder hands reaching at twelve and nine, spins in opposite directions matching the pounding beats.

Again and again hammering my body in fast flowing moves. Suddenly the record fading, a deafening roar filling the casino. Hands on hips catching my breath, sweat burning my eyes Darb, Kim, Cesar, and Jako instantly at my side.

"You did it man, you did it!" Jako hugging me.

"Well done Gethro, nice dancing man!" Cesar shaking my hand, our respect as dancers straight from our hearts held tightly in crossing hands. I had given my very soul, I had nothing left to give.

Russ coming towards us, "We didn't want a gymnastics display." Walking to the judges, Mike Walker at their side.

"Tough. That's the way we dance around here!" My agitated reply.

"Fuck him Gethro. What's he know about dancing, you pissed it!" Darb wrapped around me, Kim bursting in smiles holding me in her arms. Russ calling us to the front of the stage.

"First of all I would like to thank our dancers, please give your appreciation!" Four of us in a line a thundering roar, whistles, clapping hands held high, a sea of endless faces. Slowly a chant growing loud then louder echoing around the casino Gethro! Gethro! Gethro! A counter chant Cesar! Cesar! Cesar! The atmosphere a roaring volcano exploding before my eyes. Kim squeezing my hand, emotions welling inside me, would we complete our dream? Brent and Bolton lads at the bottom of the stairs screaming our names. My eyes raising to the balcony, there a girl holding my gaze, jumping, waving her arms. No way it can't be?! Never! Rain cheering with Mickey, leaning over the balcony, I felt a glow of happiness for her. Arms held high clapping above my head, I too cherishing the moment, riding the sea of emotion.

"The judges' scores are as follows, only one point separating the dancers." A hush of silence. "First place goes to Steve Cesar!"

A thunderous roar filling The Casino, old and new styles had clashed. I applauded from the heart, after all he had won fair and square. Cesar graciously accepting his fifty pounds prize. My heart dropped, our fairytale over. There would be no King and Queen of Wigan, Cesar had taken the crown. Russ moving down the line, "Sorry what's your name again?" Kim shyly whispering her name. "In second place is Kim!" Again roars and cheering reverberating around The Casino, at last Wigan had found their Queen! My heart bursting with pride, a rush gear could never equal, Darb and Jako leaping in jubilation. Again the chant echoing around The Casino Gethro! Gethro! Gethro! Russ handing me an envelope, "In third place is Ghetto!" The deafening roar drowning out my name. Sharon accepting her prize, The Cats 2nd, 3rd, and 4th, a reminder of the dancers in that club!

Destiny playing her hand, little did I know the impression I had left with one of the judges. "You were ripped man!" "You pissed it Gethro!" A chorus all around us falling into a sea of arms and hands, pats on the back the floor rewelcoming us. I hadn't won it would have been a perfect night but Kim did. She was the best dancer of all the girls in The Casino that night and proved it. To our little band and all of our friends she was the Queen of Wigan's floor.

"Gethro man!" Jimmy laughing, lifting Kim off the ground with ease. Winston joining in hugs, the depth of our love as brothers, Mona at my side.

"Hey up! You won that hand's down mate! But I've seen you dance better."

"Fuck it Mona. It was what it was man!" I had no time for resentment, I was too happy and I had nothing to prove. Mona returning my money, not even bothering to count it, our friendship deeper than that. The heat of the club unbearable, Martin Ellis screaming down the mic driving the atmosphere wild. The night a boiling inferno, a dancer retaking the decks.

All of us hitting the floor nothing held back, the atmosphere contagious, the emotion of the night swallowing our souls alive. Darrow Fletcher "Gotta Draw The Line", Sandi Shelton "You're Gonna Make Me Love You", Larry Williams & Johnny Guitar Watson "Too Late", Dean Parrish "Tell Her", Fred Hughes "Baby Boy" Joe Hicks "Don't It Make You Feel Funky", Mr. Floods Party "Compared To What", Al Wilson "The Snake", Willie Mitchell "That Driving Beat", Al Kent "The Way You Been Acting Lately", Rita Dacosta "Don't Bring Me Down", The Spellbinders "Help Me", Frank Wilson "Do I Love You (Indeed I Do)", Jackie Lee "Oh, My Darlin'", August & Deneen "We Go Together", and Duke Browner "Crying Over You", anthem after anthem Martin Ellis crouched over the dexks, a darting figure surrounded with records riding the atmosphere as only he could, more DJs taking over others milling around. Keith Minshull, Dave Evison, Richard Searling, and John Vincent Wigan's floor now in full flight, if you left your spot it was instantly gone.

Dancers giving it all, creating a barrier of bodies, kicks and spinners, energy levels increasing with every beat. Jimmy, Kim, and Winston in Mr. M's. Jako, Mona, and Darb dancing at my side. My head spinning, on fire burning with sweat, drink after drink pouring through my body, I had to get off this floor. Moving through The Casino, gear raging through me pats on the back, Soulies acknowledging our dancing others still chasing gear. Pausing on the balcony I had never seen such a beautiful site. Waves of energy sweeping the dance floor, spinners captured in fluorescents, flashes of light at blinding speeds. Wigan's floor in full flow a tangled mass of bodies not a gap between them. Three thousand arms spreading, reaching skywards, hand claps of thunder echoing in the roof Bobby Freeman "I'll Never Fall In Love Again" a sound we all knew and loved. Girls in every direction dancing, youthful figures clinging in sweat. Shirtless Soul brothers leaping, turning, twisting crowds six deep line the floor. Others seated at tables encircling the balcony mesmerized by the sight below. A tingle running through my body, I was part of this club! I belonged here! This was my world, one I lived for a totally underground scene for those who had discovered it!

"You nearly did it Gethro!" Startled I turned around, Darb smiling at my side.

"It was never gonna work mate. It was a load of bollocks, no one dealer will ever run this club."

"Yea but they know we've arrived."

"They do now I sold those tickets." Both of us bursting in laughter, arms around our shoulders the love I felt for my friend, my brother. Our journey had been long and now we stood on a pinnacle, as always side by side.

"You lost that competition as soon as you walked into his office Gethro."

"I know, I had that feeling as well. Fuck it! Who needs competitions, we live out on the floor man?! You'll never see me on that stage again!"

"Never?" His lightened expression questioning my decision.

"Never Darb. Not everything in life goes as planned mate. Anyway I blame Kerr for giving me this Celtic top!"

"Why's that?" As ever his voice inquisitive.

"You know everybody hates the jocks." Our faces breaking to smiles.

"We came close man, look at that floor see that guy trying to copy our moves, at least our styles original." The seed had been planted, the gymnastic style of our dancing was clearly here to stay.

"We missed two good clubs though Darb, The Wheel and Torch. Their dancers definitely influenced us, especially Booper.

"Yea I know what you mean." His nodded expression in agreement, our night unfolding beneath us.

"I've got to get out of here mate, I'm burning up on this gear. I'll see you in M's later."

"Later man." Our verb ling over, parting in our usual way. The balcony crowds stifling my every step, passing the record bar now on two levels of The Casino I couldn't help but smile. Vinyl detectives scouring boxes, hunched prospectors searching for gold. Hilda greeting me at the bottom of the stairs.

"You're late tonight, you been behaving?"

"I always do Hilda, you know me!" My face of innocence, capturing her smile. The hand stamp guaranteeing reentry, descending the steps I ventured outside. Billows of steam clouding the doorway, energy of dancers evaporating a refreshing coolness to the air. The crack of dawn breaking the evening sky, glimmers of light in the distance our night coming to an end. A few couples milling around, my body on edge burning with adrenaline sharpness to my vision. A peering inquisitive stare at distorted shadows I knew I had reached my red line. Deepening my breath I wandered through the car park, usually someone would shout my name, something catching my eye.

"What's my car doing here, I didn't bring it?" Inquisitively I ventured forward taking a closer look, I tried the back door. Wow! Two record boxes staring at me, as ever the opportunist I didn't turn the offer down. To me there are two types of thieves, ones who deliberately go out and steal, which I wasn't, and the opportunist, which I was. Taking my haul I casually wandered over to the coach. Mel asleep, not even rising when the door opened, his snoring louder than two jackhammers, I stashed my find. Life felt good, not bad for third prize. I hadn't got a conscience, just a memory of my bedsitter being ransacked. In some strange way I felt I had evened the score. My eyes straining to adjust the transition of night and day, the lights of The Casino pulling me back to sanity, offering me sanctuary from the outside world.

"You're back early?" Hilda smiling as I returned.

"I know, I was by myself this time."

"Glad to see your behaving at last." Her wistful smile making me blush, she knew me better than anyone, there was never any chance of that!

Our night spent dancing on the main floor and Mr. M's. Moving through the crush of the crowds, only to find one room just as packed as the other. At the top of the stairs above the men's toilets music filtering into the main room from two open doors of a wide passageway. Couples seated on worn carpet, faces of deep piercing eyes locked in intense conversations, backs slumped against the walls. Bodies strewn left and right, the night and heat taking its toll. Soulies streaming in and out of the doorway, a never-ending flow into Mr. M's. Kenny Spence on a small stage holding center of the room, above him a narrow ornate balcony encompassing the dance floor on three sides.

The room a miniature of the main floor, below sounds from The Torch and Cats sucking you in, driving the atmosphere wild. The Younghearts "A Little Togetherness", Isley Brothers "Why When Love Is Gone", The Dramatics "Inky Dinky Wang Dang Doo", Jimmy Conwell "Cigarette Ashes", The Cooperettes "Shing-A-Ling", Lee Roye "Tears (Nothing But Tears)", Denise La Salle "Do Me Right", Bob Brady & The Con Chords "Everybody's Goin' To A Love-in", The Miracles "Whole Lot Of Shakin' In My Heart", Tommy Neal "Goin' To A Happening", The Fantastic Johnny C "Don't Depend On Me", Isley Brothers "Tell Me It's Just A Rumour Baby", David And The Giants "Ten Miles High", and Tony & Tyrone "Please Operator". Jimmy easily standing out amongst the dancers. Matted headband clinging to his forehead, his shining muscular frame dripping in sweat. That fast shuffling style he had perfected, skimming the edge of the floor suited to the packed room. Kim, Winston, and Scatty joining him their dancing on the right-hand side dominating the floor. Our meetings always with bursting smiles, as we all took to the floor the tunes as good as the main room. The heat unbearable, Soulies camped along the edges others crashed out on chairs. I struggled to find space to break out to our fast flowing footwork on the small floor. The upstairs room a temporary fix to the overcrowding with an atmosphere and crowd of its own, Jimmy instantly finding a new home. After a short spell I often returned to the main room.

Our night ending in the main room, Gerry Marshall the owner of The Casino receiving a standing ovation. The Casino thundering in roars of foot stamping approval, Mike Walker at his side. The club etched in all of our hearts, a night we would never forget, both men having our instant respect.

The last three records filling the floor. Jimmy Radcliff "Long After Tonight Is All Over", now a Casino anthem, "…tonight with you for the first time I have learned what my lips are for…" hands raised to the chorus, two thousand voices singing the words, emotions of the night tearing me apart. A sadness now filling my heart, the unmistakable intro Tobi Legend "Time Will Pass You By" words so true to our moment "…Life is just a precious minute…" a testimony to our youth that thought this night would last forever, never thinking of tomorrow. All of us just pebbles on a beach, rolling in the sands of time our hearts connecting forever. Friendships that would last a lifetime, the power of our music, our underground scene that would outlive us and our youth. Tears of emotion overflowing in the well of my heart. Russ spinning the last record, his words choked with what lay before him Dean Parrish "I'm On My Way" ending our night. My world crashing around me, now just a memory, a page in a diary of time. The decaying skin of a leper, shadows turning to light the shabbiness of our surroundings unveiling before my eyes. Peeling walls of torn paper, the filth of worn carpet beneath my feet, bottles strewn across tables. The Queen devoid of her beauty now, showering in cascading light. "Come on everybody out! If you don't mind were closing," Bouncers cajoling the crowds, no one bothering to move everyone gathering at tables.

"What time's the coach leave Gethro?"

"What coach?" Playful banter that never stopped.

Chapter 46

KEEP ON KEEPING ON

Flushed with my success of the anniversary, I now branched out with the coach after all I had the float to take a gamble. The Civic in Wolvo on Friday nights trying to fill the void of The Catacombs, failing miserably. Even with top DJs frequenting the lineup Pep, Max, Colin Curtis, Brian Rae, Keith Minshull, Neil Rushton and others. Too many Divs and straights on the dance floor, often ending in drunken fights. Another drawback Wolvo squad paying frequent visits, attention we didn't need. As well as attending The Casino every Saturday which now had opened two entrances due to the crowds. We now travelled in a new direction, three hours south. Once every two weeks on Fridays we would visit the Howard Mallet Club Cambridge. Open from eight till one, not even an all-nighter, the venue well worth the effort. The huge dance floor and friendly crowd always welcoming us, Tony Dellar the DJ playing all of the top sounds Wolvo Soulies always filling the coach. In September there had been a big bust in Cambridge, it didn't take long to make contacts, local dealers eager to off load their gear out of the area. To compete against the dex flooding into the casino from Bolton, I had the perfect answer backstreet blueys buying in bulk. Our time on the road spent longer than in the club, often returning to Wolvo at five Saturday mornings. From here I would visit my stashes, gear filtered out in the week payments made in The Casino. Once again my ingenuity working like clockwork, not even attracting attention leaving the chemist bashers to occupy the squad.

Two events both involving the coach now bringing the reality of my world to the forefront. The first after one of our trips to the Howard Mallet Melvin, the driver escorting me to the back seat.

"Look I have to clean this shit up Gethro! It's not on, I found the same last week after Wigan! What's going on mate? If the owner sees this you won't be hiring any more coaches, I can tell you that!"

Blood splatters on the ceiling and back of the seat, a shudder of anger and shame ran through me at what lay before my eyes. Breaking every rule I held in my insane world, my motto "if you can't swallow it then I don't want to know." I knew who had been sitting there.

"Look I'll sort it out Melv, please don't say anything it won't happen again I promise. Come on mate, I'm sorry. I had no idea mate." Shaking my head with remorse deep inside, a boiling inferno of anger. I knew what was going on, the bastards were taking the piss. Fuck this, everything in jeopardy just because of a needle. I knew exactly what I was going to do, they'll pay for this.

Darb and Jimmy greeting me in The Octopus full of the Saturday crowd. "What's up with you?" Jimmy as always reading me like a book.

"I got a problem with that wanker!" Pointing to Ronnie on the far side of the room surrounded with his little band of junkies.

"Take it outside Gethro, not in here mate." Darb placing his glass on the table.

"Watch my fuckin back!" Ronnie looking nervous as I approached. "Ronnie pop outside, I want you to check these blueys, they don't look right to me." Lowering my voice, concealing my anger.

"Yea no problem." Both of us leaving together, settling in the doorway outside.

"Why you bringing needles on my coach?" Searching his face for answers.

"I'm not Gethro." A smirk of smugness igniting my anger.

"Look I let anything fly but not this man! Look at you, you're turning into a fuckin junkie! Come on Ronnie you were a good chemist basher, now it's got you by the bollocks!"

"Don't tell me how to run my life, who do you think you fuckin are? You're nothing but a scummy dealer!" The punch coming in a flash of lightning hitting him square in the mouth, more retribution followed as I vented my anger leaving him battered in the doorway. My heart bleeding on the inside at what I had done, a friendship lost forever. "What friendship really?" One fueled on his addiction to drugs? To not of acted at all would of opened the floodgates, Wolvo had a saying. You touched the wall a few of us did not, all of us came back. The Northern scene didn't take prisoners, when it came to gear some of us could handle it, others couldn't. I knew I was looking at a living corpse.

The coach wasn't fifty percent of the people taking gear to stay awake all night, nothing of the sorts. More like ninety-nine percent and even then I can't remember many straights making it to Wigan. The next event coming out of nowhere as we travelled to The Casino Edwin Starr would be on live tonight, December 7th, a date I would never forget. The coach packed with regulars, the atmosphere infectious, tonight an absolute sellout. The coach doors opening at Knutsford for our usual stop. A sudden silence making me turnaround sharply from the backseat. Two police officers looking straight at me, I hadn't dropped my gear and problem was neither had half of those around me. They had us all bang to rights! Everyone loaded with caps and pills!

"Turn the music off driver!" Flat cap patrol officers standing at the front of the coach. My thoughts for some reason turning to God pleading forgiveness, asking his help promising I would never again sell drugs, just get us out of this.

"Which one of you is Gethro?" I held my stance no one saying a word.

"He got off at keel mate!" Muff's voice flouting the silence, a murmur of defiant laughter breaking the tension.

"You're not going anywhere till we find him. We know he's on here, we can play around all night if you want!" The officer's voice showing a pitch of anger. "Now, where is he?" No one saying a word, the tension unnerving! I rolled the dice, after all what could I do?

"I'm Gethro."

"You're in big trouble son. You need to come with us. Stay seated, no one move!" Every step I took slicing through the atmosphere, a shudder ran through me encased in fear. This was it, the games over we're screwed! Leaving the coach in silence a two door Range Rover, their patrol car my lift.

"Place your hands on the roof and don't even think of moving." An officer staring at me in the front seat. From the open side window I could see the other officer talking on his radio, blocking the doorway of the coach. "Fuck we're in the shit now!" Suddenly he returned to the car, another patrol car flashing in blue light pulling to our side.

"You got him?!"

"Yea, he's in the back seat."

"Ok, we'll follow you." I couldn't believe what I was seeing watching the coach fade into the distance. The idiots had us right in the palm of their hands, two patrol cars following each other. My strip search revealing nothing, eventually leading to discarded underwear and cavity searches. Stashes of my belt loops overlooked, the rarest of occasions I had nothing to hide. The ensuing interview a game of cat and mouse I didn't know Benny from Wallsall and fifty-three witnesses would testify to my movements tonight. Eventually being returned to the coach the interior lights ablaze beaming wide-eyed expressions, erupting in cheering, two officers at my side.

"Right we're going to search this coach, no one move! Stay seated!" Two officers moving down the aisle, a police woman now joining them. I had never seen a more helpful crowd. Girls chatting as they opened their vanity cases.

"Here's my compact case and knickers." "Oh, they're nice. Where'd you get those from Julie?" "Chelsea Girl, Sharon." Towelettes, spare batteries, Diskatron tape players filling the seats, granny sandals, and Sasha platform wedges openly on display. Soul brothers jokingly emptying pockets talc and sports bags thoroughly inspected, a total waste of time. Their over exuberance making me smile, as they openly took the piss. The officers leaving empty handed to resounding cheers and insults of "Got any gear?" "Want some?!"

"Come on, let's get to Wigan, Edwin's on!" Melvin obliging as we roared onto the M6 the only two straights on the coach were me and the driver! Soon rectified in The Casino by blueys and dex, the night as always going down a storm.

The second of my nine lives evaporating, I had dodged a bullet I now closed everything down, not going near my stashes and playing by my rules. The hardest criminal to catch is one who switches on and off, listening to my karmas heading my close call. In the back of my mind Christmas around the corner, turkey not so appealing behind bars. Our last three weekends of the year spent in The Casino, a trip to the Howard Mallet now holding all-nighters on a Friday and two all-dayers, one at Derby on the 29th and the other at Whitchurch on January 1st. Christmas spent with my family, the only one I had my Soul brothers and sisters dancing to Northern. Fifty all-nighters and all-dayers in one year plus all our other clubs and venues, our dedication had been relentless, our passion second to none! Every detail recorded in my diary, times, dates and memories all of my emotions locked in the pages. "Why do you keep that?" Kim looking over my shoulder, smiling at my meticulous writing "I may read it one day lover." Closing the page I felt I had lost a friend.

Chapter 47

TOP OF THE POPS

Little did I know what lay in store for me. Would this be a year I had the Midas touch? Destiny paving her way, everything I touched turning to gold. The coach running like clockwork, our fame on the scene spreading as we travelled the length and breadth of the country, imposing our style of dancing on every floor we stepped on.

A record filling The Casino towards the end of last year was "Footsee" by The Chosen Few. Released on Pye Disco demand label it had entered the charts in mid-January at number thirty-eight. It quickly gained momentum by late January, it was number twenty-five and rising. The record held no interest to me, it was a catchy instrumental with a driving beat but it sounded manufactured. Not what I would call a natural Northern classic like Hoagy Lands "The Next In Line" or Jackie Wilson "The Who Who Song". The B side of Footsee, "7 Days Too Long" by Chuck Wood, that's a Northern tune! The story as I knew it at this time, was Dave McAleer while working for Pye Disco Demand, a subsidiary of Pye Records, discovered the instrumental on Roulette USA. Lucky for him Pye held the rights to the Roulette catalogue in the UK. He or someone then reworked the record, speeding up the beat to give it Northern authenticity and with the help of a few Casino regulars added car horns and crowd noise. It became one of the first commercially successful remixes of a previously released record, the original artist being The Chosen Few from Canada.

Although I did hear they were session musicians, who they were in reality, I hadn't got a clue? With the record riding high in the charts Pye had a problem. A telegram dropping on my doorstep would give them their answer. Jako and I had been asked to contact Dave McAleer at Pye Records with the view of us teaming up with other dancers from The Casino. We would represent the record on Top Of The Pops, a hugely successful musical show with 15 million viewers that aired every Thursday on BBC 1.

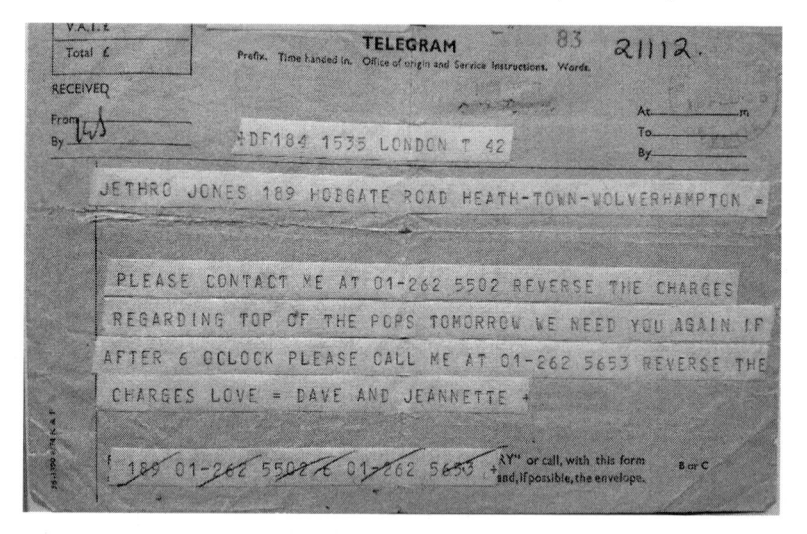

> TELEGRAM 21112
>
> DF184 1535 LONDON T 42
>
> JETHRO JONES 189 HOBGATE ROAD HEATH-TOWN-WOLVERHAMPTON =
>
> PLEASE CONTACT ME AT 01-262 5502 REVERSE THE CHARGES REGARDING TOP OF THE POPS TOMORROW WE NEED YOU AGAIN IF AFTER 6 OCLOCK PLEASE CALL ME AT 01-262 5653 REVERSE THE CHARGES LOVE = DAVE AND JEANNETTE +

The reason I jumped at the chance was simple and personal. I had suffered the show's pathetic resident dancers week after week as my foster parents drooled over their dancing. It would be my perfect answer to them kicking me out if I appeared unannounced on their TV screen, blowing their precious idols off the floor! I found the shows dance routines to be distasteful, based on a sexist nature. Female dancers prancing about a stage, scantily dressed showing off their so-called charms. It's what the public wanted, fair play to them but my attitude towards dancing was different. Deep inside I wanted to make a statement for the youth of our generation. To show how we moved and connected to music, but most of all how to really dance!

Arrangements were made, we would travel by train and be met by a representative from Pye Records at Euston station. Four of us would be from the Midlands Jako, myself, Winston, O'Mally and Steve Powel. From Wigan would be Ann Rogers, Tom and Kipper, all well-known faces in The Casino. These three had been responsible for the horns and clapping on the remixed record, hence the name Wigan's Chosen Few. The stage was set, we entered Shepherds Bush Studios on Wednesday the 29th of January to do the recording. Transmission to take place at BBC Studio 8 run through from four in the afternoon, final transmission from seven thirty onwards. I didn't even feel nervous, why would I? We were from another world, Wigan Casino still an underground club. Some of its best dancers were about to deliver a message with a massive culture shock!

Our dressing room a hive of activity, Ralgex liniment massaged to bare legs. Ann adjusting her hair in the lighted mirrors, all of us just enjoying the moment, taking the piss out of each other.

A knock on our dressing room door calling us into the main floor. Following the production assistant we entered the studio. The room wasn't that large, stages of various sizes were set in different areas, each had a capitol letter, a small crowd congregating around each one. Floor assistants stood to the side with clipboards in bold letters with the words "Clap!" Above our heads a metal grating suspending banks of lights, corresponding numbers were being adjusted to various heights.

Two large cameras on wheels moved across the floor. Pans people were warming up for a dance routine Cockney Rebel checking their instruments on the opposite stage. Toney Blackburn, the DJ for the show, standing with a microphone in his hand, a makeup artist adding touches to his perspiring face. None of us were star struck, taking everything in our stride yet here we were rubbing shoulders with household names. Gathering around a production assistant we went over the script. The acts we would be appearing as defined with specific times. At the top Toney Blackburn would introduce the show in area E. The following acts would be on live, each given designated areas, others appearing on film. The Glitter Band, Queen, Andy Fairweather, Lowe, Pans People, Alvin Stardust, Mac and Katie Kissoon, Cockney Rebel, and Wigan's Chosen Few I felt a twinge of pride at our involvement, we would be dancing in area A. Suzi Quartro would end the show.

None of us missing a beat as we waited patiently in our area, watching the hive of activity around us. Tony Blackburn having to do a couple of takes on our introduction finally the record filling the studio, we hit the floor. Jaws dropped, the crowds gathering around us backing away as Jako launched into a somersault. I followed with a handspring landing into the splits, our rehearsal turning into a disaster. Dancers fanning out, leaping in every direction. They had never seen anything like us and immediately the music stopped!

"What's up?!" Jako bursting to laughter, coming towards me, stepping around a camera I too laughing at the commotion we had caused.

"I think they got a problem Jako. They ain't seen nothing like us." Winston grinning, now standing at my side. The production assistant and floor manager approaching after talking to the cameramen.

"We're going to do long shots and aerial shots, can you keep to a smaller area?"

"Who's in charge here?" The rep from Pye Records joining us, everyone pointing at me, I felt embarrassed.

"There's no way we can dance in this small area, that's the way we dance. We never even really got started." The assistant politely acknowledging my comment, turning away and clapping his hands.

"Ok I want the crowd in a big circle please! We'll do a run through!" The music restarted and once again we hit the floor with the same enthusiasm, all of us letting it rip. The studio full of startled faces at the speed of our dancing, the moves all of us brought to the floor. Spins and drop-backs, splits and handsprings cameras flying left and right trying to keep pace with our movements. Our time on the floor just over three minutes, the record fading to cheering from the crowd. Cameras switching to Tony Blackburn in lighted area E as he introduced Suzi Quartro. All of us stood watching the filming of her act in silence, our time on the floor had gone well.

After a short recess we reentered the studio, final transmission unfolding the same as the run through, our dancing equally intense. Watching the show from start to finish it all seemed so false to me and nothing like I had seen on TV. Some of the acts seemed to me to be lip-syncing their songs, Pans People giving their usual display of dancing, the whole show completed in just over in thirty minutes.

"Gethro, someone wants a word with you." Pye's rep beckoning me to a small group of people, a gentleman stepping forwards.

"Hello, I'm the choreographer from Pans people. Who is yours, I would like to meet them?" I smiled at the stupidity of the question, shaking my head and tapping my shirt.

"We don't have a choreographer, there are no set moves. We dance from the heart." As we mingled on the floor I collected a discarded script, a memento for Kim's scrapbook.

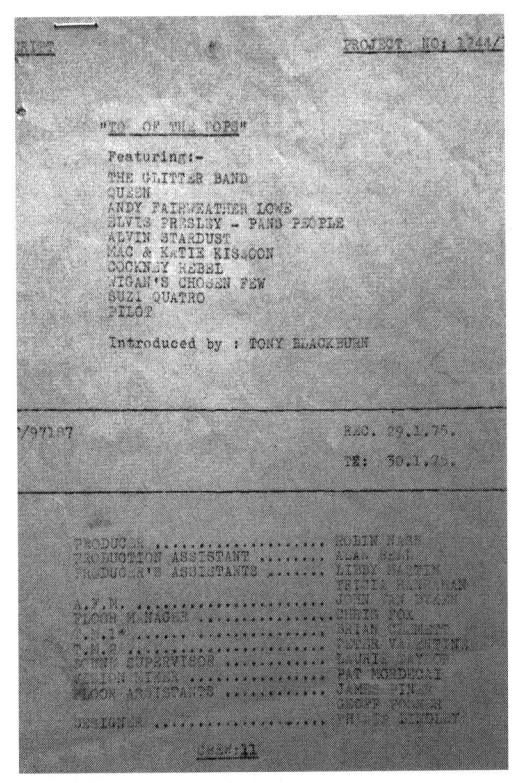

Crowds gathered around asking for our autographs, so this was how fame really felt? Signing my name as Gethro, Wigan's Chosen Few I felt a cringe of sadness, in reality I was as false as the show. Finding solace in my thoughts, our dancing making the statement I had wanted, it really was that simple to me. "We had come to dance."

Various dignitaries entering our dressing room, Dave McAleer shaking our hands, thanking us for coming. Later that evening taking us on a tour of Pye Records. Walking through the studios I paused at a window, Barry White smiling at me as we exchanged waves. An icon of the seventies, he seemed just a normal guy to me.

The show being screened the following night, our dancing having the impression I had wanted. That weekend in The Casino to many we were heroes, they felt proud of what we had done. To others we had sold out the scene for self-gratification.

On the floor I gave them my answer in one of my best displays of dancing, daring any of them to take me on! None of us realized the impact we had made on TV that night giving inspiration to so many, an alternative to the normality of the seventies. We were the first ever dancers to appear on a British TV dancing to Northern. A generation burst to life, as others sought to leave the shackles of the pop culture, many following in our footsteps. From our humble beginnings the legacy of our dancing created a pathway for others to follow, to dance like us and discover the unmistakable sound of our music, "Northern Soul."

The End

A POEM BY SHIRLEY DONKERSLEY

The week is over - it's taken it's time
Going to Wigan - that sounds just fine
Once inside feel that beat
The smell of Brut and oh that heat
Now where's them friends I met last week
Looking around it's like hide and seek
Forgot where they said that they would be
Ah, there by the stage I think I see
It's taken an hour to get that way
More people to talk to, lots to say
Cross the floor - got have a dance
Here's another friend met by chance
Outside M's there's the usual crowd
We can chat out here it's not too loud
It's a load of rubbish that's being said
Almost as something has messed with my head
The people at nighters are one of a kind
And as Bob Rolf says "it's blowing my mind"
So now the nights over, I'm on my way
Hopefully to somewhere that's open all day

Printed in Great Britain
by Amazon